The Culture of Vengeance and the Fate of American Justice

America is driven by vengeance in Terry K. Aladjem's provocative account – a reactive, public anger that now threatens democratic justice itself. From the return of the death penalty to the wars on terror and in Iraq, Americans demand retribution and moral certainty; they assert the "rights of victims" and make pronouncements against "evil." Yet for Aladjem this dangerously authoritarian turn has its origins in the tradition of liberal justice itself – in theories of punishment that justify inflicting pain and in the punitive practices that result. Exploring vengeance as the defining problem of our time, Aladjem returns to the theories of Locke, Hegel, and Mill. He engages the ancient Greeks, Nietzsche, Paine, and Foucault to challenge liberal assumptions about punishment. He interrogates American law, capital punishment, and images of justice in the media. He envisions a democratic justice that is better able to contain its vengeance.

Terry K. Aladjem is a Lecturer on Social Studies at Harvard University and an Associate Director at Harvard's Derek Bok Center for Teaching and Learning.

D1561956

The Culture of Vengeance and the Fate of American Justice

TERRY K. ALADJEM

Harvard University

CAMBRIDGE
UNIVERSITY PRESS

CAMBRIDGE UNIVERSITY PRESS
Cambridge, New York, Melbourne, Madrid, Cape Town, Singapore, São Paulo, Delhi

Cambridge University Press
32 Avenue of the Americas, New York, NY 10013-2473, USA

www.cambridge.org
Information on this title: www.cambridge.org/9780521886246

© Terry K. Aladjem 2008

First published 2008

Printed in the United States of America

A catalog record for this publication is available from the British Library.

Library of Congress Cataloging in Publication Data
Aladjem, Terry Kenneth.
The culture of vengeance and the fate of American justice / Terry Kenneth Aladjem.
p. cm.
Includes bibliographical references and index.
ISBN 978-0-521-88624-6 (hardback) – ISBN 978-0-521-71386-3 (pbk.)
1. Political culture – United States. 2. Justice. 3. Rule of law – United States.
4. Criminal justice, Administration of – United States. 5. Punishment – United States.
6. Revenge – United States. I. Title.
JK1726.A423 2008
364.601–dc22 2007024634

ISBN 978-0-521-88624-6 hardback
ISBN 978-0-521-71386-3 paperback

I therefore left the problem of the basis of the right to punish to the side, in order to make another problem appear, which was I believe more often neglected by historians: the means of punishment and their rationality. But that does not mean that the question of the basis of punishment is not important. On this point I believe that one must be radical and moderate at the same time, and recall what Nietzsche said over a century ago, to wit, that in our contemporary societies we no longer know what we are doing when we punish and what at bottom, in principle, can justify punishment.

– Michel Foucault, *Interviews*, 1966–1984

That man be delivered from revenge, that is for me the bridge to the highest hope, and a rainbow after long storms.

– Friedrich Nietzsche, *Zarathustra* II "On the Tarantulas"

Hardening them to disgrace, to corporal punishments, and servile humiliation cannot be the best process for producing erect character.

– Thomas Jefferson, August 4, 1818

Contents

Acknowledgments

I am deeply indebted to Louis Sargentich and the Liberal Arts Fellowship at Harvard Law School, where I began this project, and to Martha Minow who has encouraged me ever since. The late, inestimable Judith Shklar offered sustaining comments on the pilot essay, and Austin Sarat's remarks on the project in a preface to his own work have helped considerably to frame it. I am extremely grateful to Danielle Allen who understood everything I was trying to do from the start, to Dana Villa for his intellectual generosity and incisive criticism, and to Patchen Markel and Peter Gordon for their friendship and extraordinary insights along the way.

My thanks as well to Judy Vichniac and Anya Bernstein for guiding Social Studies at Harvard so well, and for creating the opportunity for many formative conversations with our wonderful students and colleagues. My students, past and present, have been a constant inspiration. I thank my collaborators at the Derek Bok Center for Teaching and Learning at Harvard for their remarkably generous support and our Director, James Wilkinson, who has been mentor, advisor, and friend.

I have had inspiring discussions with Bonnie Honig, Susan Hekman, Christine DiStefano, and Jennifer Radin about liberalism and punishment. My dear friend Deborah Foster offered insights into the use of masks, among other things, and Harry Brill, Tedros Kiros, Bob Spaethling, and my departed friend Al Hoelzel offered penetrating remarks during those many sidebars at Widener Library. Any time I have run into Robin Kilson, Joel Greifinger, Henry Rubin, Michael Meltsner, or Barry Mazur they have had things to say that have made me think more deeply.

I must thank Rachel Farbiarz for her splendid comments on an early draft, Garance Franke-Rute for a thought about Rousseau, Jen Hui Bon Hoa for her most perceptive remarks, David Finegold for taking me back to Plato, Travis Smith for his thoughts on Hobbes, Donna Conrad for her keen editorial eye, Shirley Kosko for letting me vent about the death penalty, Paul Kirchner for sharing his thoughts on this topic too, Meredith Petrin for pointing out how much more there is to say, Virginia Rivard for challenging me and for reminding me of Poe, Lynne Layton for her discerning thoughts and psychoanalytic insight, and Toby Yarmolinsky, a wise and thoughtful friend who has a hand in everything. I thank Phyllis Menken of course, Wendy Whiteaker, Andrea Cousins, and Arianne Dar for years of patience and support, and Susan Fox and Richard Hill for their great forbearance over my social limitations. I have always wanted to thank Wendy Artin, an artist of the soul, for her prodding on the matter of grief when I was too young and cerebral to fully appreciate its importance. I thank Sally Matless, a thoughtful reader, Alex Blenkinsopp for his fine attention to detail, Camilla Finlay for her aesthetic assistance, Diane Andronica for her technical skill, Micaela Janan for his thoughtful comments, and Judy Salzman for her wise counsel. I especially thank Jasmin Vohalis who read over my shoulder at times and has an extraordinary grasp of language at a very early age – she is a wonder.

I am most grateful to my late father, Nisso Aladjem, my mother Hélène Corry, my stepmother Charlotte Aladjem, and my sister Anne Hutchins for their unqualified support. My brothers Peter Aladjem and Thomas Corry have sustained me in more ways than I can say. I am deeply grateful to Elizabeth Thulin for her patience and enduring friendship. There are not words enough to thank Susan Youens, dear friend and model of productive scholarship, whose wisdom and experience have guided me in this project as in so many things. I owe an odd kind of thanks as well to those who have led me to examine my own "emotional register," if not always in flattering ways, as it has been instrumental in shaping this work.

I am deeply grateful to my editor Beatrice Rehl, the Syndicate, and the staff at Cambridge University Press, for their thoughtful guidance in the production of this book.

Preface

When I began this project I had no idea how colossal it would become or that it would so completely change my view of America. For nearly a decade it has made me rethink our foundations and reassess our driving passions, and it has been something of a personal odyssey as well. Some time ago, in my second or third year of teaching a course called "Prisons and Punishment" at the University of Massachusetts, Boston, my colleague Jennifer Radin and I arranged what we thought would be an instructive and highly civil debate about the death penalty. This being Boston, I expected the class to be roughly divided on the topic, if anything fewer for than against, and that arguments on both sides would emerge quite naturally.

To my surprise, the class irrupted. Those who supported the death penalty vastly outnumbered their opponents. At first I was prepared to write this off as a matter of campus demographics, but it struck me that something was terribly wrong. The arguments on the one side were not so much arguments as they were expressions of outrage. The students on the other side cowered, and as I tried to fill in and help them make their case, to venture the usual concerns about human dignity or compassion, my arguments seemed hollow and fell completely flat.

In that moment I had made a discovery. America was not what I thought it was. The debates that had traditionally divided it were no longer made of the same stuff. Suddenly it was clear that something frightful was moving beneath the surface. Human rights, the rule of law, the Constitution, had almost nothing to do with what these kids thought about "justice." Instead it seemed that they had all been victims, or knew victims of violent crime, or were wholly identified in this way even if they didn't. Not only did they lack compassion or any concern for the rights or person of the offender, but their unseemly outbursts were openly, and almost entirely, about revenge.

This, of course, would hardly seem shocking in the years to follow, and that early encounter proved to be an indication of things to come. Soon there were "victims' rights" advocates everywhere. The polls told us that nearly 80% of Americans supported the death penalty. The law itself became increasingly open to expressions of vengeful sentiment, from the Omnibus Crime Bill and the War on Drugs and Megan's Law, to victim impact statements and mandatory sentences. "TV justice," as I had begun to chart it, was concerned with little else. On shows like COPS, on Court TV, and in virtually every crime drama, a fictive, compensatory American sense of justice had made its way into the public consciousness – it would soon find a corollary on millions of "true crime" Web sites. At least since the beating of Rodney King, the agents of law enforcement had internalized that justice to such a degree that *real* justice, like the Miranda warning, seemed only to be an annoyance. It was this same shadow justice, it appeared, that set the stage for the Bush administration's tactics after 9/11 – to get the terrorists "dead or alive," with contempt (as at Guantánamo or Abu Ghraib) for the rights of anyone who got in the way.

But where had this vengefulness come from? How had we gotten this divided sense of justice? Why were we now so comfortable with the apparent contradiction?

To answer these questions about America, it was clear that I would have to go head to head with the tradition. I would need to examine those liberal theories of justice, punishment, and law that had gotten nowhere with my students, to see why they were deficient. This would mean examining the very idea that "rational justice" like ours arises with the taming or transformation of revenge, since that now seemed to be in question. This was the problem that I first presented to Harvard Law School for the Liberal Arts Fellowship that would launch my inquiry. I proposed to look at the practice of the death penalty and the deep controversy surrounding it in the context of that tradition. As a political theorist interested in the founding of our laws, my search for the roots of the problem would lead initially to Locke.

Are people naturally endowed with a "right of punishment" as Locke surmised, I wondered? Is that right truly derived from reason and not to revenge? As members of society, do we consent to give that right over to the state, and is the state then the bearer of a right of punishment that is free of revenge? Can vengeance and justice be so easily set apart? Is vengeance left behind in a "state of nature," or is there something amiss in this accepted formulation? That nice, reasonable argument seemed to account for much in our approach to punishment and the constitutional thinking of our founders, but it could hardly explain or accommodate the anger of my students. The rational calculus that leaves vengeance to the side now seemed unsupportable in light of what they had taught me about the deeper motive and how it animates thinking about justice. This presented a paradox at least, or perhaps a fatal flaw at the foundation of democratic thought. I would raise this question in several papers on "Revenge and Consent," and formidable scholars, like the late Judith Shklar, encouraged me to pursue it.

It was soon apparent, however, that this inquiry only scratched the surface. I left the Law School still wondering what it was that had been left out of the account, what indeed was seething underneath. The trouble with vengeance clearly concerned a great deal more, and if it was not something rational that explained the way we punish, then what, exactly, was the nature of the irrational demand it had placed on justice?

In pondering this, I was reminded that the problem, at least as it surfaced in America, always seemed to concern murder – the punishment of death for the loss of a life. Did that mean that the burden of assigning our "right of punishment" to the state had, in some sense, meant suppressing or giving up our grief? Is that what so troubled my students, that the legal process of judgment and punishment failed them at this level, or that the society had lost the means or its ability to mourn? And if there was anger, indignation, and grief in their reaction, did I not owe it to them, and to the victims they championed, to address the question on the terms of those emotions themselves?

The problem clearly concerned something about emotion and the rational structures of the law. There were plenty of theories about "emotion" impinging on rational thought in psychology and philosophy. But there was a more particular problem here, an *affective reaction* to collective loss that was operating throughout the culture. It seemed to me that feelings of loss, or "affects of broken attachment" as I came to call them, were making specific demands on justice. It now appeared that vengeance, as a societal mechanism, must be a powerful and psychologically necessary means of binding unendurable memories of loss – the loss of loved ones, or of victims more broadly. It appeared that all the language of redress, recompense, or rectification on behalf of victims, had this at its core. I now suspected that the "retrospective interest" that is usually associated with "retribution" by philosophers contained a more complicated and more pressing need to effect time and memory in the face of grief. Upon reflection, it seemed that virtually every society had some way, either by ritual or religion, to resolve the "rage in grief" (Rosaldo) that is fueled by such powerful memories. Each had a way to inscribe the painful past within a moralizing scheme of explanation. It appeared that this, or rather the lack of it, must be the source of the difficulty in ours.

I then read all I could about this phenomenon in other cultures. René Girard had noticed something similar to this in *Violence and the Sacred*, but the specific problem of memory and grief, as I now understood it, introduced something new. Those grief-driven memories would need to be resolved here, as they have elsewhere, in terms that make *moral* sense of the loss. If violence had been bound in rituals of sacrifice for Girard, and we have none to speak of here, then vengeance of this order would have to be resolved in punishments that "make a memory" (in Nietzsche's phrase) but also offer vindication. The aim of punishment that had motivated my students was driven by a kind of self-deception, a wish to make it fulfill this function, and to remake the past as something justified. In the vast majority of American movies, on television, and in almost every novel (since they all seemed to involve a death) I noticed that the culture was replaying this theme over and over again – denouncing, displaying, and punishing the latest horror, and trying to reconcile mortal loss within a framework of good and evil.

The problem of revenge had thus led back to the problem of "theodicy" as Leibniz had first understood it, and as Weber adapted it for a secular world. This, in Weber's view, is the social and psychological need to ratio-nalize reward and suffering. It is what religion has always done in binding vengeance and, it seemed to me, what our secular society and its justice now fail entirely to do. This must be why so many have returned to religion in America, and why religion (at least on the Christian right) has taken such a punitive turn. It must be why people look to punishments like the death penalty with so much zeal and so much talk of hell and damnation. In considering this, then, an extraordinary hypothesis presented itself: If our world is such a world, and it has lost its capacity for this sort of explana-tion, could we have reverted to the vengeful prototype? If American justice and other such modern things fail to rationalize suffering or to account for good and evil, has vengeance, in some sense, come to take its place?

In the course of my inquiries, I had puzzled over an American impulse to "restore morality" through punishment, as it is called for by certain retribu-tivists and so-called revenge utilitarians. There are many who want to bring back the anger or "disgust" of punishment to that end – my students had been nothing if not *morally* indignant. Might this now impose religious demands, or rather, the demands of a proto-religious and vengeful theod-icy upon our system of justice? Is this why our presidents – Reagan, Clin-ton, and notably George W. Bush – now speak so openly of evil? And if vengeance, with its need for self-justification and vindication, is also full of deception, can it truly be *moral*? Indeed, where it is driven to alter the past, or insists on the righteousness of punishment or victory at any cost, is it not remarkably *amoral*, authoritarian, and substantially at odds with the democratic interest in "truth and justice"?

This, then, was the argument that I had failed to make to my students, the intuition that must have been palpable for Locke and our founders: Vengeance insists on its own righteousness – no matter what. Fine retribu-tive arguments (Kant, Hegel, etc.) could scarcely mask the vengeful sen-timent that secretly animated their aims. To accept its claim of moral or factual certainty, and to give it expression within punishment, is to per-mit something absolutist, something profoundly undemocratic, to become dominant within our justice – as it has clearly begun to do. The trade-off in imposing capital punishments, mandatory sentences with their facile denunciation of "evil" today, is thus not between "concern for the victims" and some misplaced "compassion for their tormentors," as my students would have it, but bctwccn *vengeance* and *democracy itself.* This is the choice that our society now must make, and that it has so far made rather badly.

Now it was clear that I could not address this argument only at the level of the theories of punishment (retributive and utilitarian), though I would certainly have to engage them. It would not do to rehash the history of American vengeance, from the revolution to frontier justice, to lynching, vigilantism, the displacement of native peoples, and the Civil War; to racial backlash and so many military encounters, although this is relevant background that others have covered. It would not be enough to trace the punitive practices of the law or the resurgence of capital punishment and now of torture, though these things clearly inform my inquiry. It could not just be about the petty revenge that seems so commonplace in America – from the vindictiveness of reality TV, to soap operas, gangsta rap, and road rage, though this is part of the phenomenon in question. It would be too much to present the evolution of revenge, from its biblical to its modern variations as Susan Jacoby has done, though it is important to frame the question here too as a matter of Western experience. It would have to be an argument made with all of this in mind, a retracing of the problem that both demonstrates how vengeance has become a distinctive force in America and why it is so troubling for our democracy in particular. This is how I make the case:

In the first chapter, I take issue with those who claim that we are suffering from a moral crisis *as such* in America. I suggest that our crisis is rather more about vengeance, the wish to rectify harm, and the particular want of meaning that accompanies it. I suggest that widespread dissatisfaction with liberal democratic justice intensifies this impulse, and that it is expressed in increasingly punitive terms. This is evident in the anger of American politics (particularly of the right toward so-called liberals), in the response to the attacks of 9/11, as in the depictions of "justice" broadly in the media. I trace this contemporary problem to a failure within the liberal tradition to resolve the problem of revenge, suggesting that Locke and the American founders had swept it under the rug. They, in turn, had relied on an old assumption that vengeance can be tamed by reason or transformed into justice. I explore this in several iterations, from Aeschylus to the Christian proposition that vengeance belongs only to God (Romans 12), in the "myth of enlightenment" (Adorno and Horkheimer), and in the philosophies that seek to justify punishment as a matter of reason. I engage Nietzsche to suggest that the rage in grief and the need to rectify memories of horror were not then, and are certainly not now, readily contained by these more rational resolutions of punitive justice. On the contrary, because these rational formulations have failed, vengeance reasserts itself in a way that now fuels a dangerous political reaction and threatens to remake justice itself.

In the second chapter I demonstrate how America has been reinventing its justice in just this way, on TV and radio talks shows, and in reaction to crime and terrorism. Conservative intellectuals (Stanley Brubaker, George Will and Dan Kahan, James Q. Wilson) call for a return to harsh or shaming punishments and the reinvigoration of moral disgust. Yet in this, I argue, the culture precipitously reconstitutes persons as objects of blame. In the courtroom, and in virtual simulations of crime and justice, the public reads in what it wishes, obsesses over bloody details, and interjects a vengeful story line replete with victims and villains and satisfying conclusions. This cultural obsession is no simple intrigue with crime and violence, I insist, but an expressly American need to generate moral meaning – to rationalize matters of pain, death, and cruelty within a moral scheme that is fundamentally religious. It is, I argue, an attempt to produce a secular theodicy of good and evil within a democratic society where such things are highly problematic. In America, revenge against "evil" people (sociopaths or terrorists) thus becomes the hallmark of a dangerous proto-religious impulse. It may look like a more benign return to religion or "moral values," but it now stands in for both with potentially disastrous consequences.

I have suggested that the vengeful effort to alter the past and "make memory" is a matter of self-deception – yet the danger this poses to truth and justice still needs to be established. In a third chapter, I demonstrate how this works and look beyond the American case to illuminate it. In many defining instances (Oedipus, Othello, Hamlet), vengeance has had the character of a performance driven by delusions of self-righteousness. I argue that Western notions of identity (a tradition of sovereignty) is both informed by and threatened by this. I take up the play of eyes that one finds everywhere in representations of revenge to explore the matter – "an eye for an eye," making an offender "see." I turn to Oedipus as an archetype of this problem of subjectivity, and to his own self-punishment as a paradigmatic instance of revenge. I take up the question of what "must be seen" in revenge (Othello) and the need to "make another see" (Kafka's punitive device) with an eye to contemporary instances of the same thing. I consider why masks are so important to the self-deception of vengeance. I weigh the need for audiences, spectators, or legitimating publics in them. I expose the need to manipulate audiences to states of pity, as in the eighteenth-century executions at Tyborn, England, and how it relates to the wish to "excite pity" in tragedy for Aristotle. I consider the special nature of the "catharsis" in punishment, how it may come to supplant moral feeling, and how it is operative in the demand for "closure" that Americans seem so quick to place on punishment today.

Finally, in a fourth chapter, I show how this vengeance is essentially authoritarian and a threat to American law and to democratic justice as such. Democracy has at times indulged vengeful tendencies, yet its interest in rights, liberty, and the fallibility of the state stands opposed to them. Now, however, when the Supreme Court asserts the state's "interest in the finality" of judgment, especially in the verdicts of capital cases, it affirms a vengeful, self-certain kind of authority with pretensions to infallibility. I weigh this by examining the successful 1997 death row appeal of one Roy Criner, and by reviewing the claims of his zealous prosecutors. I suggest that a certain skepticism or openness to doubt – beyond the legal test of "reasonable doubt" – is the best recourse against a vengeful authority in such cases. Even or especially a punitive apparatus that is armed with DNA testing and modern forensic techniques should recognize that it might fall prey to vengeful distortions.

In the end, I argue that holding the lawbreaker accountable, where such tensions prevail, requires something special. Its proof against him must be tempered by democratic doubt or skepticism toward state power of this kind. This accountability must have a special obligation to truth and under-standing (recalling the South African experience of the TRC). Democratic punishments must thus do their best to foster responsibility or *democratic* accountability. Because they should not be the repository of a self-certain (vengeful) public morality, they can neither redress the public anger nor mollify private grief. The case against vengeance and irrevocable punish-ment therefore presents itself as a matter of democratic necessity. I maintain that if we are to rescue democratic justice from our culture of vengeance, the way that we punish and act toward others as a democracy must be sub-stantially reconceived.

A Note on Liberalism

It is a difficulty that so much of this book is posited against the background of liberalism and that I aim only indirectly to make that complicated tradition clear. But nothing begins in a vacuum, questions of meaning arise in contexts of meaning, and liberalism, roughly speaking, is ours. Of course, to say that it is "ours" in a society that boasts of its diversity is also problematic. It can only mean that I refer to sensibilities recognizable to some, shared by many, or meaningful at moments to all.

When I refer to "our liberalism," then, or sometimes to the liberal tradition, liberal democracy, or secular society, I am referring to a distillate of three ingredients: The first is the familiar legacy of political theory from Hobbes to Locke; from Mill to Rawls, which sets out terms that encompass the debates between our own political liberals and conservatives – what should be public or private, the relationship of citizen and state, the idea of a rational subject or sovereign individual, the extent and limit of his or her freedoms in association with others. The second is that host of laws and institutional practices that comprise the constitutional system of American law and justice – terms of suffrage, representation, individual rights and liberties, and practices of punishment – that are much indebted to the first. The third is the effluence of norms, images, and assumptions that shadow, reproduce, and often distort those traditions in the broader culture and its media. "Liberalism," in these dimensions, is necessary to, if not identical with, "democratic" practices, or at least those of our particular democracy.

Admittedly this is no pure or philosophically precise definition, and it may frustrate the political theorist or legal scholar who aspires to such things. Exploring that frustration, however, is the point and it would beg a question I want to pose about theory and its relation to the social world to provide yet another theoretical exposition that reduces the muddle. Rather, I am writing in the troubled margins of that tradition to question their placement, and because it is necessary to do so if one is to discover its faults. To understand the problem of vengeance in America, that is, one must look critically at its liberal resolutions, and with suspicion on the western myths and traditions that have long informed them.

If there is anyone to whom I address this inquiry, therefore, it is Americans who are aware of the worldly dilemmas posed by this tradition and who appreciate its ambiguities even as they value it, whose assumptions have been challenged, say, by Nietzsche, and who might have him in mind when they think about politics or watch TV. These are the good citizens, I suspect, who will help us to discover what sort of punishment is best suited to a pluralist democracy (and not just a liberal one), and who may rediscover, lest we forget, why it should not be vengeful.

Liberalism and the Anger of Punishment

The Motivation to Vengeance and
Myths of Justice Reconsidered

Our liberal democracy is incapable of generating its own moral guidance, say the critics. It articulates "rights" but not "the good," says Michael Sandel. It has abandoned the virtues, says Alasdair MacIntyre, and the traditions that once guided a way of life. It has tried, argues Habermas, but cannot "administratively reproduce" the motivating morality on which it has always relied. As its formal justice presents issues in terms of individual rights or states' rights in the law, it frequently misses what is more deeply at stake. It is unable to give people their "just deserts," insists Stanley Brubaker, to punish wrongdoing or reward merit, or to recognize the worthiness of those who work hard, pay their taxes, and answer first to their God.[1] In the pursuit of its comforting legal abstractions, one might say, liberal democracy and its justice have ended the bitter feuds and religious wars that have threatened perpetual vengeance, but at the expense of the commitments and values that once made that democracy worth having.

I begin in partial agreement with this lament, yet with the suspicion that it paints its target too easily, aiming at the weak underbelly of certain theoretical constructs of liberalism when the real foe lies somewhere else. Liberalism surely is a body of thought that has tried to extricate itself from such local entanglements and to rise above particular cases. In matters of law and public life, the 'real' individual with all of his or her concerns and devotions is sacrificed to the 'abstract individual' with such disturbing regularity that one might long for a simpler time when a sense of good or moral duty seemed less confusing, when justice, perhaps, was more basic, and the punishment fit the crime.

Yet it is precisely this longing that has been overlooked by those who offer their diagnosis at the level of failed ideology or lost values. They rush too quickly to say what is missing – classical virtues, moral education, religious instruction – to see what has happened on the affective side, where the passions aroused by such things may be less concerned with civic life or moral regeneration than they think. They do not see how the anger that Americans express in declaring their "War on Drugs" is as much at stake. Or how the "outpouring of grief," after the Oklahoma City bombing, and the wish to see the perpetrator put to death express the same frustration.[2] They do not weigh the eagerness with which Americans met their enemy in the Gulf War, or search for one in the "War on Terror," or their special indignation over the World Trade Center attacks and their astonishment that anyone should hate us so much. They do not see how these things are linked; how the gut feeling with which so many Americans cheered the death penalty in the 1980s or still cling to it in the face of DNA evidence that innocents are being executed reflects the same cathartic need to give expression to an otherwise inexpressible rage. It is not a lack of values, exactly, that explains the public anger at this level, but something more pressing in the sense of moral vacancy. It is not simply moral failure that drives Americans in this pursuit, but a singular distress that has left them preoccupied with mortal loss, unaccountable grief, and the vengeful expiation of injustice.

In the work that follows I want to suggest that the source of this distress lies deep within our conception of justice – not so much within 'justice' as liberal or legal theories elaborate it, but in the tension between that system and the strong public feelings that now run counter to it. This distress is on the one hand, an expression of frustration with that justice for not doing more to protect us, for not being simple and effective. It is on the other hand, a result of the failure of that justice to grasp the nature of such strong public feeling, and to define its proper relationship with it. That failure, I suggest, reflects a longstanding inability of liberal justice to address the problem of vengeance and to face its implications. It has left us in a state of contradiction, with a system of justice that denies vengeance, and a culture that is utterly obsessed with it.

Ever since Locke made "calm reason" the central condition for a justice based on "consent," that same justice has tried to check the vengeful impulses at the door. It has deluded itself into thinking that because it is practically and philosophically necessary to do so, that it could actually be done. The difficulty, it appears, is that along with the beliefs and values that this justice consigns to a private sphere, it has left *those* feelings out there too – the anger at slights or offenses to honor, vindictiveness, moral self-certainty, which had all found greater comfort in earlier systems of justice and which seek, or rather seek again, to be admitted to this one. That liberalism had presumed that the world could be divided between reasonable subjects who make contracts and adhere to rational principles of behavior, and irrational people who do violence, break contracts, or take the law into their own hands. It has produced a world in which vengeance and justice appear as opposites – in which one need not worry how the two might really be entwined, or how their interdependence must always present a dilemma for democracy.

I want to suggest that the very abstractions of such liberal thinking have ariscn with the dcnial of that intractable connection – that notions of natural law, consent, rights, tolerance, even distributive fairness as it bears on punishment, depend implicitly on keeping such things from sight.[3] Where they are dismissed, I maintain, they have festered, and where they have festered, they have insinuated themselves more deeply within the culture and its practices of justice. I propose, therefore, that the reluctance of liberalism to confront this difficulty might prove to be a more worthy target than whatever else seems 'missing.' If the problem is not one of lost virtue or values that might be restored within the culture, that is, but of a more obstinate inability to reconcile grief, rage, guilt, indignation, and vengefulness – the affects of *broken* attachment – then it is a problem of different magnitude. It is a problem of such magnitude, because those affects independent of their former content and detached from the things that once made them seem virtuous now make unseemly demands upon our institutions of justice.

Indeed, what is called "justice," on TV or by most Americans, now appears to be as much a manifestation of those demands as anything deserving of the name. When Americans say they want justice, they most often mean something angry and punitive. They may call for it in the name of 'religion' or 'family values,' but not at first to restore those things themselves. Such justice would address the more immediate feelings that arise when a family member is murdered, one's home invaded, or one's faith is challenged – the feelings that attend *ruptured* faith or the *loss* of home or loved ones, although they may be experienced vicariously or with indignation on behalf of others. It might express the "reactive feelings" that Nietzsche elaborated (at least "hatred . . . rancor, and revenge"), which arise when a person feels "aggrieved," although they may be politicized directly with a different connotation.[4] Such feelings would seem to be part of the "visceral register" that William Connolly finds to be excluded from public life, but which nevertheless make their demands upon justice.[5] It is in facing these reactive feelings as such, I argue, that we will discover more about what is missing than by echoing the common lament.

* * *

In order to do this, however, it is important to see how this problem is at once a much older and larger one. It will be necessary to go to the root of our sense of justice. It will be necessary to examine the fears and longings that have always lain beneath its surface and the complex means by which that justice has tried to resolve them. To do this we must travel in the shadows of the old debate between utilitarians and retributivists where those highly irrational things were supposed to have been resolved within "rational justifications" for punishment – where a 'pain for a pain' could be inflicted without so much emotional investment. We must look beyond

notions of "natural law," or "justice as reason" or "justice as fairness" for
that matter, insofar as they exclude the thing that troubles us, at the risk
of discovering a 'justice' that is concerned with a very different sense of
fairness, one rather more torn and internally at odds than anything that
those theories could address. We must see how that troubled sense of justice
has overtaken a liberal one, and how its sensibilities of justice are now
themselves at risk.

To begin with (Chapter 1), we will consider how the vengeful impulse has
become so persistent and so well accepted in American politics and culture.
We will see how it finds expression in American law and punishment even
as it is formally denied, and how the culture both wants and remains deeply
ambivalent about it. We will see how it has lain in wait in the liberal tradition
more broadly – in the theories of Locke and Hobbes, Mill and Hegel as each
has tried to resolve it. We will trace this tension to an older, mythical idea
attributed to the Greeks that vengeance can be transformed into justice. We
will consider how this notion is carried forward both in biblical resolutions
and in the "myth of enlightenment" that still bear its marks. We will engage
Nietzsche to help us see how vengeance is still with us, and what is most
deeply at stake in it.

Next (Chapter 2) we will consider the pain of the victim of violence, and
see how it has become an obsessive interest in America. We will consider
how the public reaction to violence has produced an elaborate alternative
conception of justice, and how the prospect of a justice without vengeance
has become highly problematic. Here, we will notice how a new kind of
retributive justice, replete with victims and heroes, has replaced a more
formal justice in the public eye. We will ponder the way in which that
'justice' attempts to resolve matters of pain, cruelty, and death – how it has
become a thing of nearly religious significance that functions (in Weber's
sense of the term) as a theodicy of good and evil.

The problem will be illuminated (Chapter 3) as we consider the nature
of the vengeful impulse as it has been addressed in other times and places.
We will weigh the dramatic (or for that matter theatrical) and deceitful
means by which it claims to be righteous and just; as in certain tragedies in
which, as Aristotle reminds us, it achieves a distinctive catharsis. Here too,
vengeance will present itself as an inexorable need to alter time and painful
memory. It will appear as a personal imperative with public implications,
which, like the hope of "redemption" for Nietzsche, seeks to "...recreate
all 'it was' into 'thus I willed it'."[6]

We will conclude (Chapter 4) by noticing how that troubling impulse
informs the move to the right in American politics; how it finds expression
in the law, and in irrevocable punishments like the death penalty. We will see
how the legal insistence on the finality of verdicts in such cases amounts to a
claim for the infallibility of judgment, and how this is at once vengeful and
dangerously authoritarian. We will consider how that attitude bears on the
outcome of notorious capital cases, leading to factual and other distortions.

We will contemplate, as we look to our democratic origins, how a less vengeful sort of legal authority might leave room for doubt (an awareness of its own complexity and imperfection), and how this bears on our thinking about mercy and forgiveness. Throughout, we will confront the difficulty of a system of laws that attempts to manage the demands of the same vengeful impulse, and does so rather poorly. We will notice, with Camus, that when "the law ventures into the blind realms of being, it runs a terrible risk of being impotent to control the very complexity it attempts to set to order."[7]

* * *

What are the blind realms of being that liberal law cannot fathom? The question might best be answered from the vantage point of those who have lived their lives in accordance with the law and rational principles, but find that such things fail them in the face of pain or mortal loss. In *Culture and Truth*, the noted anthropologist Renato Rosaldo discusses the effects of personal trauma on his life and work in a way that is especially revealing in this regard. He begins with a scholarly reassessment of his efforts over many years to make sense of the practice of headhunting among the Ilongot tribesmen of the Philippines. He then ponders the difficulties of maintaining objectivity for an observer of culture in a moment when it has been punctured by a devastating experience.

In an earlier account of the practice, Rosaldo had dutifully recorded the great apprehension of the tribesmen at the prospect of the legal prohibition of their headhunting ritual: The song of the celebration "pulls at us," says one in defending it; it "drags our hearts, it makes us think of our dead uncle."[8] Yet for all of the care and calculated detachment of Rosaldo's inquiry, the allure of hunting strangers' heads by those in mourning had remained a mystery to him. He could not see, he now tells us, how his own intellectual commitments, his method, his science, the very rationality that made the question seem pressing to him, had also made the headhunter's longing quite impenetrable. Only in the course of enduring his own grief over the loss of a loved one would he come to see the force behind the Ilongots' words fully, and permit himself a different understanding.

His wife Michelle had fallen to her death during one of their research trips. A tragic loss, one might say, a terrible thing, which, however, should have no bearing on the scholarship or methodological commitments of the anthropologist. Ordinarily the occasion might be addressed in a dedication at the beginning of his next book – a private matter sadly laid to rest, a tribute, perhaps, to his partner's own academic achievement noted in passing. But for Rosaldo the experience could not be captured or set aside just so. It would invade every aspect of his awareness, forcing a different perception of his life and work and of the headhunters themselves. It would require the rethinking of his approach to everything.

Only now could he see more clearly how the illusive practice of the Ilongot had itself been a response to such a loss, a highly ritualized and urgent undertaking essential to the spiritual well-being of the people. In struggling with his own inability to comprehend this, disrupted as it was now by personal torment, he was at last able to see the decapitation of strangers and the discarding of their heads as a means of purging grief and expressing an otherwise inexpressible bereavement. The discovery of the Ilongot's pain through his own would not only test the methodological limits of his objectivity; it had forced an encounter with his own undetected affective screen, and with that of his culture as well.

What is striking in this account for the student of American society is not the problem of method, or the veracity of the insight it provides into head-hunting, exactly. It is the particular bewilderment of the liberal, western anthropologist. He had taken little notice here of the peculiarity of purging grief by disposing of the heads of strangers, or of the striking absence of accountability, blame, or retribution in the act. What concerns him, he admits, is his own "inability to conceive the force of anger in grief."[9] Yet in this remarkably honest reckoning, Rosaldo presents himself as the perfect reflexive artifact of a distinct incapacity in our own culture. He had been unable to grasp the *rage* in grief until the sudden death of his wife had shocked him into a different awareness. In the wake of inexpressible tragedy, he tells us, he is able to see his own "heaving sobs without tears as a form of anger,"[10] and it is only then, he believes, that he can understand the headhunter's quest. In grief, the missing piece is sighted, the sake for which the violent deed is done, the cause or reason for wanting to express it.

In the same unwelcome epiphany one can see that the moral lapse, loss of community or "heart" that so concerns the critics of liberalism, must involve something similar – a disturbing lack, one might say, in our own collective means of addressing unendurable memories of loss – or that register of intensely painful emotions.[11]

Of course, the headhunter offends other things in liberalism besides the predilections of the dispassionate observer – its prohibition against such hurtful expressions of faith (that would make the former a criminal in spite of his right to believe in them); its insistence on restricting punishment to rational agents who are directly at fault; its sense of the rights of those punished, so clearly at odds with the headhunter's militant notion of 'the good.' But here the noteworthy offense is the Ilongot's unabashed linkage of grief and rage and its purgation by violence, that coincidence of emotional and symbolic expression that is wholly lost to our own legal and funereal practices. Now, it seems, this conjunction of things is implausible, quite insupportable within the confines of a liberal culture that no longer understands, but must nevertheless endure something very like the headhunters' rage.

So it is that Rosaldo's insight captures an almost unbearable duality within our own identity. It is quite the same mix of emotions that the presidential candidate Dukakis evoked when he could not seem to feel or express his outrage when confronted with the prospect of the rape and murder of his own wife during a televised presidential debate.[12] It appeared, on that occasion, that this reasonable and decent modern man had wholly internalized the legalistic imperative in the management of his own affects. He seemed to exemplify a distinctly liberal (and masculine) ordering of despair, muted anger and moral restraint that is starkly at odds with the anguish that other men at other times might have expressed at such a thought – so much at odds, these days, with public feelings about justice.[13] The fact that the candidate's reluctance received more criticism than praise, or that the self-control that would have seemed admirable at one time should now seem cold and contemptible, is at once highly suggestive. It is quite the same quandary that burdens the American debate over the death penalty, and troubles the soul of any one of us contemplating it. Grief, rage, and violent purgation are here, but not at home here, and if it seems that liberalism has lost its heart, it may truly be that motivational conjunction at the heart of vengeance that has been so painfully cut out.

It had eluded Rosaldo. It could not be spoken by Dukakis. Such feelings must be bracketed and kept apart from such considerations of justice, and of course they have no place there.[14] But on this occasion, and if it should for a moment seem that those limits have been instilled in the man who would lead the nation, or might somehow impinge upon a threatened world of moral feeling, he cannot be permitted to win. The candidate was *right* to hesitate. Vengeful rage does not belong in the office of the Chief Executive of a democracy, and how impertinent the moderator's question would have seemed at any other time. But it is now equally clear that Americans want something more from their leaders. They must exemplify moral self-certainty. They must be passionate defenders of the home, family, and nation, like those men of aristocratic pretensions in the old (if still electable) South. They must seem to unite public justice and private morality, to identify and denounce "evil," as every successful candidate since has learned to do. They must express indignation – as Americans wish *they* could all the time – and it is far less important that they grasp the proper limits of a neutral state, or of a rational, dispassionate law.[15]

It is an indication of the times that Americans could not resist speculating about how the candidate could have responded differently – that he would 'track down his wife's murderer,' that he would 'deplore the evil deed and want to kill the perpetrator,' and only 'reluctantly obey the law.' Yet in that moment, one can see something still more disturbing at work. An *imaginary* justice has sprung up in opposition to legal and rational restraint and to all that was once sacred in justice. It strains for recognition within the media, it unites those conservative 'NASCAR moms and dads' and the Christian right in their thinking about pedophiles or Al-Qaeda; it operates in fiction, in fantasy, and every medium beyond the law to challenge all that is staid, ponderous, or properly hesitant about liberal justice and its entirely unsatisfactory punishments.

Consider this fictional account of the loss of another wife, and the central place it seems to occupy in this culture:

> I was monstrous with the grief of it, homicidal for revenge. Of course I'd believed that this was the kind of thing that happened to *other people*: gang members, crack heads, the foolish, the unworthy. And now it seemed that any ten coked-out dudes lounging around the street corners abusing the English language or begging change in the subway station were not worth the life of my lovely, blue-eyed Liz. I looked at every teenager with a gold chain around his neck as if he were the one who had killed my wife. *That guy could be the guy.* I thought about buying a gun and just driving up to Harlem and picking off someone, some poor bastard as retribution. Why the fuck not? In the great balance sheets of justice, it seemed reasonable. . . .[16]

There is clearly no room on the balance sheets of *this* justice for any restrained liberal sentiment, for the rule of law or the concern for rights or equity. This man, at this moment, could not be further from the dispassionate observer interested in truth. He is hardly prepared to recognize the rational principles of law. As he contemplates an indiscriminate retaliation, it is not at all clear that reason will prevail as it did for Dukakis, or that the balance of justice really matters at all to the disturbed mentality in which one life equals ten.

What is compelling in this character, the narrator, our 'hero,' however, is not that his passions are those of a traumatized and *exceptional* man who must be reined in by reason and justice. It is that he is so ordinary and that it has become so unsurprising to hear him and others validate the theme of white, middle-class revenge. What is compelling, quite beyond the implication of racial backlash (more of this in Chapter 2), is that his predicament and his fantasy so precisely mirror the common ones. In America, his grief and this perverse sense of justice insist on being heard, and it is only by joining him (or the likes of him) over and over again in fantasy that we keep from acting it out. The distinctive longing of this poor man, and his frustration with liberal justice, must seem strangely comforting, even affirming to the American at rest with the novel, caught up in the ambivalence of the moment, ready to discard the restraint of the law, and yet paralyzingly aware of the consequences of doing so.

* * *

Of course, this man's dilemma reminds us that even as liberalism once based its claim for punitive justice on a 'right of self-protection,' the 'sanctity of property,' 'public safety,' and 'security,' it has always been deeply afraid of revenge. Liberal thinking, so to speak, has always shrunken from the anger of the one vengeful individual. The dangerous fury of the renegade, or solitary "natural man," is what first strikes its theoretical imagination. For Hobbes, the man without laws faces "continual fear and danger of violent death . . ." and is quick to "revenge all injuries. . . ." Yet even those who are disposed to act *rationally* for Locke, like the "Indian in the woods of America," do so for fear of being like these others – the "savage" who threatened civilization for Mill,[17] the headhunter, coked-out dudes. Nothing is more frightening to the inhabitants of this culture than the "keening cry" of anguish from the wilderness, in Rosaldo's phrase,[18] the person who lashes out and is scarcely ruled by reason. No system of thought is more aware that the man who takes the law into his own hands becomes an enemy, or that his vengeful anger is anathema to its governance. Everywhere such desperate individuals remain the objects of fear in America – the drive-by shooter who avenges a gang killing, the Unabomber, Timothy McVeigh, the disgruntled employee who shoots his co-workers, terrorists who must themselves seem vengeful and irrational.

Historically, this society has been equally afraid of its own collective vengeance – as much afraid of the vigilante as the outlaw, wary of lynching (though not enough) and of the retribution of the people assembled.[19] The "mob," wrote Gouverneur Morris, "begin to think and reason. Poor reptiles! . . . [T]hey bask in the sunshine, and ere noon they will bite. . . ."[20] In the background, there has always been Hobbes' fear of the "seditious roaring of a troubled nation,"[21] the threatening crowd or angry mob that must be kept at bay. And where the natural state in which men find themselves does provide a happier context for Locke and his American followers,[22] even he confesses his fear that here, "self-love will make men partial to themselves and their friends, and . . . that ill-nature, passion, and revenge will carry them too far in punishing others. . . ."[23]

Now, the rage in grief, the keening cry, and the angry mob together comprise the dread of liberal culture, and are at once its most basic ingredient. It is this above all that must be subordinated to rational principles of justice, transformed or bound in cautious legalism.[24] The mythical and philosophical ground of our liberal origins is rife with such accounts. The imperative of suppressing vengeful impulses, one might say, is so insistent that it is axiomatic, and it has come to be taken for what is natural, universal, and true.

If vengeance had been given over to the Lord in the Christian tradition, it would be left behind in a state of nature for Locke and supplanted by the rights of self-preservation and punishment. These 'rights' in turn are happily conferred upon the state by the 'consent of the governed.' In the broader tradition, vengeance would variously be set apart from reason and "judicial" punishment (Kant); dismissed as a matter of particular or merely 'subjective will,' and distinct from the retributive right of the state (Hegel); or transformed as by a "common consciousness" into a useful principle of collective authority (Durkheim).[25] While it is sometimes credited as a source of self-respect, bravery, or public virtue in that tradition, it is always something lowly, merely personal or animal in us as well. In every liberal variation, there is the same supposition: Vengeance, that knot of grief and rage that demands a remedy and will not let go, can somehow be divided from its better aspect, detached, converted, or transposed into legitimate punishments, so that the rational law may proceed free from the taint of its pernicious effects. Precisely as Clytemnestra's Furies were compelled by the Goddess to accept a home in Athens,[26] the anger of vengeance is tamed in the philosophical expressions of our justice. But in the same breath it has been distorted, miscast, and almost certainly underestimated.

* * *

Suppose, then, that we do not accept this characterization or the assumptions that inform it – that we do not imagine that vengeance is so brutish and irrational, or that it can be so easily tamed or kept out. Suppose that it is rather more insistent, intractable and clever – a devious agency capable of insinuating itself where it is least expected. This vengeance would make its way within the most rational constructs of justice, even or especially where the latter contrives to punish with precision and detachment. Then, the mythical idea that vengeance can be converted or set aside might seem suspicious. The liberal philosophy, and the justifications and practices of punishment that follow from it, would be open to a different scrutiny.

On this account, vengeance must seem less like the wild beast that has been barred from entry, and more like the uninvited guest at a masquerade. It appears among us in judicious disguise,[27] and while everyone wants to know who or what is hidden behind the mask, they can know it only by its representations. 'Blood,' 'honor,' 'God's justice,' even 'the rights of victims,' then, would appear as the valid traces of its public presentation. And if its true or universal nature could not be readily perceived, it would be recognized by its legitimating symbols – the sword in the lower hand of the figure of Justice; the apparatus of 'painless' execution; or in most every claim to have found the 'just measure' of punishment. In the effort of concealment, therefore, vengeance might appear as many things – the venting of righteous anger, the vindication of good, the condemnation of evil, the administration of just deserts, of right over wrong, getting even, a restoration of balance. Surely as it takes up residence within the rational terms of punitive justice themselves, its involvement with them would seem more intimate and complicated than before.

If it is in the nature of the liberal justifications of punishment to disavow vengeance, that is, it is in the nature of *vengeance* to *claim to be justified*, respectable, a thing of value. The very attempt to legitimate itself – its claim to reverse injury, or to 'right the balance sheets of justice' – is thus an essential aspect of its disguise. Notably, it *seeks* to establish its currency and it asserts its own validity.

Hence, when Americans speak of a 'right to revenge' today, the coupling of vengeance with rights (in that idiom) gives the former a coin of expression other than itself by which it may enter the more legitimate economy of moral exchange. Just as everyday exchange relations must find a medium like gold or silver to establish their relative value, the bloody exchange demanded by revenge enters the moral economy as some other, purer currency of justice. Where there is no question of the true standard of its 'value,' and the exchange into which it enters has no fixed referent of the sort, say, that "labor power" provided for Marx, then vengeance seeks some other article of worth to represent itself – a culturally specific residue by which to measure anguish or its own ability to displace it – 'honor,' perhaps, or 'fairness.'

Vengeance therefore, cannot be discussed apart from its expression as a *quantum* of suffering to be lessened in the victim by vanquishing the offender, or as an amount of good that punishment does for society, or as a quantity of desert that might be gauged on the scales of justice. All such things are efforts at precision in the measurement of pain and proportionate reaction, which again have no essential substance of their own apart from that representation, but which do indeed manifest the wish to give suffering a finite, measurable character. So we find that vengeance is exacted in different pains and privations through the ages – in the agony of the criminal who waits for a blow to come, in imprisonment, or time deprived of liberty, in bodily inflictions, whip strokes, scars, or inscriptions that aim to deliver a message, which have all been 'justified' means of punishment (on utilitarian, retributive or other grounds) at one time or another.

If all of this makes the distinction between vengeance and justice seem less certain, however, liberalism itself has another, most ingenious means of sustaining it. Its division of the world into public and private spheres corresponds exactly with the distinction between rational, calculable, legitimate expressions of justice, and those intolerable private emotions that must be suppressed or left aside. The imagined revenge of our grieving husband is *illegitimate* from that liberal standpoint, not only because it is dangerous and indiscriminate, but because such things must forever remain private. That system cannot entertain it publicly as a question of honor in the way that others might,[28] just as it cannot indulge a venting of collective grief, of the sort that Rosaldo recounts in the headhunters' highly public ritual. It can, however, and most certainly does entertain it as a private fantasy.

Even where things 'merely personal' are categorically dismissed as being extraneous to considerations of justice, they retain an odd *ad hominem* bearing on it nevertheless. It seems wholly appropriate then, that in Mill's founding argument for liberal justice, *On Liberty*, his own enormous grief at the loss of his wife Harriet Taylor – of the "great thoughts and noble feelings which are buried in her grave" – is sealed off in an epitaph at the beginning of that most rational treatise.[29] By Mill's own account, the world of intense feeling had always eluded him, and scarcely ever touched the world of logic and reason that otherwise occupied his thoughts.[30] Personal anguish, a most private thing, must be bracketed, for that reflection on public life and the place of the (private) individual within it to begin. In this emblematic (some say, rather male) liberal formulation, the questions that bothered Rosaldo or might plague the renegade or vigilante are likewise set aside, so that the more abstract considerations of individual liberty, the 'public sphere' and its justice, can be entertained properly.[31]

Much as money, that crude article of public exchange, should have nothing to do with love or friendship, justice should have nothing to do with vengeance in that cleansing division of the world. Such personal motivations should be locked away in a private place, while that justice is meted out as its own public medium of exchange. But of course, justice exists only on the condition of having kept such motives in check. Its very character depends on how this is done, on where it stands in relation to them – on how it resists or enlists them in its cause. If vengeance corrupts liberal justice, it would seem that the latter has been substantially dependent on it as well. The reactive assertions of our democratic revolution; the vindication of rights as a matter of self-respect; the defense of 'self-evident truths' for which so many have given their lives; these are cornerstone of that justice too.[32]

On the one hand, as Judith Shklar suggests, "... revenge is uniquely subjective, not measurable and probably an unquenchable urge of the provoked human heart. It is the very *opposite* of justice in every respect, and inherently incompatible with it." On the other hand, she recognizes also that the "wild justice" of which Bacon had spoken is a "real passion," "blame" a psychological imperative. "Legal justice exists to *domesticate, tame, and control* all forms of vengeance in the interest of social peace and fairness."[33] Justice must exclude, and justice must enlist the vengeance that inevitably makes demands upon it. And in this, we may perceive a fundamental paradox of liberalism: That intractable subjective urge which must be confined to a private place is nevertheless driven to make a generalizable public claim. If it is the opposite of justice, justice cannot do very well without it.[34]

Of course there have been numerous attempts to resolve this dilemma in the early liberal discussions of vengeance. It has variously been conceived as a threatening evil that must be eliminated, a natural passion requiring the restraint of justice, or a rational response to harm in itself that is a valid source of justice.

For Hobbes, with whom the conversation so often begins, the law must be established against that brutish condition in which men "revenge all injuries" done to them,[35] and yet "revengefulness," for him, is also basic among the passions, a "desire, by doing hurt to another to make him condemn some fact of his own."[36] In his *De Homine*, vengeance is driven by hope and fear and would make evildoers "repent." It is distinguished from mere anger, as it is a "long-term will," which, as well as compelling repentance, may "frighten others away from doing injury."[37] Beyond its futile, backward-looking aspect, that is, vengeance itself contains what we would now recognize as a utilitarian interest in effecting future justice.[38] Vengeance, therefore, is divided within itself. It represents panic, irrationality, perpetual war, and a vain hope insofar as it dwells on the past, but it can and should be directed to the "future good" as natural law dictates.[39] Government, then, in *Leviathan,* is set up against the "desolate conditions of masterless men," and should entail the "coercive power to tie their hands from rapine and revenge." Nevertheless, its Governors derive their own strength and glory from the "*vigor*" of such men.[40] Law is set up in opposition to vengeance but is dependent upon vengeance in this respect, and Hobbes at least is forthright about the need to bind it within the coercive power of a foreword-looking justice, and to hold it in reserve against an enemy.

The ambiguity that gives vengeance its place in justice for Hobbes, however, is all but lost in the theory of Locke. What concerns him is the way in which a "natural right of punishment" is surrendered to the state. That "right" (which is, significantly, uncoupled from rapine and revenge and rooted instead in 'self-preservation') is bounded by reason and implicated in justice from the start.[41] By the authority of a 'natural law' that already has this predilection, that is, every man may "bring such evil on any man who has transgressed that law as to make him repent of doing it. . . ."[42] The wish to induce repentance however is at once an inclination of rational men who are 'sovereign to themselves,' and proceeds in accordance with the laws of nature and of reason. That "right" is thus ready made for consensual transfer to the state and confers sovereignty and legitimate punitive authority upon it.

The problem of vengeance would seem to be solved for us thereafter if that well-mannered, rational sort of retaliation against transgression is dominant in the first place, and the anger of Hobbes' 'masterless men' is already subordinated and forgotten. So it is by similar reasoning, that Adam Smith could identify a primary sentiment for justice that seemed entirely free of bitterness and acrimony: "In order to enforce the observation of justice . . . nature has implanted in the human breast that consciousness of ill desert, these terrors of merited punishment which attend upon its violation as the safeguards of mankind, to protect the weak, to curb the violent and to chastise the guilty."[43] What a noble sentiment for justice we are born with in this estimation! What a wonderful thing to be so conscious of ill desert, so dedicated to the common good, so dutifully wary of punishment. And how removed from the grief and rage of vengeance that instinct for justice now appears. Vengeance and war are set off before the law, yet quite openly as justifications for it in Hobbes. But for Locke and Smith and the thinking that follows, it is replaced by a primary instinct or rational inclination toward justice. Insofar as it has told the story in this way, the liberal tradition must be credited with two great accomplishments – it has purged vengeance from considerations of justice, and it never looks back on that motivation seriously again.

* * *

Now of course, and although such naturalistic accounts are no longer fashionable, something of the same logic has survived in the prevailing justifications for punishment. Either vengeance is divided within itself such that its better aspect serves the higher aims of reason (which is how certain retributivists like Kant and Hegel make the case). Or, if just punishment cannot be derived from rational impulses of a first order, it still follows from the pursuit of rational ends, and thus has nothing to do with revenge (as utilitarians like Bentham and Mill maintain).

As different as they seem, then, it is striking how retributivists and utilitarians both privilege that relationship between reason and punishment, and how both, owing no doubt to that same liberal predilection, remain dominant in considerations of punishment today.[44]

In utilitarianism, of which we see premonitions in Hobbes and Locke, punishment is undertaken for the *sake* of reason or rational aims. It is undertaken to protect society as one such aim; intended to reform or rehabilitate the offender and to provide demonstrable benefits for the future good of all. There should be nothing of vengeance here, since this 'consequentialist' justification for punishment does not look back upon the crime, and is disassociated from any such retrospective or compensatory inclinations. It is grounded prospectively insofar as its ends are the deterrent effects of punishment upon criminals or on crime in general. It holds individuals to account for the effects of their actions, taking their crimes into consideration only so as to punish them *enough* to serve as a warning to others who might be similarly inclined.[45]

In retributivism, by contrast, punishment is justified for the *sake* of a very different good – not to achieve practical ends, or even, for that matter, to satisfy the individual who has been wronged. Rather, it would weigh the offense of a particular crime so as to offset or "expiate" the greater "outrage to morality" – the damage done to collective "moral consciousness" as Durkheim put it – or for Hegel, on different grounds, to affirm and restore an "abstract right." For Kant, of course, the offender is held accountable to that aspect in himself (*homo noumenon*) that by its very nature accords with reason and reason's law.[46] Although the terms of retributive accountability to higher justice may vary – from religious conceptions of sin and atonement, to secular systems of merit – such punishments have the aim of advancing a universal morality.[47] By definition, persons as moral beings are implicated in such a moral scheme, and are punished for their failure to live up to it because they deserve to be. This must be distinct from revenge, because imposing discomfort upon them should restore only the moral order in which the conditions of desert have already been established or ordained.[48]

The utilitarian punishes prospectively, with the aim of greater happiness in mind and without looking back upon the crime. The retributivist has a retrospective interest in finding compensation for the crime, in service to a greater moral balance.

For all of their differences, again, as justifications for punishment, the two theories appear to be engaged in a related enterprise. The efforts of both are entirely consistent with the liberal project of denying and enlisting the vengeful impulse. Both validate the infliction of pain (giving it an abstract status) to match or counter the effect of a past injury (proportional punishment). Both make something else of it (an inclination of revenge itself, as we have said, that only *seems* to serve rational ends). For their claims to work as they do, retributivists and utilitarians must thus make comparable assumptions about the nature and measurability of the pains suffered at the hand of another, and about the efficacy or moral worth of inflicting the commensurate pain of punishment in response – that *pain*, no less, can be inflicted in good measure without some other psychological investment.[49] Each would punish in proportion to the crime; the one by weighing, matching, and negating its moral force, the other, by offsetting its effect. Each proceeds without anger or grief, although each, fortuitously, offers a clear reason to punish a murderer with death.

For the utilitarian, says Stanley Benn, "the good that comes from punishment may outweigh ... the intrinsic evil of suffering deliberately inflicted."[50] For the retributivist, according to Murphy: "The criminal, having engaged in wrongful conduct in the past, deserves punishment. ... In receiving punishment the criminal pays a kind of debt to fellow citizens. ... [He] must pay in some other way (receive punishment) because it would not be fair to those who have been obedient if the criminal were allowed to profit from wrong doing."[51] Although we can never know the precise amount of pain (death, or time in prison) that deters people from certain acts, the utilitarian assumes that we can. Although we cannot know how much pain inflicted offsets an injury, the retributivist assumes that we must. And the very fact that each presumes to know the nature and moral efficacy of pain without further elaboration suggests that both have a prior commitment to its use.

Our two theories of punishment, so much opposed, thus meet on the ground where vengeful intentions are denied and pain measured and inflicted to effect an exchange that serves some higher purpose – actions deterred; debts repaid, the rage in grief transposed – either of which might be accomplished by the same punishments and compensations, and which, no less, has made their long collaboration possible. This is quite the same ground on which liberalism (Locke, Hobbes, etc.) once found them united in a way that kept revenge at bay, and it is deeply indebted to much older suppositions about justice. One might say that the very abstraction of pain, for these transactive purposes – even as it generates punishments that seem disinterested in inflicting pain for the sake of revenge – is precisely what allows a *measure* of revenge back in.[52]

* * *

It is significant then, how Mill resolves the problem of revenge and introduces rationality and the calculability of pain instead in his founding account of utilitarianism.[53] First, he acknowledges a "natural feeling of retaliation or revenge." Yet, he says, "this sentiment, in itself, has nothing moral in it; what is moral is the exclusive subordination of it to the social sympathies, so as to wait on and obey their call." A vengeful private feeling is thus subordinated to rational, public, or social sensibilities that make it 'moral.' Upon suffering an injury at the hands of another, one may feel an immediate "resentment" that runs the risk of becoming indiscriminate, but that feeling becomes a "moral feeling" when one holds back and "considers whether an act is blamable before he allows himself to resent it." That patient, calming pause, and the implicit concern for a "rule which is for the benefit of others," together make the punitive response a moral one, and of course, not vengeful resentment, which they repress.[54]

If it is "natural to resent and to repel or retaliate any harm done or attempted against ourselves or against those with whom we sympathize. . . ." and that inclination is connected in the first place with an "impulse of self-defense,"[55] man is also possessed of a "superior intelligence" that allows him to generalize the same impulse. So it is that two distinct things combine in just punishment: the "animal desire to repel or retaliate," and the expansion of that principle to all, once we reflect on it, as "intelligent self-interest." Just punishment derives its "energy of self-assertion" only from the former (vengefulness), but its "morality," strictly speaking, from the latter.[56] It appears that the impulse to "self-defense" at work in the initial inclination to retaliate is rarefied in this logic, subjected to judicious reflection, and hooked up directly with a generalizable interest in the common good and public safety, which is to say the general *utility* of punishment.[57]

Rancor and resentment are entirely washed out of the account then, even as something of their "energy" lingers. There is no suggestion that they might smolder within the "intelligent self-interest" of a more *patient revenge* or affect the judgment of what is "blamable" more tendentiously.[58] There is no suggestion either of how the special considerations of that judgment might really be brought to forget the crime, or purge itself of those complex motives toward the criminal, as in Hobbes' forthright "desire to make him condemn some fact of his own."[59] Rather, it is assumed that the process of interrupting "resentment" and introducing the proper thoughts and considerations can be free of any festering vengefulness, and will enable a purer calculation of justice. The public coin of punishment, then, derived in this manner, will reflect its usefulness only to the aim of general happiness, which may now be meted out with great precision.

It follows that in supporting the use of capital punishment for the crime of murder, Mill can claim to be able to weigh that relatively "short pang of death" against "immuring [the convicted murderer] in a living tomb," or prison – the latter being worse and less humane in his view – and to know the deterrent effects of the fear of such punishment upon the public good.[60] Having followed Mill's prescription, the utilitarian is not at all concerned here with the wickedness of the offender himself or of the particular offense that might have led to one punishment or the other. But he or she is very much concerned to convince the public that the one punishment is the more efficacious and more humane course of action of the two – although the reason for its being humane, under the circumstances, remains something of a mystery.[61]

That public in turn, Mill insists, would be able to see that the punishment of *death* is the better choice in any case – since it has the power to *seem* most terrifying as a deterrent – if only it were not so easily "shocked by death in general and in the abstract, as to care too much about individual cases."[62] He wants them, in effect, to abandon their prejudice against death as a punishment, and care less about the life of the offending party (for which he nevertheless professes humanitarian concern), so that they might embrace it as the single most terrible and efficacious punishment (his feelings about a 'living tomb' notwithstanding). He is, no less, asking them to set aside the one prejudice about pain and death in favor of another, which of course, opens the door to all sorts of other prejudice in assessing one pain in response to another. And in the inevitable *valuation* of pain that this entails, that utility becomes porous to other interests.

As Mill's critics point out, in turning his attention away from the crime and the criminal to focus exclusively on the effect of punishment, the utilitarian has no reason intrinsic to his argument for restraint (being humane). He has no reason for keeping the punishment proportionate to the injury, or even for punishing the guilty party as such (though there are utilitarian solutions for everything). Beyond this, however, in the conditions he has set for the reflection that should transform "resentment" into calculated punishment, Mill presumes a great deal on the public perception of the infliction of pain, and its deterrent effect. He hopes to set aside the "shock" of death (in the public eye), so to impose the better shock of its deterrence; suggesting, as it were, that death is not so terrible, so that death may become *usefully* terrible. The difficulty with this is not that the logic is wrong; it works perfectly if one accepts Mill's premises. It is that from the setting aside of an initial resentment to the suspension of feelings about pain and the selection of the *proper* terror, it depends on people thinking or feeling a certain way about pain. This can hardly resolve the matter, especially in a democracy, where what they think varies, and matters quite a bit.

If Mill succeeds in his argument that the punishment of death is warranted on utilitarian grounds, then the claims that make that conclusion palatable do not rest upon precise shared knowledge about the relative pains of punishment (here, of course, prison might work just as well), so much as on his own assumptions and the rhetorical ability to convey them. To be sure, the pause that *he* makes to "consider... before..." in ridding himself of resentment allows him to insinuate the convenient suggestion that the pain of death is at once more humane and more terrifying, and that the harm that might be done by imposing that terror on the public (by the threat of using it, or as a deterrent) is of measurably less concern, and may be disregarded. The *measure of pain* here is a tissue of guesswork and warmed-over prejudice that refers back all too readily to that initial "resentment."[63]

So again, the "pause to consider" may be filled just as easily by different assumptions about pain or death and their utility. The same punishment may be defended, as is often the case in America today, by a vengeful, retributive claim that some crimes call for the punishment of death precisely because it is the *most* terrible and *least* humane thing to do to a person, but is nevertheless *deserved*. The argument may be bolstered by the claim that the observance of desert in this way has *its own* utility, and that only the public threat of severe punishment will sustain it.[64]

In the leap of "intelligent self-interest" that the utilitarian expects us to make, therefore, that pause in which resentment or vengeful feeling is made to "wait on and obey" the "social sympathies," the utilitarian makes three questionable assumptions about the 'rational' apprehension of pain: First, that it could or should detach or suppress the reaction to injury and the memory of the initial pain from its pronouncement on the person who inflicted it (the conjunction of feeling pain, resentment, and wanting to inflict pain in retaliation, now as abstract "resentment"). Secondly, that it can know the precise effect of different pains upon the offender, and concern itself with these in isolation from the first. Thirdly, that it can measure or know the relative import of the threat of such pains on others and calculate their deterrent effect (or some other utility). Each assumption involves moralizing judgments about the nature or measure of pain, and each, leaves ample room for other "social sympathies" or vengeful prejudices to creep back in.[65]

* * *

By contrast, retribution may be taken as a just cause of punishment if it is derived from a 'universal aspect' of revenge that is already distinguished from its purely subjective or personal aspect. This is Hegel's enduring formulation, taken in part from Kant. In Hegel's view, that distinction can be established by virtue of the fact that there is a determinate "value," that is, an "implicit character" by which a crime and its punishment can be equated at a certain level of abstraction,[66] so that the "measure of punishment" can be "derived from the act."[67] In respect of that value by which a "crime and its negation" are ideally connected (and which can only ever be *approximated* in punishment), "our idea of a thing [an injury] is raised above its immediate character to its universality."[68]

In this, of course, Hegel is careful to confine himself to the task of justifying punishment at the level of "abstract right," and not at the level of the "Understanding" – those merely practical or parochial (and approximate) attempts to measure it. At this level, punishment is undertaken out of respect for the will or reason of the criminal, which has implicitly been engaged in the criminal act. It honors him (as for Kant) by acknowledging his "right" to be punished as a rational being. "Revenge" can only be "just in its content in so far as it is retributive," which is to say, insofar as it addresses injury at the level of this abstract right, but not as something "subjective," "contingent," or "particular."[69]

Here, in effect, Hegel has consolidated the wish of all retributivists (that there be an equivalence between the crime and the punishment) by assigning that equivalence to a higher plane and rendering its abstract character as something beyond reproach. The compelling, transcendental cleverness of this, however – the rarefication of a purer revenge, retribution – is also its difficulty. As Hegel sets himself the task of justifying punishment at the level of abstract right, he has divorced himself from the problem of particular punishments and placed them categorically outside his interest. Yet as he acknowledges, they must be meted out (approximated) in ways that consult a less rarefied aspect of revenge.[70]

Now the very separation of the justification from the application of punishment that is achieved in this reasoning permits practitioners of punishment (who may think that they do not operate on the level of mere "Understanding") to act upon 'subjective, contingent or particular' understandings anyway. They may seek "equivalent" punishments of a more mundane sort *under cover* of the supposition that an abstract equivalence can be found in principle. In this, and related arguments, the abstract justification of retributive justice begs the question of its inevitable particularity, and the fact that it is always *also* a local, highly interested matter. The state that implements that punishment finds itself in a curious position that is, when the stripe is laid on a criminal's back, or the switch is pulled, and the "universal" is made painfully particular.[71]

Thus, and where Hegel at least distinguishes between local punitive practice and the universal justifications for it, many retributivists appeal directly to intuitions about 'desert' or to 'common sense' (in a crude approximation of his logic) offering them up as something generalizable, universal, or true. "Desert," for George Sher, "is central to our pre-reflective thought." It is a matter of intuition, but also of convention and belief. The *justification* of that perfect principle must therefore begin with a "canvassing" of "our less-than-perfect consensus about the particulars of what people deserve."[72]

Other retributivists, like Ernest van den Haag, are similarly less intent than Hegel on distinguishing the justification from the practice, and far less abashed about introducing vengeful bias or intuition as its legitimate basis. They want to distinguish the 'motive,' which is revenge, from the 'purpose,' which is "doing justice" even though the latter should fulfill the task of vengeance. 'Doing justice,' that is, must be undertaken by the courts and legitimate authorities, which are guided by a moral "consensus" (the next best thing to universal truth), but this consensus, which gives them their legitimacy, is and should be openly retributive.[73] Where such circular retributive arguments rest on a popular 'sentiment for justice' or retributive consensus they are often riddled with first person appeals – "We aim to restore" "We punish to expiate. . . ." These arguments go on to present 'intuition' (like Sher) and colloquial understanding (that mere Understanding which was insufficient for Hegel, having now slipped through Hegel's loop) as a philosophical justification that has general validity. If they look back upon a crime for its intrinsic moral "value," then, that abstract universalizable quality of justice discerned in the effort is entirely laden with the vengeful, parochial understanding of its worth.

* * *

The ground on which retributive and utilitarian theories both fulfill a function for liberal justice regarding vengeance may now be seen more clearly. First, it seems, the abstraction by which retribution rises above the subjective tendency in revenge and toward "infinite" retaliation for Hegel[74] is quite analogous to the appeal to general utility that is achieved in the patient reflection that follows an injury for Mill. While the appeal to reason is undertaken differently in each, both formalize the liberal fear of revenge by rejecting its subjective aspect (and the pain and anger of grief). One does so in virtue of abstract right, the other of utility, as they have been doing since Kant and Bentham. In this, however, each justifies the infliction of pain (and notably not just penalties, fines or demotions!) by means that must seem troubling from the standpoint of reason and the respect for persons on which it also depends – that it honors the criminal and his rational will for Kant and Hegel, or that it deters those with reason for Bentham and Mill.

Both theories put pain and reason together again in an ostensibly less vengeful way. As we have said, to sustain their general or universal claims for punishment at the right level of abstraction, both must entertain comparable and unsupportable assumptions about the rational apprehension of pain – that the pain of an injury can be known or assessed (its *value* for one; its *effect* for the other) relative to some greater scheme or end of justice. Or, that one can impose pain upon a particular offender in such a way and to such a degree as to affect his reason (or that of others for the utilitarian), or to serve Reason in general (rational morality or 'right' for the retributivist).[75] Both, therefore, underestimate the extent to which those unsupportable assumptions are really necessary to their claims, and the extent to which they may be faulty. In making such assumptions about pain, that is – that it can be measured, repaired, matched, or put to better use – neither has quite answered the formidable question that Nietzsche posed to all those who "naively" seek some "purpose" in punishment, namely: "How can making suffer constitute a compensation?"[76] Both still assume that reason, and not something else, dictates that the present pain of one person can either redress the past pain of another, or serve some greater purpose in relation to it.

By a trick in time and memory (one that forgets the initial crime and resentment it provokes as such) both theories offer an abstract exchange that would supplant the initial pain and reaction to an injury. The utilitarian looks beyond it, weighing the future 'benefits' of punishment, which should also offset its consequences. The retributivist looks back on it, but sees only its moral 'worth.' The "compensation" in making suffer in either case is achieved by the sleight of hand that makes it seem timeless (unhinged from the precipitating incident and the concerned parties then and now), impersonal, measurable, and universal – but not vengeful, present, immeasurable, and highly personal.

Dedicated as they are to its measurement, and the commensurability of harms and effects, neither theory appreciates the sense in which the injury is also a persistent present memory charged with its own pain and anger – an insistent thing disguised by its own efforts. Neither appreciates the extent to which the vengeful reaction of the victim asserts *its own* 'universality' or 'interest in the good of all' or might initiate an exchange of pain for pain on its own terms. The retributive impulse to find a just measure of punishment and to make the offender pay for his crime retroactively, and the utilitarian wish to make punishment in the right amount serve a future purpose, both take the reaction out of time (temporal experience). Both miss the sense in which the memory of that crime persists and is resistant to measurement, and rages against every attempt to find equivalence or simple compensation. Certainly philosophical justifications of punishment must set aside such things, the crime, the horror, and the rage of loss and grief in order to *be* justifications. Yet each harbors an a priori commitment to the infliction of pain to match an injury in a way that belies its own reasoning. Each tries to rationalize the rather particular pains of injury (or broken attachment) in a way that makes that impossible task seem viable and just. Each in that sense is an excuse masquerading as a reason after the fact.

The point, then, is not just that the two theories fail to produce rational justifications for punishment (they do at least articulate the better reasons for undertaking it), but that in their attempts to do so, they have also rationalized and displaced the *immeasurable* pain of loss and the *irrational* rage in grief with presumptive alternatives. This may be as much the wishful thinking of each theory as anything justified by its argument.[77] So it is that the debate itself has masked a common enterprise in which the two sides are complicit. Both confirm the story that vengeance can be left behind and pain inflicted for a better purpose; both frustrate the impulse that they also indulge; both permit vengeful interests to insinuate themselves in the rational practices of punishment. This is because both proceed from the underlying assumption that reason and justice can do something transmutative with pain and anger in the first place – a supposition drawn from the Greeks and underlying the enlightenment, that is among the oldest sustaining myths of western justice.

It is on this shared ground, therefore, that the two justifications together are now institutionalized in American legal practice – we have retributive prosecutors and utilitarian institutions of punishments, and neither disputes the fundamental legitimacy of the other. Neither questions the idea that there can be an exacting moral calculus of pain, or that it can be measured or applied without vengeance. Neither questions the premise that a justification on this order can be found. And neither is very surprised by or abandons its connection to vengeance. So it is that in the current debate where the public seems sharply divided, each theory looks to the other to shore up its inadequacies, and there are innumerable attempts to reconcile the two.[78] For all practical purposes, one might say, the controlled opposition between retributive and utilitarian impulses is essential to the justification of punishment in America today, and finding the proper balance between them *is* the current liberal project insofar as punishment is concerned.

American Variations

That proper balance has been the subject of a rather pitched battle in America of late. At first, it seems, liberals committed to individual rights and utilitarian reforms related to punishment have been under assault by retributivist challenges from the right.[79] But since those founding arguments about punishment are in fact so porous, the same liberal utilitarians have been able, and surprisingly willing, to accommodate retributive aims, and to openly acknowledge their debt to vengeance.

Many American utilitarians would combat the effects of crime by severely punishing criminals to deter or to reform them, while hoping at the same time that this will rectify their crimes and restore the virtue or the moral health of society. These "revenge-utilitarians," as they have been called,[80] insist that a dangerous impulse toward private revenge can be distinguished from a morally better, and more useful, "governmental revenge."[81] The latter, they say, serves a higher retributive purpose, which has its own utility. For some, such public punishment should actually reduce the incidence of private revenge by satisfying that fundamental impulse in healthier and less dangerous ways. For Ernest van den Haag, again, revenge thus plays a "major role in retributive punishment," much as the "sexual appetite" "finds sanctioned satisfaction in marriage."[82] If feeding that appetite seems vengeful, the justification for satiating it through punishment remains a rational and utilitarian one, since it would channel public anger usefully toward retributive ends to restore a principle of "desert."

While some American retributivists are less interested in satisfying an appetite for vengeance than van den Haag, they still consider the connection between public anger, harsh punishment, and decisive moral standards to be essential. Stanley Brubaker, for one, wants to resuscitate a claim for punishment that he traces to Aristotle. Expressing public disapprobation through punishment, he says, works to distinguish the "beauty of character" from the "ugliness of character." Deserved punishment thus affirms the virtues in a way that has the quality both of a personal and social intervention:

We praise and reward people to express our appreciation of their deeds and our admiration of the beauty of character their deeds bespeak, elevating, displaying, preserving, rendering more secure the things we care about. We punish and blame people to express our resentment and disapproval of their deeds and our detestation of the ugliness of character their crime bespeaks. At both ends of the spectrum we intend the deserved treatment to penetrate deep into the self, to mark our judgments of the person in virtue of the deed.[83]

That our "detestation of . . . ugliness," in Brubaker's words, should "penetrate deep into the self" is hardly a new wish. But his is a rather more bitter expression of retributive sentiment than one finds elsewhere. To enter and "mark" a person in virtue of his deeds is, as he intends it to be here, openly hostile to liberal conception of individual rights (more on this in Chapter 2). It is frankly more comfortable with vengeful punishment than most other retributive theories have been. This is because Brubaker is intent upon reviving the anger of punishment as such, the very thing that liberalism has sacrificed, by "taking out of political life the things men and women love most and thus would be most likely to become angry about – God, country, virtue – and focusing instead on the relatively tame concerns of material well being."[84]

Here, however, it is as if restoring the feelings attached to those missing values, the dearness or jealousy with which they were held, would restore or repatriate their *meaning* too. In this scheme, retributive punishment should do the job of reconnecting the disapproving *affect* to the host of threatened moral values, and in that way repair the moral deficiencies of the system – which is not at all Aristotle's point, but is very much an American tendency as we have said. Brubaker's critique of liberalism, then, would seem to affirm what we have noticed: Liberalism, as such, "cannot punish," as he says, or at least it cannot justify punishment of this morally constitutive sort. But when it *does* inevitably punish, it draws inspirations from much that is properly beyond its scope – ideas about virtue, notions of beauty; "the things we care about." The hope then is that the virtues might be rejoined to moral feeling in retributive acts of punishment, to compensate (quite usefully) for the deficiencies of liberal justice. Curiously, this retributive critique of liberalism and its moral vacancy boasts of a certain social utility. It offers anger or moral indignation as a counterweight to that liberal deficiency in the same way that it accuses liberalism of doing, and it is rather more a symptom of than a solution to the same problem.

Insofar as the usefulness of punishing more (or more angrily) in order to restore virtue inspires American retributivists, the attempt to justify punishment philosophically gives way to efforts to rationalize or valorize the feeling behind it. And if this is not the only thing that guides them, there is quite enough of it out there to constitute a trend.[85] There are many, of course, who are determined to restore the righteous anger of the community and who insist that public outrage itself should be taken as the source of moral and legal justification. That anger for them, expresses the immediacy of moral revulsion, and not the highly self-conscious, reflective transposition of resentment that we find in such thinkers as Hegel or Mill. It appeals to something immanent and "unselfconscious" about mortal feeling of the sort one finds everywhere in retributive and conservative literature – namely to the indisputable character of moral claims; the simple authority of tradition.[86]

It follows that the familiar, first-person construction that Brubaker deploys would seem to supply all that is needed for such a common sense rationale: "We praise . . . to. . . ." "We punish . . . to . . ." as it might reaffirm the favored affect: ". . . with admiration, detestation . . ." to assert the decidedly unreflective validity of vengeful self-assertion. This then affirms the American impulse not only to restore virtue and merit (which again is gaining currency even on the left), but to restore the invective of condemnation; or indeed, the haughtiness of calls for the punishment of "unworthy" persons by those who think they deserve "praise and reward" themselves. This of course is the sense of "moral superiority" that makes punishment serve rank and social order, and with which "merit" has been bound to "privilege," which we will take up in Chapter 2.[87]

In this American retributivism there is a shift in emphasis from the Kantian and Hegelian claim that 'you deserve to be punished for your crime (by virtue of that which is rational in you, for the former, or in respect of universal reason for the latter) because it is right to do so,' to 'I or we deserve to punish you.' This is the very different rhetorical gesture one finds in arguments like Brubaker's that sets the righteous (or the self-righteous, and not just their reason) above the wicked. Yet it is not at all clear that this attempt to make moral hierarchy consonant with the social hierarchy – those who take themselves to be deserving of punishing the undeserving – will restore the proper values or empower the right persons.

If the older retributivism would produce a rational calculus of fairness aimed at rewarding merit (that which is worthy in all of us – a precursor to liberal egalitarianism), the latter is animated precisely by such anti-egalitarian sentiment.[88] In a sense, it *does* admit the rage in grief that has seemed wanting in liberal discussions of justice, but does so by hitching the disembodied anger arising from a pervasive sense of victimhood[89] to a general dissatisfaction over the loss of 'desert' (especially for those who think it was theirs to lose), which is, of course, quite the opposite of connecting a rational retributive impulse to universal right, and far more vituperative than any ordinary moral indignation.[90]

As this sort of American retributivism would place itself above revenge by enlisting the anger of revenge rather directly, it gives the latter a special legitimacy: One judge rather benignly suggests that the "'morality of consent'" intrinsic to a democracy demands that it should heed a public sentiment for revenge and retribution.[91] Yet such thinking also reactivates an older, decidedly undemocratic mode of legitimation in which vengeful anger, moral rectitude, and political authority are connected quite differently. Like this older vengeance, that is, it seeks advantage wherever it can; it discovers evil everywhere (as we shall see); it claims moral superiority for all the right people; and falls with disproportionate weight on the poor and on the weak. It is not surprising, in this context, that the language with which Americans announce their war on drugs, call for "three strikes" in sentencing criminals, or appoint a Drug Czar to combat crime is so quick to invoke such nondemocratic sources of authority.[92]

Within the Law

American law has long labored under the weight of these inclinations. While it has tried to accommodate them, mixing retributive and utilitarian principles in a number of ways, it must do so within a constitutional framework that limits punishment but gives the legislatures a great deal of latitude in its application. The Supreme Court, one recalls, is only charged to consider the meaning of "cruel and unusual" punishment under the Eighth and Fourteenth amendments. It does not weigh the specific rationale or type of justification for punishments imposed by the States. It has no means or mandate to decide whether utilitarian or retributive practices should prevail (there are complicated precedents for both as one sees in the remarks of the Justices), and it is agnostic about expressions of vengeful anger, until or unless they infringe upon established rights.

On the one hand, as the defender of those rights, the Court and the law must not allow the anger of the victim or of the community to influence its actions. The police should scrupulously observe the rights of the accused and give them a clear verbal warning as to their nature.[93] Victims of violent crime must sit silently during the trials of their tormentors. Attorneys must not use inflammatory language to influence a jury. Prisons should detain felons for a time to curtail their actions and deter others, while corporal punishment, and devices of public humiliation, like the old stocks and pillories, are prohibited and have long been considered "cruel."

On the other hand, the law harbors a retributive aspect in the person of the prosecutor, in courtroom procedures that register the anger of victims, and in "victim impact statements."[94] State by state and with federal approval, the law has been responsive to demands to make the prisons more painful and to bring back shaming and corporal punishments.[95] With the restoration of capital punishment in the majority of states, no less, the Court and the legislatures have clearly been less concerned to protect individuals with rights from vengeful excess than to defend the "states' rights" to punish them, and in assuming this posture has become a kind of floodgate for the public anger.

In 1987, for example, the Supreme Court still resisted the use of victim impact statements to recount the suffering or express the anger of victims and their families in capital cases. Justice Powell had argued for the majority that "any decision to impose the death sentence must 'be, and appear to be, based on reason rather than caprice or emotion'" (*Booth v. Maryland*).[96] Powell's equivocation concerning appearances now seems prescient in light of the Court's reversal of that decision in 1991 (*Payne v. Tennessee*), where it insisted that the appearance of reason in the state's courts could be maintained even in the face of the same sort of provocative appeals to sentiment.[97] Indeed, the conflation of 'appearance' and 'reason' that sets the standard for the Court here accords perfectly with the prevailing "revenge-utilitarian" sentiment, and Justice Stewart's own earlier claim that such punishment can best prevent "vigilante justice, and lynch law," by satisfying a public "instinct for retribution" (*Furman v. Georgia*, 1972, J. Stewart concurring).[98]

Such is the legal (and moral) ambiguity of the moment: "Retribution is no longer the dominant objective of the criminal law" (*Williams v. New York*, 1949)[99] as Justice Stewart had affirmed in *Gregg v. Georgia* (1976), "but neither," he continues, "is it a forbidden objective nor one inconsistent with our respect for the dignity of men."[100] "Indeed, the decision that capital punishment may be the appropriate sanction in extreme cases is an expression of the community's belief that certain crimes are themselves *so grievous an affront to humanity* that the only adequate response may be the penalty of death."[101] In the 1958 decision against the death penalty, *Trop v. Dulles*, one recalls, the Court had linked its interpretation of the meaning of "cruel and unusual punishment" to that notion of the "dignity of man," and this in turn to "evolving standards of decency."[102] Now, however, as the public makes new demands upon the law, such standards have "evolved" in quite another direction.

For all of this, however, the law is not simply a reflection of public sentiment, and the Court's resistance to the more emphatic expressions of anger is revealing. It permits legal retribution as the only "adequate response" of the community, but it still holds out against cruelty or capriciousness in punishments that are grossly disproportionate to a crime, or that reflect a pattern of racial bias – retribution, one might say, up to the limit of a discernible infringement on civil rights. While the Court acknowledges an "instinct for retribution," it can muster only jurisdictional (states' rights) or utilitarian reasons for assenting to it, not daring, it would seem, to call it by another name. It follows that as the public frustration with the law creates a tension *within* the law, the latter gives expression to vengeful interests in the rather constrained, prudent language of its decision – "...that certain crimes...are so grievous an affront..." – even as it denies vengeance (or the appearance of vengeance) everywhere else.

It should not be surprising on this ground that the decisions of the criminal courts still frustrate the strongest retributive impulses (the rage in grief in capital cases), such that the latter seeks other avenues of expression. Increasingly, victims of crime pursue remedies in civil court hoping to "recover" in monetary terms what they are unlikely to in punitive ones.[103] Elected officials call for 'legislative relief' for the suffering of victims, demanding systematic and harsher punishments like the mandatory prison terms and "three strikes" laws in many states, or the strict, uniform sentencing code of the Comprehensive Crime Control Act.[104] While such policies purport to be exacting, to reflect fairness and "truth in sentencing" (and decry the interference of "liberal" judges),[105] they turn on a revenge-utilitarian logic that prefers to err, with considerably less precision, on the side of spite.

Ironically it appears that the wish to impose punishment that arises more frankly from anger rests precariously upon the retributive and utilitarian claim to render abstract measurements of pain and suffering *without anger*. This leaves us (or contemporary retributivism at least) in something of a quandary. On the one hand, in order to fulfill retributive and utilitarian expectations, the law must seem to be precise – six months for drunk driving here, one to three years for burglary there. Yet on the other hand, in order to satisfy the public anger, it must justify harsher or rather *more* punishment that is quite out of proportion, and without proof either of its deterrent or its ethical value.[106] It appeals to 'universal rational standards' that are in fact contrivances of local prejudice – a 'consensus,' that is (this being a democracy), which is taken for a universal standard.

So it seems that a very great deal has slipped in with that expressed desire of the states and legislatures to punish more, and the courts' efforts to honor this while punishing 'only enough' to deter.[107] If the law pays lip service to higher retributive and utilitarian sentiments even as it indulges the public anger, the presumption about pain in both – the abstraction of pain from anger, its measurability and convertibility into another quantity or value – becomes all the more untenable. The law, it would seem, can maintain this facade or appear to be rational in this way only if something else reinforces it – the wishful or mythic predilections of the culture.

Behind the effort to justify punishment, that is, one finds an informing myth of justice that makes this all feasible. It has been an article of faith that pain and anger can be channeled justly, and that punishment is somehow elevated in the process – that vengeance, in the story taken from the Greeks, can be transformed into justice by divine or other intervention. That myth of conversion is pervasive. It is so deeply ingrained in the culture that even the formidable critics who examine it most closely have left its central premise undisturbed. It is to this compelling myth, as it emerges in several variations, that we now turn our attention.

The Supporting Myth

In their *Dialectic of Enlightenment*, Theodor Adorno and Max Horkheimer trace the genesis of modern justice to the ordeal of Odysseus and his personal struggle with vengeance. The conversion of the latter takes place in a series of steps, which are at once highly revealing. From the start, in their estimation, Odysseus "... is the self who always restrains himself." Above all, he is the world-historical character who sacrifices his own impulses, rededicates his energies, and sets the stage for the history of civilization as "the history of renunciation," in which reason and law then become possible.[108]

The particular moment of renunciation that is pivotal to those thinkers occurs as Odysseus waits and weighs his actions before attacking the monster Polyphemus – a moment of restraint in which the will to vengeance makes way for rationality; in which there is at once a spontaneous "adjournment of action," a certain "patience" (like Mill's pause), or "perseverance."

In this, they say, an "objective principle" of self-overcoming (imperative denial) has been established for the first time, as Odysseus consciously defers his revenge and internalizes the idea of doing so. It can be generalized beyond the one character and the particular myth thereafter as a societal principle of restraint:

> ... his behavior still openly features as spontaneous intention something that is later concealed in total imperative denial, in order thus to assume irresistible force in the subjection of everything natural. With its transference into the subject, with its emancipation from a mythically given content, this subjection becomes "objective"; objectively self-sufficient in comparison with all particular human aims, it becomes universal rational law.[109]

For the authors, what appears as the spontaneous curtailment of impulse is really the advent of subjective self-possession; an historic act of tremendous will representing nothing less than the emergence of modern subjectivity. Yet subjectivity – at least the solitary, spontaneous subject represented by Odysseus – can scarcely bear the strain of its own effort. It must subject itself to the "imperative denial" of all things natural, a denial that becomes both a governing force within the modern individual (conscience) and an objectifiable basis of law. Subjectivity, in that sense, has been freed from the subjective impulsiveness of the moment, and made into something greater and more enduring. Again, this all occurs in the "deliberation" that precedes Odysseus' calculated act of vengeance:

> Already in Odysseus' patience, and unmistakably after the slaughter of the suitors, revenge becomes legal procedure: the ultimate fulfillment of the mythic compulsion becomes the objective instrument of domination. Justice is restrained revenge. But since this legal "patience" is formed on the basis of something outside itself (nostalgia for the homeland), it acquires human characteristics – even traces of confidence – that point beyond the specific revenge that was refrained from.[110]

In other words, the particular moment of restraint becomes a generalizable restraint – a pause and "legal patience" that stays the vengeful hand for practical reasons and with immense difficulty. But the nature of the deliberation (and the colossal effort that goes with it) must be weighed within the context of the myth. Adorno and Horkheimer remind us that the subordination of vengeance is *strategic*, and that it is brought to serve the aim of getting home (he will take his revenge later). Odysseus sets this vengeance aside momentarily to pursue that other aim (he does not make it serve justice, as he would, say, if he had put the monster on trial). It seems, then, that the strategic subordination of vengeful intention, for our authors and at that pivotal point in our story, comes almost casually to serve rational justice, and that the subjective patience of our hero seems all too easily to join with the objective restraint attributed to the law.[111]

If "Justice is restrained revenge," for Adorno and Horkheimer, it is also *harnessed* revenge. It is now a matter of expedience, in which neither the aim of the mission (getting home) nor the ultimate revenge upon the monster needs to be renounced or sacrificed. And with patience, we may add (which does not merely point "beyond" a specific revenge) Odysseus gets both kinds of "justice."

One can see then how the heroic effort is undertaken in a series of steps in this account. Spontaneous intention must be renounced, patience prevails, and the subjection of impulse is ultimately internalized as an objective principle. For this to occur, restraint, and for that matter perseverance, require a measure of forgetting. Odysseus, we are told, "forgets his life,"[112] and in so doing, his renunciation appears as a fait accompli, which may then prevail as an objective principle of the law. In this, there would seem to be a thoroughgoing conversion of that which had been restrained and of the restraining act as well. The triumph of reason (even for those critics of reason) seems complete, and here ever after, rational justice (utilitarian and retributive reasons for punishment among other things) may proceed without referring back to that very incomplete renunciation that first made them possible.

Once an initial act of vengeance has been forestalled, that is, and myth has legitimized the deed, the supposed transformation of vengeance entails a certain amnesia. Yet that story line of enlightenment notwithstanding, Odysseus (or Homer who is no creature of the enlightenment) insists upon keeping alive in memory the very thing that cannot be subordinated to reason or patience so easily. The terrible and unforgettable image of retaliation will never let us entirely forget it, or regard its transformation, quite in the way that Adorno and Horkheimer do,[113] as something fully accomplished:

> ...So with our brand we bored the great eye socket while blood ran out around the red hot bar. Eyeball and lash were seared; the pierced ball hissed broiling, and the roots popped.
> One sees a white-hot axhead or an adze plunged and wrung in a cold tub, screeching steam – the way they make soft iron hale and hard – just so the eyeball hissed around the spike. The Kyklops bellowed and the rock roared around him, and we fell back in fear.[114]

The anguish of the villain is recounted in great detail in what follows. Odysseus himself cannot forget its less 'strategic' purpose, and even as one confederate begs him not to "bait the beast again," he proclaims his wish for revenge – "If I could take your life I would and take your time away, and hurl you down to hell!"[115] While revenge may succumb like all "spontaneous intention" in the myth of enlightenment, it actively resists the amnesia by which the myth, or any justice that follows, might hope to convert it. Reason and law, it would seem, are not at all the unambiguous victors here.

Surely this idea of conversion becomes commonplace as more modern myths represent the victory of reason with a kind of ritualistic inevitability. At first it seems, for example, that the vengeful Furies of Aeschylus' *Eumenides* represent an unforgettable, unquenchable vengeful anger. In the familiar singular voice, they accost Orestes and reproach him for the murder of his mother:

> ...you'll give me blood for blood, you must!
> Out of your living marrow I will drain
> my red libation, out of your veins I suck my food,
> my raw brutal cups.... [116]

The stark equivalence of blood for blood ("agony for mother-killing agony!" they say) is burdened by a lust for vengeance that is scarcely modified by reason, patience, or any interest in restraint or proportionality. But soon after the intervention of Athena, those vengeful spirits begin to show another side:

> We are the Furies still yes
> but now our rage that patrolled the crimes of men,
> that stalked their rage dissolves...
> ...Strike the balance all in all and god will give you power;

the laws of god may veer from north to south –
we Furies plead for Measure.[117]

All at once, the vengeful spirits seem ready for that unlikely transformation, willing, though one may question their sincerity, to accept the judgment and the tutelage of the stronger Goddess.[118] With a final warning to those of criminal intent, one recalls, the Furies, unquestioning and obedient, take their place upon the stage of justice as Athena directs them, fixed for the moment to a Stone of Unmercifulness, from which they face the accused, as he in turn stands by the Stone of Outrage. Athena has taken her place between two urns into which ten Citizens of her choosing stand ready to cast their ballots to decide the case.

In that one extraordinary moment, the relentless, bloodthirsty spirits of vengeance relent. Their deference to the wise Goddess, like the seemingly spontaneous restraint displayed by Odysseus, is represented as ordinary compliance to the law. Modern justice, and perhaps its most compelling image, have been born.[119] Of course, it is not clear why they relent. It would not make sense to us that they become so reasonable at a moment's notice or succumb so readily to Athena's instruction, unless we were predisposed to accept such reasoning (or to regard her powers as absolute in the way that they do) and unless we have already learned to take such Odysseus-like efforts of self-overcoming for granted.

In the play, the shift is made palatable by the continued presence of the Furies. Their behavior does seem more reasonable. They have undergone a dramatic change in which their anger is made manageable, if not satisfied. Their movements are restricted on the stage; their inclinations anchored, proclaimed, and balanced by those others present on the tribunal. But we know them too well already to see them only in this light. They have had their say in earlier scenes, and they must still represent a tension within the justice that is being staged for us. We know that it is only by their complicity or willingness to still their rage that this tension seems resolvable, and that their unlikely compliance seems strained in that moment of willed (or is it forced?) conversion.

So it is that Fagles, the modern translator, identifies a paradox represented by those "spirits of the avenging dead that can also bring regeneration." Yet, in taking their "merger with Athena" so completely to heart, he suggests that "Athens will now go forward under the guidance of her goddess who embodies justice and compassion, the equity of Heaven and the energies of Earth."[120] In this, the transformation is wrested from paradox – if not completely in the mysterious movement of the play, then in the retelling. And the myth of modern justice is secured in both.

As always, a frightful thing must change its nature, a force reacts upon a force and bloodlust becomes Good Measure. Gods (their motives unquestionable, their power to effect a change implicit) require the payment of moral debts and a settling of accounts. Society needs balance for the good life to proceed, and invariably it is some thing or agency other than revenge that makes that exchange possible. In the one instance, the extraordinary self-control of a hero turns his revenge upon a Cyclops to the service of a greater destiny. In another, vengeance is recast by spirits who accede to the demands of the intervening goddess (or the staging of the playwright, or the translator's flourish). All are catalytic devices of plot or rhetorical effect promising that vengeance can be transformed, or that its champions will be restrained, seated, or kept in their place precisely as they will in all the juridical proceedings that follow. That justice (not vengeance) can be exacted by a surrogate, judge, or executioner (as modern law requires) makes sense only in a world where it is imaginable that personal grief and anger, or the quantity of suffering brought on by a grievous crime, can be dispossessed and represented by another persona, force, or substance – that indispensable magic that myth supplies and makes appear ordinary.

It follows, then, that even when anthropologists, psychologists, or political philosophers weigh the transition to modern justice in more analytical ways, the same wishful alchemy is very much at work. Each account offers us a different vision of how some deeper social force or mechanism drives or explains the transformation of vengeance into justice. Invariably we are presented with an economy of forces other than revenge to explain what is actually at stake in punishing. Punitive retaliation is really about preserving the social balance of violence, says one. It is really about preserving the balance of honor says another; it is about venting sadistic desire says a third. As each theory provides significant insights into the mechanism of the supposed conversion, identifying the means, the hidden economy or catalyst differently, each suggests ways of resolving an irresolvable tension. Each contributes to a story of modern justice that may yet be viewed with greater suspicion.

Theoretical Iterations

In *Violence and the Sacred* – perhaps the most comprehensive contemporary treatment of the matter – René Girard suggests that the emergence both of ritual sacrifice and of modern justice is rooted in the fear of unending "reciprocal act(s) of vengeance."[121] The containment of that violence, says Girard, has been paramount in every society, and punishment serves essentially the same social function as sacrifice once did in containing it. To punish the "sacrificial victim," throughout time, thus gives violence the necessary abstraction to allow for its prevention. In "primitive" societies initially, and by furnishing such a symbolic outlet, the "sacrificial process prevents the spread of violence by keeping violence in check."[122] This is the same aim, he suggests, that is served surreptitiously in modern society by the institutions of punitive justice.[123]

Here, the old liberal fright at the prospect of endless feuding in a state of nature is revealed as a kind of social imperative, or market force within a hidden economy that must be institutionalized in order to preserve peace. That "economy of violence" is not concerned with the "expiation" of a crime, or any sense of personal vindication as such.[124] Rather, it concerns the largely impersonal societal need to deflect violence, and has a particular interest in selecting the sort of "surrogate victim" that least invites further vengeance.[125] This expressly amoral social imperative therefore helps to explain why the sacrificial victim need not be the guilty party in every case. It would explain the headhunter's killing of strangers. It explains modern deterrence, and other seemingly indifferent aspects of punishment, which have been cloaked in "judicial guise" in Girard's phrase, so that the more direct aims of vengeance do not seem to be in play.[126]

For Girard, then, modern justice is built upon a fear of violence that is long forgotten but still deeply ingrained – and doubtless he is in some sense right. Even the modern insistence upon punishing only those individuals who are guilty merely rationalizes the deeper economical need to prevent the spilling of too much blood.[127]

Yet in the very effort to distinguish this amoral function of retaliation, Girard has taken vengeance, properly speaking, out of the equation. His formidable account could arise only within a world in which utility has come to dominate – its inglorious "balance" being quite alien to the self-understanding of retributive punishment or to any idea of desert – and it is ready made for that world too. It is, moreover, alien to any attempt to rectify the harm that has been done in spilling blood, or to moralize suffering and the punitive responses to it.

Certainly modern justice depends on such imperatives more than it cares to admit. Liberal law, like ritual sacrifice, is in some sense set up against the prospect of interminable violence. But in that analysis, the economy of violence hypothesis eclipses the reasons for punishing, those motives that concern us here, its insistence upon expiation, vindication, and the moral assertion against violence.

It may be tempting to overlook such things, for that reason, when examining the more formalized sorts of vengeance that arise in so many systems of honor. Christopher Boehm, for example, offers an account of "blood revenge" driven by a dynamic of duty, pride, and collective dignity that presents a similar functional hypothesis. In the tribal societies of Montenegro, the killing of a clansman for a clansman seems to have affected the balance of violent acts, as Girard suggests. Yet for Boehm, the economy in question is not one of bloodletting violence as it might be represented in sacrificial currencies. It is a matter of collective honor (embodied in the practice of the feud), which for those people becomes tangible, measurable, and morally charged in its own right. Vengeance, in this respect, is not just a dangerous force that is curtailed by such ritual diversions. Rather, it has its own self-conscious interest in the containment of violence, as clansmen kill only enough to secure a delicate balance of honor among them.[128]

It is possible elsewhere then, for elaborate economies of *pride and honor* to displace the simple economies of violence in a great many ritualized practices, ranging from the extremely violent exchanges of the Sicilian vendetta, to the highly formalized (and far less violent) rituals of the medieval duel which Kiernan has discussed at length.[129] If Athena's restraining hand may not be so evident in Girard's account of the imperative to equalize violence, or in Boehm's balance of honor, that is, it is evident in the self-restraint of the individual who acts with honor (codified, restrained vengeance). Yet such an individual is guided by a greater duty – like the less impulsive Odysseus, perhaps. In displays of honor, restraint is also formalized within clear rules of behavior. Ritualized vengeance, one might say, when it is driven by such a code of personal obligation, modifies a more erratic or spontaneous vengeance, and gives sacrificial violence a higher purpose – fighting or killing to serve honor. Honor transforms violence and the persons who perpetrate it. And vengeance (or so the story goes) can be seen as progressing from mere violence and sacrifice *through* honor and *into* justice.

As Edward Ayers reveals in discussing the origins of American justice, however, that progression has not always been a smooth one. For Ayers, an abiding interest in honor and revenge in the old American South was neither transformed nor simply thwarted by a superior Northern liberal justice, as is commonly believed. Rather, the old Southern sense of collective honor had begun to collapse on its own already under the combined pressure of capitalist encroachment and evangelical piety. It was the internal decay of that greater system that would lead to the displacement of personal honor by a more egalitarian conception of "dignity" that properly belonged to the North. Honor and dignity thus appear as defining opposites: "Dignity might be likened to an internal skeleton, to a hard structure at the center of the self; honor, on the other hand, resembles a cumbersome and vulnerable suit of armor that, once pierced, leaves the self no protection, and no alternative except to strike back in desperation."[130] With honor, that is, "you have exactly as much worth as others confer upon you." Slights are intolerable, the system inflexible. In the competing legalism of the North, "each individual at birth possesses an intrinsic value," which would ultimately prove to be more accommodating, egalitarian, and successful as a principle of justice.[131]

Nevertheless, and even in this revealing account, the transition from honor to justice appears as something of a rout. If honor did fail on its own as Ayers suggests, the brawling and dueling of the South that ensued would seem to be too unruly for the modern world and its superior justice. Yet if Northern dignity did not simply displace Southern honor, however, one may argue on similar grounds that the two already shared enough to make the transition feasible.

Owing in part to their common European roots, aristocratic honor and bourgeois dignity had long ago made their peace in certain practical and legal respects.[132] If, for Ayers, "the heart of honor was the respect of others," a related sort of respect would no less underlie the claims of Northern justice.[133] The rights and privileges of the Old World, steeped as they were in vengeance and honor, would inform the "abstract rights" of the new. The rules, rituals, and abstractions of honor, whether or not they could leave the baser inclinations behind, had been incorporated within the prevailing ideals of dignity and the rights of man, so that honor (and its residual vengence) would not so much give way, as be absorbed within the better justice to come.

One might say that having traversed through systems of honor that required its attenuation and rationalization, vengeance had been made ready for the complex modern systems of moral accounting. Even where its cruder aspects were resisted (as by certain evangelical Christians of the American South),[134] vengeance had already made its way within religious schemes of good and evil. It had already been propounded in an ethic that promised to serve higher, rational ends.

So it is that for Weber, vengeance intrinsically possesses a rational aspect that is suited to religious purposes, and is deeply rooted in the psychological need for a "rational theodicy of misfortune." The latter, he insists, has an important part to play in the modern world, where it is particularly necessary that there be "...an ethical interpretation of the 'meaning' of the distribution of fortunes among men," and where the need for this has "increased with the growing rationality of conceptions of the world."[135]

Beyond the ritualized containment of vengeful violence that honor might achieve, religious systems must offer "rationally satisfactory answers to the questioning for the basis of the incongruity between destiny and merit" (sic); an "individual redemption ethics," for example, in which compensations for undeserved suffering and death occur in an afterlife.[136] There is, in Weber's words, a basic "metaphysical need" for such an "economy of salvation" which, through the medium of priests or magicians, identifies the factors to be blamed for suffering and the rewards that make up for it. Vengeance is rationalized in such a scheme as a divine tool of compensation that satisfies this need, and survives obliquely in the belief that those who benefit, but are unworthy, are destined for hell.[137] On this view, *theocratic* vengeance has been enlisted within a religious moral economy concerning far greater balances. Now it appears that the grief and violent rage that seek formal expression in systems of honor are diverted and forgotten in those rational, theological systems of merit – a necessary precondition to the abstractions of liberal law – which, of course, is both an extraordinary insight, and the claim of those systems themselves.

To "bring such evil on any man" in Locke's phrase, "to make him condemn some fact of his own" for Hobbes, however, still seems to contain more rancor than such rationally transformed vengeance would admit. That abiding liberal concern seems to refer back, at least, to an earlier Christian treatment of the same impulse. One that is not yet so well rationalized in the scheme that Weber identifies. One that is less concerned with redemption, and more concerned with the dangers of retaliation. This, of course, is the effort to induce guilt in the offended party for wanting his own revenge or for acting on it. The vengeful impulse would ultimately be placed in the service of theodicy, as Weber suggests, but only by those complex psychological means set out at its origins – the proscription that would put vengeance in the service of conscience, while consigning the force of its anger to a higher authority.

"Dearly beloved," instructs Romans 12 (19-20), "avenge not yourselves, but rather give place unto wrath: for it is written, Vengeance is mine; I will repay, saith the Lord. Therefore if thine enemy hunger, feed him; if he thirst, give him drink: for in so doing thou shall heap coals of fire on his head." Quite apart from the amoral resolution of vengeance in Girard's economy of violence, or its binding in systems of honor (and beyond its subordination in Weber's rational economy of salvation too), there is an immediate, imploring need to displace vengeance with a sense of higher moral obligation; to separate out its better aspect, as it is now seen to reside in the heavens. The charge intoned by God is at once a declaration of His moral supremacy and a prescription for changing a system driven by worldly vengeance and mundane honor into one of abstract conscience and higher duty.

It follows therefore that the mysterious task of "giving place unto wrath" is not just a matter of sacrifice or simple subordination of rage to duty, but a far more subtle psychological proposition as well. It can be accomplished only in the exchange of simple goods for moral goods. Giving food and water, the symbolic currency of kindness, should ignite the "fire" of shame in one's enemy, and kindle guilt (its reflective aspect), while making room for the more judicious vengeance of the Lord.[138] Secreted away within that transaction, then, another moral exchange is undertaken. For one to give sustenance would seem only to be an act of placation toward one's enemy, but here it introduces a pause in enmity – supplication – that allows God's law to enter. People must be good to one another; *only* God punishes, as Athena portends in calming the Furies.

In that extraordinary moment, then, vengeance is psychologically reversed by the exchange of one sort of "good" for another (ordinary goods become moral goods), and it is made ready (its wrath giving place) to be subordinated within a theodicy of misfortune.[139] Once vengeance is the object of religious prohibition, the Christian plan is to effect its transformation through guilt and into guilt – *through* guilt, for presuming to have a power that properly belongs to God, and *into* that guilt which falls as charitable "coals of fire" on the heads of one's enemies. This then is guilt *both* as an internalized condition for those mortals who would punish and for those whom they would punish, *and* as a manifestation of God's judgment – both within and upon all whom only He may judge and punish. The fact that punishment is "deserved," or that an eye may be taken for an eye elsewhere, seems less important here than that vengeance is replaced by guilt and subjected to a higher authority in an *economy of guilt and subordination to God.* This, of course, is where the force of conscience is meant to stay the force of vengeance, a necessary condition not only for the more rational calculations of theodicy, but for that liberal idea that the state assumes the "right of punishment" by the tacit (or acquiescent) consent of the people. It is the foundation too of much liberal toleration, and distinguishes those many American Christians who grasp it from the more punitive Christian right.

* * *

The story of the transformation of vengeance into a largely secular justice is thus not complete without an account of the binding of vengeance by guilt, understood as a matter of individual conscience – or ultimately, as a structural disposition of mind.

Freud (and psychoanalysis) provides just such a story as he explains how the individual psyche is made ready for the civilizing process. The psyche has been made ready, as it were, by an unconscious predilection toward self-control that first finds its footing in the "primordial ambivalence" experienced by an initial band of brothers toward their father. For Freud, the world historical emergence of guilt begins with the killing of the primal father by those sons who had loved and despised him (hence the ambivalence), and who fear his enduring aggressiveness in reprisal for their crime. This fear ultimately comes to be internalized in a way that is constitutive of the psyche itself.[140]

Ordinarily, the aggressive instincts associated with self-preservation would be indiscriminate and enormously dangerous to others. But here, in that primitive state, the feared aggressiveness or reprisal of the father stands as a perpetual force against them. It may thus turn those instincts inward so that they comprise the individual's superego. Once internalized, they confront the violent and demanding aspects of the ego (or for that matter the id) so that people "renounce the satisfaction of this vengeful aggressiveness."[141] As the force of these aggressive instincts is internalized and becomes its own agency within the psyche (now contending with all manner of desires), a conversion quite analogous to that of "giving place unto wrath" has been effected. The intra-psychic transformation of vengeance occurs in an *economy of internalized aggressive energy* of which guilt is the painful, if necessary, result.

Guilt, then, is vengeance and aggression turned inward, its energy bound to other purposes. The ego now confronts the pressure of the superego, the sons band together and renounce vengeance in favor of religion, and ultimately (we may suppose) consent to democratic law. Hereafter, to find another guilty or to feel guilty are two sides of the same coin. Vengeful anger (and guilt) may arise, either because one blames oneself for failing to prevent an injury, or because one unconsciously wished it to occur. The more the vicissitudes of that instinctual economy are revealed, the more the Judeo-Christian, ultimately liberal trick of turning vengeance against itself, appears to have found a sound psychological basis. Yet even as psychoanalysis describes the healthy process by which vengeance is brought into the service of conscience (as every analyst knows), guilt and aggression have their own perverse currency within the psyche, and this account of the emergence of conscience also masks the more indiscriminate and amoral aspects of the same impulse.[142]

* * *

Nietzsche, of course, would seem to be the least complicit in such tales of conversion, as he sets apart the better punitive impulses from the more vengeful ones that do ultimately make their way into liberal morality and law. Nevertheless, he offers two accounts of the origins of punishment (one being his own rendition of the emergence of conscience) that seem not to concern vengeance directly, but help to identify its place in the human experience.

First for him, in a most primitive state, the emerging autonomous individual must acquire a "memory of the will."[143] He must acquire this if he is to have the "right to make promises" that depends on having such a memory.[144] Once that is achieved, that individual "reserves a kick" for "those who promise without the right," and a "rod for the liar," thus enacting the part of conscience. Yet conscience, the capacity for guilt and responsibility, is at first "burned" into him to become the "dominating instinct" (recall Freud). It is burned into him by the punishing effects of "torture and sacrifice" that endure in memory; those ingenious punishments and penal codes that presage modern law and justice and which, in this capacity, have little to do with revenge.[145]

Secondly for Nietzsche in another vein, the aims of punishment are best exhibited in the primitive relationship between a "creditor and debtor"[146] – a punitive dynamic that involves persons who make promises, albeit now with a different moral salience, which does not concern revenge either. Here, the creditor seeks compensation for an unpaid debt by inflicting "indignity and torture" upon the debtor.[147] This is not yet punishment that is undertaken because it is "deserved," however, which is a later development. Rather, the pleasure he takes in such cruelty itself is his primary compensation. His enjoyment of the position of superiority that he assumes in inflicting it (though he may be of lower rank) offers him a "foretaste of higher rank," which allows him to partake in the "right of masters."[148] Although he may never be of such rank, the posture in which he enjoys this is quite the same as that of noble men who were once "active aggressive, arrogant"[149] – who were possessed of a "better conscience,"[150] who punished freely without guilt; who themselves take a certain justified and, "profound joy in all the voluptuousness of victory and cruelty."[151]

The joy of punishing without the burden of conscience therefore has attributes of a more direct kind of vengeance that once accompanied honor,[152] but where it attaches to the position of mastery (or is found in the hands of the nobles elsewhere) it is always something more pure.[153] On the contrary, it is the slavish reaction of the downtrodden themselves that has always harbored the more treacherous impulses; the *ressentiment* of slaves toward the nobles, charged as it is with the "reactive" feelings of envy, jealousy, and festering vengeance.[154] Revenge of this sort is clearly lodged within the revolt of slaves against their rightful superiors – a force of relentless unforgiveness – ultimately an abstract or "imaginary" revenge, which has (regrettably for Nietzsche) been encoded in Judeo-Christian ethics and becomes entangled with modern justice.[155] Insofar as justice survives this assault, however, it is because that noble morality has set a "stronger power" against such *ressentiment*, ultimately turning "grudges and rancor" into a better, impersonal sort of law.[156]

The truth about punishment in this vein, and what dignifies it, is that it is born among the better motives of creditors and nobles (those who imagine or possess higher rank and punish without the burden of conscience, though each has a different place in things), and remains decidedly more pure and forthright than that slavish revenge. Among the Egyptians, Nietzsche reminds us, a "creditor could inflict every kind of indignity and torture upon the body of the debtor," and the creditor's satisfaction in punishing the shirking debtor bears its own self-justifying "logic." He seeks a certain "recompense in the form of a kind of *pleasure* – the pleasure of being able to vent his power freely upon one who is powerless, the voluptuous pleasure '*de faire le mal pour le plaisir de le faire.*'"[157] Hence, Nietzsche's answer to his own question – "How can making suffer constitute a compensation?"[158] – appears at first to be that the sadistic pleasure of cruelty is taken in repayment for that which has been irrevocably lost – "money, land possessions of any kind..." – an *economy*, as it were, *of cruelty and sadistic pleasure.*[159]

Like the curtailment of bloodletting by sacrifice (Girard) and the Biblical exchange of goods for guilt, it seems once more that an essentially amoral substitution of things has been identified by Nietzsche and that the "valuating animal" man, who contrives equivalencies everywhere, has magically produced another one here.[160]

As the creditor seeks moral repayment in this peculiar currency, however, it is not just that a sadistic enjoyment is traded for an injury. Nietzsche makes much of the "*festival* pleasure" of cruelty in this exchange as well. There is an exchange of the pain of one for the pleasure of the other. But the sense of moral right attaches to something else, something haughty and related to social rank – a publicly acknowledged exercise of force.[161] The efficacy of the exchange, and even the pleasure in such punitive cruelty, one might say, lies in the freedom to vent one's will with *righteousness* – that masterly "voluptuousness of victory," which is also quite free of guilt. It is at once the pleasure of exercising this power with approbation, in having "a warrant for and a title to cruelty," as Nietzsche puts it, that makes it not simply sadistic cruelty, but cruelty that is freely applied or withheld, and above all, admired by its audience.[162] It follows that either a creditor or a noble man may take pleasure in forgoing the punishment of his inferiors, because he can, quite literally, afford fairness and mercy in the bargain.[163]

On the one hand, punishment seems to be satisfying as the indulgence of sadistic pleasure. On the other hand, this haughty pleasure derives from something more – the "exalted sensation" and esteem that accompanies the "right of the masters" – though Nietzsche has not exhausted the implications of that here.[164] The latter is a quality that he has disassociated from reactive revenge in order to claim it for a better, nobler justice that will be purged of such vengeance, or for a time when righteous masters punish without shame.

But who is to say that the enjoyment of that freedom to vent cruelty with right – or that better justice he associates with it – can be so readily distinguished from the indiscriminate and self-righteous joys of vengeance as such?[165] In revealing the "truth" about punishment that is (what is best, more honestly cruel and masterly, and what is worst, most "reactive," resentful, and vengeful), and in exempting his rarefied 'nobility' from the latter, Nietzsche conceals what is vengeful in the *nobles* and everyone else who takes pleasure in such punishment.[166] The aspiration to righteousness and to vindication, the need to occupy a place of power with seeming legitimacy; the condescension, arrogance, and even resentment (if not *ressentiment*) that is no stranger to honor – all of these are as much the impulse of the noble as the slave.[167]

This of course is why it is now possible for *these* "vengeful" impulses, cloaked in 'fairness' and legitimacy, to make their 'noble' claim upon the law in a highly reactive contemporary American context where retributivists call for greater punishment.[168] Here, a righteous venting of cruelty linked to privilege is all too accommodating to its own resentment, rage, and grief, and finds it all too easy to denounce the 'abstract revenge' of liberal justice – those very rights and principles of equity that arose from our own struggle against slavery. This is a vengeance of *condescension* rather than envy (*ressentiment*) of a sort that Nietzsche did not take to task – an "imaginary" revenge of would-be nobles.[169]

If Nietzsche is more forthright than most in insisting that enjoying cruelty was once at the heart of punishment, the attempt to ennoble that cruelty and to disassociate vengeance from such noble efforts remains suspect – as suspicious at least as what we now make of it in legal punishment. Against the vengeance that makes its way into the law as *ressentiment*, that is, Nietzsche held out the possibility that a more honest, less reactive punishment without it might be 'redeemed' by the more noble man of the future.[170] Yet in suggesting that vengeance may be displaced by the indulgence of a purer, better cruelty, he lets the very vengeance that is inseparable from such cruelty back in, and has inverted, but not unseated, the myth of its conversion into justice.

The Enjoyment of Cruelty or the Management of Memories of Horror

There is another part of the story as Nietzsche tells it that may help to explain the relationship between vengeance and justice in a way that is not tied to this line of reasoning. Once again, man is the animal "with the right to make promises," and promises – enduring commitments ruled by conscience – are dependent upon memory.[171] It is as a creature with a "memory of the will" that man acquires a "conscience" and conscience, once more, is impressed on him by bloody punishments.

Punishment then is certainly "a festival, namely the rape and mockery of a finally defeated enemy" (a cruel pleasure, if not a vengeful one), but it is also "the making of a memory...."[172] The latter is accomplished no less, as "only that which never ceases to hurt stays in memory."[173] So it was too in the practice of the ancient "memory arts," as Frances Yates has rediscovered them, that even the most ordinary image could be made memorable "by introducing one stained with blood, or soiled with mud or smeared with red paint, so that its form is more striking..."[174] Those well-crafted, memorable images that constitute violent punishments in Nietzsche's consideration surely serve similar purposes.

To make memories in this way must therefore be a complicated proposition. Not only do cruel punishments impose a memory to produce conscience, one might say, they put cruelty in the service of the promise. They reconstitute memory to suit the demands of conscience, and in doing so meet the demands of justice. If man "creates a memory for himself" in punishing, that is, he does not do so only to shock or make memorable for the sake of establishing his conscience. He must do so as well to *manipulate* memory and reverse cruelty, making use of both in the name of conscience.

The memory effects that Nietzsche helps us to see in punishment are threefold. First they play a vital part in producing conscience, even if, as he allows, they are not very good at inducing conscience in an offender.[175] Secondly, they indulge cruelty enjoyed from a superior position that alters the way the punisher is perceived or remembered – as vindication (although Nietzsche does not emphasize the point). Thirdly, they create a memorable spectacle or lesson for all. Punishment is thus demonstrably "cruel" on the way to being "exalted." It aims to reverse the past and to proclaim that reversal to all as a matter of publicly affirmed conscience. It must be this character of punishment – those very mnemonic effects – that link the creditor's (more noble) cruelty to vengeance, and certain disturbing aspects of liberal punishment.

Thus, and although he did not mean it this way, Nietzsche has unearthed a constellation of punitive interests in which vengeance, memory, cruelty, and law are all deeply connected.[176] Now, we might say, it is not the venting of cruelty or the enjoyment of the power to vent it, as it is first taken as compensation by the creditor, that is at stake. Compensation is to be had in having the power to enlist cruelty to change the past. This is the pleasure as it were, of exchanging one bloody past for another, of punishing and 'making a memory' not only to produce conscience, but to displace the memory of an injury and seemingly reverse its consequence.[177] Between the pleasure in cruelty, and the satisfaction of constructing that substitute memory by way of punishment, lies that pleasure in altering the truth – a species of self-deception as we shall see – that makes the idea that an injury (or debt) can be repaid or undone in this way seem entirely plausible.[178] This festival of punishment enlists cruelty, memory, right, and truth in ways that Nietzsche does not credit, and what is 'festive' in it is precisely the transformative pleasure of revenge. The latter shifts the world by its own magic, and if man, noble or otherwise, is the animal who makes promises to secure the future, he is also one who rectifies the past and alters the truth to suit his present wishes.

Evidently, the complex pleasures at stake in this are not fully explained by the joy-in-cruelty hypothesis, nor has the latter fully answered Nietzsche's question, "how can making suffer constitute a compensation?"[179] Rather (and especially when the crime in question is a great deal worse than the simple failure to pay a debt), they prompt a different set of questions. How does the cruelty of punishment act to compensate for, relieve, or erase such terrible memories? How does it bind the rage in grief? Why have he and other "genealogists of morals" (as he calls them) been so oblivious to the need for *this* compensation in their efforts to discover a 'purpose' in punishment?[180]

Initially, Nietzsche insists, punishment "tames men but does not make them 'better.'" Yet later with its help they develop a "bad conscience," the 'internalization' and 'inhibition' of impulses that ultimately accompany the creation of the "soul."[181] But once this becomes its aim, we may add, punishment obtains another purpose as well. It tries to justify and make sense of its own cruelty, or rather (if we extend the argument), *out* of its cruelty. That proud creature that remembers and "deserves" now also seeks validation against the suffering and indignity that he does not deserve, and against others for what they deserve. In the moment of judging, whether to be cruel or merciful in punishing one who has wronged him, he seeks vindication, expiation. He wants to make the offender take back or repent of his action, and perhaps foolishly, to induce a "sting of conscience" in him.

In the moment when he stands over the offender flogging him with all his might in the certainty that he is right, he also knows that he is tragically wrong and that this action will not produce 'right' or achieve its aim. The action is satisfying, however, as the wronged man insists to himself and to others that the punishment has indeed been effective. He insists that a wrong has been made right; that the past and memory have both been addressed, that conscience has been served (at least abstractly) if not repaired in the offender, and that 'morality' or 'desert' have been restored in the enactment. By such punishment (and such demonstrative cruelty), the crude image of what he has suffered is carved in duplicate within the offender (and made memorable), such that his pain appears as the proper vehicle for undoing the harm that he has done. Like a voodoo doll, it is linked by the likeness of that image (plausibly, rationally) to the cause of his suffering and to the memory of the injury to be discharged.

Yet as soon as cruelty is caught up in the need to make memory in this way it becomes a *proof against proof.* It performs an impossible reversal that is affirmed nevertheless before witnesses. It would rectify unendurable memories of suffering by changing the equation of suffering itself – undoing the effect of pain through pain, insisting against all doubt that this can be done.[182] Thus, in systems of honor, a sense of obligation or debt is met by addressing the injured party through an injury (a slap, a thrown gauntlet), a slight by a slight for all to see. The claim of most every punitive power to undo suffering by reversing its effects (even in the utilitarian case by making something useful of it) still bears the mark of these origins. This must be close to the heart of the Judeo-Christian tradition and the residual vengeance that Nietzsche saw in it. The hope of redressing a particular harm is at once a source of faith, redemption, a wish, and a promise to undo harm and suffering in general.

The compensatory pleasure that Nietzsche's creditor and others take in possessing the power of cruelty, once again, is also a pleasure in being recognized as having such power over the villain, and in virtue of this, the power to reconstitute the memory of the crime. He, and others who do likewise, would create a memory – of himself as being powerful where he had not been before; of the offender in a posture of regret in spite of himself, and of the terrible consequence of the latter's misdeeds which is here established before witnesses. He acquires the power to retell the story of the crime (or unpaid debt), and to underscore its message by the reversal and the reinscription of pain.

If its aim is not the sadistic pleasure of cruelty per se, it is more precisely that of publicly humiliating one's tormentor and obtaining approval for the act. In its more modern variation, it is the satisfaction of rationalizing the punitive act as being laudable and moral – of legitimating such public humiliation and the authority that undertakes it. The wish to be recognized in this way is at once more personal and vindictive than the headhunter's quest, yet public enough in its posturing to insist on its high reputation or "standing" as law.[183] If, on the one hand, it reflects an almost infantile desire to be acknowledged in the eyes of another, to induce a memory or a pinch of conscience, it also aspires to affect a legitimating public (or audience) by the moralizing (and most memorable) pain of shame.[184]

So it is that at the dawn of liberal justice public floggings often required the additional humiliation of nudity.[185] Even in laying the philosophical groundwork for that justice (which would ultimately be free of such things) Kant allows for the "humiliation of pride" for an offender of high standing, suggesting that if such a man has offended the honor of another, he might be required to make a public apology and also kiss his hand.[186] So strong, and unquestioned is the impulse to right an injury and rectify the past this way, that it is commonly perceived as the source of self-respect, as of all the respect and reciprocity underlying reason and law. But this, notably, is 'self-respect' that is dependent on the humiliation of another (a peculiar privilege attached to the position of mastery). Its real pleasure – the compensation it finds in making another suffer – is to convince oneself and others that one has been uplifted or ennobled by the shaming of the other: that painful memory will cease, when humiliating punishment has put an end, in Aeschylus' phrase, to that "relentless anguish gnawing at the heart."[187]

Now, and if cruelty had been pressed into the service of justice and the creation of memory in one way in Nietzsche's argument, I maintain that the impulse to humiliate employs cruelty to affect memory and produce justice in other ways as well. Vengeance entails an *economy of memories of horror* – an economy that aims to rectify the past in multiple ways.[188] Purging the memory of victims, inducing recognition in offenders, changing the story for those who bear witness in memorable acts of humiliation – all are essential means of rectification. Even the covering myth of the conversion of vengeance into justice, I maintain, turns upon this underlying need to reconstitute the past. And the most rational justifications of punishment are caught up in the wish to effect memory in this way too.

This is most apparent when one assumes that the paradigmatic crime is not the breaking of a promise or the failure to pay a debt, but the killing of loved ones – mothers, fathers, children, siblings, husbands, wives. It is this sort of crime (and dreadful memory) for which the Furies pursued Orestes through the ages, for which clans have fought wars, and which our liberal politicians have such difficulty addressing.[189] I suggest that all those other 'economies' make sense in light of this – the moral economy of desert touted by the retributivist; the utilitarian calculus that puts the pain to better use; the "economy of salvation" in Weber; of violence in Girard; of honor in Boehm; of aggressive instincts in Freud, and of guilt; suffering and subordination in the New Testament; even the Nietzschean exchange of the joy in cruelty for an injury. All attempt to redress the past in some way; to transpose pain, horror, grief, and guilt by rearranging time and memory; to transfer pain from one party to another; and to disguise the effort involved (a kind of power, a sort of 'might') as something rational, moral, quantifiable, legitimate, or 'right.' All such efforts would displace an unendurable past by offering some impersonal quantity in its place. It is that very moralizing abstraction of vengeance, I argue, that has long anticipated the move to a rational modern justice.[190]

If the wish to rectify the past does seem to have a logic of its own, however, or to serve rational ends, it is never identical with them. Where it is (obsessively) concerned to take the measure of a crime in the attempt to alter the past or exchange memories, it is really not interested in equitable punishment as such. Where it is (desperately) concerned with fairness at one level, it has no commitment at all to a 'fairness of proportionality' of the sort that concerns retributivists and utilitarians.[191] On the contrary, it seeks to establish memorable punishments that vanquish and exceed the memory of an offense where it can no longer vanquish or humiliate an enemy with as much effect. It aims 'economically' to get the *better* of the bargain.[192] It expresses the need to manage grief and rage 'efficiently.' Its unique restorative power may appear as a benefit for society or an affirmation of 'desert,' even where it is really more self-serving. It may look very much like self-defense or an act of self-preservation as for Locke and Mill, yet the true motive of the protection it affords is either retroactive ('retribution') or concealed within projections onto the future as 'deterrence' ('utility').

In this, the impulse to rectify owes more to its own need to affect time and memory than to any greater reason, truth, or imperative of 'necessity.' This is why the claim among utilitarians that they would punish only enough to deter seems disingenuous.[193] It is why the collective anger of retributivists, for all of their protests to the contrary, can so easily be vented upon the innocent, the surrogate, or the scapegoat. It is why aggrieved persons today who are concerned only with victims' rights may be more anxious to get on with the punishment than to be sure that the right person receives it, and why, at the level of motives that are not taken seriously enough, this is quite often preferred.[194]

Finally, this wish to rectify the past would convert memories of horror, diminish and displace them. Yet rectification, psychologically speaking, is also a distortion[195] – an act of self-justification that makes its claim *as* greater justice (in spite of the truth, and in order to alter the past), which is not really an exchange or balance or a proper economy at all. It is significant, then, that this *irrational* proclivity is so deeply entwined with the rational practices of law and the justifications for punishment. To be sure, the 'neutrality' and 'universality' that reflect the rational character of the law have been more open to its influence than one might think.[196]

* * *

The aspect of creating memory in punishment that Nietzsche calls to our attention now has further implications. Vengeance, as the author of *Wild Justice* suggests, is the opposite of the impulse to "forgive and forget."[197] The authors of *Vengeance: The Fight Against Injustice* concur, saying it "does not allow one to forget" as forgiveness demands.[198] In light of its odd economic rationality, however, I suggest that the objective of vengeance is precisely to forget, or more precisely, to consign to a quieter memory that which rage, guilt, or humiliation might otherwise turn into an obsession.[199] If one cannot wholly forget a particular horror, one can displace or exchange it, minimize its hold upon the present, and hope to put it to a different use. Those punishments that have been 'justified' in so many ways thus do not transform vengeance into justice, blood, honor, or anything else, but are continuous with it in this respect. Each provides a currency in that exchange, a way of representing and redistributing intolerable memories, a way of managing or reconciling the rage in grief.

In every culture, it appears, such exchanges do much more than punish crime. They provide a means of remembering that which a people must, but cannot bear to remember in the making of their justice; a symbolic currency that allows such things to be represented as justice, a mode of rectification: The bloody crucifix and the stylized cross each differently recall the unjust suffering of the martyr and displace it. His pain (and all pain) must be recalled *before and instead* of the betrayal and cruelty heaped upon him – which would otherwise call for revenge – a precise forgetting that makes way for forgiveness and the vindication of such suffering in God's justice.[200] Timothy McVeigh's vacant execution chamber lingers in memory, his crime eclipsed if not forgotten. The denuded image makes a memory that attests both to the inability of the state to rectify the injury, and the current imperative of making the attempt.[201]

Now this has extraordinary implications for understanding the cultural crisis with which we began. One may venture a hypothesis. If vengeance seeks a reparation of memory and reinstatement of moral feeling that is both a source of liberal justice and contrary to its basic tenets, then the increased interest in vengeance reflects the heightening of that contradiction. It is a sign, perhaps, that the ill-founded attempt to rationalize punishment and to deny its vengeful aspect has reached a point of intolerable stress, and that a crack in the foundation has begun to affect the edifice.

Once again, it is not our 'lack of values' that is at stake in this, but a need to rectify suffering in a way that gives it value and makes it part of justice again. Thus, when the legal system fails to be morally decisive or to punish in convincing ways (one thinks of O. J. Simpson, the Menendez brothers, or Susan Smith), a great many people revile the verdict. Their dissatisfaction with the result is at once dissatisfaction with justice at this deeper level – with its inability to redress harm, to make sense of pain, cruelty, and violent crime. The lack of a convincing legal resolution is, more deeply, a failure to rationalize suffering, and the failure of justice at that level heightens their interest in revenge. Vengeance returns, in this sense, not as an expression of higher morality, but where higher morality no longer fulfils its function. It is thus expressed as frustration *with* justice (displaying images of McVeigh's gas chamber conveys something of this), or a wish to put 'values' back into justice. It insinuates itself within the most mundane legal pronouncements, where its message can be read plainly between the lines.

* * *

One can see this even in the most ordinary execution notices that appear in the press from time to time. Those brief wire service announcements are surprisingly consistent in tone and structure and appear only to fulfill the requirements of legal notification.[202] If one looks closely at their content, however, and reads them as an American might, one can make out just what is struggling for expression. Every year there are dozens of declarations like the following:

Associated Press (April 7, 1992)
A triple murderer made an obscene gesture as he was put to death in the gas chamber yesterday in Arizona's first execution in 29 years. Donald Eugene Harding, 43, was executed just after midnight following a flurry of appeals. He was pronounced dead 10 1/2 minutes after cyanide pellets were dropped into a bowl of sulfuric acid beneath his chair.... [203]

After describing Harding's "throes of death" and a repetition of the "obscene gesture," the notice informs us that Attorney General Grant Woods was "among the witnesses." After that, the details of Harding's crimes are recounted. At first glance the report seems impersonal and straightforward, and like the event itself lacking in any malice. The courts have ruled, the arguments have been weighed and the punishment, now long after the fact, seems anything but vengeful.

Yet in this brief column, just 225 words, a distinct frame has been imposed on memory, pain, and anger even as the perfunctory language and well-worn phrases recall a familiar American story. There has been a "flurry of appeals," we are told (the clock ticking, the Warden waiting for the Governor's call, the fatal 'pellets dropped'). Euphemism is reserved for the defiant "gesture" (expressed here in the active voice), but not for the terrible crimes detailed in the passage that follows. *It* is "obscene," while the execution, for all the understated death throes, is like any other public event at which better manners should be observed.[204]

It is unsurprising that the reportage begins in the moment before Harding's death. Yet this ordinary choice reverses the sequence of crime and punishment, accomplishing in retrospect what punishment would do to memory. The ghastly event now precedes and overshadows the memory of the crime as if to diminish it. In due course, Harding's victims are named, and the details of the crime retold (they were "robbed, hog-tied, beaten and shot"). As horrifying as the depiction of their fate must seem, it is secondary in the order of retelling – succinct, economical, matter of fact, and past tense.

The objective flatness of the language works almost as a provocation. The words are well chosen to capture the villain's indifference toward his victims, and quite capable of provoking anger now. But here too, the anger that is summoned is more general. It is grief for all victims – Harding "was linked to at least three other slayings," his death a blow for justice everywhere. The certainty of punishment is affirmed accordingly – the refusal of the parole board is expected, the inescapable chamber, the unequivocal effect of the fallen pellet, the clipped column itself a testament to the finality of judgment and the inevitability of deserved punishment. All remark upon seriousness and legitimacy of the event – even as one senses that the suppressed anger of the nameless author (at Harding and perhaps the punishment itself) has only momentarily been suspended.[205]

If it is not itself a bit of vengeance, the story bears all of the markings of vengeance. First, and in portraying Harding in a posture of permanent defeat (he will never be remembered in any other way), it has done the work of fright and humiliation to affect the exchange of memories. Secondly, as vengeance requires, we must know the state of mind of the condemned man (he is *compos mentis* at the time of punishment such that his conscious suffering may be likened to the suffering he has caused; which is why the "obscene gesture" is so important), just as we must know that he had *mens rea* in committing the crime.[206] Beyond the good liberal arguments for restricting punishment to those who are sane and rational, that is, linking the humiliation of the moment to the memory of the crime depends upon his being in full possession of his faculties. A message must be conveyed and received with certainty, as in all face-to-face encounters of revenge – as if to make the offender rethink his actions in spite of himself, to undo the effect he has had on memory and time.

Thirdly, that message is affirmed before an audience. Readers imagine having witnessed the event, even as the Attorney General stands in for them in a way that makes it palatable. The announcement that reaches them is no 'spectacle' like the old public executions (that 'cruel festival' would be too much for liberal sensibilities to bear),[207] yet as they read, but do not see (photographs are not permitted), the faint spectacle of a spectacle admits vengeful feeling with just the right amount of detachment.

Fourth, time is of the essence in this short text. Not only is this execution the first for Arizona in 29 years (we are still hearing this of executions; the first woman, the first Asian, as if the novelty is what makes the moment newsworthy) but the trial is long over and the offender has waited an eternity on death row. Time heals, but time also punishes, as Nietzsche reminds us – vengeance waits and savors its passing.[208] Not only does the threatening power of the offender seem to wither across time; time does the hurting until the moment when it ends (duly noted at "10 1/2 minutes past midnight"). Fifth, time freezes in the recorded moment of finality, an exacting measurement that makes the memory of what is otherwise an incalculable event – the end of a life – now seem entirely calculable. The stamp of time marks the occasion like the date on the receipt for a purchase or the hour on a punch clock. A fair exchange has taken place, a death for a death, and balance has been restored.

Sixth, the event is shrouded. The announcement, like the vengeance it conceals, dignifies and also amplifies the punishment. The executioner and the condemned are not masked or blindfolded these days, but hidden within the chamber to lend them dignity, somberly depicted if not quite seen. So too the ritualized language ("throes of death," "pronounced dead") conceals and makes the violent ending seem proper, clinical, and just. Now the impression left to memory is that of deserved and final justice (as vengeance would want too) of certainty and inevitability that must transcend the ambiguities of law and legal punishment. The crime, the pain it has caused, the disruption of life and time, the infliction of pain in compensation, all achieve coherence. The very thing that strains credulity now makes perfect sense, as it declares to us that 'justice has been done.'

* * *

Here, where the formal act of justice meets the public eye, the phrasing of the press release is clearly a product of the times. The rage in grief vies for expression in the exacting prose as it does in the punishment itself, and the facade of legal observance scarcely conceals the difficulty. The effort seems strained, although it is all that can be done under the circumstances. Here again, an underlying assumption of liberalism has been called into question, and to all the other troubling dichotomies that characterize that tradition,[209] we may add another: The separation of vengeance and justice as it has been rendered in myth and taken up by our theories and practices of punishment is highly suspect. It is an ideological device of immense importance to the tradition of liberal justice. Yet it is impossible to maintain if one looks closely at that justice, its practices of punishment, the motives behind them, and the forms of public expression that they most frequently find.

In reviving the question of vengeance, then, and laying it directly to liberal justice, I have raised a set of troubling questions about the nature of democracy itself, public anger, and the punitive authority of the state. If our 'crisis' is not only about the loss of moral guidance, merit, and virtue, but also concerns these frustrated vengeful interests, do the latter now make impossible demands upon our democratic state? Do such demands threaten what is left of the reason and neutrality of that state? Should such a state based on the will of the people heed the public anger, or resist it? Does the latter pose dangers to democratic authority itself, to truth, fairness, balance, and reason, such that they must be rearticulated or defended more forcefully? And given this dilemma, how should a democracy properly punish? In the end it will seem that there are two sorts of answers to these questions: We can envision a democratic state that capitulates to the demands of public outrage, restores corporal and capital punishments, and celebrates retribution as a means of restoring merit and virtue. Or, we can perceive the inadequacy of vengeance as a source of moral restoration, recognize its perils, and devise punishments that minimize the risk.

Having exposed the danger of vengeance to scrutiny, I maintain, it will be very hard to pretend that the democratic state can or should accede to the public anger, or that it would have the desired effect if it did. Just as clearly, we can no longer presume that the 'neutrality' of the state will hold up against that anger in the old liberal way. The problem now, is not that the state is never really neutral, as so many critics of liberalism have maintained, that it caters to special interests, or has an unfair secular bias, but that the interests of vengeance imbedded within its justice are intrinsically opposed to such neutrality.

When the liberal state punishes with vengeance, that is, it is confused about the very nature of its authority. Its restraint and impartiality are threatened, and the old idea that it should be the repository of a 'retributive right,' derived by reason, nature or otherwise, proves to be as deceptive and self-serving as it is fictitious. This much of liberalism may be founded on a mistake – revenge is neither left behind in nature nor comfortably transformed in legal justice. It is more insidious and better concealed than it has appeared to be in theory or in the myths of its conversion, and it must be confronted more forthrightly than it has been so far.

In the next phase of our inquiry, then, we will try to discover where vengeance is hiding in this culture and what deeper needs it is seeking to address. We will ask how the forces of rage and grief have found new forms of expression in the public preoccupation with crime, violence, and every sort of enemy or 'evil'. We will see how memories of horror are being managed in this, and how this extraordinary process seeks to do for our secular society what religion has done elsewhere in making moral sense of suffering. As we proceed we might well heed the warning that Nietzsche had offered in a different context: "... the 'wild beast' has not been slain at all, it lives, it flourishes, it has only been – transfigured."[210]

2

Violence, Vengeance, and the Rudiments
of American Theodicy

In a word, the old gods are growing old or are already dead, and others are not yet born.

– Emile Durkheim[1]

What are we doing when we watch, over and over again, the image of the twin towers collapsing, and the TV returns us inexorably to 'ground zero'? Is this the compulsion to repeat that Freud recognized in those who suffer mortal trauma? Perhaps, but why do we look within the scene to explain the terror or to find the meaning of 'evil'? Why does the camera, at first uncertain, seem finally to fix its sights and the one image linger in memory? What is the obsession with the wound, the scarcely suppressed anger of the news coverage, the mournful celebrity telethons for the victims, the return to the scorched earth at the site for each commemorative event? Is this the rage in grief that is so difficult to express? Is it the beginning of our revenge – not of a simple, obvious kind, but the conflicted sort that we have discovered? A symptom, perhaps, of a society that denies vengeance as a matter of its formal justice, but is obsessed with it nonetheless, a secular society that now makes something almost religious of it? Surely it is an attempt to 'make a memory' in the way that Nietzsche called to our attention, and to make moral sense of suffering as Weber thought necessary. Yet one sees how quickly we produce the list of suspects on the Most Wanted list and pursue Osama bin Laden – wanted "dead or alive." One can see by the ease with which it is all done, that this is not something new, but an established means by which the culture responds to every violent disruption and quietly redefines its justice.

Consider another American scene: The talk-show host nods sadly, as an expert on crime recites statistics on the particular violence that is the topic of the day. The frame shifts from images of horror to close-up faces in the studio audience whose shocked expressions find sympathy with our viewers at home. In that moment the audience reacts as one – with fear, anguish, revulsion – as the expert offers data on crimes of this type, suggestive psychological phrases and pious-sounding remarks to guide it through the trauma. The expert reminds them that ours is a "culture of violence" or something like it.[2] The phrase has a diagnostic ring to it (like "culture of poverty") that is at once analytical and disdainful. Those who invoke it stand apart. They survey the carnage with a certain detachment, if not the objectivity with which others once viewed society's ills.[3] This host and expert always let us know how disturbed they are by what they see. They shake their heads like clerics who share some higher knowledge. Once, perhaps, as journalist and criminologist, they might have contemplated the reasons for the crime in question, or enumerated incidents of violence on TV. Now, having remade themselves as "victimologists,"[4] they ponder its effects on those who suffer, the grieving family and friends, who will join them momentarily on stage.

It is virtually the same scene with every crime or new disaster. They are so predictable that we scarcely notice how they consecrate an obsessive interest or how the presence of the expert and the manipulation of points of view elicit a particular public reaction. We scarcely notice how the repetitive performance, the involvement of victims' families or friends, play upon the prevailing feelings of loss, and how the talk-show ritual with its facile religious moralism and faint 'reflective' commentary is just satisfying enough to manage the shock and keep us from asking deeper questions about it.[5] It is all so solemn and tastefully done, that no one asks how the summoning of attention to scenes of violence or the ascent to that seat of judgment fulfills a greater function, or what sort of catharsis is achieved as a result.

Of course, no one notices how the arrangement of justice on this stage – the changed characters, their altered poses and affects – has reversed the one that Aeschylus built for a very different scene of justice. Here, the Unmerciful face the Outrage of the day directly, and confront the violence with much less restrained vengeance.[6] No one suspects that the ceaseless observance of violence on so many stages like this serves to maintain that arrangement as much as it does anything else.

Split Justice

It is significant that the influence of the TV experts goes unchallenged in this arena, and that others who might comment are left out.[7] There is no place here for truly objective observers or for theorists who really know the tradition of law and liberal justice. For them, such inverted scenes of justice have little to do with the real thing. The events on this stage do not belong to a public sphere in which questions of justice might better be considered. That forced dialogue is not the sort of democratic discourse that should properly take place there. On the contrary, for such liberal scholars, justice is what rational individuals *would want* if only their minds were not cluttered with such daily terrors – if they could engage in pure debate about what's best for society, or find an ideal, unencumbered space in which to express themselves as citizens.[8] The problem of contemporary violence is one thing – tragic, indecipherable; the public outrage – a mere epiphenomenon; justice, rightly speaking, must be free of both.

It is a defining aspect of the culture, then, that this sort of theory and more mundane notions of justice have fallen to utterly different spheres. Of course those theorists read about violence like everyone else and see the spectacle on TV. But they also read the *New York Times*, books, and journal articles steeped in the liberal tradition. They occupy a different conceptual and moral universe from Americans who only watch the talk shows, read the tabloids, surf the cable channels, or listen to Rush Limbaugh approvingly. If they put down Rawls at home and reach for *The Star* at the supermarket (priding themselves on their connection to the common man) they cannot quite share the mindset of those who are violently sick of violence, who are ready to strike out at youth gangs, the homeless, or crack-addicted mothers – for whom "justice as fairness" could mean only an 'eye for an eye.' These theorists are not like those who would publicly humiliate criminals, 'lock them up and throw away the key,' or would remove the televisions and weight rooms from the prisons, and castrate or execute sex offenders – Americans who blame those intellectuals themselves, with their abstract notions of rights and justice, for the failure to punish decisively in this way; for producing a "victim culture,"[9] and a "nation of cowards."[10]

It is striking however, that so many of these intellectuals try to be like, or are conciliatory in addressing those other Americans. If certain conservative intellectuals acknowledge their anger as a sign of 'moral awakening' as we have noted, a great many liberal intellectuals regard it as a symptom of moral vacancy, and call for a justice of revived 'moral feeling' to address the vacancy. In America these days, there are even 'progressive' thinkers who want to claim the public anger as their own, and who would dearly like to integrate it within their own more properly liberal schemes of punishment.

Jeffrie Murphy, for one, has connected "resentment," which he deems to be a type of "anger," to self-respect. In doing so he would revive elements of a Kantian "character retributivism" with its concern for "personal virtue," to accommodate the sort of moral feeling in question precisely in making judgments about punishment.[11] Adjusting Hegel for the times in a way that is comparable, Mark Tunick advances the idea that what "'every human being feels'" (namely the feelings of retribution that Hegel had credited) should have a distinct place in punishment. Feelings of retribution should be paramount in this notably American rendition of Hegel's argument, even if people now feel them in a "less than ideal reality" (or rather without Hegel's ideal scaffolding).[12]

Taking his departure from Nietzsche, Robert Solomon has expressed his conviction that the "law is a vehicle for the expression and satisfaction of emotions, specifically revenge." Yet significantly he would disregard

Nietzsche's alarm at such things in order to cultivate an expressly "liberal" sort of revenge that "has the capacity for rationality, prudence, and cultural shaping."[13] With Durkheim in mind, in still another American appropriation of this kind, Mark Osiel applauds the generative effects of public outrage in producing 'social solidarity' and advancing the good moral health of the society.[14] Most boldly perhaps, with shades of Aristotle like Brubaker above, Dan Kahan advocates the "progressive appropriation of disgust" as a mission that he finds compatible with liberalism. He contends that the "proper course for liberalism is not to obliterate disgust, but to reform its objects so that we come to value what is *genuinely* high and to despise what is *genuinely* low" and, of course, to punish people accordingly.[15]

While it is hardly surprising, given the argument here, that these worthy scholars find so much of vengeance in the liberal tradition and its progenitors, it is striking that their eagerness to awaken it in this way so completely outweighs their fears. One wonders why the return to *feeling* and the more vengeful elements of the tradition does not arouse greater concern, and why the path to 'virtue' and better justice – even if it must awaken the emotions – should lead back through 'revulsion, disgust and shame' in particular?[16]

* * *

Apparently that impulse common to Kahan, Brubaker, and others – to restore virtue by "detesting" or "despising" what is truly unvirtuous or immoral – is quite oblivious to the problem that is posed where the 'virtues' are contested and anger is indiscriminate.[17] This has been the case in America at least since 1987 when the FCC suspended its requirement under the "fairness doctrine" to give equal time to opposing viewpoints on radio talk shows.[18] Since that time, of course, talk radio has made the emphatic expression of moral feeling entirely ordinary, and it has made resentment, anger, and the denigration of others a standard practice in virtually every discussion that pertains to 'justice.'

Where this has become the norm, however – one that is expressly antagonistic to the achievements of democratic 'progress' – it is hard to imagine how progressives can 'appropriate disgust' without compromising everything they intend as progressive. Democracies like our own must certainly entertain anger and bitter argument as a function of healthy disagreement. But as those progressives surely know, such caustic expressions of moral revulsion are dramatically at odds with other precepts of democratic discourse and democratic justice – respect for others, reciprocity, and a commitment to truth – as Habermas has so carefully enumerated them.[19]

Disgust, on the other hand, is monological and overtly hostile to discussion and to truth. This is especially apparent in the monologue of the angry talk radio host who entertains the views of others only to reinforce his own.[20] The chief rhetorical strategy of this self-styled expert is to dismiss conflicting evidence, to suppress or talk-over opposing points of view. His principal aim is to castigate the misfit, the member of a minority, the feminist, or the criminal – anyone who might take comfort in 'liberal political correctness' or seems overly protected by rights and liberal justice.

Listeners find this compelling not because it is the truth as a matter of veracity, but because it is undeniably a *true* register of what they, or 'every human being' feels. It is especially compelling because that 'moral feeling of disgust' (like other affects of broken attachment) is so effectively detached and redeployed in the moment. In that moment too, the invective is itself a form of verbal retribution aimed not only at the one object of scorn, but at the very norms of discourse, rationality, and truth that once sustained progressive liberal justice.[21] On talk radio such expressed anger is taken to *be justice*, to be more genuine and sincere than any restrained, procedurally bound liberal justice. The 'appropriation of disgust' in these circumstances is hardly a winning project for liberals. It aims at the heart of those very principles and safeguards that sustain liberal justice, and is implicated in a far more extensive process of recrimination than it might seem.[22]

* * *

Evidently this process is well under way even in the most credible efforts to revise our practices of punishment. In *Thinking About Crime*, for example, James Q. Wilson promotes a practical scheme to lower the crime rate that reconceives both the target and the purpose of blame. In his lauded work of the 1970s and 1980s, Wilson, the conservative, expressly utilitarian policy maker who seems not at all concerned with moral feeling or the denigration of others, supplies exactly what is needed to connect deep-seated resentment to an otherwise rational (liberal) conception of punishment. Crime, in his estimation, results from largely rational sorts of behavior, a series of false steps along a path that has been littered with the wrong incentives. For Wilson, calculated choices underlie even the most irrational acts, and those choices can be altered only by instituting a more coherent system of rewards and penalties.[23] A practice of decisive deterrence, swift and certain punishment – and certainly not the liberal social engineering policies of welfare – is thus the best way to address crime and to improve a crime-ridden society.

At first this seems to be quite consistent with a liberalism that privileges the 'rational individual,' and exempts those persons who lack the capacity for reason from culpability. Yet Wilson's conception of agency in fact does something of the reverse.[24] Where crime is entirely the rational choice of badly motivated individuals (he later attributes this to bad character),[25] that old saw of a 'rational, responsible, culpable individual' becomes a back door through which a different kind of blame may enter – one that is quite compatible with moral revulsion and the newfound disgust. If, on the old liberal account such a 'rational individual' would be held accountable by virtue of the faculty he was *supposed* to have (in spite of his often irrational choices and actions), here, for Wilson, he is held wholly and immediately accountable for the failure of a capacity that he always, in fact, *does* have.

The criminal, defined this way, may become the locus of unremitting blame that can be assessed without hesitation by an unassailable authority – no longer by cautious procedures that weigh and determine the state of his reason, but by a system that simply ascribes it. On the one hand, then, Wilson seems to see in the criminal precisely what liberalism has always seen – a rational human nature worthy of respect that can be addressed by reasonable incentives.[26] On the other, the 'rational response to rational behavior' hypothesis makes it remarkably easy to find fault, because any claim for the relative *irrationality* of the criminal or his acts is a priori, and by definition, open to contempt.[27] In the end, Wilson, the actual expert, takes up the moralizing attitude of the TV expert as he applauds prosecutors who "throw the book" at criminals. The utilitarian strains in his argument give way to the usual first-person appeals of the retributivists, since, "[a]fter all, we not only want to reduce crime, we want to see criminals get their just deserts."[28]

* * *

One can see how the very conception of persons and responsibility – of identity itself – is under revision in this, and how that restructuring of blame is at once something more general. In a society that lacks moral direction, and suffers violence and disruption as a result (a society that has relied, perhaps overly, on the idea of 'rational identity' to provide that direction) people desperately want reassurances about the stability of that rational core. If that core identity seems to suffer fragmentation or "dis-integration" (as so many postmodern theorists maintain), this precipitates a longing for fundamentals in which a fractured identity seeks to be made whole.[29] In such a society, the very idea that the agent of crime is a *unified, temporally intact, rational subject* has tremendous compensatory value. It can be invoked in response to crime or violent disruption, and applied to every criminal. If the latter (defined this way) is not a scapegoat precisely, he is nevertheless an antidote to that same problem of identity.

Revenge against him, whether by retributive or utilitarian means, is thus the revenge of society against this failing in itself. In punishing him for his impaired reason society reaffirms its threatened rational identity. Of course, such a society cannot allow him to be (or appear to be) insane or irrational in a way that mitigates blame and gives credence to his excuses. He may seem reckless or stupid and be ridiculed for his bad choices, but he is a *responsible agent* who has made them nonetheless.[30] Here, it appears, contemporary society has played a kind of Kantian trick – blaming the purportedly rational being for a failing of his reason in a way that secures the hegemony of reason. Yet here too, 'reason' becomes the catchall for a great deal more – personal virtue and 'the good' – common ground for such disparate thinkers as Wilson, Brubaker, Kahan and the talk radio host. Reason is the measure of a person's worth or deficiency, its perversion an invitation to detest. It is not surprising in this context that the punishments directed at criminals scarcely address their *reason* in any genuine sense at all. It is not surprising that the very capacity of rational agency that once stood opposed to revenge is now wielded against them as an instrument of this society's redoubled revenge.[31]

So it is hardly enough these days for the object of blame to be reconfigured abstractly. As the old paradigm becomes imperiled, people demand a new set of correspondences, new punishments fitted to new and secure definitions of the agent and the crime. They want a more confident knowledge about what is normal, right, and true of the sort that Wilson provides, but they want it to be more tangible, bodily, and secure. They would be comforted perhaps, by the old connection between truth and beauty that intrigued Brubaker, the unquestioned correspondences of physiognomy, the phrenology of the 19th century, or the Nazi catalogues of racial and other body types. This, of course, is precisely what the stylists of talk radio have grasped as they suspend truth and bend 'discourse' to reshape justice from within. They make their own vulgar assertions about the worth of persons – their beauty, ugliness, or bodily eccentricity – to refresh the fading prejudice against the 'types' whom they so readily despise.

Once again, in denigrating those persons and reducing them to their attributes, they revile the very rights (or 'political correctness') by which liberal society had allowed them to be something more. But if that effort seems illiberal and anti-rational, it is now quite in keeping with such recast notions of liberal 'rational agency.' Bad people are what they are (like ugly people, fat people, people who 'choose' the wrong sexual orientation, addicts who can't say no), not in spite of, *but because of their reason* (their 'will,' or what they stupidly think). In this view there is no more mystery to the connection between intentions and actions, or mind and body.[32] Now rather, the imagined transparency of those agents of wrongdoing, makes them seem fully revealed.

The problem therefore goes deeper. If, as Foucault argued, the power of society once inhered within an exacting knowledge of persons and bodies, creating the strategies of normalization and discipline that characterize the modern period, now it goes searching to refresh its motives and to establish its knowledge on different grounds. Power, in this sense, can no longer proceed on the old assumptions about persons, and the moral firmament that once secured them has been revised. Now it is no longer a 'disciplinary knowledge' and 'control of the body' alone that drives this effort, but knowledge of the mind, motives, and condemnable character of the criminal – an object of blame as we have said – that would counteract the 'dis-integration of identity.' It is an imperative of knowledge, wielded to such purposes, therefore, to connect the body, mind, reason, moral feeling, right, and law *again* in a way that reinforces that identity and underscores that power. This is the sort of *morally purposive* identity that had been established, for example, when the church and state were one, and which has suffered a uniquely modern disruption.[33]

If 'power' aspires to obtain certain 'knowledge,' that is, it is not knowledge for the sake of discipline exactly (as Foucault suggested for an earlier time), but knowledge that enables *moralizing* judgments that address such severe disruptions of identity. It is not so much 'knowledge of the body,' as precise, visceral certainty about whatever threatens the body, and who or what is to blame. This, we might say, is exacting evaluative knowledge of the specific terrors that violence awakens and that religion once resolved: pain, death, and cruelty (as we shall see), as of those rational, evil persons who bring such things upon us.

This is why Americans needed to know for certain what the 9/11 hijackers did or said; precisely what they must have been thinking at the time, and how their captives responded in every detail. It is why television is so obsessed with forensic reconstruction, and why the motives of violent criminals and the inner workings of their minds are so much in evidence at trial.[34] It is why so many Americans think they know that the guilty are guilty, and say, as if it should settle the matter, that they have a gut feeling that corporal or capital punishments are just. Justice – or *power as it is again being justified* – now operates on substantially different grounds, and entertains these older, viscerally reassuring kinds of validation as well. It does this by cultivating an exacting knowledge of the criminal or his 'reason' so as to construct memorable and meaningful punishments. It does this, increasingly, in microscopic and obsessive examinations of the violence itself.

Devil in the Details

What do we make of the intrigue as millions of Americans follow the trail of evidence in the Simpson case? Is this just prurient interest in violence and murder heightened by a fascination with celebrity? Or is it driven by the racial dimensions of the case? Surely, all of this matters. But why such extraordinary interest in the *details*? Why is it not enough to know 'what happened'? The sequence of the chase, the capture, the discovery of each bloody piece of evidence must all come under scrutiny. For hours as O.J.'s white Bronco is pursued by news and police vehicles, the networks search for meaning. From the moment of his arrest, the media ask, 'do we make too much of our heroes?' Too much for what, the question implies: to catch them and punish them, as they deserve? Is it that the trouble occurred in an interracial marriage? Certainly not. The talk shows congratulate themselves for setting aside the question of race, for not holding Simpson to a different standard (even as they do). For all of the attention that it gets, the fact that the case pits a celebrated black man against a system of justice that has historically favored well-off whites largely recedes. Neither his race nor his celebrity status should cloud the question of his guilt or innocence. That question will be addressed if we just stay tuned for the details.[35]

Now, Simpson could be any man accused of such a crime. Questions of race, equality, celebrity, spousal abuse, and murder all fall into place. As the media sift through them, the priorities of justice are reconstituted in the process. The accused is sedate (or sedated), now (paradoxically) just another rational agent seated in the courtroom where at last, a justice of *desert* will rightly be applied.[36] This can hardly be a matter that concerns a 'justice of *equity.*' Racial prejudice should not be a factor (even though, by an extraordinary trick, it is the deciding one).[37] In deference to the latter, Simpson is acquitted as his attorney plays the "race card," but few who know the *details* truly imagine that he is innocent.[38]

This above all must be established in the current period, and the Simpson case marks a turning point. It is longer a time of 'civil rights' in which the inordinate inequities of the system might be righted in a court of law. The last decade of the millennium is a time of *retributive justice*; one in which the deserving are rewarded, and the guilty (rational agents that they are) receive certain punishment, one in which the system and its punishments are presumed to be just.[39] Yet even as the verdict seems to challenge that assumption, a retributive justice is asserted by new and extraordinary means. The public is saturated with forensic information about the crime itself (and others like it). The trail of blood has TV experts wondering, 'could so much evidence have been planted?' And 'Is DNA testing 100% valid?' An old photograph of the victim's bruised face brings on the talk show topic: 'Stalking and Spousal Abuse.' Is that what happened here? A thematic interrogation of the evidence reveals how this, and other crimes of its nature, might seem to be redressed with greater certainty.

The same cycle is repeated with every notorious case. There are pictures of the crime scene in the news, careful reviews of the evidence, tearful interviews with witnesses or surviving victims. Long before there is a verdict, we are privy to the syndrome that would account for such events. It is some new type of 'abuse,' they say, another kind of 'traumatic stress' or even 'celebrity excess' that warrants a new or different punitive response. There are assertions that this case is only the 'tip of an iceberg,' expressions of editorial outrage, a review of the many other cases exhibiting such tendencies. This is followed by close attention to the trial, the jurors, and the judgment and punishment, which, it is fervently hoped, will fit the syndrome as well as it fits the crime. Finally someone is held accountable, if not by a verdict of guilt in an actual court, then in the court of public opinion, or at least, as for Simpson, in a subsequent civil trial.[40]

Here it would seem, the blank, transparent, blamable individual is the slate on which new priorities of justice can be written. The phenomenon is discrete. Like other scenes of justice it is carefully arranged to have the right effect, and one can readily see what is at stake. Beyond what the one man did or what he deserves, beyond any mitigating effects of insanity or racial impropriety, it is an effort to make sense at the limits of sense, to account for each disturbing detail, to delimit the horror by category and type, and to condemn, vociferously, the most threatening sorts of violence.

'Senseless acts,' 'random violence' – these are things that hold special fascination for Americans. If the intrigue seems to be with violence, celebrity, or race (as in the Simpson case) it can be traced to this imperative as well. It is no longer enough for punishment to balance the scales of justice. Grief and rage demand an answer. Americans ask, with indignation, "how could this happen?" Or, as on 9/11, "how could they do such a thing to our innocents?" The movement proceeds from shock, to outrage, to a hopeful moral classification by which such violent characters and their unspeakable motives will be made known.[41] Crimes for which the reasons are unfathomable; crimes that resist categorization or that occur at the extremes of wealth, poverty, or depravity; crimes that should seem unimaginable to the ordinary citizen, are what preoccupy the public imagination.

It is front-page news when a "Central Park Jogger" is thought to be brutally raped and left for dead by a gang of youths who were, as one puts it, just "wilding."[42] The extreme viciousness of the act, the way it typifies violence against women, and certain incongruities of age, class, and race make the case a lightning rod for refreshed outrage. But it is the inexplicable amorality of the crime, the difficulty in grasping it as a rational act or intention that is called to attention in the stunned editorials and by the distinctive term used on that occasion. Now the allusion to a threatening nature, the moral depravity of youth, the sound of that unfamiliar vernacular in the news, the violation of a place of sanctuary and the activity of middle class leisure – all compound the horror that intrudes like a cry from the wilderness, demonstrating, once again, how liberal justice has failed to contain those irrational things at the limits of its 'sense.'

It is precisely this sort of intrigue that characterizes so many colossal accidents and random acts of insanity – those unaccountable events to which the media would lend the accountability of a violent crime. The media must discover what is blameworthy; categorize, document, and make the horror comprehensible. The space shuttle Challenger explodes on takeoff. Within hours the search for the culpable O-rings and their manufacturer hastens to fill the void.[43] Newscasters wonder: "What could go so wrong?" "Who is at fault?" – as they would again when the Columbia burned on reentry. Television quickly generates a story, complete with heroes and villains, visual mock-ups and expert speculation on the probable cause in order to fill the silence. "Who failed to warn us of the Tsunami?" – the news shows ask. What should the warning system have looked like? In New York, speculation of this sort began even before the second tower was hit. It is now intolerable to have 'dead air' without this sort of commentary, and we cannot long endure such inexplicable or arbitrary events.

The imperative is the same when the culprit is easier to identify. The former employee of a fast food chain storms an outlet with a rifle, killing scores of patrons. The bloody scenes are everywhere. The talk shows wonder: "What could make this happen?" Does the 'disgruntled employee' represent a new syndrome?[44] The rampage of an alienated high school or college student seems less threatening if the motive can be determined or this type of mass murder defined. Jeffrey Dahmer is arrested; interest grows, not just because he is a serial killer, but because people need to know how the handsome, well-mannered, middle-class white man can also be a sadistic homosexual cannibal, and whether he is a new type of violent criminal that must now be categorized and blamed.[45] The shows ask: 'What *is* Dahmer?' 'Does child abuse make serial killers?' The nature of the interest reveals itself as the shows wonder, 'is this insanity or is it evil?' and as always, 'should there still be an insanity defense?' Even as the media generate consensus on this point (it is evil and a *blamable* form of insanity it turns out) audiences are comforted to know just what sort of rupture Dahmer has introduced into the sensible world, how his crimes compare to others, and what species of condemnable creature he must be.

As the wish to make sense of the horror persists over time, the public wants to know every step in the killer's thought process and what it reveals about his malevolent intent or the nature of his crime. If it is useful to know precisely how the World Trade Center towers collapsed for 'reasons of security,' or what the terrorists must have known of their design, that knowledge is indispensable to the vengeful calculus and the assessment of blame as well.[46] From the first instant in which it is divulged, the news provides the 'inside story,' the probable culprits, a plausible sequence of events, the elements of the crime that might reveal its motive, and, by implication at least, the nature of the 'evil' behind the act.

In every visual medium (if less obviously on the Internet) violent crime is reported with enticing warnings to 'sensitive viewers.' On the dare, virtually everyone is bound to see it, and the prevalence of such scenes – the vividness and repetition with which they are shown – owe as much to this imperative to expose, as to any increase in the actual incidence of violent crime.[47] Wounded victims and morbid bits of evidence dominate the offerings of the local news. Taglines like 'shocking crime,' '. . . traumatized witness,' '. . . the ski mask worn by the killer,' '. . . the rope used . . .' the '. . . bloody scene of the murder,' the '. . . exact position of the bodies,' accompany the flow of images, giving it all a distinctly familiar cast.[48] Where actual photos cannot be found to accompany them, specially enhanced stills or snippets of animation supply the essential elements of the story.

In the details there is endless room for forensic speculation and the artful manufacture of the evidence provides precisely what is needed for vengeful thoughts to enter and reconstitute the memory of events. By filling in the gaps, a hypothesis emerges, a detective's hunch, a plot complete with motive and conclusion.[49] In America you can see it all, and something magical and (almost) meaningful occurs in having seen it. A kind of vindication of sense over senselessness is nearly complete, and the triumph of good over evil is (almost) achieved in the process.[50]

It is striking then, how this impulse may even affect the outcome of notorious cases or the way they are perceived. Having followed the bloody trail of evidence into Simpson's bedroom, the public imagination could not rest with his acquittal and would ultimately need to script a different ending. The experts predicted (correctly) that Fred Goldman would win his civil suit on the same facts.[51] Even if they had been wrong, however, most everyone (adjusting for racial disparities) would suppose that Simpson was guilty.[52]

Armed as they are with knowledge of the details, audiences can impose their own meaning or 'moral' on a case no matter what the court has decided. If the wealthy, famous defendant is found guilty, people delight in the reversal of fortunes. As knowledgeable witnesses to the proceedings, they are comforted to know that even such celebrated individuals who do bad things will get what they deserve, and that goodness still has its rewards. Yet if such a person goes free, like Simpson, or is scarcely punished, their cynicism is affirmed in a way that is nearly as satisfying. Knowing the details as they do, they may imagine that *they*, at least, would have decided differently than this judge or that jury.

TV now provides them with innumerable opportunities to second-guess the court and reach their own conclusion. If the verdict is displeasing, they can identify with the victims or dissenting jurors who are interviewed in the news. Remarkably, they may register their discontent in network viewer surveys or on countless blogs if they wish. When the real outcome is too deeply disturbing, the fictional medium that brings them the news frequently lets them see how it *might* have come out differently in a 'docudrama' that changes the story or its ending.[53] In the turnabout made possible by so many small observances (and by audiences that think they know best) that compensatory justice tricks fate and restores a sense of 'just deserts' precisely where it is lacking.

Here too, however, and since that purposive reading of the details begins well in advance of the trial itself, the old connection between truth and justice is distinctly undermined.[54] What might have been a simple democratic exercise of airing the facts publicly (the act of a free press to advance the truth and protect persons from persecution) now has a decidedly different cast. While the 'facts' might mean one thing for a jury, that is, they are now burdened by narrative expectations that run entirely counter to the democratic interest in truth.[55] Here, the *truth* is no longer a version of events supported by the facts, but a *story* that must be told – the villain is exposed with a measure of certainty that the courts cannot achieve and the tricks of the media do better to approximate. Jurors are said to exhibit what attorneys call a "Perry Mason syndrome." They expect the facts to 'speak for themselves' or that the felon will be unmasked at the trial. They expect that the prosecutor or the state's witnesses will *solve* the case with perfect accuracy just as they do on *CSI*.[56] Where *that* truth eludes the grasp of the law, jurors may well imagine that the charade of justice is in the courtroom, and the real justice is on TV.

On this cusp of fact and fantasy (truth and would-be justice), crime reenactment programs engage real police officers and victims (or actors, it seems not to matter which) to relive the actual events of a crime and its solution. Programs like *COPS, Rescue 911, True Stories of the Highway Patrol, America's Most Wanted*, Court TV's *Forensic Files*, or APB News' *Crimesolvers* or NBC's "To Catch a Predator" (teamed with Perverted Justice and local law enforcement)[57] showcase the pursuit and humiliating capture of fugitives while viewers assist (in some cases) by calling a 900 number. If such programs seem to cater to the retaliatory fantasies of only a narrow demographic, 'fact-based' TV movies offer different points of access to anyone who is left out.[58] Certainly there is no place in the 'truth' of this justice for "reasonable doubt," hung juries, or acquittals. Mistrials or unsolved or unresolved cases are unacceptable in this scheme of things, and few who watch such shows can distinguish the ineptitude of the law itself from this fantasy of its perfection.

The irony in this, of course, is that audiences think they have become hardened to a 'reality' about justice that is not in any simple sense a *reality*.[59] When cynical Americans imagine that they know all about violent crime and injustice, or that they can see through the fraud and distortion of the law to the 'real story,' it is this wishful construct that they see as much or more than any truth. 'Real American justice' is no longer distinguishable from its fabrication, and it is as likely to be generated on *Judge Judy, Judge Joe Brown*, or in the space before the TV screen as in any real court of law.[60] So the medium that joins fact and fiction (even better than its talk radio counterpart) conflates its 'realism' with a wish for moral certainty in a way that is entirely opaque to self-scrutiny. As Americans think that they *see through* the fraudulent medium to the truth of every case, that is, they see *only* through that medium, and grow contemptuous of any reality that complicates its 'truth.' Legal technicalities that confound the simple story of good and evil, or cast doubt on their reading of the details – rigorous standards of proof upheld by 'liberal judges,' mitigating circumstances or the presumption of innocence – all must offend their 'realism.'

What is disturbing about this from the standpoint of an older dedication to truth and justice, then, is not just that is blind to the *particular* truth of a case in the way that simple or ordinary revenge might be. It is rather that such blindness has become a *systemic* feature of justice that aims to rectify cultural deficiencies that have nothing to do with the facts of the particular case. Paradoxically, that is, as this story of justice enlists the details, it sacrifices the particulars of the many cases to fill a greater vacancy in meaning – to provide righteous heroes, unmistakable villains, and triumphant endings. Like the stories told by children around a campfire to help contain their fears, this one too is offered as a palliative. It is repeated again at the edge of the lawless condition where liberalism has built its justice. And those who listen now seem far more interested in reaching the vengeful conclusion than in discovering the *truth*.

Sadistic Pleasures, Vengeful Fantasies, Victim–Heroes

The intrigue with violence and vengeance must now look quite differ-ent in light of this pervasive story of justice. The Nietzschean proposition concerning the satisfactions of punishment must look different too. It is not so much a matter of taking the pleasure of cruelty in compensation, or 'making memories' in the process. It is rather a matter of the need to tell a particular story, to underscore and fix it in memory; to make it seem true by the infliction (or the depiction) of pain. Thus, if it is tempting to attribute this intrigue to a first-order 'pleasure in cruelty' – to say that the same sadistic fascination that once drew crowds to gladiatorial contests now fills the coliseum of our own licentious culture – this does not explain the moral imperative that guides that American story line, or the special need to pass judgment in the end.[61] When young men flock to Action/Adventure movies, it might seem that the vengeful plot is only a pretext for their sadis-tic enjoyment. Yet its claim to obtain 'justice' is equally important to their satisfaction and to the show's ultimate success.

Of course there are films that play upon sadistic drives, but the more sub-tle and effective ones indulge a series of competing impulses. There is an enticement to join in the violence (sympathetically filmed from the perspec-tive of the felon); revulsion at the effects of violence (exhibited in all its vivid details); a twinge of conscience (a sympathetic view of the victim); finally, an invitation to imagine doing violence in order to stop the violence. If there is no single sadistic drive at work in this, the plot negotiates a series of emo-tional states to validate the sadistic action – fear, envy, mistrust, remorse, grief, guilt, outrage, vindictiveness; the pleasure of cruelty in revenge – so that a succession of morally driven releases compounds the sense of a justi-fied (or warranted) cruelty in the sympathetic reaction.[62]

That American intrigue, therefore, can be nothing so pure and direct as the German notion of *Schadenfreude* suggests. It is far more conflicted and in need of excuses.[63] The suffering of others may seem pleasurable, but only on the condition that it is justified within a fantasy of revenge – a fantasy, for that matter, in which it is enjoyed from a position of nearly paralytic rage and frustration. Surely Americans are not running out in great numbers to commit cruel acts of retaliation, or taking pleasure in punishment *directly*. They do nothing so noble as they sit in front of their TV sets, decrying the restraint of the law and rooting for a harsher jus-tice – complaining and (rather more *masochistically*) enjoying their com-plaint at once.[64] There can be no *simple* sadistic pleasure in this, since the pleasure in question is derived entirely within that paradigm of conflicted justice, and is achieved only in imagining the series of steps that would overcome it.[65]

In America, the way out of the paralysis is thus clearly marked. The sadistic impulse certainly does find expression, but only when it is matched by sympathies at the other pole – not sympathy for the one who punishes, but for the one who has been harmed and would retaliate – in *masochistic sympathy*, or identification with the victim. Evidently the fascination is not just with violence and cruelty, but also with the condition of the victim who suffers it, and the reversal of that condition in *morally vindicated* cruelty. Where that is the case, it is not surprising that American audiences so strenuously applaud the vengeful feats of victim–heroes; those who righteously rebel against some circumstance, and are wholly unrestrained by law or the exigencies of superego.

At the level of the story, this sympathy for the victim manifests itself in the theme of 'fighting back.' Small persons, weak persons, injured persons who find themselves in such terrible straits that 'anything goes' retaliate with such immediacy that it seems, at first, like self-defense – American underdogs are always in the right, their retaliation always justified under the circumstances, and even maltreated or outmatched *criminals* can be heroes.[66] Courage against incredible odds, superhuman strength triggered by anger and the ensuing justifiable carnage, are all what makes them heroic. There is invariably a personal vendetta, a life-and-death conflict between two principal characters in which the whole world (or at least many lives) hangs in the balance.

For the most common sort of hero, however, the law itself is a special handicap as he is driven by frustration with justice itself. The usually masculine, Caucasian prototype is distinguished by his need to overcome the limits of the law, to punish the 'scum of the earth,' 'slime-balls' or just 'scum bags' precisely as the frustrating, impersonal, public courts cannot. That hero – usually an alcoholic, divorced and disillusioned police officer, himself a victim of violence, disgraced by the same courts or liberal judges – has frequently been suspended, is off duty or has been forced into early retirement to become a private detective. Despite those defects of character and the hindrance of his legal position, we are assured that it is within him to do good. Invariably he finds the inner fortitude or honor to make it personal as he avenges the death of a partner, a family member, or a friend, so that he is a transparent, rational agent equal to his foe.[67] He always becomes personally involved with his clients and abuses his office to help them when he must. He invariably scoffs at the *Miranda* rule as he captures or kills his opponent such that he is the opposite and the antidote to everything professional, detached, and frustrating about the 'justice' of the law.[68]

Where the boundary between real and fictive justice is itself in question, however, the effects of this heroic type can hardly be innocent. It now plays a significant part in the self-conceptions of nearly everyone involved in criminal justice. As the police themselves (Homeland Security or other "first responders") are increasingly aware of their heroic status, and as it is fed back to them continually in the media – emulation forms a feedback loop. Real officers play for the camera even as their crime scenes become stage sets for the fictionalized news. They invite cameras along for an arrest.[69] Detective Mark Fuhrman is indistinguishable from the racist character he claimed to adopt in the tapes that compromised his testimony, and later became a media consultant on the strength of that same ambiguous identity.[70]

Inspired by example, officers of the law who should not exhibit revenge behave as if it were their job to *punish* suspects – they say '*alleged* perpetrator' through their teeth, and recite "a right to remain silent" while administering a hammerlock.[71] And in watching videotapes of Rodney King and others being beaten, one must wonder whether it is just sport for those involved, or that imitative self-righteousness that really guides their actions. Now, virtually the entire apparatus of law enforcement acts as if it were a moral authority: judges scold, prosecutors boast of their conviction rates, prison guards humiliate, and the prison system is rife with persons intent upon teaching offenders a lesson. On the model of the TV victim–hero, that is, law enforcement has acquired a personal dimension that it was never supposed to have. While this does nothing to restore justice, it presents the dominance of good guys over bad guys as if that were the same thing.

Of course, that heroic paradigm now bears directly on the shift from a justice of equity to a justice of retribution. If, for a time, the beating of a black man by police would have been regarded as an instance of racial injustice or a violation of civil rights (in which the agents of the state would hardly seem heroic), now the discussion turns on whether, or how, the one man resisted the police. Did his personal conduct at the scene reveal him to be a villain or a victim? Was the chokehold warranted? Was Amadou Diallo reaching for a gun or a wallet and what did it look like when the police shot him 19 times? Or were the police in some sense justified in thrusting a baton in Abner Louima's anus?[72]

Violent events of the sort that once raised deeper questions are now read as human interest stories that portray individual victims fighting back. Selfless risks taken during a rescue, stories of personal retaliation against gangs or of hapless citizens withstanding attacks consistently overshadow the less palatable issues of racial injustice. Rodney King is re-made as a hero, not for exposing racism, and not even for his selfless appeal for peace at the trial of his persecutors, but for having occupied the victim position so compellingly. This is why attempts to put the ensuing riots in the old frame of racial conflict seemed so incongruous at the time. Scenes of looting in the LA of the '90s looked eerily like those of the '60s, but would not survive the image of a lone white truck driver being dragged from his vehicle and brutally assaulted by a few black men, only to be rescued by others. The fact of persistent racism would ultimately seem too obvious and too dated to warrant much attention on this occasion, but the tendency to look within the violence for a personal story of justice, to define heroes and villains in spite of their race, to focus on the 'one man and his story' – citizens who rescued the truck driver or the shopkeeper whose livelihood was ruined by looters – made the moment, and the 'justice' at stake in it, seem suddenly quite different.

To say that America is racist on such occasions misses the point, as much as saying that it is too violent. Of course it is violent and racist. What is striking, however, is that it is struggling to rationalize these failings and to redefine the moral points of resistance to them on a plane of fictive justice and exaggerated personal heroics where race and the prior terms of justice are of diminished importance. This certainly has racial consequences; indeed it may engender a new type of racism. But again, its primary impulse – its *modus operandi* – is to put the justice of retribution and desert above that of equity and to restore the individual contest.[73]

If, at a defining moment in history, as Nietzsche suggests, the 'law' became "impersonal," attaining "the reverse of that which is desired by all revenge that is fastened exclusively to the viewpoint of the person injured,"[74] now there is a *reversal of the reversal*, and of the very impersonal standpoint that made that justice of equity possible in the first place. Yet paradoxically, restoring the paradigm of the individual contest does not restore the viewpoint of the person injured as such. On the contrary, since anyone may participate in that contest in principle (or rather, in imagination) and heroes black and white may all play equal parts, they all may share that *victim's viewpoint* with a measure of 'equity.'[75] This of course is what permits the 'individual principle' to be generalized in a *shared fantasy* of collective retribution without any true or particular attention to the victim and the victim's point of view.[76]

Now, this heroic character as a generic type is a perfect vehicle for the inversion of liberal justice – a reversal that makes vengeance its general principle without entirely sacrificing an interest in equity or persons with rights, or fully engaging the personal standpoint of vengeance either.[77] Such heroes are blank, transparent, often racially indistinct,[78] essentially pure and good, like the action figures made of them for children. They may be completely identified with the victim (the masochistic pole) – like the firemen and police officers killed at ground zero, or those Americans who are made heroes simply because they are victims. They are heroes, that is, insofar as they provide points of equal access to the imaginary victim and the fantasy of fighting back – a sense of restored agency that offers an escape from the paralysis induced by violence (if only in imagination) and reflects the extraordinary ambivalence with which vengeance is presently expressed.[79]

An American Idiom

The fact that this occurs in fantasy and that there is so much imaginary revenge is a testament to that particular American ambivalence. When our fictional heroes finally exact vengeance, they do so with sufficient torment to remind us that the impulse is not entirely at home here. Their expressed frustration reminds us that it is forbidden in the proper enforcement of the law, only implied in the phrasing of an execution announcement, and that Americans are still dimly aware of its dangers. The word 'vengeance' is often spoken here, but it is ventured with trepidation in the odd space between private grief and public outrage. If it seems timely and familiar, it must also seem strange and oddly out of date. It is a source of both shame and pride, and as a point of access to the moral crisis that has concerned us here, its strained usage is immensely revealing. When an American says, 'I want revenge,' it is likely to be whispered with irreverence, or shouted in defiance to the law. The phrase has a decidedly different connotation than in those older, more forthright "cultures of vengeance," where an offense to honor would demand a direct response.[80] Yet it is invoked with this in mind, as if to revive that aspect of its former meaning.

It must be an instance of this uniquely American ambivalence, then, when the father of a girl who had been raped and murdered in 1993 offers praise for the execution of a murderer in a similar case, insisting all the while that "this is not vengeance." The unfortunate man's denial is striking in light of his enormous anger, and the pronouncement would seem disingenuous if nearly every American did not grasp the pained, impacted meaning of his words:

This is not vengeance, this is not deterrence – this is justice, God will blame them. My God is a vengeful God. I don't believe in forgiveness. When we say "forgiveness of our sins" in church, I can't say that. I can't forgive them. I want them to rot in hell.[81]

In the seeming contradiction of a vengeance that is not vengeance, a number of things vie for expression: the disavowal of merely personal revenge; the intolerable sense of loss that still demands something like it; the dismissal of the church and its forgiveness (and of any lesser sort of punishment); the affirmation of an absolute justice.

It must be significant, then, that in the moment of such determined fury both the church and the established secular interest in 'deterrence' should give way to that other sort of justice. For that aggrieved American, as we others can see, the abiding desire is scarcely concealed in the disclaimer of the moment, and the very incongruity of his denial invites an older, vengeful God to displace the more forgiving Christian God of the present.[82] Just outside the courtroom, in the moment of manifest grief and rage, there is an irresistible impulse to make the pain of mortal loss meaningful by vindicating a timeless sense of justice – a justice, to be sure that occupies the past and present at once.

A striking thing about the word "vengeance," then, is the temporal impropriety with which it strikes our American ears. Its evocation of the past is at once an equivocation about the present. In the moment of shock and moral revulsion in which that present seems unbearable, victims search backward through imagined pasts to find solace for their grief – in God's justice, frontier justice – all in an attempt, as for that one inconsolable father, to salve a painful present memory with a more venerable and universal one.[83] Now, when one recognizes the word "vengeance" as the bearer of anachronism and nostalgia, one discovers a distinctly American problem of meaning – a different tension in it than one finds at other times and places. The pain of the present, the rage in grief, looks backward to find resolution. Its frustration with present justice leads not just to personal, but to divine retribution – or rather to some crude, faintly recalled version of the latter.

The problem of meaning that the word bears is therefore precise. As a response to the violence and death of the moment, it is at once a reaction to the moral deficiency of the present and a lament for what has been lost. Americans who experience this do not simply suffer a crisis of 'modernity,' 'values,' 'meaning,' and so forth; in a way that makes them pawns of history. Rather, they have a problem *with* history, and have fixed their sights upon the facile moral and religious resolutions of the past precisely because reason, freedom, and liberal justice do not give them secure or meaningful moral foundations now. The idiom of vengeance thus expresses *a wish to make justice meaningful again*, a reversal of the reversal, or inversion of justice, that would mend broken attachments; address devastating loss, and more broadly reestablish the meaning of meaning. The seeming anachronism of the word is at once an expression of faith that people may recover the means to grasp the violence and cruelty in their midst – all that should be reconciled in a world that makes sense, but which seems to have made sense only in the more certain justice of the past.

Evidently this nostalgia for moral expediency is still caught up in the old religious paradigm of good and evil. Whether it is couched in legal terminology, aired on talk radio, or expressed in demands for more punishment, that wishful impulse cannot be distinguished from the spiritual element it now recalls. Although it seems odd to say so, in our predominantly secular society,[84] it is still a problem of theodicy.

Theodicy and the Liberal Aporia of Evil

In forging a contraction of the Greek words for god and justice, Leibniz originally meant the term theodicy to refer to his resolution of the dilemma presented by the persistence of evil in a world created by a single, omnipotent, good, and just God. For Leibniz, that great paradox of monotheism could be resolved only by demonstrating that "God co-operates morally in moral evil, that is, in sin, without being the originator of the sin, and even without being accessory thereto. . . . He does this by permitting it justly, and by directing it wisely towards the good."[85]

While such reasoning may seem to have resolved the theological difficulty, the question, or rather the persistence of the question, clearly reflects an imperative of a different order. In recognition of this, for example, Weber adopted the notion of theodicy to refer to the psychological need to rationalize reward and suffering in general, even, or especially, in a world that has been "stripped of its religious and ethical meaning."[86] To be sure, says Weber, ". . . even a meaningful world order that is impersonal and super-theistic must face the problem of the world's imperfections." To underscore the point, he offers the example of those German workers who rejected the "god-idea," less because they had been convinced to do so by reason and science, than because religious explanation had failed them in that essential respect.[87] Beyond an interest in the vindication of God's authority, the psychological imperative at work here entails the need to see that good is rewarded and evil punished, whether or not there is a god.

If Weber is right about this – and that our modern secular society has gone so far in this direction that it no longer makes reference to a "god-idea," God's justice, or to any extrinsic reason why good should be rewarded and evil punished – then we must wonder where else that need is being met.[88] For the Christian faiths, theodicy had concerned the worldly path to salvation or the ultimate destination of the soul, either of which might compensate for the misfortunes of this life.[89] In a secular world of competing beliefs, however, where there is no universal scheme of salvation to contain the problem of good and evil, people look elsewhere for such comfort. If it is not to be found in the heavens, that is, they may hope to find it in more immediate worldly rewards as Weber noticed, and the notions of justice that sustain them. Where good is rewarded, success is attributed to merit, and misdeeds are punished we may add, there may be a modicum of redemptive satisfaction. The terms of reward and suffering provisionally make sense, and the philosophical claims that reinforce them (retributive, utilitarian) assume particular importance.

This is complicated however, since it was those very rational notions of reward and punishment that undercut the idea of God's final judgment in the first place – both that secular idea that punishment should advance universal laws (Kant and other retributivists),[90] and the utilitarian hope to serve the 'future good.' If those liberal notions of reward and punishment once undermined the idea of God's ultimate justice,[91] that is, and these notions now fail people too, they must look to something intrinsic to suffering itself for answers to questions of this kind. They must try to find a simpler idea of good and evil that is less dependent on god, salvation, or destiny, and to find explanations of reward and suffering in things that are rather more mundane.

A *secular* theodicy thus finds consolation in the elements of misfortune themselves, in reading the immediate, causal nexus of suffering – the source of pain, death and cruelty – to find means of redress, and by punishing those who are responsible, or finding scapegoats (as for Weber's German workers in the end).[92] This is why the public moral searching is done on surfaces, in the details of a crime scene or in second-guessing a verdict, and not so much in scripture, or in examinations of conscience. People want to find the meaning *in* the act because they cannot bear to be reminded that it may no longer have meaning of the sort it would obtain in a convincing theodicy.

This is precisely how 'ground zero' has become so symbolically important in the search for moral explanation. It was inevitable that the otherwise meaningless, empty pit where so many lost their lives would become a place of national mourning. Yet it is as much an aporia or perplexity that has opened up where theological and rational explanations have failed[93] – a site of contested memory (and contested monuments) where many still search for the meaning of 'terror' or hope to discover the nature of evil.[94] As the absence of a moral or religious consensus on those questions now makes them more pressing, answers are sought obsessively by returning to the act, the crime, and to the traces it has left in the unhallowed place itself.

Like other such efforts, however – picking over body parts, or searching for signs – this is more like attempts to divine the intentions of the gods in the entrails of an animal than any theological meditation on the nature of good and evil.[95] It cannot quite be an instance of "secular religion," since it appears where both secular and religious instruction fall silent. If it is a theodicy, it is rather more 'pre-' or 'post-' religious than the term has implied so far. There is something almost superstitious in it; something perhaps that aspires to be religious, but has not yet, or again, attained that level of refinement. In this, the affects of broken attachment make their interest known. It is what links the least religious elements in the victims' movement to the Christian right – and those who pray for the "Rapture" and think less of a forgiving Christ.[96] Both look for signs of a sort that prefigure theological explanation, and if they differ in other respects, their deeper motive is substantially the same.

It would be a mistake to think of these people as being conservative or religious in any ordinary sense. They are far more reactive and regressive than either term would suggest. While they may still try to rationalize suffering religiously, or appear pious and disapproving as we have seen, they are not so much religious as they are *proto*-religious. As they return to moral constructs that prefigure religion, what they aspire to, more properly, is a *post*-secular theodicy.[97]

While these Americans are uneasy with what liberal society has brought them (great freedom, moral ambiguity, etc.), they indulge its liberties and hope to find something good or redemptive within them. Destiny plays out for them in games, lotteries, or contests on TV and in identifying with the winners. Where there is no full-blown theodicy in which God has a proper place and plan, it is enough that luck is on their side – that 'our team,' 'our forces' or 'true believers' achieve victory. If God will not necessarily save them, it is vital that their enemies be vilified, and meet defeat. They rationalize their misfortune with what is immediately at hand. They want to name the tormentor – the cruel agency that causes suffering, pain, and death – and yearn to restore the expressive force with which it once could be called "evil."

Secular Evil[98]

It follows that the current conception of evil really must be distinguished from anything that has preceded it. The word, as it is has been revived in secular or post-secular discourse, has a very different connotation than it did when it occupied the center of the established moral universe. Those clerics who openly welcome the return of the discussion of evil today would be well advised to notice that difference. If, for example, George W. Bush seems to share their concern by taking every opportunity to identify terrorism as an "evil" and terrorists as "evil people," they might observe that he is appealing to *extralegal* and *irreligious* sensibilities of justice when he pronounces the terrorists "wanted dead or alive."[99]

Now if one listens carefully to the voices of moral outrage in America, one can detect the precise moment of exasperation at which they abandon rational or theological considerations, and resort to the older term of denunciation. Even the most erudite liberal politician expresses his philosophical doubts concerning the existence of evil, and in the same breath announce that he has "seen evil," nevertheless.[100] With increasing boldness, every President or candidate for high office must make similar claims in denouncing the 'enemies of liberty' if he or she is to secure a "moral base."[101] 'Evil' remains just outside the scope of rational inquiry – a moral outer limit to which a just, secular society should not appeal, but to which it inevitably does appeal in establishing the parameters of its justice.[102]

Hence, when Jean Baudrillard offers the suggestion that evil has virtually passed away as a category of understanding, he does so almost regretfully, and in a way that reflects its ambivalent status. On the one hand, he suggests, the marginalization of the category of evil reflects the moral vacuity and sterility of the modern period. On the other hand, it signals a transformation in the meaning of evil itself:

In a society which seeks – by prophylactic measures, by annihilating its own natural referents, by whitewashing violence, by exterminating all germs and all of the accursed share, by performing cosmetic surgery on the negative – to concern itself solely with quantified management and with the discourse of the Good, in a society where it is no longer possible to speak Evil, Evil has metamorphosed into all the viral and terroristic forms that obsess us.[103]

"We can no longer speak Evil," he continues – it has been lost to the liberal 'discourse on the rights of man.' Yet it has "metamorphosed" for us into such things as the Ayatollah Khomeni's terroristic Islam (an "archaic microorganism" he calls it, or so it seemed at the time).[104]

We cannot "speak Evil," but there it is. Baudrillard's lament at its passing is at once a recognition of its importance as a boundary condition to the state of liberty in which it cannot properly be discussed. Once upon a time, it seems, liberalism put limits on the condemnation of evil, making its pact with the many devils and its bargain with the many priests. It said, in effect, that in order to enjoy freedom we must suffer a measure of evil, or suspend our certainty concerning what it is. It created a space free of judgment against evil, in which such judgments must be made nonetheless. Yet when they *are* inevitably made, we might add, they reflect that initial compromise, and the enormous moral dislocation that came with it.

If the charge of evil is not made effectively in the liberal "discourse of the Good," that is, it is now lodged from the periphery to compensate for the effects of liberty themselves. An American conception of evil, therefore, is not the evil of witches' spells or demonic possessions, or of a devil that steals souls or tempts the weak to violate commandments. It is rather a function of those disparate energies unleashed in a condition of rights and liberty.[105] This evil, it would appear, is conceived in response to the uniquely modern anxiety that Sartre had termed "*angoisse*"[106] – the particular distress arising from having too much freedom and too much choice.

One notably American version of this has been voiced by Susan Smith's pastor in the attempt to explain why she might have drowned her two children: "We believe we have free choice and that with free choice comes evil. Evil exists because we have freedom."[107] Apparently those who choose evil, like Smith, define in the negative what it means to lead a moral life in a context of relative liberty. It is not only that bad choices or faulty reason make them blameworthy, as for Wilson. The fact of their freedom implicates them in evil nearly as it had in the Augustinian tradition.[108] Yet that evil must now be assessed in a context that promotes freedom, and be condemned in a way that counteracts its worst effects.

More precisely, in secular society where freedom and rational choice are the principal source of 'good,' threats to freedom are a primary source of evil, as are – abuses of freedom, or the very excesses that accompany it. Those who misuse their freedoms (the deranged mother, sexual predators, drug addicts, corporate thieves), those who massively threaten the freedoms of others (snipers, other serial killers, more sexual predators), those who openly condemn our freedoms (Al-Qaeda, the Taliban), fall most neatly into that category.

In this, the transparent, blamable subject assumes more definite proportions as well. On the encounter with violent crime, Americans want to name the culprit and expose the motive. Charles Manson, Ted Bundy, Timothy McVeigh are – they want to say – "evil." But this is an evil of a certain cast. Such men *choose* to do murderous things that a free society cannot permit *and* flaunt their freedom to make that choice at the same time. They abuse others and threaten their freedom (life, liberty, and pursuit of happiness), and flagrantly hide behind the laws that protect it. These are the crimes of rational men on the edge of sanity who test the limits of reason and sanity. Their 'warped reason' is revealed as the obverse or negation of that which belongs to the upright citizen – the very reason, once again, that defines what remains of the liberal 'good.' Theirs is a psychology of malicious intent, one that must be made as open to public viewing as the stocks or pillory had ever made the criminal.[109]

The evil that is exposed in this, the worst evil of all, is the psychological disposition of the amoral individual who freely chooses to rape or murder innocents to satisfy his own perverse desires. Locally this must be the pedophile or mass murderer.[110] It may be foreign leaders who abuse people in ways that our laws and liberties could never countenance – Idi Amin "eats his subjects," Saddam "gasses his own people."[111] It is almost impossible, where this paradigm prevails, for Americans to conceive of Osama bin Laden as a man of faith or convictions who might not be driven by such base or sinister inclinations.[112] In this context, it is hardly surprising that it is an American who has engaged a transparency of evil hypothesis to account for the Nazis as "willing executioners."[113] Such are the 'monsters' everywhere in news and fiction, 'sociopaths' as they are commonly called – the perfect embodiment of contemporary evil.

The sociopath, then, is an ideal type that is crucial to this paradigm. He is utterly rational and calculating about his crimes, lacks a moral faculty of any kind, and openly enjoys killing. He is not a person who suffers the delusions associated with psychosis, or other sorts of insanity, and who might be excused.[114] This diagnosis does not recognize his unconscious motives (its antipathy to Freud and psychoanalysis is absolute).[115] On the contrary, that particular disorder – its seeming coherence, transparency, or consciousness – is precisely what is worthy of blame. It is an indication of the times, therefore, that this 'type' corresponds precisely to the latest American standard of legal culpability: "guilty but insane." This is a finding by which, in many states, such persons may be treated medically for their illness and punished for their wicked behavior concurrently.[116] By that assessment, the 'guilty mind' of the felon (*mens rea*) is implicated regardless of its status or intentions. Insanity is no longer the exception that tests the rule, [117] and the once rare sociopath becomes a standard by which sanity and evil can both be judged. His *reason* and his *will* do what had once been the work of darker forces – he alone is the 'originator of moral evil, that is, of sin.' And neither God's will nor his illness as such have much to do with it.

The inversion of 'reason' that began for us with Wilson is now virtually complete. *Reason* is always and for everyone transparent and intact. It is no longer just a mental capacity, but the very crux of our morality (if good people control it and evil people choose not to). So it appears the very faculty that established the secular world has been retrofit to a vengeful, post-secular theodicy, much as the 'wicked soul' or 'original sin' had once fit another. But of course, to identify the evil and expose it in this way cannot explain it this time either. In the end, the hyper-rational sociopath is as opaque to a secular society as God's will and evil had been to its predecessor. Now, in describing this netherworld between reason and insanity – that impossible place in which we try to trick and keep the devil – we beg the question of theodicy and awaken the problem of evil again. For a time, evil explained it all; why we suffer, why others torment us, even why we die. Yet the sociopath's rational, deliberate cruelty, his very indifference to pain and death, only makes these questions more pressing.

The trouble with this is not just that we are in danger of reviving the old notions of 'satanic agency' (as the work of Delblanco and others suggests).[118] Rather, there is a need to solve these underlying mysteries once more. These are things that were attributed to malevolent forces before theology addressed them, and which our rational world has long stripped of magic. These are things that cannot be resolved without a unifying faith (or the headhunter's devotion) and which our liberty seems only to make worse.

It follows that the theodicy of the moment is concerned to explain the particular varieties of pain, death, and cruelty that arise most forcefully in a context of liberty. It is concerned with pain, but especially the inexplicable or chronic pain that can neither be treated, nor attributed to a specific agency or cause. It wants to explain death, but primarily the unexpected death of the young, or the undeserved death of the murder victim. It is interested in cruelty, not just the sadistic cruelty of the sociopath, but everyday cruelties that test the limits of liberty. For every unaccountable misery in our secular world, there is an effort to find the blamable aspect, to identify some small evil that can be remedied or resolved within a greater theodicy of revenge.

Pain

Physical pain would seem to be the most immediate of those concerns. If it has become improper to speak of evil in a liberal secular society, as Baudrillard observes, we still equate bad things with the pain or discomfort that they bring. Everyone at least agrees on this, pain itself is bad (if not the mysterious force causing it), and is one thing everyone holds in contempt. "Evil" too is casually defined as that "causing ruin, injury or pain."[119] In a society of so many faiths (and yet diminished faith) this would seem to be the common denominator, the irreducible, concrete universal of human experience that should transcend our differences and bind us in a common morality. Even utilitarianism, that expressly irreligious doctrine that makes unacceptable pain the moral limit of its judgment, depends implicitly on it being invested with some greater meaning.[120]

For all of that seeming agreement, however, pain is the site of considerable disagreement. When an American youth is caned for acts of vandalism in Singapore, there are many who abhor the illiberal cruelty of the punishment, or the inhumane disproportion between the pain inflicted and the good it should accomplish. There are others who applaud the simple justice of such corporal punishment, and the pain applied for the young man's deeds.[121] The meaning of pain, that liberal 'lowest common denominator,' is itself in dispute, and is quite unable to advance or underwrite moral agreement.

This is because pain, in spite of the definite impression that it makes, offers no stable basis for judgments of that kind. It offers nothing intrinsically to determine how much is enough in punishing, as we have said, and nothing in itself to clarify what it means to apply it (whether in retribution or for reasons of utility). It is of little use either in resolving differences between those two philosophies of punishment.

The notable thing about pain is that it is not at all a measurable *quantity* of experience, but an immeasurable quality of experience – one that threatens, as often as not, to be endless and intolerable. Yet that very illusiveness is why there are so many attempts to quantify it, and why it is so frequently miscast as a relation of cause and effect. Because it is so insistent, it is frequently mistaken for a cause or motive that can be measured and addressed, although it must follow from some action and is quite beyond measure. That must be why it seems reasonable to remedy a pain by inflicting a pain, and why that appears to be entirely coherent even when it is not.

This of course is the ineffable quality of pain that is the knot of our difficulty with punishment. As Elaine Scarry suggests, it is in its very nature to be inexpressible and indefinite, a quality that finds no point of comparison outside itself: "Physical pain – unlike any other state of consciousness – has no referential content. It is not *of* or *for* anything. It is precisely because it takes no object that pain, more than any other phenomenon, resists objectification in language."

Yet if pain has no referent, in Scarry's estimation, it is intrinsically ill at ease and cannot remain self-referential for long. It strives at once to be expressed as something other than itself. On the one hand, as she says, "Physical pain does not simply resist language but actively destroys it, bringing about an immediate reversion to a state anterior to language, to the sounds and cries a human being makes before language is learned."[122] On the other, we may add, those sounds and cries are themselves a form of language, a first step by which pain inevitably takes on other meaning.[123]

If it is characteristic of pain that it cannot be explained, but that it demands explanation, then it is (more properly) an effect *looking* for a cause that aims to be expressed in thoughts or words for the sake of its own containment. If it is never so stable as to be the 'answer' that punishment would make of it, it is very much a source of the demand for such stable answers. In reflecting on the nature of pain, for example, David Morris recalls Barkin's comment on that interrogative aspect of its character: "To attempt to understand the nature of pain, to seek to find its meaning, is already a response to pain itself. . . . In those instances in which pain is intense . . . its demand for interpretation is most naked, manifested in the sufferer asking, 'Why?'"[124] In the moment one suffers one must know the reason, and wherever pain threatens to be unendurable and endless, the wish to know its source at once entails the hope of knowing its end.

The context of meaning in which that question is framed and answered thus bears significantly on the experience itself. Painful experience in a secular context, informed by medical conceptions of disease and its etiology, must be very different from the pain that is conceived as religious penance, or, in Morris' example, as Job "understood his boils as unquestionably a punishment sent by God."[125] The distance between the question and the answer – which opened up so many more questions for Job – in this case between 'Why am I in pain?' and 'Because God is punishing me' – is itself charged with sensation. Any lag or uncertainty in the explanation must be agonizing, as the screams of the child suggest (Scarry), and *not knowing* what pain means, as for Job, must surely make it worse. This is not to say that pain hurts *only* because of what it means, but that Nietzsche's claim that "pain hurts more today" may have some credence if one takes it to mean that things do 'hurt more' in a context where such explanation is deficient.[126]

In the West, as Morris suggests, a pervasive deficiency of this kind can be attributed directly to the Hippocratic tradition. At one time, he reminds us, doctor–priests concerned themselves directly with this interrogative aspect of pain as they "mediated between the physical and spiritual worlds as specialists in the art of interpretation." With the advent of the diagnostic medicine, efforts to intercede between external causes and their painful effects have substantially displaced those older ones.[127] Now, Morris maintains, medicine concentrates nearly all of its interpretive energies on intervention, giving it a virtual monopoly over the physical dimension of pain and disease. If pain hurts more for this reason, then, there would seem to be less of it, and the rationalization of suffering seems to have been left almost entirely to private religious counsel and the alternative therapies. Medicine promotes its monopoly of diagnosis and treatment so effectively, Morris insists, that it has produced a virtual cult of "pain relief" in which Americans think of "pain-free life as something like a constitutional right."[128]

There is, of course, another side of the story. Even as the new model of medicine came to be established during the Enlightenment, it had acquired a unique explanatory power of its own. It seemed remarkable at the time, for example, that Rousseau should take comfort in the newfound understanding of a painful affliction that had troubled him for years. After the successful diagnosis of an untreatable prostate problem by the skillful probing of one Brother Côme, followed by a little conversation, he notes that he would at last more easily endure his pain knowing that "I should suffer a great deal, but live a long time...."

Thus having been successfully treated over so many years for diseases I had not got, I was finally informed that my complaint was incurable but not mortal, and would last for the rest of my days. My imagination was restrained by this information and no longer showed me the prospect of a cruel death in the agonies of stone.... Certainly since that time I have suffered much less from my malady than I had done before....[129]

The new medicine answers the questions 'what?' 'how?' and 'how long?' which constitutes a reason of sorts, and in so doing, its interpretive effect remains comparable. It attends to the mental state of pain, if only as an afterthought, yet still keeps the frightened imagination within bounds. Here we might say that the 'how' 'what' or 'what to do' stand in for the more spiritual 'why,' to achieve nearly the same analgesic effect that comes in declaring 'because...' This, of course, is the same sort of substitution that a secular theodicy makes in its rather clinical pronouncements against evil.

Now it seems that the modern entitlement against pain to which Morris refers, coupled with increasingly effective explanations of this kind, has placed an extraordinary burden on the knowledge of causes and the hope of a cure. The question 'why am I in pain?' persists, and diagnostic language still has the character of faith – a cult of pain relief is still a cult; Brother Côme is presumably still a priest, and medicine, as always, finds itself mediating between the physical and spiritual domains.

It is in this guise that modern medicine so frequently ascribes causes where they are not known, and offers medications for things (like depression) without entirely understanding their efficacy.[130] It reassures those who suffer nonspecific ills by giving them their proper anatomical name (with the suffix 'itis') and recommending treatments that doctors "prescribe most." Yet, if such partial explanations seem to lack those moral and spiritual dimensions that Morris finds missing, they acquire one directly. The sense of entitlement against pain, together with the interventionist attitude of 'heroic medicine,' now gives them a distinctly moralizing character.

It is often quite enough, that is, on the terms we are entertaining here, to know what the pain is and how to treat it. If proper objective medicine should 'interpret only in order to intervene,' moreover, that intervention now has the character of 'fighting back.' It 'beats back' throbbing pain. It 'declares war' on AIDS,[131] it 'fights battles' against cancer, it 'defeats' SARS or 'stockpiles ammunition' against Bird Flu. It pursues a 'cure' as if it were a kind of justice in which returning to the 'state anterior' to the illness or injury (both in the curative *and* retributive sense) now appears as its own sort of entitlement. Thus, at a time when reason and science remain inadequate to resolve suffering, and medicine itself is implicated in the failure, pain-freedom appears as more than just a right – it is what worthy Americans *deserve*. In a world where there is no theodicy of good and evil, and 'bad things happen to good people,'[132] a microtheodicy of pain relief insists that such things should be overcome as a matter of *meritocratic principle.*

This is why so many ailments like headaches, stomachaches, backaches, and hemorrhoids receive special attention in this culture. It is not only that these elusive disorders are more plentiful and annoying than other afflictions, but that they are susceptible to the binding of meaning that this thinly informed entitlement provides. The graphic depictions of pain on television make them seem unwarranted and beatable. Those kinds of aches and pains are normal, one can see, yet one has a right to feel *indignant* about them – all things being equal (normal, healthy) they seem particularly 'unfair.'[133] One *should* be able to take a Tylenol to make them go away. By definition such ailments are attributable to proximate causes – the food was bad, the chair too soft, the TV too loud – and the treatment fits the ailment as the punishment fits the crime. A great many Americans ask, 'what did I do to deserve this?' And whatever the answer, a reprieve is to be had in the latest convenient remedy.

Pain freedom therefore constitutes a realm of entitlement and heroic resistance at once – not quite those antiseptic or "prophylactic measures" that define the modern world for Baudrillard, but *anesthetic* ones – the same morally defensible sphere of desensitized indifference that Americans protect with guns or by driving minivans and SUVs. It is the same relative pain freedom that audiences obtain through masochistic identifications with the pain of others – the narcissistic preoccupation with their own pain as it is mirrored in theirs, that lets them experience it without real empathy or too much feeling.[134] It is, of course, the same condescending insensitivity with which they want to see pain inflicted on those who *cause* pain, to assert that their own pain is more important, or that they are somehow virtuous for having endured it.

This may help to explain the extensive experimentation with pain on the margins of this culture. If pain 'hurts more' now and there is a morally charged notion of pain relief on the one hand (entitlement – a narcotized norm), there is pervasive, amoral numbness on the other. The very desensitization that is a response to the meaninglessness for some Americans may thus be experienced *as* meaninglessness for others. Self-inflicted pain in this context appears to be a way in which the absence of meaning and feeling can be entertained meaningfully. This would account for the prevalence of certain sadomasochistic practices that are undertaken almost as a form of worship.[135] It explains why so many young people find it compelling to pierce themselves, and why inmates in all sorts of institutions engage in self-mutilation.[136] Some people, estranged as they are from that pervasive culture of pain-freedom, pinch themselves to vitiate the numbness. For those who are so thoroughly caught up in this condition, who have no prescribed way to feel, the pinch of pain is (almost) liberating.[137]

Now it appears that there are those who cultivate a certain numbness, and those who seem to feel too much and fetishize the pain of others – the heartbreak or unexpected calamity on soap operas, the suffering of victims – so as not to feel their own. Both are caught in the same paradigm. One is numbed into indifference, the other caught up in its parody of indifference. Each finds different drugs to suit its disposition or ameliorate its discomfort. Each takes different risks – perforation, tattooing, slamming, skateboarding, bungee jumping; watching sports, soap operas or "reality-competition" on TV – to flaunt or dull the pain.[138] In the end, the paradigm of moralizing numbness remains. It affords a kind of invulnerability (if not an afterlife); a place of relative safety and self-preoccupation from which to render judgment (a kind of secular heaven) on all that is unfair or undeserved (a certain evil), and fend off all the pain that goes unanswered (a sort of living hell).

Death

The question posed by pain and the fear that it may become interminable is closely related to the question of death, or what it means to die and what happens thereafter. In other times and places, the prospect of death has been rationalized as an end point to the pains of earthly existence. It has been seen variously as a point of crossing, an escape from misery, slavery, or degradation. In the Christian faiths, death offers an opportunity for atonement and salvation. It is a point of final judgment in which one must face the possibility of eternal damnation, but may hope for a place in paradise. The prospect of such judgment places one's life and death in the context of 'eternal justice' and 'destiny,' so that the weight of such concerns, and any doubts attending them, are substantially displaced onto the future.

In a secular context, however, death does not hold such promise. There is no guarantee of escape or salvation and its weight falls entirely on the present. In the absence of compensatory final rewards or ultimate redemption, there is increased anxiety over the prospect of one's own death; there is no convincing way to bind one's grief or to manage the experience of the death of others. It must be for this reason (among others) that the 'return to religion' seems so all-encompassing in this society, even as so many seek other, more tangible kinds of relief.

In secular society, the prospect of death without final reward has thus become an entirely compelling reason to pursue more immediate, earthly rewards.[139] It is why many Americans seek consolation in the great variety of preoccupations that *anticipate* some benefit. Where there is no hope of salvation or future compensation, that is, there is tremendous pressure for people to get something like it now – not just the trappings of success that serve as an emblems of one's destiny, which Weber noticed in a different context, but signs of advantage that bear on more imminent success.[140] They take any means to effect chance, fate, or good fortune to make life in the face of uncertainty (and certain death) seem as predictable and rewarding as they can.

Where there are no guarantees of salvation, to be more precise, the particular pain of this anxiety can be numbed or offset by various strategic purchases or low-risk wagers that seem to bear on the future. This explains the obsession with luck, lotteries, and other gambling in America if not elsewhere,[141] and the widespread sentiment that it is wise to hedge one's bets about the afterlife – to give to charity or do good deeds just in case there is one. It explains the financial (and spiritual) success of televangelism, and the warranty aspect of the life insurance and funeral industries, which together have produced an elaborate micro-theodicy of death.

The industries related to death cater to this mentality by observing a code of service that seeks to convey the impression of assurance and reliability. Secular death, so to speak, occurs under the auspices of licensing commissions and of state regulated insurers, lawyers, and morticians who keep the uncertainty to a minimum. Wills are read; the intentions of the deceased are honored. If the premiums have been paid and the estate well settled, the survivors are provided for into the future. One can know how one will be remembered in the obituaries, what sort of service or eulogy there will be, whether one will be interred or cremated. Certainly one may face death and die within one's faith, but not without a substantial secular infrastructure becoming involved. Living wills,[142] hospice care, and funeral homes serving all denominations are in place to address one's final needs.[143] Now the innumerable commercial services of the funeral industry – embalming, shrouding, hearse-led processions – seem to smooth one's passing. And if the terms of salvation are elusive, a luxurious, well-accessorized casket should get one to a better place.[144]

By Jessica Mitford's memorable account, the funeral industry has generated a euphemistic commercial discourse of "pre-need planning" and "eternal slumber" that has come to affect the comprehension of death itself.[145] Where it appears that this society had performed "cosmetic surgery on the negative" for Baudrillard, or made a cult of "pain relief" for Morris, now in Mitford's phrase it has 'anesthetized resistance,' to that commercial jargon of death and its comforting message.[146] What is striking in this is not its spiritual emptiness per se, but the fact that it is so ingeniously (and so *meaningfully*) addressed in these commercial terms;[147] that a present outlay for some future benefit should seem so reassuring. Where earthly rewards have such bearing on final rewards, the anesthetized state with which one may now face death is yet another instance of entitlement.[148] Now as the industry (not priests or theologians) becomes the relevant authority in this arena, its reverent sales talk combines the terms of material success, desert, and spiritual destiny so effectively that religious leaders envy and seem compelled to emulate it.[149]

For the most part, the bereaved themselves accept this all without question. Their suffering puts them at the mercy of the faithless industry, and their grief should remain a private matter anyway. But of course, the secular treatment of death is in no way adequate to the problem posed by death itself, or to the distinctive anxieties associated with it.[150] As reassuring as they seem, immediate rewards are not final rewards, wagers are not winnings, and the comforting sales pitch does nothing whatsoever to answer the question 'Why?' Even when psychologists counsel survivors on the 'stages of grief' in the tradition of Elisabeth Kubler-Ross, it helps them only to anticipate their emotional states to 'cope with the loss.'[151] It guides them in the moment, but it does not give them the answers they need – it offers no rationale or reason for their suffering, and surely no 'because. . . .'

In this secular society, where such questions are not effectively addressed to the heavens and the answer does not seem to be forthcoming, there is nowhere for their grief and rage to go. The bereaved cannot quarrel with God or fate convincingly,[152] they cannot beg forgiveness for their anger, or pray for a loved one's immortal soul. Beyond immediate or proximate causes, there is nothing and no one to blame. Instead, they address their anguish to the dead themselves, in whispers or fragments of writing, with mementos and other small offerings that comprise the latest sort of public lamentation. American monuments to collective victims – the Vietnam Memorial, the AIDS Quilt, and the plans for ground zero – now make room, quite literally, for just this sort of expression.[153] Those inspired creations provide a place to reconcile painful memories and connect the past to future hope, to register regrets and wishes for the departed – a crack in the wall, a patch of cloth, a common space in which life, death, and final justice might seem to be connected as they would certainly have been connected in an earlier theodicy.[154]

Of course the very inadequacy of this sort of remembrance and the lack of suitable explanation now generate a great deal of speculation on the nature of death itself. There are innumerable books on death and dying in as many disciplines, and while these do not provide answers either, they have generated a consensus on how the matter might be discussed.[155] Observations on parapsychology are offered in the same respectful tones as religious commentaries on death, so that the 'acceptable' ways of speaking have formed a kind of truce. There is widespread interest in 'near death experiences.' Ghosts, angels, reincarnation and all sorts of phantasmagoria associated with the afterlife seem more credible. As these 'unknowns' are taken seriously, a generic conception of death is generated in just the right measure of obscurity to suit its secular status. In films like *Ghost, Flatliners, The Sixth Sense* or *Dragonfly*, fresh souls of the dead make the same restless procession. There is usually a light toward which the wayward spirits move – a vague, nonsectarian, probable God or heaven looms in the background as they are pursued by shadowy forces of evil. But of course, they cannot reach their goal until their own misdeeds or murders have been avenged or something disturbing about their lives has been set right by the living.

In this expectant American mentality, the world *might* just make sense – there might be angels among us, there could be cosmic justice, the dead might hear us or be saved by our efforts, and if this does not produce religious feeling in those who grieve, a sense of 'mystery' passes for 'awe' with nearly the same consequence.[156] This speculative state of mind is at once one of anticipation, something like hope (if not providence), which suggests that death may yet be rectified or have meaning. It is fertile ground for the wager – death might be redeemed if we play it right, if we whisper the right words and make sure there is payback or compensation wherever we can – secular redemption seems possible if there is the right sort of revenge.

Of course, the ubiquity of inexplicable death – especially death that results from violence or unanticipated disaster – heightens the need to effect outcomes or futures in this way. Where such death is not clearly subject to God's judgment, or its cause is difficult to assign, the wager becomes more complicated and there must be room for finer assessments. Certainly those lesser deaths – deaths due to accident, safety failures, or mere negligence – may not require such extreme compensation as those resulting from murder. There must be room for other kinds of repayment, a proportionate revenge, a calculus of pain and suffering that maintains the illusion of control and adjustability, and which, when it is called for, can exact "additional" compensation.[157]

In these finer adjustments of the scales of justice, the 'degrees of culpability' and 'scale of damages' may be set out in advance. If a death cannot be predicted, an actuary may assess its probability, risk, or likely impact nevertheless. If death is indemnified to the right degree, it may seem to have been anticipated; its compensation judged and preordained. In life insurance, estate planning, and the many statistical efforts to predict the financial effects of death, prognostication functions almost as prophecy.[158] In civil suits, at least, the impact of a death can be weighed after the fact in awarding damages, such that the living might seem to have influenced this much of 'life' after death.

In a world where such accounting is possible, there should seem to be no accidents or unattributable deaths. This, of course, is the impulse that drives the extreme litigiousness of American society in matters of 'wrongful death.' It is why physician's malpractice and hospital incompetence suits are so costly, and why the national debate about awards limits, like other matters of punishment, falls precisely along party lines.[159] If there are no final rewards, at least there is *financial* reward, and that expectation is so pervasive that a death without recompense would seem to have been a death in vain. Now indeed, when several thousand people are killed at the World Trade Center there are interfaith services, but the main attraction is a telethon to raise money for the victims' families – and if the latter agree not to sue the airlines, they can avail themselves of a victims' fund that pegs payouts to income along standard actuarial lines.[160]

Finally, then, the innocent victim of murder is of special interest. At last a needless death of immeasurable consequence that could least be anticipated, one that cannot be redressed in this way, one that calls the meaning of death profoundly into question and cries out most for final judgment. Like the unclaimed surfaces of collective monuments that bear the missives of individual mourners, the image of the innocent victim is the preeminent empty space on which the public lament is written. The face of the high school cheerleader bludgeoned by her abusive boyfriend announces the 'senseless waste.' The yearbook photos of children killed in school shootings or victimized by gangs are held up to proclaim the horror, the victims of terrorism get their pictures on Oprah.

On the one hand, this is a testament to that fine modern sentiment for justice that Richard Rorty identified in "the ability to shudder with shame and indignation at the unnecessary death of a child."[161] On the other, it *uses* the victim as a symbol to stimulate moral feeling, to activate disgust, to engage the sentiments; to make death seem comprehensible overall.[162] The victim, as *symbol*, is Christ cut down from the cross to be anyone (it could be you or your child), and like the suffering figure of the Savior, it insists that every death will have greater meaning.[163] Those who shudder with indignation for the victim may do so less for the one child, than for themselves, and for all whose deaths do not 'count' properly (or cannot count until their murderers are caught and punished). And since Christ has indeed been taken down, they no longer say, "forgive them . . . " and they have no moral alternative to venting their rage and grief in vengeance. The very horror that could not be anticipated (or insured against), and for which there may be no final judgment, demands worldly payback. The risk must be eliminated, the bet hedged with the certainty of God's judgment. This must be why Americans are so inordinately invested in the death penalty. They go to church and may have their doubts, but they sleep better at night if they have that too.

Cruelty

We have noticed how the effort to demonize one sort of cruelty is the closest that we come to identifying and condemning evil in a secular society. This, again, is the extreme sadistic cruelty of the sociopath who brings pain and death, and who epitomizes the 'rational individual' gone wrong. In a liberal society, after all, it is supposed to be irrational to want to harm others, to break the golden rule (or violate Kant's categorical imperative). Those who wish to harm others either strain that paradigm of willful, rational action or remain woefully outside of it – the nasty characters entertained by Hobbes or Machiavelli have long been offered as exceptional cases in a world more properly described by Locke. It is for this reason that we forgive children for their cruelty, and excuse the hurtful effects of insanity, and why we reserve punishment for rational persons who have committed deliberate acts. It is why we fetishize and condemn the lesser cruelties – bullying, road rage, and careless indifference toward others.

On this ground, there does appear to be a liberal basis for singling out people who are malevolent, for distinguishing their 'malice aforethought' and punishing them accordingly. Nevertheless, knowing and assessing the intentions of such persons, discerning the degree or nature of their 'cruelty,' have been notoriously difficult in our system of justice.[164] This is why we punish people for their actions, but not their motives, penalizing them in equal measure whether they are vicious and mean spirited or not. In an older theodicy, intentionally hurtful people would be deemed evil and would face certain punishment in the afterlife, but such cruelty as a standard of judgment has been particularly vexing for us. Somewhere along the way, as we have privileged reason over the darker motives, the moment for such assessments has been lost, and it has become difficult for us to denounce cruelty without equivocation.

If we could not "speak evil" for Baudrillard, then, Judith Shklar has made it clear that we cannot 'speak cruelty' very well either, and that liberal society has been quite unable to condemn hurtful actions in such simple moral terms. In her provocative meditation on modern liberalism, *Ordinary Vices*, Shklar points out that "Philosophers rarely talk about cruelty" anymore – "They have left it to the dramatists and historians."[165] She finds this to be deeply troubling, and makes it her task (as a liberal) to resuscitate the discourse on cruelty that once mattered to political philosophy – to "put cruelty first" as an object of moral denunciation as Montaigne had done, and in doing so, to provide the basis for what Michael Walzer has termed "a moral psychology for liberals."[166]

To that end, and in a way that is rather more subtle than those other attempts to restore moral condemnation that we have considered, Shklar returns our attention to the forgotten roots of the liberal tradition itself, and to those long-standing humanitarian concerns with vindictiveness and cruelty that had once been close to its heart:

By the eighteenth century these were very common concerns, especially in England, where secular humanitarianism had begun its extraordinary career. It was never to be without its enemies. Religious rigor, the theory of the survival of the fittest, revolutionary radicalism, military atavism, masculine athleticism, and other causes hostile to humanitarianism never abated. Nevertheless, taking cruelty seriously became and remained an important part of Europe's accepted morality even in the midst of unlimited massacres. Putting cruelty *first* is, however, a matter different from mere humaneness.... Putting cruelty first has therefore been tried only rarely, and it is not often discussed.[167]

The moral stance against cruelty, it would seem, has been there all along, but it has never been made a sufficient priority. Shklar suggests that restoring emphasis to that strand of thinking might now help to offset a dangerous imbalance.

How curious it is, however, to suggest that liberals need to be reminded of their grounding moral psychology, or that so much should turn on this particular sensibility. For Shklar's project to become necessary, there must have been a more serious deficit than this to begin with – a deeper reason for the lapse; a moral or psychological dilemma of greater proportions. On the one hand, in order for liberal "humanitarianism" to take on its more muscular opponents, it would indeed need to condemn certain vices of character on what had once been religious grounds. Yet on the other hand, it had already begun to defend liberty – the sort of liberty that had its origins in resisting religious persecution – and that would soon part company with condemnations of character of this kind. In its secular form, that liberty would foster rights and toleration, and *give up* the more perilous hunt for vice or cruel motives.

Shklar is well aware that early liberal humanitarianism relied heavily upon Christian judgments of character to establish its claims. But she is equally aware that such pursuits would be abandoned in the elaboration of liberal law and political philosophy. Liberal law had clearly perceived the danger in this reliance, and it had left off chasing after 'bad character' because it was painfully conscious of the problems of equity that this would raise, and the intrusiveness of the law that it would require (worthy modern concerns that were not yet evident to Montaigne). By virtue of its interest in liberty, no less – in acknowledgment of such Christian sensibilities *and* the need to set them aside – liberalism would have to confront the danger in condemning cruelty *itself*. This is precisely the concern we may add, that has ceased to matter to the people who *do* talk about cruelty all the time in the tabloids and on the more sensational TV shows. Those who would be as willing as Shklar to 'put cruelty first,' but pursue a far more facile sort of condemnation than she has in mind.

Instead of addressing the danger that this revived disdain for cruelty might pose for a liberal democracy, however, Shklar reminds us that the liberal dislike of such things has really been there all along. She suggests that this attitude might restore our moral vision, or bridge the gap to the more virtue-oriented moralities, if it could only be accessed properly. As she suggests, "[i]t seems to me that liberal and humane people, of whom there are many among us, would, if they were asked to rank the vices, put cruelty first. Intuitively they would choose cruelty as the worst thing we do."[168]

Doubtless she is right about the "many" liberals, but it is striking that she must rely here on an aspect of character that they would display if asked, and that her appeal is made to an intuitive self-assessment that this ought to elicit, but not to liberal claims about human nature, or to any religious commandment against vice. Significantly, the ground of the appeal has shifted away from those older ones. It seems instead to turn on a private sensibility that liberalism has merely harbored or tolerated. Indeed, the conditional sense in which the many 'would rank vices' seems to offer the assurance that the very moral hegemony that *should no longer* reign in a democracy can be counted on nevertheless. It is additional evidence, perhaps, that frustration with the seeming moral vacuity of liberalism produces a theodicy of its own, that it invites the ranking of *virtues* and the return of moral condemnation and vengeful judgment.

To imagine their own response to Shklar's hypothetical question, then, would seem to allow liberals to avoid the more difficult questions that their system ought to pose to *them*: 'What is *wrong* with simply condemning cruelty?' 'Who will decide what is cruel, and by what standards?' and, 'Is there something inherently dangerous (or dangerous for liberal democracy) about moral condemnation of this sort?' Cruelty, it seems, is all around us, cruelty repels us, and we may certainly enjoy having the opportunity to say so. But thinking liberals who do ask such questions cannot rank cruelty chief among vices because they know that ranking vices has always gotten them in trouble. They know, or should know, that introducing a hierarchy of vice or virtue into a pluralist egalitarian society is highly problematic.[169]

To her credit, however, Shklar does not wish to rely entirely on the intuition of some liberals to sustain her moral claim. She locates an abiding concern for cruelty within the liberal credo itself, within a strand of liberalism that "underwrites" the better-known liberalism of rights.[170] Instead of the old "liberalism of *natural* rights," she suggests, we need to rediscover and heed a "liberalism of fear," one in which rights are seen as the "politically indispensable dispersion of power." This is a liberalism that "institutionalizes suspicion," and in which the stand against cruelty can itself be seen as a foundation for other rights.[171] "Why put cruelty first?" in this context, she asks, and then answers: "Because we have rights." And since the liberal commitment to rights can be traced to a fundamental "fear of fear"[172] in which the opposition to cruelty is implicit, she feels justified in assigning it priority.

But this of course is only one way to read the tradition, and it is hard to know what sort of morality this 'fear of fear' would produce. Again, it might make one shudder at those cruel things that induce fear (the murder of a child), or it might institutionalize the response to fear in a way that becomes hardened and indifferent. It may entail a fear of its own reaction to fear as for the liberalism that cowered on the edge of a threatening wilderness for fear that it might loose its reason to revenge. Or, for that matter, it might lead one to react against fear, without enough healthy suspicion of the vengeful cruelty that is involved in suppressing other cruelties, which is the very problem we are facing.

Shklar knows perfectly well that rights, for this reason, do not overtly contain fear or prevent cruelty – they scrupulously avoid such things because they are so much less susceptible to the judgments that a rational society can make than those positive freedoms delineated by specific rights. Yet intuitively for her, rights involve respect for persons and an implicit "irreducible" right to be "protected against the fear of cruelty," and against all tyrannies great and small.[173]

But again, that fine attempt to discern the common moral thread begs the question of liberalism's essential ambiguity on this point.[174] What about the right, one might ask, to be cruel or indifferent toward others that *also* follows implicitly from the more formal rights?[175] Must we not tolerate a great deal of psychological and even physical cruelty if we going to defend personal liberty? What of those "tendencies to cruelty inherent in searches for autonomy" that Rorty calls to our attention?[176] What of the ambiguities of legal rights – as when the rights that protect one's home and property also protect the abuser?[177] Or what of rights that protect the parent who withholds medical treatment from a child who is deathly ill, and which might be deemed cruel? What of the contested right to terminate a pregnancy (in the view of many)? What of the 'right of the state,' as many see it, to inflict painful punishments? Rights, in other words, can be cruel themselves, even if they are necessary to protect persons in liberty from other cruelties. If the idea of rights contains a narrow basis for a claim against cruelty, that is, it can scarcely preclude cruelty as such, or provide a reason to rank it *worst* among the vices. To the enemies of a true liberalism of rights, lest we forget, the moral ambiguity that arises with rights would seem to be the 'cruelest' thing of all.

If one agrees with Shklar that rights guarantee a range of personal freedoms against certain (cruel) intrusions, then, it might be more accurate to say that they have *arranged* cruelty in order to make the moral pluralism, individual liberty, and market freedoms of democracy possible. Evidently, rights have been carefully constructed here so as not to oppose cruelty in every sense – the cruelties of capitalism, so vexing to an earlier Christian humanitarianism,[178] or the cruelties of the law – which is precisely why the reaction against liberal moral ambiguity has been so vociferous in America. This must be why our society has needed to establish its own order of cruelty by way of standardized punishments. The American "ranking of vices" (as it is found in current criminal sentencing guidelines for example) has hardly put cruelty first in a way that diminishes its own brutality. Anything like a right against "cruel and unusual punishment" has clearly lost ground to the right of the punitive authority itself to be cruel. At best, one might say, the notion of rights keeps open a space in which the moral stance against cruelty is continually debated. Yet we may take the hint (or rather the warning) that we are remaking rights (and ranking cruelties) surreptitiously in ways that narrow that space all the time.[179]

It is not surprising, therefore, that in declaring the "first right" to be the right "to be protected against the fear of cruelty," Shklar wants to insinuate a moral link between cruelty and "evil" that forecloses this debate by make precisely the sort of moral assertion that liberalism should find troubling:

People have rights as a shield against this greatest of public vices. This is the *evil*, the threat to be avoided at all costs. Justice itself is only a web of legal arrangements to keep cruelty in check, especially by those who have most of the instruments of intimidation closest at hand.[180]

On the one hand this is a remarkably honest acknowledgment of the problem we are facing – a deficit in the meaning of contemporary justice, and the need to fill it with a more pragmatic liberalism that has its moral priorities in order. People live behind a shield of rights that protects them from cruelty, but in accepting the terms of that protected space they have forgotten how to condemn cruelty as an evil. Since cruelty persists, it now seems wise to refresh the condemnation they would make if they could only remember how. On the other hand, Shklar's concession to a "liberalism of fear" leaves the door open for those enemies of liberalism who would exploit her "first right" and take the opportunity to define evil in whatever way they wish.

It is useful, then, to recall how a very different first right (or "first law of nature") once underwrote all other rights for liberals – that of "self-preservation."[181] For Locke, self-preservation, and *not* fear, gives one the right to deploy hurtful acts against all sorts of threats and intrusions. It permits one to resist those acts with a degree of indifference toward the threatening party, if not with gratuitous cruelty or for the sake of revenge. Such self-preservation is a matter of rational, justified resistance (among other things) to the intrusion of self-assured moral judgments (for him the Church of Rome), but not to cruelty as such. Surely notions of 'rights' grounded in this way grew up *against* the excesses of authority that arose from such judgments – by various persons or institutions (the Inquisition), and against punishments that justified their own cruelty as a weapon against "evil" and *its* cruelties – precisely by taking cruelty out of it.[182] Rights, one might say, have emerged in opposition to the simple, unambiguous denunciation of cruelty, as, for example, when early advocates of rights opposed the witch hunt, because they saw how quickly it could be turned against *any* idiosyncrasy or perversion that was thought to be evil or cruel.

Instead of reviving the condemnation of cruelty, then, thinking liberals might recall that rights are *themselves* a series of bargains struck among the cruelties that privilege the preservation of the individual – bargains made by thoughtful people who have recognized that zealous condemnation leads to its own tyranny and that liberty as such entails a paradox of cruelty.[183]

It follows that in ranking cruelties (as they would eagerly do if asked) and making that bargain to suit themselves, Americans harbor a rather self-serving sense of priorities concerning what qualifies and what does not. The system of capitalism could not appear to be cruel to them for very long, or economic growth as such, for all its casualties. Exploitation of laborers abroad or poor working conditions are not perceived as the chief cruelty, nor is the psychological torment of exclusion for minorities, nor the hurtful prejudices perpetuated in the name of 'family values.' It cannot be the careless uses of the environment, driving bigger cars, slaughtering livestock, or killing game that count as cruel.

It is no longer even slavery, oppressive kings, or communist dictators that are the cruelest enemies for Americans. Rather, it is whatever threatens their entitlement to these things – their 'right,' primarily, to buy and to own things, if not some principle that applies more broadly. What counts as cruel, then, is whatever threatens these liberties, the killing of our civilians, *not theirs*, their (alleged) ability to use 'weapons of mass destruction,' the combined threat of those governments in the "Axis of Evil" to our freedom if incidentally their cruelty to their own people. Beyond this, however, the ranking of the cruelty of others now defines a realm of *protected cruelties* for Americans – the measure of our indifference toward those others and the way we rank their pain relative to our own. This implies a degree of insensitivity or "incuriosity," as Rorty puts it, born of our own "private obsessions with the achievement of a certain sort of perfection," which makes us "oblivious to the pain and humiliation we are causing."[184] It suggests that our anesthetized indifference has produced a micro-theodicy of *permissible* cruelties.[185]

Missing from Shklar's account, then, is a sense of how the moral stance against cruelty may mask these biases, and of the disturbingly close relationship between liberty and cruelty that is implicit within them. In setting up cruelty as a moral limit, the moral–psychological paradox of liberty – disdain for the very cruelties it fosters – seems nearly soluble. At first, the ranking of vices with cruelty at the top promises to function on behalf of the rational framework that sustains liberty, and to keep those darker motives in check.[186] The trouble is, however, that if Americans (many liberals included) were asked to rank their *pleasures* with any degree of honesty, cruelty would certainly be among them, especially that with which they denounce others or inflict the pain of punishment, or like to watch it being done. Not only do certain biases creep in as they rank the cruelties, that is, but the denunciation of cruelty affords its own satisfactions when it functions *as* a moral limit – by privileging its own cruelty in 'legitimate' acts of vengeance.

Hence, any attempt to banish cruelty to the periphery of liberal society is outmatched by a need arising within liberty to explore it, and to keep it always within sight. This is the American inclination to test its limits constantly, to imagine doing and undoing those acts of cruelty that we have considered; to know it as if by some inverted empathy, and to return from the edge of that knowledge morally unscathed. If there is some delight to be had in the liberty *of* cruelty that follows from rights (the freedom even to do cruel things), then, still greater pleasures may be had in that cruel denunciation of cruelty without ambiguity – in watching yet condemning violent movies, in enjoying yet deploring the cruel expulsions on Reality TV, or in reviving the older satisfactions of casting out demons. Again, this is not just the 'pleasure in cruelty' that Nietzsche thought was once the true currency of punishment, but the vengeful satisfaction of knowing that one's own cruelty is exempt – a position of *morally vindicated cruelty*. From that perch, Americans can manage their dread of pain and death, contain their memories of horror, and arrange cruelty to secure a protected, relatively painless place *in liberty*.

Now the state of relative liberty in which we live is rife with temptations of this kind, and full of such unseemly gratifications. One might say that a distinctive psychological condition of our liberty is its envy of cruel excesses denied. Where that is the case, the denunciation of cruelty is never a simple moral undertaking, and to imagine that such things are 'genuinely' worthy of disgust (Kahan) is to misunderstand its complicated status within liberty. Cruelty, like evil, is always present 'in denial' – we must always know where and what it is – which is why Americans love to imagine the hateful extremes of liberty, and "love to hate" the cruelest excesses in their midst.[187] Just as the pinch of pain disrupts their sense of meaninglessness, or the shudder of indignation affirms the moral limits of their community, this observance of cruelty gives them a momentary sense that they are right. It provides the hope that the moral crisis will subside and that the questions posed by inexplicable pain and death will yet be answered.

At last, these questions seem less disturbing if the motive force that brings them into being can be determined – if pain and death are *caused* by cruelty, and we think we know what that is, then an answer can be found in punishment. The moral uncertainty of liberalism recedes when pain, death, and cruelty line up for a whipping and a self-assured post-secular theodicy seems to know just when and how to administer it.[188] Here of course, the "institutionalization of suspicion" that Shklar advocates (to keep the punitive power of the state from becoming cruel)[189] is no match for the moralizing pressure that this intrigue has placed upon punishment. No mere 'suspicion' will stop the punitive practices of justice from becoming increasingly cruel. If liberalism stands a chance against this, no less, it lies in acknowledging its own complex relationship with such things, and retaining that acknowledgement in institutions that protect rights, but do not so easily denounce cruelty.

It is a fine thing to be against cruelty. But the heirs to liberalism must remain vigilant about their own hypocrisy in these matters, and suspicious of attempts to make it a priority or to equate it with evil.[190] In putting *rights* first, of course, as it had done to protect us from the very cruel excesses of government that concern Shklar, that system had denied itself the ability to enforce a clear moral dictum against cruelty, and retains only a limited democratic basis to condemn anything else. Again, in resisting such public 'tyrannies,' it has invited a range of private cruelties, excesses of liberty and violence, which have left liberals and liberalism internally at odds. This is why so many want to *sanctify* 'rights' (and bracket the cruelties that invariably attend them), and to make them look more like a 'moral system.' They want to extend the notion of 'human rights' to those who suffer cruel oppression without fully addressing the paradox of that imposition

(Rawls' "Law of Peoples"),[191] or to amend the regime of rights with a sense of virtue (MacIntyre again, and Kahan) to contain its excesses. They seem unwilling to face the contradiction, to see just how much liberty has indulged cruelty on the one hand, and instituted cruel punishments to make up for it on the other.[192]

So it would seem that the denunciation of cruelty, like the appropriation of disgust, is a most precarious place for liberals to stand, until and unless they acknowledge how much they are caught up in that impulse, or the extent to which they already indulge in a ranking of cruelties as they cherish their liberties and craft their punishments to protect them.[193] The task, it seems, is to put the problem of *vengeance* first – not to rank it as a vice – but to recognize how the uniquely *authoritarian* cruelty of revenge has become the organizing principle of that same impulse, and to see how it is inimical to a justice of rights. The challenge is to interrogate our own great interest in such things, to rearrange our priorities around them in a way that is more honest and better suited to a system of democratic rights and freedoms.

We have now identified the phenomenon and the dilemma. First, it is evident that the crisis in America that appears to be about lost meaning is also about vengeance, as the rage in grief demands a moral accounting. Secondly, and because liberal society cannot address such things in the way that the religions used to do, and since it never resolved the problem of vengeance either, that demand now falls heavily upon its institutions of justice. An inversion of the meaning of justice is therefore under way at the deepest level. Its interest in rights and liberty has now been compromised by what we must acknowledge to be an interest in theodicy – that human need to make moral sense of pain, death, and cruelty – which is exacerbated in liberal society, and which demands a simpler accounting of good and evil.

Now indeed, as this needful cloud descends upon the system and the sensibilities of justice, the safeguard of rights and the restraint and compassion of liberal law are all in jeopardy. Under the guise of 'moral restoration' and too often in the name of justice, rights give way to severe punishments, the Constitution is twisted to new ends, and 'democracy' is reduced to popular whim. What presents itself as 'moral progress' is thus rather a retrogression, full of dangerously misplaced nostalgic yearning.[194] The rage in grief, those affects of broken attachment, have been set loose like the Furies, and much of what passes for morality or religion in America is a manifestation of that revenge.

In recognizing this, we have reached a very old impasse. Liberalism and its justice had once provided the best protection against vengeance, but liberalism has produced a need or moral vacancy within itself that invites its return. If, on the one hand, we give in to the temptation to meet that need, imagining that the culture suffers a "*lack* that must be filled," as

William Connolly observes, then we will surely succumb to more sinister motives.[195] In that event, even Judith Shklar's thoughtful restoration of liberal moral precepts may become confused with those other calls for moral regeneration.

Yet on the other hand, if we notice how much the public anger does try to fill that void by any means, we may be alerted to the danger. Instead of calling for new efforts to institutionalize our "suspicion" or "fear," or for that matter to revitalize our 'disgust' by way of punishment, we would be suspicious of such moralizing efforts wherever they arise, resist those impulses, and develop punishments that are less self-assured, moralizing, and severe. In direct opposition to this impulse, we would institutionalize democratic humility or "doubt," and conduct our moral discussions in this spirit. Now instead of imagining that we can rediscover a 'moral foundation' implicit in reason or rights that stands against cruelty or revenge, we would see how the latter is already implicated in the former. We would acknowledge that the rage in grief and the moral desperation that we have tried to keep out cannot be kept out, despite the very good democratic reasons for trying.

In the end, if we heed this warning, it will become clear that the most challenging choice before us is not between moral decay and more vengeful punishment (as the political right would have us believe), but between vengeance and democracy. Democracy, then, must have a better grasp of the forces it has unleashed, and a clearer reason to stand against them.

Before we turn to the question of how democratic justice might address this problem therefore (Chapter 4), we must further consider the nature of vengeance itself. We must contemplate the means by which that seemingly personal impulse makes its demands upon a public stage. We must see how it has been a central to the Western self-understanding since the Greeks, and how the arrogance of vengeful self-assertion bears on matters of recognition and sovereignty that are so important to that self-understanding. We must see why it is so troubling in these dimensions – how the vengeful need to alter time and memory lends itself to deception and self-deception (engaging Freud and Sartre) and how this has been exhibited in performative, or for that matter, theatrical displays from Oedipus to Hamlet. Here we will see *why* that assertive impulse is intrinsically authoritarian, and how it does damage to truth and ultimately to democratic justice.

3

The Nature of Vengeance

Memory, Self-Deception, and the Movement from Terror to Pity

> We are the skilled, the masterful, we the great fulfillers,
> Memories of grief, we awesome spirits
> stern, unappeasable to man,
> disgraced, degraded, drive our powers through;
> banished far from god to sunless, torchlit dusk,
> we drive men through their rugged passage,
> blinded dead and those who see by day.
> – The Furies, in Aeschylus' *Eumenides*[1]

> Thus the will, the liberator, took to hurting; and on all who can suffer he
> wreaks revenge for his inability to go backwards. This indeed this alone is
> what revenge is: the will's ill will against time and its "it was."
> – Nietzsche's *Zarathustra*[2]

As we turn to the Greeks and others who know the matter well, we should
consider personal revenge. In conflicts at work, or in bitterness over a failed
relationship, one thinks of getting even, imagining the pleasure of it while
remaining alert to the dangers. Such private fantasies are exceedingly common, and if they have not been formally consulted so far, they have quietly
informed our inquiry. It may seem, for example, that a certain sympathy with
vengeful feeling – for a grieving spouse or victim – has enabled us to perceive a liberal deficit. Knowing these fantasies and their limits in ourselves,
we may suppose that we have special insight where they are concerned,
that we can perceive their bearing and proper limits within the present
world. We might think that we can know them and control them even as
we control our tempers.

It has become clear, however, that if we rely too heavily on that internal
sense of measure, we indulge a misconception. Such thoughts and feelings
appear only to be private ones having little to do with reason, theodicy,
or a public interest in justice. If we consider them only in this way, we
may miss the deviousness of the impulse as it operates in this dimension.

94

We may fail to see how vengeance turns the most private concerns into public, self-serving accounts, and why it is no longer very clear to us what is public and private (or rather personal and vengeful) in the realm of justice. Perhaps it is time to concede the point, if not to give in to it completely, to recognize at least that the personal aspect must be taken seriously in this way. Perhaps in seeing how the private impulse *prevails* upon the public, or by what psychological and even theatrical means it aims to be convincing, we may better understand its nature.

This, of course, is the quality of vengeance that Aeschylus and Shakespeare (among others) have perceived so clearly – vengeance as it is a palpable, corrosive force in personal identity that affects the realm of public justice. In appealing to them for guidance in this connection, we will consider how the perceptual demands of vengeance have played a part in the establishment and self-understanding of Western identity – in the moment of 'recovery from terror' (Plato) as it bears on the establishment of conscience, in assertions of 'sovereignty' (Hobbes), and ultimately in the 'recognition' that we expect or would defend in a democracy (Honneth). We will see how this involves deception and self-deception (with the help of Sartre and Freud) in a way that is destructive to that identity (as in *Oedipus Rex*), and ultimately to the justice that depends on it. After examining modern displays of punishment (eighteenth-century England), we will consider how vengeance engages every theatrical device (masks, plot twists, audience manipulation) to remake the world, to alter time and memory, to achieve a 'cathartic' resolution (Aristotle), and make its very public claim.

* * *

"The Politician's Wife," a Masterpiece Theatre production by Paula Milne, offers a fantasy of personal revenge that is especially instructive for these purposes. In the opening moments of the story we encounter the "unsuspecting wife of a distinguished and adulterous parliamentarian," who just this moment has been made aware of her husband's infidelity.[3] The press has surrounded her house, and she has been informed in a most public and humiliating way. Almost at once, as word of her calamity spreads, the expectation falls on her to play the part of a supportive spouse. The party faithful hope that she will use her position and good influence to preserve the political fortunes of her husband, a conservative defender of 'family values,' and to diminish the impact of his evident hypocrisy. This, at first, she seems willing enough to do. Yet as she discovers the extent of her husband's deception, and even as her quiet dignity in the midst of crisis wins her praise, she exacts a perfect revenge.

Privately she stops defending him, hinting to his colleagues that he may be treacherous in more ways than one. In a discreet moment she confronts the other woman face to face, and with a whisper in the ear of a friend has her banned from the exclusive restaurant where she and her husband are members. Even as the wife seems to be loyal and forgiving in public, she contrives a rendezvous for her husband and his mistress, and covertly tips the press as to its whereabouts. And if this were all not ruinous enough for her philandering spouse, she invents a real-estate fraud and sees to it that he is publicly implicated.

Playing upon the sympathy that she has won as his victim, the wife now effects a reversal of fortunes. Publicly her husband is discredited while she is praised. Privately, she knows and ultimately he knows that she has engineered his demise. In a striking final moment, we find him gazing up at her image on a television monitor as he leaves the country a ruined man. She is being interviewed after winning his former seat, and is poised to replace him as a party leader. In the end, it would seem she has obtained everything that had been his: his power, his prestige, the lofty moral perch that he had disgraced and used to mislead her, and from which she now looks down on him enjoying her singular victory.[4]

This private revenge is of course a most public revenge. It proceeds in the 'guise of justice,' one might say, but is obtained in exertions of concealment and disclosure that are far more calculating than that phrase implies. On the one hand the wife's success *depends* upon the strict observance of a distinction between 'public' and 'private.' On the other, she must violate it secretly and repeatedly to make it work. To be sure, what had been a private affair and a most personal insult has been made painfully public and can be reversed only in that arena. Everything that she does publicly to forestall the damage to her husband must serve privately to punish him. The reversal of fortunes is obtained only by taking his place, exchanging her private role for what had been his public one.

Not only has the old distinction between public and private been violated here, and personal revenge taken in the name of justice, but it is all done with smoke and mirrors in a way that alters the very nature of the 'public.' Indeed, the wife makes her case to a 'public' that is no mere abstraction of politics or justice. This is no discreet democratic arena, or rational 'public sphere,' but a kind of public that is uniquely susceptible to her appeal – an *audience*.[5]

For her revenge to succeed, all of the various parties must now be (or appear to be) entirely convinced. The husband, his supporters, even his mistress, must seem to accept her façade as genuine, and to sustain it as mutually reinforcing audiences.[6] They are inclined to do so, no less, because each has something to lose if her efforts against him are revealed to be anything but just – she has arranged things that way. Yet even though *we* know that *she* knows that *he* knows how he has been bested (which is the essence of the matter), the extended audience must not seem to be aware of it. The best revenge for the wife is not (as the saying goes) in 'living well.' Rather, it is in living especially well in the shoes of her tormentor while *appearing* to be just and virtuous in the eyes of everyone who had once held him in esteem. Evidently *this* wife is not at all the sort of passive victim we encountered above. She could hardly be avenged by a protector, or for that matter, by the paternalistic legal system that she has so clearly outmatched.[7] She is vindicated instead as she captivates and transforms the legitimating public of justice itself, making it her own private audience, and as such, her ally in deceit.

Revenge thus always contains a host of performative elements. Its representation as justice consists in making complex theatrical appeals to a variety of split and reconstituted audiences. In all such plays or performances (*The Politician's Wife*, *The Oresteia*, *Hamlet*, talk-show scenes of justice, aspects of the public trial), there are players within the play who must be convinced, and a secondary audience (ourselves, perhaps, as we watch) that is enjoined to see the crime, the perpetrator, the victim, and the punishment in a given way. What may be doubted by the first audience is repeated and made certain for a second, and rebounds again upon the first such that an act of clarification, *re-iteration*, is intrinsic to the revenge. Only by masking her intentions and fooling these publics, then, does the avenging party overcome doubt and punish with impunity.[8] In this, and for all of her concealment and trickery, she must obtain *recognition*, not only in the eyes of those other audiences, but in the eyes of her tormentor too.

So it is that this demonstrative visual play engages the avenger in a series of face-to-face or like encounters, each striking a bargain on her behalf (with her husband's mistress, with her husband as he imagines her seeing him, with herself as she imagines being seen by him or his supporters). The visual play is thus instrumental to the reversal – the reiteration of the wife's message before different audiences facilitates the essential transposition (her taking her husband's place). At the level of the plot, these audiences conspire to affect the story line, to validate the reversal of roles (as of cause and effect), to change the outcome of the story from what it might have been had the crime gone unavenged. This, in turn, implies the possibility of altering time, memory, or fate itself.

Now this dubious proposition is foisted upon an audience that is transfixed by the pain or humiliation of the offender (the ultimate performance). Yet even as this display has the appearance of moral 'desert,' fairness, or balance, it must exceed the crime in its severity if it is to have the desired effect (punishing the husband for a fraud he did not commit). In the final act of vengeance, something disturbing flickers in the visual field (the wife's image fills the television screen, the eye of the screen momentarily fills our own) and reality has been emphatically reconstituted. Her pain, and the cruelty she has suffered suddenly *make sense*, if not at the level of public justice, then as a statement of a more personal and dramatic kind. But now too that statement must register as a *public* satisfaction, a vengeance significantly, that has corrupted a democratic process (or formal justice) to insure her personal and political victory. The final message has been conceived and produced in the play of eyes, with masks, audiences, and twists of plot, which we now take up here.

Of Eyes

Why is it that a person seeking justice still speaks of getting "an eye for an eye"? Is it because such personal vindication is best achieved before the eyes of others as we have said? Is it that reading the eyes of someone who offends us is so much a part of assessing his moral status (whether he is sorry; whether to forgive or to condemn him)?[9] Or is it just tradition that makes this the preferred metaphor, a convenient way to invoke the seriousness of the Mosaic Law, or a means, as good as any other, to stress the need for balance in seeking blood for blood? Perhaps. But why is it the *eyes* that have survived for us? In excluding the long chain of couplets in which the Old Testament places the payment of an eye for an eye[10] – that exacting exchange of 'life for life,' 'tooth for tooth,' 'hand for hand,' 'foot for foot,' 'burning for burning,' 'wound for wound,' 'stripe for stripe,' which, taken together insist upon balance and good measure – why have we kept only the eyes?

Susan Jacoby insists that the very exhaustiveness of the original passage implies great precision or restraint, and that this belies the claim that Jewish Law is an especially vengeful law.[11] Do we now stress the *opposite* in keeping just the eyes? Or do we favor the reduction to eyes because it has a different psychological force and resonance than the rest? Is it that the blinding anger that great injustice provokes in us is entertained, even as it is laid to rest in that grotesque ocular reference? Does the proposed exchange recall the visual apprehension of some horror, and at once blot it out? Is it a homology, perhaps, for the wished-for effect on time and memory, of replacing the one terrible sight with another? Or is it just a debt we owe to a time when curses chased curses, and the threat of punishment followed one everywhere, of 'all-seeing eyes,' or 'evil eyes'?

The taking of an eye recalls that pivotal moment in the emergence of 'enlightenment' (as Adorno and Horkheimer identified it), when cunning and reason first turned to justice. It recalls equally a time when the idea of punishment still harbored a simple, honest hatred and the Cyclops got his due.[12] On the one hand the reference to eyes in matters of justice implies restraint, good measure, the strategic turn to fairness or higher purpose. On the other, it refers to the unbalancing effects of anger upon perception, a struggle within, or that instant in which, as Nietzsche admonished, "a small dose of aggression, malice, or insinuation certainly suffices to drive the blood into the eyes – and fairness out of the eyes – of even the most upright people."[13]

The invocation of eyes thus scarcely conceals its reference to another, more infantile wish to control sight and affect pain or fright. When children imagine that they can make themselves invisible to some danger by covering their eyes, or hide their eyes from things they cannot bear to see, or cover their faces in embarrassment, it is an attempt to do something of this sort. It is all an effort of erasure, self-erasure, and self-affirmation; a concealment that facilitates a change in perception and self-perception, an attempt to *remake themselves and the world as they might wish it to be*. Safety, a sense refuge (even for the most upright people) begins with the end of sight – a return to the womb, as it were, a retreat from the world.

It seems that the adult must want something similar in demanding an eye for an eye and in the appeal for 'closure' at the end of a devastating ordeal; to occupy some safe perch, seen but unseeing[14] (as the politician's wife now fills her TV monitor). "An eye for an eye," then, is less about balance than it is about acknowledgment. It is about seeing and being seen, or rather, effecting the same magical conversion that the child would over something trivial, and that the adult does in moments of severe loss or trauma. It expresses quite the same wish that we find in that great kingly gesture of putting out one's own eyes in self-punishment (as we shall see in a moment with Oedipus), which has been taken both as a point of origin for modern justice, and of the sovereign, modern individual as well.

* * *

In a defining state of enmity between sovereign persons, a condition far from safety that creates the need for justice and peaceful government, Hobbes recalls how the eyes of distrustful strangers play a special part: "But though there had never been any time wherein particular men were in a condition of war one against another, yet in all times kings and persons of sovereign authority, because of their independency, are in continual jealousies and in the state and posture of gladiators, having their weapons pointing and their eyes fixed on one another...which is a posture of war."[15] When men are compelled to fight each other or are in a condition of jealousy or threatened sovereignty, wary eyes must be a tactical necessity. At the same time however, they must acknowledge the folly in their battle of wills, and in the attempt to find safety (an effort of reason driven by fear) they look beyond their impasse and find themselves "drawn to agreement."[16] Justice is obtained in wresting sight (although this is not Hobbes' point) from the initial warlike encounter, and in coming to see the virtue of "interdependency" in which there is "no *mine* and *thine* distinct."[17]

Beyond the essential distrust that propels men to the establishment of a civilized polity for Hobbes (and quite apart from the sort of reciprocal recognition that would later issue in a contract for Locke),[18] there is something else at work in the initial exchange of gazes: an instant of recognition, perhaps, in which justice first finds its footing *in the eyes* of another. "Sovereign" persons in this tradition – princes who make compacts and citizens for Hobbes and Locke – in the act of seeing and being seen, demand respect for themselves or their reason from persons who may at any time disregard both. Respect is won as the threat of vengeance is forestalled and they may at last dare to look away. In one way for Hobbes and in another for Locke, a threat must be neutralized before trust is established and justice is pursued, and both identity and justice must be persuasively and performatively affirmed *before another*.[19]

Eyes and Identity, Recognition, and Repulsion

Sartre retains something of this (even as it disappears in more Cartesian philosophy) as he addresses the visual play that he regards to be vital to the establishment of conscious sovereign identity at its most basic level. For him, the emergence of 'consciousness' itself is established intersubjectively, as it first apprehends or is apprehended by others. There is something embattled, even destructive that is characteristic of such subjective awareness:

> It can happen therefore that due to the very impossibility of my identifying myself with the Other's consciousness through the intermediacy of my object-ness for him, I am led to turn deliberately toward the Other and *look* at him. . . . I direct my look upon the other who is looking at me. But a look cannot be looked at. As soon as I look in the direction of the look it disappears and I no longer see anything but eyes. . . . This means that in my upsurge into the world, I can choose myself as looking at the Other's look and can build my subjectivity upon the collapse of the subjectivity of the Other. . . .[20]

One's subjectivity and one's very consciousness as a subject are constituted in relation to an Other. But since the Other's consciousness and "look" are impenetrable and useless as a vehicle for one's self-construction (one sees nothing but "eyes"), one perceives the Other in this awareness and chooses to construct oneself accordingly. The denuded eyes of another thus prefigure something generalizable (abstract subjectivity, a self-referential consciousness), but in the same moment they are reducible, a *mere vehicle* of self-construction, which is at once more primitive and more troubling than any such abstraction.

That reduction, says Sartre, thus entails a certain "indifference" toward the Other – a narrowing of the eyes perhaps, a willingness to use, if not quite exploit the other.[21] Here it seems that this indifference toward the Other (its negation which turns on the reduction to eyes) is a necessary step in the building of one's identity, or all identity, and that even the recognition of the Other, reciprocity and the more rarefied abstractions of western identity, turn on this assertive solipsism. Indifference thus enables the very abstraction of consciousness, reason, and the impartiality so central to that identity, and to the Lockean (liberal) recognition of the Other. It lends itself no more to this, we may add, than to mere self-assertion of the sort recalled by Hobbes – a wish to be recognized at the *expense* of another, perhaps – or to the *other-negating* self-righteousness of revenge.

Hence, even in a Hegelian scheme in which recognition and reciprocity have a different salience, the all-important "totality of consciousness" is conditional on the "appearance of the actions of the other against my totality," or, as Axel Honneth reads this, conditional on conflict, crime, or a mutual violation of claims to subjectivity.[22] Not merely abstract recognition, then, but an embattled relation of the one toward the other in which subjectivity passes through a moment of uncertainty (not knowing the other's consciousness for Hegel, indifference for Sartre) thus characterizes the vital mirroring in which subjective consciousness and universal ethics both become possible. One might say that modern ethics, insofar as it concerns 'sovereign' beings (their value in relation to one another for Hobbes, subjective consciousness here, or any 'privileging of the subject') becomes possible in the interplay of eyes, of recognition – and of *indifference*, its essential opposite, which is never far from revenge. 'An eye for an eye,' one suspects, must reflect something of this relation too.

* * *

Yet there is another thing about the eyes, very old and deeply intuitive, which makes that proposed exchange *seem* like a moral one. In a state of fright, one looks away and must promptly regain oneself or one's moral center. Indeed, the 'wide-eyed flight' from terror recalls something implicit in the reductive indifference toward others – that fear, self-erasure, regaining composure play a part in recognition and in perceptions of injustice that bear on identity. This may be characterized by a state of being drawn and repelled at once. In looking upon a scene of such horror that it threatens to disrupt one's identity, by all accounts, one's eyes seem to detach from the scene and from oneself and to become virtually opposed to oneself. One's eyes register fascination and revulsion simultaneously – a rupture of self we might add that ultimately makes moral self-observation and 'moral feeling' possible. This is the same inner conflict one may feel in the observance of punishment, as we have noticed, and which Plato captured so well in relating the story of Leontius, son of Aglaion:

On his way up from Piraeus outside the north wall, he noticed the bodies of some criminals lying on the ground, with the executioner standing by them. He wanted to go and look at them, but at the same time was disgusted and tried to turn away. He struggled for some time and covered his eyes, but at last the desire was too much for him. Opening his eyes wide, he ran to the bodies and cried, 'There you are, curse you; feast yourselves on this lovely sight!'[23]

In this scene, evidently, 'others' have been reduced so horribly and with such indifference as to cause a split in identity at the sight. A disowned and disassociated appetite (one, perhaps, that feeds on the collapse to which Sartre alludes represented here by 'feasting' the eyes) sets itself over and against a better aspect of the self – a kind of 'detachment' that again presages the self-observing aspect of conscience. But *these* eyes seem to act on their own volition and may thus be isolated and blamed, as in the biblical admonition: "if thine eye offends thee, pluck it out."[24] They are driven to look upon the offending spectacle, even to the point of disgust. In this, they embody a unique opposition – an opposition of the self to its own appetites from which the self may in principle retrieve itself, curse its appetites, and restore its ethical unity. When the thing in sight elicits outrage, no less, it is crucial to regain control and to unite the self at any cost.

If there are certain things the eyes must see in the precipitous reestablishment of identity, then, there is a great deal that they cannot bear to see. The scene of unspecified horror draws them; the crime in which a loved one has been hurt turns them away. One wants to know about it, but does not dare to look. Like Leontius, or the child who covers his eyes and hopes to disappear, one wants to be shielded from its horrors. Now, when we speak of the period of 'denial' that accompanies grief, we refer to a protracted version of the same impulse – the shrouding of pasts that cannot be faced or looked upon. A complicated wish that is harbored in "an eye for an eye," therefore, is the wish to *remake the past and the self* in relation to it, and to constitute the remade vision as something sustainable and just.

In the moment that one blinks and looks away, the flicker in the visual field initiates a reconstitution of threatened identity. And while this may be at the source of all sorts of moral claims for the sovereign subject – honor, conscience, rights – it is the beginning of revenge as well, an initial false step from which others will likely follow. In this, of course, one alters the memory of events, the sight lines in which they are perceived, one's own posture relative to them, and one alters the 'truth' in a variety of self-serving ways.[25] Perhaps this is why the optic play in *Oedipus Rex* remains so powerful as a comment on what a man can or cannot bear to see in being ethical, and what justice wants to know or see of 'truth.'

Oedipus

We may recall that it is on the word of the blind prophet, Teiresias, who is privileged to see the truth, that Oedipus comes to see that which he had not seen but wishes mightily that he had foreseen – the terrible crimes of patricide and incest for which he now cannot forgive himself. The prophet knows, but will not reveal the truth, because he also knows "How dreadful knowledge of the truth can be when there is no help in truth!"[26] He knows, in effect, how easily mortal eyes can be deceived and what exaggerated pain must come from seeing that for which there is no hope of retrospective correction. If he is ambivalent about the kind of assistance he can render Oedipus in his quest to see the truth, it is because he knows that truth must come in its own time, as the Chorus informs us, and that time serves an all-seeing justice that is out of mortal reach:

> But all eyes fail before time's eye,
> All actions come to justice there.
> Though never willed, though far down the deep past,
> Your bed, your dread sirings,
> Are brought to book at last.[27]

Oedipus is heroic, we are told, because he struggles to discover the truth of this justice and to overcome his mortal limitations, denying, or rather forsaking, the eyes that have so terribly misled him. For Eli Sagan, among others, he is a hero who struggles against "the human desires not to know the truth, not to recall the past, not to remember what has long ago been repressed," a hero who seeks to conquer his own "inner blindness." Sagan persists in this psychoanalytic vein: *Oedipus the King* is a "play about insight, memory, the capacity to deal with those things that have previously been repressed."[28] For his forthrightness, to be sure, Sophocles had assigned Oedipus a noble ending.[29] Yet the machinations of time and truth in the story, and the play of eyes that give them substance, now make that reading less compelling.

Oedipus, we recall, is first moved to save his city of Thebes from a plague of great misfortune, the cause of which is that crime of his own doing. It is only upon discovering that the cause of all this misery is the death of the King Laios (not yet revealed to him as his own father whom he has murdered) that he is publicly committed to discover the truth and to avenge the death. Though he takes up the son's part in avenging the death of his predecessor (a king's debt to a king)[30] it is not at all because he has a repressed knowledge of their true relationship. Rather it is because this, in the timeless state of all-seeing justice, is what vengeance demands.[31] Now that justified vengeance precedes, drives, and shapes the very search for 'truth.' The latter is thus undertaken with a measure of reluctance (needing to know but not quite daring to see) and is unlike any other search for truth.

If Oedipus had repressed the killing of his father (or evidence of his true identity at the time that it occurred) and then later struggled for insight, *this* would be a "heroic" effort in the psychological sense that Sagan wants to credit. In that case, a very different order of time, truth, and justice would prevail. Then Oedipus might be driven to accept the truth pursued so openly, to face and accept himself in light of its devastating revelation, and not turn against himself so wantonly in such a self-destructive act. But Oedipus is *not* facing a repressed memory, or 'facing the truth' in any simple, factual sense. His crimes had never before been known to him, and he pursues the 'truth' of the past on the terms of a wholly different kind of heroism.

As the story unfolds, Oedipus is heroic on the premise that fate has brought punishment to Thebes (for a crime that he has unwittingly committed, and must in any case avenge), heroic in the pursuit of *that* truth, which is not at all the search for inner truth or for the truth as it might be pursued (also heroically) to exonerate him in a more modern court of justice. One might say he goes blindly after truth – blindly, because he is unable yet to see it or the consequences of discovering it, and is ill prepared to assimilate it once he does. And while he accepts the consequences of his actions on the terms by which he remakes them – as self-punishment for a crime, putting out his eyes – he cannot bear to accept them otherwise. He is far more eager to bring the past "to book" than to accept its consequences (in the more profound modern psychological sense) for his present life.

The particular means of punishment that Oedipus selects for himself speaks to this. On the one hand it is a self-effacement so absolute that it seems to pay for the crime almost perfectly. It is better targeted, one suspects, than the simple exile or execution that awaited lesser men of the day. Since the crime follows from a distinct blindness to past truth, it seems fitting that Oedipus should pay with the eyes that have betrayed that truth. Yet on the other hand, the self-blinding is an expression of torment. It reflects the impulse *not to look* upon another truth even as it lies before him (the corpse of his mother; his bride, the mother his children – Jocasta). *This* truth is a product of his misconceptions and misdeeds, the shattering present effect of pasts he could not control but which he would now, in the throes of rage and grief, remove utterly from sight.

If it was the hope of revenge (to avenge his father) that drove his interest in truth in the first place, an equally unforgiving turn of events now follows upon the discovery of truth. As Oedipus reels at the sight of Jocasta's suicide (one recalls that she could bear the revelation no better than he), he seizes her golden brooches and plunges them repeatedly into his eyes. In that terrible moment – a moment itself too ghastly to be looked upon directly, which is recalled for us as convention dictates, only by a messenger – Oedipus addresses himself not to *her*, not even directly to himself, but with striking detachment, to those ruptured eyes themselves:

> No more, no more shall you look on the misery about me,
> The horrors of my own doing! Too long you have known
> The Faces of those whom I should never have seen,
> Too long been blind to those for whom I was searching![32]

It is not a blinding grief for his beloved that is the primary emotion, nor even guilt (in any simple sense) for what has transpired – if it had been, she would still be foremost in his thoughts. It is a kind of self-directed blame to be sure. Yet beyond that it is an extraordinary manifestation of revenge. His *eyes* have betrayed him. They have failed to see what they should have seen, allowing him to live the life and enjoy the fruits that he should never have enjoyed. *They* must be punished for their blindness, revenged upon for their failure to see the crimes of the past, and for the lie that they have permitted to endure into the present. In so doing, however, Oedipus has torn his eyes from the scene and the lifeless body that lies before him, turned them away from love and grief for the woman who had made and filled his present life and the children she had mothered, and toward an irredeemable past. It is all accomplished in a single gesture; a gesture which looks, at first, like any other self-flagellation of mourning. The astonishing act of self-punishment is distinguished, we must suppose, as an act worthy of a king, a king who concerns himself immediately with justice (his debt to Thebes), and displays a noble willingness to take the blame.

Yet in the very gesture that *appears* to express a forthright acceptance of his own guilt, it is his accursed *eyes* that he sets apart and punishes, and to which he addresses himself as if to an alien thing. Now his guilt is objectified (even personified) in them. If the 'truth' is to be restored by punishing those eyes, it is in the deluded belief that their past blindness will be magically undone in the act of blinding them now.[33] The very thing that seems so pure, so honest, and so accepting of the truth is also an equivocation before the truth, a wish to change it. Now *this* present along with Jocasta disappears thereafter in the play, and the pitiable noble man (at once a king and prototypical sovereign) dwells upon the past in precisely the attitude in which vengeance has always made its ignoble claim upon justice.[34]

It is in that very inversion of time, or rather in the equivocation before the present and its truth, that the ambiguity of truth so often noticed in the text reveals its deeper nature. Karl Reinhardt tells us, for example, that it is in Oedipus' sightless state "that his real seeing begins, in the form of recognition out of the night of blindness, recognition which is self-recognition."[35] This is surely an aspect of the playwright's intentions. Yet Reinhardt also reminds us that what Oedipus discovers with his new sight is not "reality" in any meaningful sense, but rather (as he puts it) the "irruption of truth into the structure of appearances."[36] Significantly, the very self-recognition brought on by an 'irruption of truth' is not simply *the* truth. It is, rather, a distinctive temporal domain that vies with the 'structure of appearances' and for a place in the unfolding tale. The latter, we may add, is the world *as it appears, but should never have been* – an impossible tense for which there is no linguistic expression, only dramatic representation – a world, now, of ruined reputation that must not be permitted to endure into the future and which Oedipus repudiates in denying himself the very sight of it:

Could I have joy at the sight of my children – born as they were born? With these eyes? Never! Could I look upon the city of Thebes? The Turrets that grace her walls? The sacred statues of her gods? I was the curse of Thebes! Could these eyes look upon the people? Never![37]

By his blinding, then, Oedipus steps out of one temporal domain – the irredeemable *present* Thebes, that "structure of appearances" – into another.

The world he chooses instead, the alter-world of yet another tense, is a world in which all is revealed (and *all is as it should have been had the past and the truth been known*), a world of perfect all-seeing justice where his crimes could never have occurred, where his life would have ended in childhood, and his city would never be imperiled;[38] a world no less of rectified memory, precisely as vengeance would construct it.

This world of course is equally impossible, and if it can be known by gods and oracles, it cannot be entered by mere mortals. Oedipus, as the prophet has foreseen, cannot find 'help in truth' in knowing such a place – as hard as he tries he cannot go there. Yet precisely because "truth" is divided in this way between an unacceptable present and an unattainable past, there is a third world to which Oedipus might obtain – a world, we might guess, to which one of the "three roads" that met at the site of his crime now leads[39] – a sightless "prison" that exemplifies the dilemma that has left him caught between the other two:

I would spare nothing to build a prison for this defiled body where sight and sound would never penetrate. Then only would I have peace – where grief could not reach my mind.[40]

This tomb-like place that could never be attained is a timeless world of stasis, forgetfulness, and escape from pain. It is a world where his soul no longer "aches from the memory of its horrors!"[41] This is as close as Oedipus can come to a life of contentment lived out to its end in ordinary time to which the final passage of the play refers,[42] a sort of limbo that is unlike either of the other worlds he straddles. This is the place of peace that is wished for in a state of intolerable pain, a world that captures and contains the fault of misbegotten action (literally, figuratively) as vengeance insists – a prison in which punishment (that of his tormentor; now that of himself) would be his escape, and within which he can hope to vanish even from his own sight.[43] He looks for it still at the gates of Colonus: "A resting place, after long years, in the last country, where I should find a home among the sacred Furies."[44]

Of course Oedipus can never build such a place for himself, and yet in putting out his eyes he has already made that wishful condition a permanent feature of his existence. In making his guilt, horror, and longing for escape manifest in this way, he behaves quite as the wishful child he is still in relation to the parents he has offended – which is very like what Freud had noticed in a different connection.[45] Here, however, the chosen self-punishment is not just that of a child reckoning with conflict and guilt on the way to adulthood. It is a more tormented choice, one might say, than even the metaphor of castration admits – the choice of an adult who is ashamed of the consequence of his actions, one who reels at the intolerable sight, reverts to the deluded state of a child, covers his eyes, and hopes to disappear.[46]

As a blinded man, Oedipus virtually gets his wish for self-erasure, an ending of sorts to guilt and grief, the realization of a wish no longer to see the world and what it has become, or to continue his existence there. As a child might, he remakes himself by externalizing a self-destructive impulse that arises from humiliation. As for the child, his wounded eyes become an emblem for others to see, at once a mask of atonement behind which he may hope to enter a less humiliating and accepting place, or imagine his restful confinement.

The self-effacement that is undertaken in recognition of the 'truth' for Oedipus is therefore also an act of *face-saving* before the audience of gods, oracles, and Thebans that demands its own version of truth and permits him, in spite of or because of his injuries, to go on living. The effort to undo an intolerable past in which he has been implicated requires a massive reconstruction of the self, and if our hero is ashamed and cannot bear to see himself in light of his crimes, he must at least appear to be changed before that imaginary audience. If the terrible self-mutilation is an act of vengeance and self-justification as much as guilt, it is also an act of vanity,[47] and as an act of vanity it is also a work of distortion.

Now then, when the modern critic asks how Oedipus' resolution is 'heroic and just,' that question invites the more pressing one, 'Is it revenge?' – to which the answer must be 'Yes, perfect revenge,' with all of the vain and wishful distortion that attends it in the moment 'one cannot bear to look.' Blindness is punished by blindness. The painful past is acknowledged but retold in light of the punishment that looks to be its just reward, and in the process the avenger and the offender, although they are the same, both appear to be reconstituted. A thing has been 'faced,' but in a manner that fulfills a desire to abolish vision and alter memory, precisely as vengeance wishes to acknowledge, to forget, and to remake its object. Like all 'blind anger,' that of our hero may seem courageous in the moment, but if there is a streak of vanity in it, there is also an element of cowardice. To be sure, in the splitting of sight that permits a judgment of the self, the observing self (that, again, which makes conscience or superego possible) now observes itself from a *preferred* vantage point, an imagined perch from which the frightening truth *and* escape from it may both be kept in sight, like that from which Oedipus imagines his tolerable 'prison.'[48]

Thus, even the 'denial of self' that is applauded in so many heroic Western epics – that calculating self-denial by which Odysseus steadies himself against danger and temptation – now seems suspect. It is suspect if, like other sorts of psychological repression, it passes through a moment of dread and looking away, a moment in which 'brave' self-control builds its barricades and arranges its sight lines.[49] The self-denial here is precisely the same sort of 'front' and narrowing of sight that permits our hero, like all great princes and military leaders, to face the future with his chin up, with an altered countenance that exudes confidence. And if such a thing is necessary to obtain victory, the entitlements of nobility, frontier justice, or even adulthood (or again, the repressive agencies of superego, conscience or law), it is also the sort of psychological denial that set those young kings apart as they remade the world, and turned their extraordinary exertions of might into right.

What Eyes Must See: The loved one lost; proof; the villain caught

Of course there is a great deal that vengeance wants to see. If all-seeing justice waits to reveal the truth in time, vengeance (at first) is far more impatient.[50] It seeks visual confirmation of the crime and the offender's guilt and may proceed from certain knowledge, but may be just as quick to manufacture it. Such is the case when Othello demands that his servant Iago bring him "ocular proof" of the betrayal of which Iago has accused Othello's wife, Desdemona.[51] In order to provoke the undeserved revenge of his master, one recalls, Iago then produces Desdemona's handkerchief and contrives a story of infidelity to go with it. As soon as the visual offering has been made and accepted as "proof," one sees how quickly a deception is sealed, and how readily the vengeful Othello sees only what he wants to see.

This proof, of course, is hardly proper evidence or cause for certainty, but a manifestation of his own need for certainty, which is an entirely different thing. Othello is eager to embrace it, it would seem, because the one truth (evidence of betrayal; a romantic rival) is easier to accept than another (self-doubt, fear of his inadequacy, recognition of his own blindness). And as much as the former seems to enrage him, 'proof' of it keeps the dreaded thing safely in sight so that this impetuous man takes comfort in making his lesser fears manifest.

Similarly, when the politician's wife discovers an undergarment belonging to her husband's mistress in her home after news of his betrayal has reached her; she dwells on it for a moment, but needs no further proof. The artifact serves to deepen her knowledge of the past and of the crime – with 'proof' her troubled imagination works upon memory to restore the truth as she *should* have seen it (that other past of Oedipus). With such proof in hand she may sharpen the one truth, focus her blame, displace the painful awareness of her failure to have seen or foreseen it, and thus revise the intolerable memory. The remnant of the injury, the proof of the crime, then, can scarcely be looked upon objectively or with indifference. This is why criminal evidence must be scrutinized so carefully, and why forensic reconstruction is, as we shall see, so fraught with difficulty.[52]

What one wants to see can thus easily obscure what is. Such distortion is what "driving the blood into the eyes" in Nietzsche's phrase is all about. If one wants "certainty" in vengeance even at the risk of inaccuracy, it is the certainty of a secured perspective or *consoling* vision. If one cannot restore a past that has been ruined by a devastating wound or murderous crime, such proof permits one to see it as one wishes. And even when it does reveal the truth, it may yet seem to open one's eyes to a betrayal after the fact, in a self-satisfying way.

Upon revisiting the scene of a crime that involves the death of a loved one, the survivor is already looking for something solid with which to grieve. The mourner longs to look into the eyes of that person once again, to search them out or call them up. As memory and imagination conspire in this way, one may think one has performed a kind of rescue that makes that person whole or visible again, as if some magical penance has been done in daring to look back.[53] The intense desire 'to see again,' as it is recounted for us in the plight of Orpheus, is both a wish to commune with the memory of the loved one and to pull her back from injury by returning her (here, by way of reconditioned sight that works that 'penance' in reverse) to the world of the living.[54]

It is striking, in this regard, that – in the process of grieving for her murdered daughter – one mother expresses her profound gratitude for being taken to the site of her death by the father of another murdered child, who seems to understand that imperative of grief precisely. "I wanted to see the last sight she had," explains the mother – not the crime or the punishment, at least not right now.[55] If she can never look into her daughter's eyes again, grief offers this last hope to see what *she* had seen, to catch the sight, as it were, of the child who is otherwise lost to her. In daring to look upon the scene, the courageous mother communes with her dead daughter by a kind of visual identification, a function of grief that is quite beyond revenge, but which, like the imperative that drives Orpheus, severely limits her perceptual field.

Vengeful persons, however, suffer far more dramatic effects on the sight lines of their grief. They return obsessively to those scenes as if to alter them. They may seem to see them clearly for the moment, but their disrupted sense of identity, their ineffectual agency, the shaken perspective that had once insured their sovereignty and sense of ethical unity (or justice) needs reparation. They are blinded by rage at their tormentors. They tear themselves from the sight of their loved ones to pursue those enemies instead. They envision their punishment in exquisite detail, and seem to see nothing but their eyes, which follow and haunt them.

To See It in the Eyes of an Offender: To make them see....

Of course, such persons want to see the punishment itself. We have noticed that the desire *to see* the criminal hurt, humiliated, or vanquished, as his victims have been hurt, is not properly part of retributive punishment. For Kant, just punishment follows from a "principle of equality (in the position of the needle on a scale of justice), to incline no more to one side than to the other."[56] It concerns the restoration of a balance implicit in the terms of rational conduct – an exchange of pain for pain – and does not, in any overt sense, need to be seen.

But again, where *achieving* that balance may involve an exchange of "hurt pride" for an "offense to honor" in his example (which raises the question, balance of what?), it invites further imagining. The 'loss of pride' that attends punishment when it is applied (and which should balance the retributive scale even *without witnesses*) is a 'loss' only as it becomes manifest in the eyes of others – as *shame* – by which "like would be *fittingly* repaid with like."[57] Where that is the case, however (insofar as the "like" of pain is determined by its effect; as experienced, observable, assessed pain), the necessary loss of face implies a relation of seeing and being seen that is intrinsic to the punishment – and is driven, in Cavell's apt phrase, by "the specific discomfort produced by the sense of being looked at."[58] It is punishment, that is (beyond what Kant would say of it), insofar as the needle on the abstract scale is balanced before witnesses, and by a substance (shame) that exists only by virtue of their presence. Even where the punishment is not so driven by shame (as one might want to say of capital punishment or imprisonment for a term) its value in the exchange is subject to a similar assessment, so that implicitly at least, it involves highly interested observers.[59]

Consequently, even though liberal punishments are justified and proceed without reference to an audience, they still harbor the vengeful wish to see the punishment take hold. Utilitarian efforts to deter persons or reform them work only if the punishment is in some sense visible. The Panopticon controls, and whatever its formal utilitarian intention, it also shames.[60] Most retributivists (if not true Kantians) hope that the offender will 'face up' to his crime in being punished.[61] 'Face *up*' so that he can be seen and so that remorse can be read in his expression, the look of guilt and the fact of guilt becoming identical in the moment. This attitude persists in the practice of requiring the accused to rise and face a jury upon sentencing. And if that ritual reflects the right of the accused to confront his accusers on the one hand, the decorum, the positioning, and demeanor of the defendant all suggest something more in the way of contrition on the other.

"Repentance," as it was first incorporated within the punishments of the American colonies, thus called for an observable change in the offender – a change both in his appearance and his own perception. Masur reminds us that during the seventeenth and eighteenth centuries here, the presiding ministers "expected the prisoner to enact the drama of penitence and redemption" on execution day. Prisoners would be admonished before an audience, compelled to read a prepared confession, and represented in the press in various states of apology. Consequently, on the eve of his execution, one condemned man offers "thanks to all the ministers of this town, who have favored me with their assistance, in opening my blind Eyes, *as to a future State.*"[62] While the claim to redeemed vision must seem disingenuous as a part of the coerced confession, it is indicative of the manner in which such punishments aim to restore appearances. It should publicly affirm that "future State" of just resolution as the corrective for a past that cannot be redeemed (Oedipus). Yet it also provides unassailable proof of the possibility of redemption. Hope turns on the lie in which the appearance – to be seen, and to *seem* to see – seems to alter what has been (and thus what will be). The persuasive power of the message now being that it is read by (and confirmed in) the eyes of the offender for all to see.

This, of course, is the vengeful aspect of seemingly rational punishments that Kafka so skillfully parodies in his story *The Penal Colony*. In that curious place, each prisoner is punished by having a message cut directly into his skin. A harrow made of glass repeatedly inscribes the "commandment that the prisoner has disobeyed on his body." Jets of water wash the blood away so that the inscription – written in an impossibly elaborate script in a way that the prisoner cannot see and in a language he does not understand – can be read by a visitor, if one should happen by. "[T]here would be no point in telling him" the content of the message, we are informed by the operator of the device, "he'll learn it on his body."[63]

The message registers somewhere, we should suppose, as in some Kantian place of reason to which the offender will never obtain. The machinery of justice, like Kant's scale and needle (the principle of "like for like") does not need to be seen for its principle to hold. But of course, as Kafka's device makes clear, it is *made* to be seen. Its intent and its functioning should have nothing to do with the prisoner's 'repentance,' yet its very indifference to him and to his state of mind defines the condition (now more real or vivid even than his suffering) in which he should learn, or *appear* to learn its lesson.

In this, to be sure, quite a different imperative announces itself. The attending officer informs us that at a certain point in being tortured to death in this manner, "enlightenment comes to the most dull witted." "[I]t begins around the eyes. From there it radiates. . . ." The officer recalls with delight how he and all who have attended such punishments have "absorbed the look of transfiguration on the face of the sufferer. . . ." – ". . . how we bathed our cheeks in the radiance of that justice, achieved at last and fading so quickly!"[64] That aim is closer to the truth of modern punishment, one suspects, than the hope that such humiliation should serve abstract justice. Here, it is fervently hoped, the message will sink in. Yet now even in a state of incomprehension and at the point of death, a message must be delivered to the prisoner that is also *for an audience*. As the mechanism of its delivery makes a show of its indifference (Kant again) for an audience that need not be there, the latter waits upon the "radiance" that registers in its eyes and eminates from those of the offender. The device seems (and yet *seems not to be seen*) to record its message within both, so that here again (if the device would only work) the look of guilt and the fact of guilt appear as one.

This, then, is what is at stake in the more blatant wish 'to see the offender suffer' and 'to make him see,' that so overburdens vengeful punishments. "[F]oul deeds will rise," warns Hamlet, "to meet men's eyes," both the eyes that expose them, and those that must be made to bear their guilt.[65] This is why punishing the eyes for the likes of Oedipus compounds the metaphorical confusion (the look of guilt, the fact of guilt) that makes the tragedy so supremely tragic, and the punishment (seemingly) so fitting. Punishing the eyes might seem to rectify a confusion, to brand the deserved message and seal it (the blinding of the Cyclops) banishing all doubt. Even as her image lingers in the culminating moment of vengeance for the politician's wife, she seems almost to be punishing her husband's eyes, as if to make them see what they ought to see.[66]

Surely it is an ordinary impulse of grief itself to want to impose such awareness within the offending eyes: "For 15 anguished years," we are told, Catherine Tyler "yearned to look into Louis King Jr.'s eyes. It was King, she always believed, who murdered her daughter...." At sentencing, even as King, "avoided eye contact...his head bowed," Tyler remained adamant in her quest – "Over the years I needed to look him in the eyes and ask about my daughter...."[67] The wish, it would appear, is to place her missing daughter within those vacant eyes, to impose her image as an article of conscience where conscience had been and remains entirely absent.

As grief turns to revenge, however, there is a greater claim upon such offending eyes, a greater willingness to confuse the organ for its sight, and to treat or abuse it accordingly. Punishing the eyes, again, promises redemption, transformation, not only for the one who suffers but also for the one who punishes. Bernhard Goetz wished he had "gouged [his assailants'] eyes out."[68] In much the same attitude, Patrick Suskind imagines a father's wish at the execution of his daughter's murderer:

And when the crowd had wandered off after a few hours, he wanted to climb up onto the bloody scaffold and crouch next to him, keeping watch, by night, by day, for however long he had to, and look into the eyes of this man, the murderer of his daughter, and drop by drop to trickle the disgust within him into those eyes, to pour out his disgust like burning acid over the man in his death agonies – until the beast perished....[69]

It seems that where the murderer is incapable of remorse or contrition, and unable or unwilling to see what a terrible thing he has done, he must suffer an infliction upon the organs of his sight. Here, at least, there is the vengeful certainty that the punishment will be recorded in them. Yet here too, by venting his anger upon the offending eyes, a father's seemingly selfless revenge becomes an act of redemption, self-affirmation, and again, of vanity or conceit, as he could bear no longer to look upon *himself* until he had tried to make that wretched man see.

To Be Seen as Victorious: Vengeance face to face

If it seems odd to have accused Oedipus of a certain vanity in choosing his disfiguring punishment, it makes perfect sense once it is construed as an act of pride (or self-affirmation) in this way. In wanting to make one's tormentor see (even if one is one's own tormentor), there is a great deal that *wants to be seen*. My pride swells in proportion to my enemy's humiliation, and if the presence of a public audience intensifies this effect, it is driven by a primitive or infantile impulse that requires only a private, internal one.

So again, one wants to be seen by one's tormentor in the moment of seeing him suffer, to be sure that he knows what he has done and to whom he has done it – "But let him come," says Laertes upon Hamlet's return, "it warms the very sickness in my heart that I shall live and tell him to his teeth, 'Thus did'st thou.'"[70] One wants to confront him face to face, if not in the more balanced sense of 'an eye for an eye,' then by demonstrating unquestionably that one has overcome the injury and is now a person of *greater* effectiveness or worth. That dubious enterprise – to be restored in the esteem of an enemy – then, must seem to register in the fellow's eyes, and is best achieved if he perceives or appears to perceive that one has been the cause of his own loss of esteem or destruction. As one of his surviving victims, for example, Andrew Scott still hoped for "eye-to-eye contact" with Timothy McVeigh on the eve of his execution and to say "you didn't break the spirit you thought you would break."[71] One's present strength or vitality, displayed in this way before one's enemy, thus seems to obliterate the ineffectuality or weakness that one has felt because of him in the past.

This is why the slaying of Hektor by Achilles has for so long exemplified the vengeful paradigm. Of course Achilles does not merely defeat Hektor in the fulfillment of his rage, but manages to restore his own image and his strength in the eyes of his dying enemy in just this way. At the time of the death of his friend Patroklos, Achilles had been occupied in battle and unable to protect him. His remorse thereafter is so profound that he is in danger of self-destruction, a fate from which only his revenge upon Hektor might save him.[72] Thus, in a final declaration to his friend's killer, he now makes himself powerful and present where he had been weak and absent before. He addresses Hektor from that position of reconstituted strength:

> Hektor, surely you thought as you killed Patroklos that you would be
> safe, and since I was far away you thought nothing of me,
> o fool, for an avenger was left far greater than he was,
> behind him and away by the hollow ships. And it was I;
> and I have broken your strength; on you the dogs and the vultures
> shall feed and foully rip you; the Achaians will bury Patroklos.[73]

Achilles then refuses Hektor's entreaty to keep his body from being eaten and to allow his own people to bury it – he is relentless in his revenge. And if he was nowhere to be seen when the late friend had needed him, he looms over his killer now, filling his final field of vision as an absolute and commanding presence. Of course, there is far too much momentum in this effort for it to end with Hektor's death, and he continues to address the fallen hero even once he is beyond hearing. He drags and degrades his enemy's corpse so to prolong the encounter. Surely he does this to place beyond doubt the very thing he most certainly doubts, the recognition he has sought to achieve in the eyes of the defeated enemy (as of gods and fellows) and which he seeks to ensure by telling him repeatedly to his lifeless face.[74]

While there may be 'honor' in this kind of recognition, it must be very different from the Kantian idea that just punishment honors the criminal as a rational being. It is hardly his "rational aspect" that Achilles addresses in the fallen Hektor or seeks to have acknowledged in himself.[75] Nor is this odd form of address a reciprocal, or properly communicative act. Rather, it is a wholly reflexive, self-serving, and irrational sort of mirroring – a declaration that makes his enemy a vehicle of restored honor precisely by dishonoring him as he looks on. In the moment, Achilles is clearly building his "subjectivity upon the collapse of the subjectivity of the Other," if not quite in the way that Sartre meant it. To be sure, punishment that 'honors the criminal as a rational being' is a proposition that is never entirely beyond such acts of honor. Like them, it is quite indifferent to the will, to the person or "look" of the Other.[76]

The 'indifference' with which Achilles ignores the pleading Hektor so as to restore his own honor is thus surprisingly like the abstraction by which the Kantian apparatus of punishment (as Kafka sees it) would do 'honor' to the reason of the criminal. Honor in either case is blind to the particular aspects of the Other and deaf to his entreaty. Both proceed as if the Other were not there; both speak to him, as it were, beyond the grave. Hence, doing 'honor' to the offender as a 'rational being' in modern justice preserves a duality in him by which he is at once nearly erased, and made to see what he should see – so that he remains a puppet in a vengeful theatre like the fallen Hektor. If that principle would acknowledge an abstract, universal aspect of another's being (recall Hegel too) by way of a certain indifference to his 'particularity,' it also does the reverse. It mirrors and affirms a superior aspect in the punisher (or punitive apparatus) such that his wounded honor – the *particularity* of his offended being – is recognized or seen as something greater, something universal.[77]

This *wanting to be seen* thus complicates claims about the communicative basis of identity, recognition, reciprocity, or equality as they affect moral or legal standing in liberal justice (or as Honneth, Habermas, or Hegel articulate such things). There is no question of wanting the *truth* about oneself to be revealed in all its frailty, or as it truly was at the time of an injury. This is certainly not the sort of liberal acknowledgement in which "subjects recognize each other reciprocally as living emotionally needy beings."[78] What should be recognized in 'honor' for the likes of Hektor and Achilles, and others since is clearly opposed to this and cannot be absorbed so easily within the liberal paradigm. Once more, the liberal project that rarefies persons and respects their reason is confounded in ways that it cannot detect by the self-concealment of persons seeking vengeance. This is because the vengeful impulse is *also* an impulse to lift up the degraded person (who is threatened in his or her particularity) to the status of universal, equal, rights-bearing subject. This is a heroic stance of sorts (if not a uniquely liberal one), in which that particularity is asserted in self-aggrandizing ways as something universal, though without any particular regard for universal justice.[79]

In a court of law, for example, the damaged party, the petitioner, or plaintiff obtains a certain abstract 'standing' before the court. Yet among other things the very abstract 'equal' standing that this allows (and which does concern universal justice) also allows a contest between the victor and the vanquished to be replayed on fair ground – this time, perhaps, to be reversed. To be "equal in the eyes of the law" as important a principle as it is, is thus also to have a hope of *prevailing*. To be successful at one's suit or litigation, especially these days, may not be so very different from Achilles' posture in revenge. Now, in the guise of reciprocity and equality, upright, law-abiding citizens seek "victory" in court – rights-bearing and self-righteous (the two being so easily confused) – enjoying a condescension toward Others upon whom they would still, as in so many conflicts of honor, *look down*.[80]

Refusing to See: The blind eye of justice. . . .

As much as this sort of recognition would see (and be seen) in a certain way then, its power, its ability to control perceptions and outcomes, turn equally upon its indifference – a kind of *not seeing*. For all the talk of the surveillance of prisoners in the disciplinary vision of power that Foucault made famous, the same surveillance retains the condescension implicit in the victory of the State – condescension, as we have suggested, which is played out in fields of sight. On the one hand in the panoptic design of the prison, "visibility is a trap," an exercise of power in which "the inmate must never know whether he is being looked at. . . ." To have this effect, the surveying tower needs to be occupied only intermittently, and this (as was the intention of its utilitarian designer) has nothing to with revenge.[81] On the other hand, that watchfulness is easily interrupted. One never knows when one is *not* being observed. An unheralded efficiency of the all-seeing design, then, is the withdrawal of protective observation – its refusal to see or to watch over inmates – or what the Court would call "deliberate indifference" today.[82] If the prisoner seems to be seen at all times by the tower or by other means, he is perpetually in danger of being beaten or raped by others when he is not. This, of course, is the implied threat maintained by guards whose inattention is as vital their attention, and who may 'look away' and leave the prisoner to others who watch and wait.[83]

When Foucault suggests that inmates are "caught up in a power situation of which they are themselves the bearers,"[84] then, that "situation" bears down on them as a nearly impersonal, mechanical sort of vengeance. They may be exposed and incidentally humiliated for purposes of security and control. Where surveillance is suspended, however, and attention and care are withdrawn, an institutional indifference does the work of humiliation. Even where official observation ceases, the accusing eye of the public follows the prisoner from the courtroom to the yard and to his cell where it hounds or ignores him. Although this was not their purpose, as Foucault's analysis makes clear, the walls seem to stare with contempt or shrug with indifference. The panoptic "eye" is at once the blind eye and the punishing eye of justice.

Evidently this 'not seeing' that is part of surveillance has its corollary in the greater exclusions of justice as well. What the law does not see – those it fails to recognize or consider to be within its scope – suffer the same condescension. The longstanding unwillingness of the courts to recognize blacks in America, to accord them legitimate status or the protection of due process is a case in point. ". . . [I]f the color is not right," declared the Supreme Court of Ohio in 1846, "the man cannot testify. The truth shall not be received from a black man, to settle a controversy where a white man is a party."[85] Here, by the monological declaration of the court, the visible mark of race makes the one party legitimate and the other juridically invisible. A blind spot is produced in which the interest in truth and common humanity is obscured, and the practices of slavery and lynching are allowed to persist within it.

Hereafter the law suffers a selectivity of vision in which it remains caught between the paradigms of "all-seeing" and "blind" justice. On the one hand, justice must be omniscient. Its blindness is a means to seeing truth, of obtaining a purer, uncorrupted vision of the sort that Aeschylus attributes to the Goddess, or Sophocles to the blind Oracle and the remorseful Oedipus. On the other hand, justice obtains mercy for all, impartiality, equity only by a sort of 'winking' as Nietzsche says, that permits it a different kind of sight.[86] Modern justice wants it both ways: to be blind, impartial, to overlook people's differences; and to see all and to entertain their differences. While it may formally do both (judicial impartiality; policies like affirmative action) the same dual impulse is compounded in vengeful punishments that pretend to impartiality while engaging in highly selective patterns of prosecution.[87] In this, the inequity of the law remains invisible (until someone like Rodney King is caught on tape) leaving many exposed to a different "justice" on the streets where the police cannot see or refuse to look. Justice may seem "blind where the judge sits," as the streetwise character in an American movie puts it, "but she's not blind out here. . . . Out here, the bitch got eyes."[88]

Sartre, Freud, and Self-Deception: What one wants to see in vengeance

Whether it is caught up in the law or not, vengeance apparently sees what it wants to see, which involves a measure of self-deception. Indeed, while a certain willfulness of sight accompanies the vengeful episodes that we have observed, it is not yet clear what sort of deviousness of mind this entails. Among others, Sartre has made the case for the impossibility of pure self-deception, or of lying to oneself in any simple sense, asserting that "... I must know in my capacity as deceiver the truth which is hidden from me in my capacity as the one deceived.... I must know the truth very exactly *in order* to conceal it more carefully."[89] As a quality of consciousness bearing on the possibility of human choice (for him), such self-directed trickery would be highly problematic.[90] To be sure, those who imagine a certain 'transparency of consciousness' in making judgments that lead to crime (Wilson) would argue that any self-deception must be "intentional" in some measure – that is, purposeful, conscious self-pretence.[91]

For Sartre, then, psychoanalysis makes the best case for such a thing being possible, but ultimately fails in the attempt. It only "replaces the duality of the deceiver and the deceived, the essential condition of the lie, by that of the 'id' and the 'ego,'"[92] and it has not demonstrated how the one agency (ego or its conscious aspect) might truly be deceived. Rather, self-deception appears to be more a matter of dishonesty with oneself (or "bad faith") than of unconscious repression (which keeps unpleasant material that is known to one mental agency out of sight of the other). "Bad faith," moreover, is far more susceptible to willful, conscious choice than anything Freud attributes to repression. "With bad faith a truth appears, a method of thinking, a type of being which is *like* the objects," it is modeled on that which it would deny and may, if with some difficulty, be overcome.[93]

The work of vengeance would seem, at first, to be more like bad faith than self-deception. Its conscious spite, its need for elaborate self-affirmation in the face of an injury, appears to require an exacting knowledge of the painful truth.[94] Nevertheless, Sartre expects the 'truth known exactly' to play a special part in bad faith that must seem troubling from the stand-point of our understanding of vengeance. The truth of an injury to which one reacts with vengeance, it appears, is never uncorrupted, never a dis-crete object that can be perfectly apprehended. The death of Patroklos, for example, is recalled *with remorse* and appears already within a con-text of angry gods and failed duty that confers meaning. It appears already to the 'mind's eye' as a reconstituted memory, on the same stage (and in the same instant) with elaborate props and fantasies designed to overcome it.

The 'bad faith' for Achilles, Sartre might say, would lie in recalling his friend's death as having been wholly the fault of his enemy, and in sup-pressing (if not repressing) his own responsibility for it. But Achilles does expressly *acknowledge* that responsibility – he just cannot bear to recall it without also discharging it. In this sense he knows the truth very exactly and does not repress it. He is driven nevertheless to convert it into some-thing else (something like and yet different from its object). We cannot imagine that this is a "choice" for him in any simple sense.

For Sartre, the capacity for internal judgment that would allow such a choice could neither obfuscate nor recoil in this way at that which it cannot bear to see. It is hardly a creative faculty that makes its own truth (like that elaborate "project of disguise" that effects repressed objects in the psycho-analytic understanding as he sees it). On the contrary, the very process of disguise, for Sartre, already "implies a veiled appeal to finality . . . an obscure comprehension of the end to be attained. . . ."[95] Yet again, the 'veiling' that accompanies such transparency is a restricted kind of knowing, one that also connotes a disguise. It is a *response* to its object, which, being a painful truth, already dictates that response and the end to be achieved. There need not be very much transparency in this, but a sort of controlled reve-lation – or as Freud intimated, a painstaking work of concealment that is not wholly aware of itself.[96]

It follows that the vengeful reconstruction of truth may well be a matter of self-deception *and* bad faith, neither wholly unconscious, nor properly subject to conscious choice. It might have properties of both, as is the case when one cringes in response to a thing, cannot resist peeking, or selects from among competing images of which one has only partial knowledge, and which are already shaded by intractable emotions.[97]

When the young husband wishes to avenge the death of his wife in the example above, he is at once haunted by her image and the past that is foreclosed to him, obsessed with visions of her death and of the retaliation that would displace it, and resigned, ultimately, to face an empty life without her.[98] Each such visualization, burdened by its own mental state, vies for his attention, and each (although part truthful memory and part fantasy) presents itself with absolute clarity. In some sense he may *choose* from among them and thus choose the path of his life. But no one of them constitutes a 'truth of which he has knowledge' over against which he might deceive himself. On the contrary, his choice is already foretold in the way they present themselves – his pain *comes from* having so little control over this self-presentation, or over the elements that make it up.[99]

The 'truth of which he must have an exacting knowledge in order to deceive himself,' then, is not the crime or the loss upon which he can scarcely focus. Rather it is a fantasy designed to counter its effects, popu-lated, one recalls, by those imagined felons on whom he plots his revenge. This imaginary revenge is a truth (of sorts) that stands in for the intoler-able truth that he could do nothing – then, now or ever – to reverse the effects of the crime; a truth which love and grief (and no mere bad faith) keep him from accepting. The "veiled appeal to finality" in this is at once a highly tormented construction which stands in a most peculiar relation to the truth – he senses its contours, flees from its shape, imagines something of its consequence, but does not dare (and cannot bear) to look. He is driven by fright and a desperate need for salvation toward a particular end (the vengeance he almost completes), and is sadly self-deceived.

The vengeful formulation, then, is not that 'I must know the *truth* very exactly in order to conceal it more carefully,' but rather 'I must construct a very exact version of a truth that I most fear, but cannot face, in virtue of which I can imagine an end or remedy to my pain.' For Othello, this means a wife's infidelity (his anxiety must have a cause), for Oedipus, it means a city that suffers terribly for his offense, for the politician's wife, a husband who thrives in spite of his betrayal. In every such case, an *imaginary and surmountable* evil, and never a truth precisely known, is summoned piecemeal so that it may be displaced by the imagined punishment that should 'fit' it so precisely.

This must be very like those extraordinary ideations that Freud noticed in pathological states of grief. In grief and melancholia, for him, the 'truth' that is concealed – the 'finality' to which an effort appeals – is no simple object of consciousness. The loved one who is lost is already invested with "narcissistic libido" which can be (and now *must* be) redeployed. To be sure, Freud's melancholic cannot let go of the object of grief or accept the loss of love, but rather replaces that loss narcissistically, by a "regression from narcissistic object-choice to narcissism."[100] This takes the form of a self-reproach (blaming oneself for the loss) which turns feelings of love and longing into hate:

> If the object-love which cannot be given up, takes refuge in narcissistic identifi-cation, while the object itself is abandoned, then hate is expended on the new substitute-object, railing at it, deprecating it, making it suffer and deriving sadistic gratification from its suffering. The self-torments of melancholics, which are without doubt pleasurable, signify, just like the corresponding phenomenon in the obses-sional neuroses, a gratification of sadistic tendencies and of hate, both of which relate to an object and in this way have both been turned around on the self. In both disorders the sufferers usually succeed in taking revenge, by the circuitous path of self-punishment, on the original objects. . . .[101]

The original lost person or object, then, is already a *narcissistic object* susceptible to this inverted treatment, such that the seeds of self-deception have already been sown in the original condition of love. It is not only because the psyche is divided (between the ego and the id) that makes the self-deception possible (Sartre's contention), but that the material that constitutes its objects (libido) makes them both malleable and subject to conversion.[102] Thus, even in the more ordinary condition of grief, there may well be a moment in which a self-reproachful condition that precipitates revenge on oneself seeks effectively to turn lost love into a more manageable hatred of others.

Yet the "substitute-object" on which hatred is lavished in such cases is also a double one (the self that is blamed, a narcissistic object, and its ally or partner in crime, who is also narcissistically constituted). Achilles thus blames himself for the death of Patroklos *and* he obsessively blames

Hektor; even Oedipus makes a criminal of himself such that the narcissistic self-condemnation turns *outward* upon another object (himself; his eyes).[103] This, of course, is an object more suitable to *conscious* contemplation, an object *that is itself* already a "veiled appeal to finality." The "deception" here is that one appears not to hate the loved one for being lost (or the loss of love itself), or even hate oneself for failing to prevent it (or for one's own miserable state of grief). One hates only the one who is blamed, whether or not he is the one who caused it, which is an enormous relief. So it is that the odd feeling of "triumph" that Freud found difficult to explain in melancholic "mania"[104] finds its more understandable corollary in persons driven by ordinary rage and grief. They must overcome that torment in themselves by finding someone to blame. And for them, there is hardly ever a moment that is *not* self-deceived.

If Sartre gives too much to the knowledge or the truth of objects in this consideration then, he may also give too much to the 'self' as a unified being, and too little to the self as having the capacity to be both the deceiver and the deceived. He may not sufficiently appreciate the divisive proposition of *appearing to oneself.* In vengeance, the self may be divided, not only in the strict psychoanalytic sense of one agency that is set off from another (the result of Oedipal conflict), but as Oedipus himself stood torn between worlds in his despairing moment of self-recognition – a self that perceives itself as another over which it must prevail so as to endure its rage and grief. In such moments, consciousness is also self-consciousness,[105] a state in which the self plays to itself as to an imaginary interlocutor or audience. The bias of that self (bias also being a strange kind of intention)[106] is that of a divided and duplicitous agency acting upon a durable stage, which reconstructs the truth in veiled and partial 'knowledge of the truth.' It would take an extraordinary effort indeed (beyond mere existential choice) to overcome such vengeful self-deception.

Hence, when I imagine that I am a conscious, rational being who rightfully punishes the one who has harmed me in order to "restore justice," I am indulging a very complex proposition. *I* tell *myself* (since there appear to be two of me; one of whom needs convincing) that the one who has done harm (whose intentions I assume to be wholly malevolent, and whom I cannot bear to contemplate without remark or alteration) can and must be punished in a way that replicates and disempowers his hold upon the past (like an effigy that represents that person and that version of the past in a form that may be changed).

In this, there are all sorts of turns into blind alleys – whether intentional or not – two selves at least contending with two possible types of protagonist and two pasts or temporal domains pertaining to an injury. At each step, a choice seems to have been made, but the choice is driven by needs and conditions established as the injured mind *performs for itself.* That interior performance, then, is not a matter of consciousness acting upon consciousness, but of consciousness *acting for* consciousness; not so much consciousness of a *thing* that is kept out of consciousness, but a thing put together for it to convince itself that its fears are unfounded. Here the self is both the engineer and recipient of its own construct; like Othello, a character whose doubts and intentions are concealed from himself by a vain and *self-conscious self-deception* – a state of being that has always been well represented by masks.[107]

Masks

Consider all the imagery of masks, veils, covered eyes, or hidden faces associated with revenge. There are masked avengers hiding their faces from the law (The Lone Ranger, Batman, the 'Knights of the KKK'); vengeful warriors in war paint (Rambo with his camouflage); hooded prisoners and executioners; gods and vengeful spirits in disguise; and all the Greek plays of incestuous murder and revenge first performed in masks. There are vengeful villains (Jason in his hockey mask) – and villains unmasked, their 'veil of innocence' torn away. Surely the blindfold on the figure of justice must also be her mask, a prop that lets the goddess play her part without revealing her true identity.

Masks may loosen inhibitions or impose them, the robes and wigs of judges (guises of the law) do the latter, being not only vestiges of austere, aristocratic costume, but vestigial masks as well. They may constitute a complete 'identification' of belief – the Shaman's mask joins him to the spirit world; the clan member wholly inhabits a totemic image.[108] Or they may reflect the more ordinary self-deceptive emulations of the mask character, a simple false front or façade, like the bravado or implied threat of vengeance that would overcome fear.[109]

On the other hand, as Susan Youens has said of the use of masks in certain operas, they may "*free* (the wearer) from façades," allowing "deeper levels of identity to emerge behind the safety of pseudo-concealment."[110] The mask builds a kind of confidence in itself, and in the wearer by admitting to its own falsehood – everyone knows it's there. By lying with a certain honesty (the disguise of undisguised trickery) it is at once a repository of other truths of identity. It is as much an "index of the real" in this respect, as of anything false. This is why Nietzsche, in Rosset's view, took such "delight in masks and the good conscience in using any kind of mask...."[111]

Yet it is the very honesty of the mask that makes it the perfect lure for the self that would deceive itself, or one who becomes too invested in the lie. One does not suppose that The Lone Ranger is fooling himself in donning his disguise, or that the deceiver is himself deceived. To be sure, the mask gives him a strange credibility, even to himself. Those deceitful costumed heroes, like Superman, who hide their identity, "never lie."[112] The face that is *openly* concealed thus reveals something paradoxical about public claims to veracity. This is also what is compelling about the 'factual simulations' on TV (Chapter 2), or the straight-faced lying and image making of presidential politics. Still it is the disguise of the mask, the deceit that is more potent for its candor, that so perfectly parallels the relationship between vengeance and justice – the former represents itself as the latter in a way that preserves a comparable two-sidedness.[113]

As actors experimenting with them have noticed, masks may thus allow a "'split' state of consciousness" in the wearer, which is at once wantonly deceptive, and convincing to the self and others.[114] The bald man thinks he is admired in his obvious toupee; the victim, though beaten, wants to look proud. Thus, when a mask is worn by the one who punishes (the interrogator, the executioner, the brave countenance of the Politician's Wife), it allows the wearer to express a part of herself, and also *not be* herself. This impersonal interruption of identity (another self-erasure of sorts) affects the identity of the punisher inwardly. It allows the *self to play to itself as someone other*, someone now capable of overcoming what she has suffered, able to convince herself and others of her rightful place of dominance in *spite* of any and all the doubts she may have.[115]

When it is worn by the one who is punished, the mask allows the punisher to proceed "impersonally" without rancor, but also without mercy. In that moment of dispossessed emotion, it splits the identity of this wearer too. If the latter is represented in a state of submission – cast, so to speak, as a permanently defeated enemy (the hooded man on the gallows or uniformed prisoner) – he no longer seems threatening. The hurtful 'truth' of the past that his presence represents has been admitted into the present on the condition of its unthreatening posture or disguise – its reenactment or retelling in this manner being another kind of lie.

If it alters the truth and the past in this way, the mask also puts its stamp upon the future. It can impose a stable conclusion, an impression that lingers, like those vengeful displays that give the moment of defeat permanence, or the character of a frieze. It is the image of Achilles standing over the beaten Hektor that endures – the magnificent helmeted faces of the warriors frozen mask-like upon thousands of pieces of pottery and in so much statuary.[116] Surely, as the image recurs, it masks lingering doubts, conceals the weaknesses of the victor, and forestalls unwanted thoughts (as of the unavenged death of Patroklos) that need never again be entertained. So the image of Macbeth facing his deserved death fulfills the same emblematic function – to be the "gaze o' th' time" ("spectacle of the age") as Shakespeare says, "... We'll have thee, as our rarer monsters are, Painted upon a pole, and underwrit, 'here may you see the tyrant.'"[117]

Such messages are still inscribed in lasting images of defeat (Nixon giving his resignation speech, Eichmann bent and listening to his accusers at trial, Saddam accepting his sentence of death), and if it is difficult to recognize the work of the mask in those 'true' representations of the media, they produce quite the same sort of enduring spectacle.

A true mask, however, is not an inanimate symbol frozen in time. It can also be reanimated. It invites new tenants (like Bentham's tower) who breathe life into its form, partaking in it as one might partake in a ritual. Masks, then, may be mimetic, communicative devices, which interchangeable wearers "speak through." Or, in the manner that judicial pronouncements are sometimes delivered, they can express themselves in shrouded, impersonal emanations.[118] In scenes of vengeance, to be sure, the disembodied voice of an avenger speaks through a mask with a special force. From off stage or behind some stern countenance, the accusing voice is serious and implacable, the detachment of ventriloquy compounding its paradoxical truth-effect. The one voice thus speaks for the many, perhaps even for the gods.[119] The speaker, amplified and cut off from accountability, brings the guilty to account.[120]

If the mask can be a vehicle for such expression, it may be the target of it too. It is frequently a device that receives or deflects blame. In this respect the mask is like an effigy or scapegoat that may be punished without fear of reprisal. Yet again, and since the mask is not always inhabited, it retains the surrogate properties of a puppet or dummy as well.

The dummy may take the blame and ridicule endlessly, or cast blame and ridicule with impunity (one thinks of "Punch and Judy"). The standard joke of the ventriloquist's performance, of course, occurs as it does both, as puppet and puppeteer insult, accuse, or punish one another. So the split in identity that is made manifest in the mask permits shifts in the burden of accountability. The 'stand-in' capability of the dummy is just what is needed either to express or to satirize the moral reversals of revenge: The initial victor becomes the vanquished; the victim assumes the guise of the aggressor; might masquerades as right; and the moral worth of the parties is contentiously reversed.

The mask thus performs a great many operations upon pride and humility, and on every sort of moral posture.[121] It may diminish, reverse, or augment such affectation depending on how and by whom it is worn – as a mark of shame for example, or a badge of honor.[122] So the very thing that permits the mask to be efficacious in such matters of identity is the apparent indifference to them that it grants the wearer. Like the effigy, scapegoat, or dummy, the mask presents a blank face or page that invites the inscription of meaning (Kafka's stupefied prisoner reflects something of this, as do representations of O. J. Simpson and other offenders discussed above). On one level, this must be like that indifference to others that Sartre thought to be constitutive of subjectivity in general. On another, it is a most useful device in moral posturing, where the reductive framing of countenances clears the way for the more self-interested revaluations of the self.

The particular 'indifference' of the mask, that which it confers on the wearer, then, is very like that which Freud had noticed in assessing the more unstable permutations of love and hate in vengeance. In speculating on the nature of a "reactive displacement of cathexis," for example, he suggests that when "[d]isplaceable libido is employed in the service of the pleasure principle to obviate blockages and to facilitate discharge . . . it is easy to observe a certain *indifference* as to the path along which the discharge takes place." Certain psychological dispositions thus proceed without regard for their origin or aim. In this connection, Freud recalls the following:

Not long ago Rank (1913) published some good examples of the way in which neurotic acts of revenge can be directed against the wrong people. Such behavior on the part of the unconscious reminds one of the comic story of the three village tailors, one of whom had to be hanged because the only village blacksmith had committed a capital offense. Punishment must be exacted even if it does not fall upon the guilty. It was in studying the dream-work that we first came upon this kind of looseness in the displacements brought about by the primary process.[123]

Owing to this "looseness," vengeance admits substitutes (a charge, we may recall, leveled at utilitarians for being exclusively concerned with the *ends* of punishment, which is also the point of the joke). Here, however, it is because libido, acting on behalf of a pleasure principle, appears to be indifferent to the aims that will satisfy it, such that the primary process is revealed in a rather humorous light. Rank's joke about the tailors and the blacksmith plays upon the very thing that seems funny about the ventriloquist and the dummy. If this pair, who are really one in the same,[124] heap blame or ridicule upon one another in a way that exposes the underlying indifference that reigns in such exchanges, then so does the substitution of the tailor for the blacksmith. The joke comes in noticing what is typical of revenge and characteristic of its efforts, that the greater aims of punishment (even utilitarian 'uses') so easily yield to expediency and *mask other intentions*. Beneath their façade lies the dangerous absurdity of that indiscriminate aspect of blame, which Swift caught in the phrase – an "odd kind of revenge to go cuffs in broad day with the first he meets."[125] The need for discharge with indifference to its aim may be the secret, too, of its apparent ability to change things.[126]

* * *

The functions of the mask as they bear on vengeful self-deception may now be elaborated: First, the indifference embodied in the mask reflects this indiscriminate aspect of revenge, the inclination to change its object and disposition toward it as by a "looseness in displacements." Its interruption of identity (erasure, cover) marks its ability to change the wearer or the subject of blame, his position in the present, and disposition toward the past. It does this by modifying the internal states of the wearer, giving cover, as it were, to his reactive states, or pretensions of superiority. The result is that it is convincing even when its deception is self-evident.

Such is the ability of the mask to efface and redefine identity. This quality is in evidence, for example, when Odysseus gave his name as "Nohbdy" before wreaking vengeance upon the Cyclops. Hiding beneath a ram to evade his grasp (pulling that wool, so to speak, over the latter's eye) allows Odysseus to remake himself as a strategic and moral victor.[127] Something of this survives too in more contemporary concealments of punishment, in the executioner's mask, in uniforms and badges of the law, or wherever self-righteous avengers gain legitimacy. The wish to be seen a certain way in states of grief or anger is thus much related to the legitimating function by which the mask seeks to present an acceptable public face (Goffman).

Where 'recognition,' 'respect,' or 'reciprocity' are seen as cornerstones of democratic society and its legitimate justice (Habermas, Honneth), this presumes a certain transparency of identity. Yet the latter is occluded by the mask (or its equivalents) in all sorts of moral posturing as in the self-righteous, punitive displays that seek to 'legitimate' the state authority.[128] Such posturing in justice, moreover, compounds the difficulty for any "veil of ignorance" that would allow the discovery of shared and generalizable principles of liberal justice (Rawls).[129] This, because that "veil" assumes certain properties of the mask too – erasing identity, conferring the mimetic power of judgment, and condemnation upon interchangeable wearers.

In revenge, there is a wish not to be recognized, or rather to be recognized as something better, less threatening, more benevolent, or just than one truly is (Odysseus in the skin of a sheep; the 'gift' of the wooden horse). This is why the simple disguise of the mask is so useful to the euphemistic aspect of revenge and in other expressions of punitive justice. It is for this reason, no doubt, that Masur found that the bodies of persons executed in eighteenth century America would be "[h]ooded and clothed in white robes trimmed with black," their corpses "enlisted in the spectacle of order."[130] Such is the "cloak of decency" or "respectability" that shrouds the most gruesome aspects of legal punishment, which explains why so many of our modern avengers, like The Lone Ranger, wear a mask *and also* the uniform of the law.

It is in keeping with these efforts at respectability, of course, that the mask deflects and channels blame. It allows the wearer to denounce others with impunity as we have seen, which is why the functions of emulation, surrogacy, and the extreme dissociative powers of ventriloquy are so useful to the masking of revenge. But if an avenger's mask protects him, his conscience may be eased in punishing others who are also masked (hooded or uniformed prisoners), his indiscriminate impulses thus preferring the more "impersonal" object of punishment.[131] This is the effigy function of the mask – a likeness that is enough like that which it represents that it may readily be targeted as a scapegoat (the original stand-in) yet different enough to be targeted without regret. Indeed, this substitution of the object of blame is only the beginning of the many other sorts of substitution that seem permissible in revenge.[132]

An extraordinary capacity for displacement thus characterizes the deceptive capabilities both of the mask and of revenge. This allows the pain of the one punished to stand in for the pain that he has caused in the manner of a sacrificial exchange.[133] This, in turn, relies upon the switches or reversals affecting the identities of players that are so notorious in stories of revenge and which are aided by masks – the evil one is made weak and the good one more powerful, or the two trade places such that the better one triumphs.[134]

So the mask introduces a quality of interchangeability, like the 'face value' of a coin, permitting the reversal of fates and fortunes (our economy of memory above). By such magic, the avenging self splits off from its 'victim self' (the idea that there are "two of me" in grief), imagining that it might revisit the past to amend or alter it. This is the temporal function by which the mask interrupts present identity, permitting those who cannot endure or 'face' the present to engage in a kind of time travel.[135] Here again, one must appreciate the power of deception and self-deception in the vengeful use of masks – a "very exact version of the truth" is perversely entertained in them. Their paradoxical truth-effect completes the illusion, like those boastful pretensions of the medieval duelists who once made vengeance an art, and who could, according to Kiernan, "*hypnotize themselves* and overawe others."[136] As the self sets out to convince itself and others in revenge, it enters a state like the "trance" of emulation (or "mask state") which Johnstone has described in actors who train with masks.[137] It is a condition, to be sure, that is highly attuned to its audiences.

Of Audiences, Gods, and Honor: Terror and pity

In revenge, as we have seen, there must always be an audience, at least in imagination.[138] The masks are worn for someone, not just for the accused on whom they impress a message, but for those who witness it as well. In legitimate punishments, too, there is invariably a public in attendance. Utilitarians deter some to comfort others; retributivists, despite their claim that punishment needs no audience to be just, implicitly summon one up.[139] But the vengeful performance of the self for the self demands a special sort of witness, one that registers the essential vanity of the act, an audience that *applauds*. The man with the toupee is convinced of his youthful looks only in imagining the adulation of others. The kangaroo court must have the gallery to cheer its finding of guilt. That reiteration (again) before primary or secondary audiences is what makes the unlikely thing seem right.

Yet if such an audience seems to confer moral legitimacy upon its object, it should not be confused with other sorts of 'moral agency' that act this way. It may be 'a public,' but not necessarily a proper judge or jury. It is not quite a superego that looks on or passes judgment within the psyche either. This audience is rather more vivid and demonstrative, a moralizing agency of a different order. It lends approval on demand, even to falsehoods, or to causes that offend the dictates of conscience. It can incite the peaceful soul to vengeance or goad the innocent to sin. So the parties to this audience may often seem to be more clearly discernable than the shadowy witnesses of conscience. They might be a perceptible moral community with which one openly engages, and which appears to exert peer pressure.[140]

This is what distinguishes a 'debt of honor' from mere guilt. For the former, an audience of peers, clan members, ancestors, or gods must be perceptible such that pride and duty are beholden to them, as to an observable, observing presence.[141] Thus, for Nietzsche, the vengeful restoration of honor rests in a visible offering to others, in a demonstration of proof: "If our *honor* has suffered from our opponent, then revenge can *restore* it.... By revenge we demonstrate that we do not fear him either." The damage to honor can be restored only in the esteem of that audience. A demonstration against fear does the restoring, not because the revenge is intrinsically moral or can relieve guilt, but because a certain acknowledgement has been won in "the eyes of others (the world)."[142]

The changing nature and disposition of audiences to punishment has thus always been important in defining it. Garland, for example, distinguishes between the "[s]pectators at an eighteenth-century public execution, visitors to a nineteenth-century penitentiary, observers at a twentieth-century correctional facility..."[143] and suggests the variety of ways and conditions on which each audience might be gratified. So too, when the duelist makes his punishing demonstration of honor he achieves 'satisfaction' before his peers only if he observes the rules of the challenge, and his actions satisfy *them*. When the penitent prays to her creator, her fellow parishioners share obliquely in the idea that she faces judgment on another plane, her faith (and their own) turns on blind observance to a punitive, observing God. When the defendant faces a judge, a jury and other authorities of the law as *habeas corpus* demands, each plays a part in seeing that justice is 'observed.'[144] Every such audience corresponds to the historical condition of blame that it affirms – dishonor, damnation, shame, guilt, criminality, and so forth – and the attitude of judgment in each reflects its different disposition toward vengeance.

In one of the earliest of these arrangements, for instance, it was supposed that vengeful spirits themselves must be assuaged – that neither the gods alone, nor the moral community of men, should have much to do with it. Antiphon, one among the "Minor Attic Orators" of fifth-century Greece, reveals that the "[t]aking of life" for prosecutors of his day constitutes "an impiety which upsets the existing harmony between man and those superhuman forces which surround him." These forces, in their eyes, are "unseen powers of vengeance" that threaten to work their will on the community.[145] They are unseen, but of course not unseeing, and the effort to appease them through punishment acknowledges both their greatness and the indeterminacy of blame. Even in the case of a boy accidentally killed by a carelessly thrown javelin, the thrower, the javelin, *and* the boy must together suffer punishment (the prosecution argues) so as to expunge the entire event and make a punitive sacrifice of all that is associated with it.[146]

Yet since the punishment must satisfy those spirits who stand apart from the human community, the condition of blame has itself become abstract and diffuse – the warding off of ill consequences by a revenge that is no longer merely personal revenge. In a shift that presages modern justice, audiences are divided between an active and a passive principle (spirits and those who await their action). An uncontainable vengeance has been contained by the 'sacrificial' justice that is designed to appease both.[147]

In the Homeric tradition, one is aware of just how meddlesome and explicit in their demands the vengeful gods can be. "Courage in the face of death," Sagan reminds us, was frequently the best cause of action,[148] but courageous action would mean little if not undertaken in the service of those watchful, warring gods. Vengeance is unleashed, directed, and valorized as an action *for the gods*, who by aligning themselves with their champions on either side of combat (and for almost any reason) would lend "justice" to their deeds. Yet as Sagan also insists, the attempt to move beyond this confusing state of affairs would only succeed in efforts to reconstitute the observing power.

For Aeschylus, he suggests, "the only escape from the cycle of killing for killing is the creation of gods who are able to nurture mankind" – the creation of a better audience of better deities, who might manifest a better justice. This, of course, would be no easy task, and for a very long time that better audience would seem indistinguishable from the potent forces arrayed against it. That audience would first need to adopt the style and tactics of certain divine beings who brought the weight of destiny (and every trick of argument) to bear upon the hearts of human agents to get their proper revenge.

In *The Libation Bearers*, the Chorus instructs Electra to "Say simply" what is right or wrong "in the god's eyes," to those who would oppose her murderous intentions: "One to kill them, for the life they took." The Chorus and the God now each constitute a different audience in favor of her revenge. Forces must be marshaled and persuasive voices heard to validate the action, which remarkably opens the door to argument and to the opposing case. Now the gods, fates, and fellows must all be aligned and in agreement to persuade Orestes too, in a moment of hesitation before killing his mother. In the end, his vengeance is a course of action prescribed by the god Apollo, foretold in the "oracles declared by Loxias at Pytho," and recalled in the moment by Pylades, the friend who stands in for and rededicates that complicated audience to the task.[149]

As soon as this sort of appeal has been made, therefore, a distinction emerges between that which is done solely for the pleasure of the gods (and for reasons known only to them) and that which is done for reasons that are given to men – from a sacrificial, to a *justified* cause of action.[150] If the former addresses unaccountable deities or mystical forces that seem opaque to human observers, the latter works by persuasion and compelling argument, and it must convince a human audience as well. This is something that Nietzsche noticed in considering two aspects of the human "spectacle" as it is undertaken for the gods. The first is the sacrificial offering of cruelty that is thought only to please them:

> . . . It is certain, at any rate, that the *Greeks* still knew of no tastier spice to offer their gods to season their happiness than the pleasures of cruelty. With what eyes do you think Homer made his gods look down upon the destinies of men? What was at bottom the ultimate meaning of the Trojan Wars and other such tragic terrors? There can be no doubt whatever: they were intended as *festival plays* for the gods. . . . [151]

Yet such things are not so meticulously enacted (or described) by men only to please the gods, Nietzsche continues, they must be "festival plays for the poets" as well. Soon that human audience would come to matter as "the moral philosophers of Greece later imagined the eyes of God looking down upon the moral struggle. . . ." Indeed says Nietzsche, "virtue without a witness was something unthinkable for this nation of actors. . . ." Virtue (and not just cruelty) must be of interest both to the worldly and the celestial observer. Now 'the spectator' is something more complex – a reflective position of gods and men taken together that confers virtue and affirms justice.[152]

The fact of an audience to human endeavors changes everything, and with it humankind seems freshly self-aware. The 'festival play' is after all ultimately *its own* as much as that of any god, and its reasons and justifications (like 'virtue') must still register in this way. The elevation of humanity to its rightful place in the observance of cruel punishment thus appears to be a necessary condition, a reflexive *a priori* of all modern claims to justice, a step in which blame and blaming first fall directly upon human shoulders.[153]

* * *

It is in this way that the odd idea of 'making the guilty suffer' before a human authority to rectify a wrong begins to make sense. Even those early state punishments that issue from a divine right of Kings seem to require heavenly assent, the approval of the Church, *and* the reflective validation of a people. So it was, in Tocqueville's estimation, that the public would play a special part in elevating and limiting punishment – the many "Kings, feeling that in the eyes of the crowd they were clothed in almost divine majesty, derived, from the very extent of the respect they inspired, a motive for not abusing their power."[154] Such an observing public would be no simple bystander to the works of God (or the ruler through which He operates), but an agent in, and the recipient of those efforts as well.

It is often noted in this connection that by the eighteenth century in Europe and the Americas, punishments were being expressly designed to induce a sense of complicity and feelings of terror in their audience. In England, as John Laurence reminds us, special events like "The Condemned Sermon" on each Sunday preceding an execution were established at places like Newgate. Here they would let the public "look at the condemned and hear the Burial Service," to witness and receive a lesson.[155] Foucault suggests that in France at this time the people were summoned *en masse* to public events in which they were expected to play a significant part:

> [T]hey were assembled to observe public executions and *amendes honorables*; pillories, gallows and scaffolds were erected in public squares or by the roadside; sometimes the corpses of the executed persons were displayed for several days near the scene of their crimes. Not only must people know, they must see with their own eyes. Because they must be made to be afraid; but also because they must be the witnesses, the guarantors, of the punishment, and because they must to a certain extent take part in it. The right to be witnesses was one that they possessed and claimed. . . .

As both targets of terror and affirming witnesses, then, the people had achieved a unique importance in those displays even as God, the Church, and the sovereign seemed to be less in evidence. For Foucault, the change is a monumental one in the transition to democracy. As the people observed and took part in the execution by *right*, and their own vengeance ". . . was called upon to become an unobtrusive part of the vengeance of the sovereign,"[156] they would come to bear other, increasingly democratic rights.

Yet by recalling the ambivalent status of these audiences, Foucault reminds us of the still more ordinary theatrical part they had to play. On such occasions they were not summoned to express their 'will,' their 'reasoned judgment,' or to 'legitimate' the event in any proper democratic sense. Rather they should register the effects of punishment as they were intended, and experience moral or emotional states consistent with rather less reflective sorts of affirmation. In France as in the Americas, high dramatic standards had been set for the performance of the executioner, the penance of the prisoner, the construction of the stage or scaffold to elicit *awe, reverence* or *dread* in its audience. If the right to bear witness seemed to be a condition of citizenship, it would be expressed in the specific attitudes demanded by the shaming punishments.[157]

A prescribed public response in viewing such things would thus be established. One hears of calm travelers strolling among the "gibbets, creaking and moaning with the bodies of criminals," which dotted the English countryside even into the nineteenth century.[158] And if one cannot know their feelings at the time (the best accounts bear strong signs of self-censorship) it is clear that they were not now intended to be casual observers, but conscripts in a cause. By the middle of the eighteenth century we are told that enthusiastic crowds had been greeting the pillory for nearly three centuries and knew well what was expected of them. On the day of the punishment by pillory of two highway robbers (Eagan and Salmon) in 1751, George Riley Scott describes the public reaction as follows: "[T]he mob, which gathered about the exposed prisoners, pelted them with turnips, potatoes, stones, etc., to such tune that in less than half an hour Eagan was struck dead by a stone and Salmon received injuries that were fatal."[159]

If the crowd was to be a proper witness (bearing this as a sort of right) it should also be a medium in which the correct attitude and proper degree of castigation could be nurtured. For many attending, it would seem to be the proper *moral* thing to join in the degradation of those notorious felons, a righteous act of disapprobation having little to do with revenge. Yet they could as easily be manipulated to other vengeful purposes – constrained to jeer the prisoner, to applaud the punishment, and to affirm the proposition that the shaming itself is a fitting vehicle of state power.

The power of the monarch and the fury of the mob could be joined together in such practices if enough forbearance, moral attentiveness, and awe would seem to be instilled in the latter. Yet if the right to witness heralded those other rights of democratic citizenship, it now anticipated a more troubling aspect of democracy as well. The tyranny of the monarch, as it was masked by and worked through those more mannered but exuberant crowds, could readily be displaced by the "tyranny of the majority."[160]

Of course the manipulation of popular sentiment for such purposes is a very old story. Yet as the humiliating punishments made their way into public life, or rather, as they began to constitute a particular sort of 'public,' they would place a discrete moral burden on their audiences. Whereas the Church had virtually monopolized the uses of shame for private moral instruction in its devotional practices (penance, self-flagellation, confession),[161] now shame would affect the viewing public differently. Shame, as a modality of public moral instruction, would thus perform a precise operation upon its audience, manipulate its *affects*, and demand a *specific* empathetic response.

The preferred effect would be carefully elaborated by the sheriffs at Tyburn England in 1784, as they made the case to discontinue the raucous execution processions that were being held at the time:

If we take a view of the supposed solemnity from the time at which the criminal leaves the prison to the last moment of his existence, it will be found to be a period full of the most shocking and disgraceful circumstances. If the only defect were the want of ceremony the minds of the spectators might be supposed to be left in a state of indifference; but when they view the meanness of the apparatus, the dirty cart, and ragged horses, surrounded by a sordid assemblage of the lowest among the vulgar, *their sentiments are inclined more to ridicule than to pity*... thus are all the ends of public justice defeated; all the effects of example, the terrors of death, the shame of punishment are all lost.[162]

Over the objections of others (including Dr Johnson who found it sufficient that the public be "gratified by a procession") these officials believed the joining of "solemnity" to "pity" to be crucial to the proper "shame of pun-ishment." Pity, it seems, should have a moral effect that is entirely *spoiled* by "ridicule." Ridicule breaks down the identification that an audience might feel with such a felon and makes sport of a most serious matter. *Sympathy* one suspects (as it would be experienced by those who decry the squalid condition he is now in) would produce too close an identification with the felon. But *pity* is just right.

When such punishment is accompanied by an apologetic statement read by or attributed to the condemned,[163] then, it should produce such a feeling in the observer – not the sympathetic notion that 'there but for the grace of God go I,' but the idea that 'as a *righteous* observer, I will never go there, and will be saved.' The trick of this public sort of pity, that is, is to *engage* the empathetic response to *undo* the empathetic response. The prescribed standpoint would allow those observers to keep their distance (or rather to approach, and to return to a safe distance emotionally and morally – Leontius better managed), to *recoil* at the sight of shame in the attitude of a *reproach*, which again, in the eyes of the authorities, is much better than 'ridicule.' So the pains of the offender should induce feelings of revulsion rather than compassion or mockery in their audience – the idea that if the wretch is in a state of misery owing to his punishment, he or she *is* a miserable wretch, or indeed a pitiable and contemptible being, both for what he has done and for what he now rightly suffers.

This, of course, is not the more *empathetic* sort of pity that Aristotle found among the enticements of 'tragedy' – those scenes to which audiences react with "terror and pity" as they observe the fate of a fully "exhibited" character of ordinary human frailty like themselves.[164] Nor is it the sort of pity one has for an undeserving victim with whom one might identify or feel compassion. It is pity, rather, for a character that is reconstituted for his audience so as to elicit quite opposite reactions.[165] In the punitive shaming of such a character, to be sure, a momentary pull of empathy should cede to revulsion, which is experienced *as if* it were a pang of conscience concerning the criminal or his deeds.[166] In his deserved shame (which is thus like but not really a tragedy), he is enough like us and not like us to induce that common reaction – which, again, is like, but not quite an empathetic one.

It seems that the orchestration of affects and moral sentiments has been as much a part of punishment as the structural arrangements of power. If the need to contain excesses of sympathy or derision on the part of observers had been keenly felt by those sheriffs at Tyburn, a need to craft the relation of shame and pity was much on the minds of their counterparts elsewhere. As those officials in England had moved to restrain the mock-ery of the execution procession by banning it, in France it is supposed to have been unbridled public sympathy for an offender that first raised such concerns. For Foucault, the decisive event took place at Avignon in the late seventeenth century. Here, the botched hanging of one Pierre du Fort led a mob moved "by compassion for the patient and fury at the executioner" to

stone and severely beat the hapless functionary. Concern over public inter-
ventions of this kind, Foucault insists, ultimately led the French authorities
to remove the crowd to a safe distance.[167] In 1775, the throng attending
an execution in Paris was for the first time separated by soldiers such that
"[c]ontact was broken" between the people and the punitive scene, reducing their involvement to "abstract intimidation."[168]

Here, as in England, the authorities had concluded that the spectacle
would incite rather than instruct the attending crowd, and it was this, for
Foucault, that fueled calls for reform and for the emerging idea among
reformers that "[i]nstead of taking revenge, criminal justice should simply
punish."[169] As this idea became widespread in Europe and the Americas,
inducements to the proper perspective would be managed more carefully.
Changes would be introduced into the punishments themselves to minimize the more incalculable effects of shame. A relatively tasteful "hanging
machine" was put into practice in England in 1783, and as Masur notes, the
gallows in use by 1822 in Lancaster, Pennsylvania included a trap door that
would "insulate spectators from what many viewed as the most revolting
part of the ritual."[170] So it is in Foucault's view that the advent of discreet, mechanical means of execution corresponds with the emergence of
a "juridical subject," or for that matter, with the "abstraction of the law
itself"[171] – an abstraction, we might add, that extends first through the
moral distancing of an audience (achieved in well-orchestrated pity) and
which never quite sheds its origin in intimidation.

In the practices of punishment of the nineteenth century, especially in
America, a great many abstract or ideal sorts of witness would appear, ranging from the incidental sorts of visitors who could occupy the 'eye' of the
prison tower (in Bentham's design and now in practice)[172] to those 'representative citizens' placed in the juror's box. Such detached, imaginary, or
hypothetical observance would be oddly consistent with liberal notions of
'tacit consent,' 'majority rule,' and the more remote sorts of 'participation'
advanced in democratic balloting and the rotating participation of representatives in the affairs of state. An *abstract citizen* bears witness (if not anyone
in particular), and any excesses, whether of antipathy or compassion, that
people had brought to such occasions would be seen as inappropriate.

Hereafter, the public presence in matters of punishment would be
reduced to that of a distant news readership and occasional observers –
there would be no more tears or thrown turnips. The jury, in Tocqueville's
estimation, would emerge as the perfect "form of the sovereignty of the
people" for the new American republic, That being a "certain number
of citizens selected by chance and temporarily invested with the right to
judge...." The jury thus embodies the abstract, aggregate reason of a citizenry, procedurally bound to remain in something of the same attitude.
The jury formalizes the right to witness, from that perspective (if not to
observe the punishment as such) and lets the "legal spirit penetrate" the
ranks of those who serve on it, so as to inform their civic character.[173] It

institutionalizes the wisdom of the people, but also instructs their moral character and redirects their affective response, and it prescribes and institutes the proper moral and emotional distance between the judgment and the punishment; those who judge and those who are punished. By virtue of its abstraction, that is, whatever other function it serves, the jury offers an improved variation on pity – an *absent disregard* for the accused as a regular feature of public judgment.[174]

Now if the abstract citizen is differently engaged – not awed by the punishment in the public square or induced to the same state of pity, but represented primarily in rational processes of adjudication – one must imagine that this audience is not thirsty for blood, but hungry only for justice. The public anger, or related sentiments, appears to be institutionally constrained. In fact, as courtroom procedure, jury instructions, and the use of the *voir dire* have evolved during the nineteenth and twentieth centuries in America, differences among jurors have been minimized and the impartiality of the jury is better guaranteed. If the jury had once been made up of well-off white men to insure its impartiality in one sense, it would soon involve others so as to minimize its bias in general.[175] In criminal matters, however, the very impartiality of the jury, the requisite detachment, and the complicated means of insuring it, would produce other expectations as well. Now jurors should not be duped by appeals to compassion, or be unduly burdened by knowledge of the punishment to come.[176]

As it freed jurors from their bias *against* punishment, however, and from compassion for the person punished, that formalized detachment introduced something new. The pity–shame relation in the observance of punishment would become one of *abstract pity*, an impersonal sort of judgment that has often passed for objectivity.[177] While jurors may not be aware of it, the deliberative posture required of them thus still bears traces of the older sort of distancing in pity. When a defendant rises to face the jury and its verdict, the practice entails a certain respect for his person, yet it may still harbor (abstractly) just what it was designed to prevent – an impulse to ridicule.[178] On the one hand, the courts seem to have found a procedural resolution to this problem, since it is the judge and not the jury who pronounces the sentence in a criminal case. On the other, the judge may be as susceptible to that impulse as the jury, since he or she faces tremendous pressure to exact humiliation, and to give expression, as it were, to the *piteous disdain* of an angry public.[179]

* * *

Where the posture of judge and jury is formally disposed to retain a measure of pity in this way, it is not surprising that shaming punishments persist, or that they exploit this very attitude in making their return. In the last decade in America, the *Times* notes, "[j]udicially created public humiliations . . . are being introduced in courtrooms across the country, usually as alternatives to incarceration. . . . Drunk drivers have to put special license plates on their cars. Convicted shoplifters must take out advertisements in the local papers, running their photographs, and announcing their crimes. And men who are convicted of soliciting prostitutes are identified on newspapers, radio shows, and billboards."[180] Shaming may be more subtle and abstract than the old stocks and pillories,[181] as the felon's likeness or reputation are now held up in his place, but it is no less inclined to ridicule than it had been at Tyburn.

Nevertheless, contemporary shaming must be distinguished from other sorts of public exposure that arise with a free press and which are intended to make punitive practices accountable to a concerned public. In America, at least, the 'right to witness' has developed into something of a constitutional 'right to know,' based on First amendment guarantees for the press and Eighth amendment concerns about the dangers of secrecy in punishing.[182] The press is allowed to report on criminal trials, but not to have cameras in the courtroom. It may enter and expose prison practices, but does not have free rein within. It can be present at executions, but not photograph or air them live. Significantly the debate over public access has thus focused upon the medium of the reporting, the uses of audiotape, still film, videotape, broadcasting feeds, and so forth, and only tangentially on the role or nature of the audiences or the person most affected. While there is a great deal of concern for the 'dignity of the proceedings,' there is considerably less for that of the accused.

A free press should expose excesses in the system. A free press also allows reporters to broadcast a police chase from their helicopters or to bring cameras along to obtain humiliating footage during an arrest. It is not clear in which spirit the attempt was made in 1991 to allow the live televised broadcast of the execution of Robert Alton Harris in the case of *KQED v. Daniel B. Vasquez* – warden of San Quentin Prison in California.[183] The First Amendment arguments advanced in the case had been challenged by the warden's expressed concern for maintaining security, but not much, at least in court, by concerns about the effects upon the public, or the prisoner who might be shamed. Legally of course, it did not matter whether KQED hoped to expose such punishment to public scrutiny in seeking to broadcast the execution, or to turn it into a degrading sort of theatre – First Amendment protections might obtain either way. But for Wendy Lesser, the case had raised deeper and more timely issues since "it posited spectacle versus procedure, excess versus restraint, bloodthirsty revenge versus bureaucratic enforcement of justice, sleaze versus high-mindedness."[184] While the argument for the broadcast in this case proved to be unsuccessful,[185] the court upheld free speech protections nevertheless, but did not address the issue of shaming or its public effect as such.

One must be suspicious, then, of claims that some greater public interest is being served in witnessing a trial (if not just the punishment), or that more edifying, democratic aims will inevitably be met in the process.[186]

This too depends upon the disposition of the audience and the underlying relations of shame and pity. In considering the notorious public trials that have addressed mass atrocities in Argentina, at Nuremberg, and elsewhere for example, which have undoubtedly had laudable effects, Mark Osiel ventures the proposition, taken from Durkheim, that such public events foster "the periodic invigoration of moral sentiment" in a people. This is because "[a]cts of violence evoke in citizens strong feelings of resentment and indignation toward the wrongdoer." "Prosecuting wrongdoers," especially by proper legal means, he continues, "also evokes – more important to Durkheimians – an awareness of sharing these sentiments with others, that is of belonging to a community whose members are united. . . ."[187]

Despite this benefit, however, Osiel is aware that the production of such "social solidarity" at any cost can lead to excessive zeal or to "delusions of purity" among the people who share in it. Accordingly, he suggests that a better, truly liberal democratic sort of solidarity arises from the procedural agreements that govern those occasions, those agreeable modes of *disagreement* that enable "public discussion" or "dissensus," and which thereby generate their own sort of moral cohesion.[188] For Osiel, this remains quite consistent with the "arousal of shared moral sentiments" that criminal prosecutions would yield in the view of his fellow Durkheimians.[189] While such trials do teach the procedural rules belonging to a regime of rights and public discourse to an ever broader audience, then, they also create a "cathartic theatre" (Osiel quotes this approvingly) that is at once a "'didactic theatre' affecting its audience." This in turn is a source of public moral instruction, or what he calls a "monumental didactics."[190]

It does not seem to bother him that in this theatre "the onlooker is *taught* what to feel," or that the audience is inducted into a kind of "sentimental education" that may not be all that different from the lessons of the shaming punishments.[191] Moreover, there seems to be quite a presumption upon the audience here (not very different from that of our moralizing media, or talk radio), that in this discourse (or dissensus), *catharsis* and *didactics* can or should be happily combined. There is a presumption as well that the discursive, democratic role of such an audience within a regime of rights will not itself be overwhelmed or distorted by that very expressive function of which the Durkheimians seem so fond. The fact that the desired "solidarity" rests in some measure upon the *procedural* aspect of the rule of law may not be entirely reassuring in this regard either.

There are many fine things about the rules of behavior that insure fairness and civility in a democratic court of law, and much that an engaged public can learn from them. And there are many other things to celebrate about a public trial (truth, the protection of the innocent, thoughtful procedure, etc.). But here, and especially in those cases where a public lesson and catharsis are being sought together in punishing, that high estimation of procedure for its *art or effect* may entice an audience into thinking that a thing 'done well' is *ipso facto* the right thing to do. The very democratic practices that were designed to foster expression and debate may then come to serve the expressive, more properly rhetorical functions of the trial.[192]

Especially where they would impose 'resolution' or 'closure' as they are tempted to do in such cases, those practices may be more inclined to produce a unified (didactic) message than to be truly 'discursive.' They reinforce the rather distorted democratic idea that well managed argument leads inexorably to agreement and to a particular truth, and not to continual dissent (dissensus) or healthy democratic disagreement.[193] Once anyone assumes that they are in possession of 'truth,' in this or any other way, they may 'rightly' pity those who are not (miserable wretches). To be sure, the most rational, procedurally well-bounded trial may thus restore the old relation of shame and pity, demanding, as such occasions often do, specific cathartic endings – *didactics* of the sort that we identify with vengeful plots in other sorts of theatre.

The Play, the Plot, and the Catharsis of Revenge as an Attainment of Pity

The satisfying ending or catharsis in a fictional revenge plot is surely the result of special effort, a careful piecing together by the author of essential elements. Somewhere near the beginning, for example, the state of things before the crime must always be exhibited. This is the quiet, normal condition that has been ruptured and which vengeance would repair – bucolic scenes in the early moments of Bergman's *Virgin Spring*;[194] the idyllic life and home of the politician's wife; Thebes before the plague of miseries brought by Oedipus; in *Hamlet*, the "majesty of buried Denmark;"[195] or Eden, lest we forget the reason for the Fall of man. As we have seen, the state prior to the crime is close to the heart of the vengeful interest. Even a purely "restitutory justice" of the sort that Durkheim had hoped to distinguish from it would restore the status quo ante in compensation for a crime.[196] The 'state prior' is thus inseparable from the condition of balance most often sought in the pursuits of justice – the idea being that the punishment will restore some equilibrium, which, even when it refers to an abstract idea of 'moral balance' inevitably recalls a happier time and place.[197]

Vengeance thus has the character of a duty to memory as to loved ones lost, an obligation to a better past. Moral accounts can be settled like monetary ones, because an affront to the past or to the undisturbed life can imaginably be compensated by payment 'in kind' for the injury, as reparation *to* that condition. The avenger thus strives to 'get even,' or to restore the 'balance of suffering,' the moral equivalent of restoring that past, to the degree that every retributive idea of 'righted balance' is an abstract residue of the same retrospective yearning.[198]

If such a debt is to be repaid by exacting an equivalent suffering, as we have suggested, however, the logic of exchange and restoration falls prey to two sorts of distortion concerning the past. First, it is in the interest of the injured party to glorify or exaggerate the virtues of a prior state (a nostalgic function of grief), which makes the assessment of 'equivalence' nearly impossible. Second, the 'equivalent' – the eye, the blood, the life taken, or for that matter the pain of the offender exacted in repayment – is never truly the same as that which has been taken or harmed by the crime. The 'equivalence,' then, is as illusory or ungraspable as the past it should address, and the analogy of a debt relationship (Nietzsche's debtor and creditor) is a somewhat strained means of accounting for it. Making it *seem* plausible to 'get even,' however, making the idea of equivalent suffering as compensation for past injury seem viable or psychologically acceptable, is the *modus operandi* of avenger and revenge plot alike. A great deal of desperate energy is directed to that end as the plot asserts the possibility of the impossible return – an irrepressible longing that validates its own temporal distortion.[199]

The imperative 'return' therefore requires a kind of motion, if not the literal crossing of time, something that nearly replicates it. The debt in question cannot be repaid effortlessly or without confrontation (although some sorts of restitution may call for that); it is satisfied only by an 'ordeal.' In that case, and since vengeance seeks payment for an injury *and* for the effort of seeking repayment *and* for the pain of knowing it cannot be had, *taken together*, the ordeal must be a gesture of exaggerated proportions. It must be a means of overcoming the original terror, every possible consequence, and *all doubt* pertaining to the effort.[200]

That ordeal, whether it is achieved in the heroic efforts of the punisher, or in the travails of those punished at places like Tyburn, thus engages (and arranges) terror and pity in the punishment as it is brought to bear on the original action (the crime or original terror of the past). It does so by an emphatic, restorative action (the new terror of the punishment) that elicits pity for the one punished and makes the victim, now the punisher, less pitiable. As Aristotle has famously observed of tragedy, "[t]error and pity may be raised by the decoration – the mere spectacle; but they may also arise from the circumstances of the action itself; which is far better and shows a superior poet."[201] The superior poet of *vengeance*, however, creates a context in which the action that has caused an injury in the past appears to be matched and superceded by a decisive action upon the present – such that the positions of terror and pity are reversed in the circumstances of *that* action.

If one has discovered that the present is unbearably burdened by the past such that the ordinary protections of the law cannot ameliorate one's suffering, there is torment, tension, and a sense that the original fright lingers and cannot be erased. In the instant one turns to face the past or the agent of past terror and attempts to *redress* an injury, one would escape the present. And if that emphatic action is to be convincing, it must also be abrupt. The verdict or 'poetic justice' should be swift, the reversal of fortunes quick and certain, and the conclusion inescapable.

Now an assertive action that seems warranted by the circumstances of past action in this way sharply reverses the path of flight from an original terror. In the sudden movement there is tension, hesitation, and release, like a burst of tears, or the shudder induced by sights of horror and in other orgiastic purgations. A vengeful catharsis comes as the movement seems to precipitate a state of equilibrium – a return to the relative calm of a spent, exhausted state which stands as compensation for the past that has been ruined and may thereby seem 'restored.' This is what makes certain abrupt reactions to pain, death, and cruelty seem 'moral' (as for those recoiling at the horrors of Tyburn), or 'justified' (one thinks again of Wilson's swift and certain punishment), or to have the character of sudden relief from suffering, which, as we have noticed, has an exaggerated importance in a context where pain and death go without explanation.

But the decisive action that matches the original trauma is not enough to achieve the catharsis of revenge as such. In the great plays, of course, tragedy most often involves revenge, and tragedy, as Aristotle reminds us, provides a certain catharsis. Yet for Aristotle, one recalls, the dramatic tragedy is only "an imitation of some action" that effects pleasure "through pity and terror" or by "exciting" pity and terror. And it is this sort of pleasure to which translators and critics have long attributed the notion of "purgation" or "catharsis."[202] In tragedy, for Aristotle, pity is reserved for those who have "undeservedly suffered" (for victims and not for all who are punished), and terror is excited by "some resemblance between the sufferer and ourselves." Tragedy is thus not well represented by the "fall of a very bad man from prosperous to adverse fortune."[203] More likely, a good or well-intentioned man (like Oedipus) will be destroyed in a way that arouses both terror and pity at once, and by a sympathetic reaction.

Yet we may add, for the special catharsis of *revenge* to occur, such 'imitative action' must take a different turn. It is not merely that "the unpleasant emotions of pity and terror ... are somehow expelled or quelled," as one critic has put it in regard to tragedy,[204] but rather, that the action moves *from* terror *to* pity, as in that rare moment when (as for Aristotle again) in witnessing certain scenes, "[a]nyone who hears the events as they unfold will shudder and be *moved to pity*...."[205] In revenge plots, that is, catharsis is achieved in a distinctive sequencing and arrangement of terror and pity – the flight from terror 'arises from the circumstances' of the original action, there is sympathy for the victim, and punishment (a fresh terror or action that sharply reverses that flight) that is accompanied by a satisfying pity (not mercy) for the agent of terror (a distortive imitation of the original action) as a means to overcoming the past.

When we speak of how the 'empathy' that is experienced in witnessing the shaming punishments can be 'internalized as conscience,' it is precisely this movement from terror to pity which allows, in both senses of the word, the observer to feel 'good.' Pity is now *achieved* in the face of terror (terror of the crime, and now of the punishment) as pity for the punished criminal (no longer of course, for the victim or oneself), as a moralizing purgation of grief and rage.[206] Whereas 'tragedy' ensues when suffering is thrust upon an undeserving character such that the observer experiences terror and pity at once, or is aghast, revenge strikes the deserving character such that pity becomes the *antidote* to terror, and the observer is released from it and is relieved.

For the catharsis of revenge to be realized, then, two additional things must happen. First, there must be a revelation, or as in tragedy for Aristotle, a "revolution" and a "discovery."[207] Only here, it is the character of the offender and of the offense that is revealed such that his 'guilt' is established as a matter of unassailable certainty. This then brings his blameworthiness into relief – a cathartic revelation or *unmasking* that invites further action. Second, that action must be exerted upon the guilty party, who, by virtue of being exposed in this way, may now serve as a prop or stepping stone in the return to the past, as to that invisible ruined state that he has brought into being.

Overcoming the offender, and any adversity encountered in the process, now replicates by ordeal the overcoming of his offending action. It rejoins the offender to that action, enlists him (once an enemy now as an ally) in his own, and thereby in *its* very undoing. Pity (of the satisfying vengeful sort) is thus achieved in a two-part motion – by the exposure of the offender for his nefarious deeds as he is hoisted and fixed in memory in their stead (Macbeth); by the public humiliation that invites condescension as we considered it in response to Nietzsche (Chapter 1) and that Americans seem to enjoy from a safe perch of entitled judgment (Chapter 2). And as a movement through condescension and pity is staged (or rather choreographed) it touches upon and 'gets over' the past.

To be sure, the defeat or subjugation of the offender is demonstrated in such a way that both the victim and the audience seem to look down upon, step over or past the offender into new territory – a destination that would also alter destiny.[208] That demonstrative overcoming might take the form of an epic journey, or a simple gesture, turn, or pivot, which, if it were only a matter concerning the eyes (as for Leontius above), would look down upon a beaten foe, but now looks abruptly backward to the crime and beyond it to the status quo ante to redeem both for the future.[209] It might be either a sudden turn of events or of the body – reeling at the sight of Jocasta, looking down at Hektor, standing high to receive the laurels for a win – the raising of the victor in all sorts of heroic accomplishments – or a pirouette of revulsion as we find it in public observances of shame and in the ascension to various states of pity.

In order to make that move effectively, however, the turn from terror to pity that enlists the offender to address the past must appear to do so in 'proportion' to his wickedness and his crime. This, as we keep saying, is a complicated proposition. The plausibility of getting even depends upon the possibility of replicating the offending action in the ordeal of punishment, which implies perfect knowledge of the offense and its effect upon the lives of its victims – its effect upon time.[210]

Its effect on time has, however, been traumatic, since time itself has been ruptured or split as a consequence of the crime. As we saw with Oedipus, there are at least two truths and two tracks in time that can be traced to or from the injurious incident, one which follows directly from the act and from the treachery of its concealment, the other, as that which might have been had the crime been thwarted and the treachery revealed, and which now in being revealed, might seem to be restored. Plot twists, fateful discoveries, and exposed double-crosses all speak to this possibility. All suggest that there are hidden causes, tricks of fate, which, if they could only be discovered or be seen now as they should have been foreseen, would imaginably 'set things right.'

With the twist, the world is not as we thought it was. While the effects of the crime have been established and blame provisionally assigned, the twist comes as a correction, a surprising revelation about the past and its true nature, like the tragic "discovery" for Aristotle, but with the implication that something devious or improper about the cause can and will be rectified. Now what once was true is proven false, and one can see through one's mistaken impression to a darker truth that changes everything.

So the revelation proceeds on two levels, bringing two tracks of time into focus in a way that implies insight, mastery, or control, which paradoxically, and for all of the irreversible effects of that fateful past, makes the vengeful reversal seem completely viable. In the moment of the revelation that comes with a twist, then, a new territory has indeed opened up, an alternate universe in which a dupe of fate (like Oedipus) might also be an agent of fate. Precisely because this revelation has proven the falsifiability of time by exposing the true nature of the crime (an otherwise untouchable past), a certain logic dictates that the same process might work backwards, so that the revelation itself provides the key to the vengeful reversal.[211]

Now it appears that if one can match the effect of the crime by the right corrective action, time itself can be repaired and returned to its proper course. The revelation of the twist reassigns guilt, sharpens blame, and 'instructs' the action so that the necessary turning of the tables, or reversal of fortunes, can be accomplished in the right proportion, and the offender rejoined properly to the action of the crime. In order to accomplish this, however, the action must proceed in a state of divided consciousness – consciousness that is split as time has been split – aware at once of the horror of the crime at its origin, and of the terror (now fully revealed) as it persists to the present – that painfully divided condition attributed to the crime and so often experienced as a 'wound.'

To act to undo this condition, to achieve peace, restfulness, balance or equilibrium is in effect to unite that divided consciousness *as* time. This, of course, is a philosophically problematic notion that is no less psychologically necessary – to unite the pain of the injury *then as now* in a singular aware-ness, as a past that is presently 'resolved.'[212] This is what seems to occur in certain states of consciousness affected by masks. The split in identity introduced by the mask which sets a present avenging self off from its formerly victimized self (allowing the self to perform for and deceive itself) also permits the temporal inversion in which the present regains dominion over the past.[213] The horrific punishment might function this way too – as for Foucault the very "atrocity that haunted the public execution . . . was the principle of the communication between the crime and the punishment, it was also the exacerbation of the punishment in relation to the crime."[214]

So the split in identity that splits time also requires a split in the action that aims to repair both. This is why the act of revenge so often involves a *double* motion as if it might affect the present and the past at once. This might be the sense in which that odd pair of examples is given in Proverbs 26:27: "Whoso diggeth a pit shall fall therein; and he that rolleth a stone, it will return upon him."[215] Again, there is present consequence and ret-rogression, a *dual purpose* in revenge (here Divine justice) of the sort that makes it extremely difficult to extricate those forward-looking utilitarian intentions from more backward-looking retributive ones, and which is best satisfied when both ends are met in a single gesture – "O, 'tis most sweet," utters Hamlet, "when two crafts directly meet."[216] Yet again, this is because the dual intent of the revenge is modeled upon the double effect of the injury – its original effect and its present effect (and the force of the rev-elation that makes it doubly painful) such that the action taken against it must be exaggerated, not just emphatic, but *redoubled,* which is also why the revenge is best reiterated before primary *and* secondary audiences as we have seen.

The sense of double punishment in revenge is therefore pervasive: killing an enemy twice in body and in soul, as Hamlet seems to wish he could do to Claudius.[217] All of the deceit, double-dealing, or two-faced character of the crime must be matched in the vengeful punishment.[218] An enemy is double damned! Hector is killed, his corpse then degraded as a distinct and redundant aspect of his being and his punishment. With more subtlety, perhaps, public shaming exploits a similar duality in the felon – revealing him now in his ruined state, in a way that recalls his humiliation at the time of capture (now reproduced in the 'perp walk'), such that he suffers in two dimensions, by two distinct discomforts. Even the awarding of double damages in civil law suits or double indemnity in life insurance coverage for wrongful death or murder (significantly, none at all for mere suicide) still bear something of the same logic.

Hence, and even as there is a doubling or mirroring of the crime *in the punishment* or the reward,[219] the plot often calls for the antagonists themselves to replicate one another, for the avenger to appear as a "double or 'twin' of his antagonist." Something like this is crucial, Girard maintains, to the "interchangeability" of "sacrificial substitutions" that play such a vital part in greater economies of violence, and the "monstrous duality" or likeness that characterizes combatants in general (in matching uniforms or armor), and the equally "monstrous double" of an inimical god or enemy.[220]

In vengeance, however, the doubling fulfills a more precise function of *replication* – a replication again, whether of the criminal or the crime that implies a magical ability to affect the thing that is replicated – a 'fit' promising access, as by a key. So the reenactment of the crime *within* the punishment, its *present presence in duplicate* is vital to its undoing, a doubling, again, that might "catch the conscience" of the villain or the spirit of his deed.[221] Of course it is that impulse to engage a 'likeness' or use replication in the displacement of a crime (that effigy function of vengeance that we discovered in the use of masks) that is most troubling to any retributive idea of balance or fairness or equivalence in punishing.

Balance as an exchange of 'like for like' may thus seem to restore equilibrium, but once it is mixed up with this interest in doubling it has ceased altogether to concern equivalence. On the contrary, the replication of the crime within the punishment aims at an uneven exchange, the complete displacement of the crime, which it must insist would do 'one better' than the criminal or his deed.

Hamlet refuses to kill his antagonist as he kneels in prayer, and would rather wait for a moment in which his death will be more than just a death: "A villain kills my father, and for that I, his sole son, do this same villain send to heaven[?] Why this is hire and salary, *not revenge.*" Rather, he insists, it would be preferable to wait, to catch the villain "drunk asleep, or in his rage," then, "trip him that his heels may kick at heaven, and that his soul may be as damned and black as hell."[222] The vengeful satisfaction is not achieved in exact, equitable compensation, a precise duplication of the crime within the punishment – mere "hire and salary" – but by exacting a far greater toll on the offender, which would undo all of the effects of his crime.[223]

Even the most calculated and best-codified assessments of vengeful punishment can thus be terribly skewed. At one time, Marongiu and Newman tell us, the punitive mutilations which had been formalized in Sardinian "code of vengeance" – to "cut off the ears for cattle theft because . . . the cattle were branded on the ears . . . to cut the throat or the mouth from ear to ear for spies" – had a precise "symbolic or reflexive purpose," but not, it seems, a strict interest in commensurate punishment.[224] Escalations of vengeful conflict can better be traced to a principle of incongruity, a tendency to excess, which is deeply imbedded in the code. Even in more recent cases, the authors suggest, an act of revenge "should . . . match the precipitating offense in kind, but may nevertheless return more damage than was received. The vengeful act should be proportional, but progressive."[225]

In the logic of vengeance, the idea that retaliation is 'proportional but progressive' is not a merely a contradiction in terms, but a contradiction that seeks by its own assertion to appear otherwise. Just as the incremental imbalance or cheat is vital to the 'exchange,' it may right the past only by *overcoming* it. The catharsis of 'getting even' is thus achieved by surreptitious excess, just as the movement from terror to pity is achieved in the observance of disproportionate punishments, which only appear to be proportionate. In maintaining such appearances, the unsustainable affective, temporal, and moral claims of such punishments are equally sustained.

This, of course, is the hidden truth of so many grotesque or exaggerated retaliations in revenge plots and the sham of so much criminal sentencing today. The punishment must 'fit' the crime, but it must also eclipse or obscure the crime completely. If it is undertaken first in respect for the victims and what they have suffered, it is compounded in escalations of pain that adjust its value upward (mandatory prison sentences do this, concurrent life sentences, or life on death row do it even better). To have utterly defeated a felon, to leave a permanent scar for a slight, thus seems 'fair' where such 'equivalence' does the work of revision. Both as a public lesson and at the level of the plot, the 'punishment that fits the crime,' takes hold as an inescapable conclusion, a *moral* of the story or final message that leaves its indelible mark upon memory. This occurs in public executions, as Foucault noticed, where that message is underscored by the "ritual destruction of infamy by omnipotence."[226] It is no less at work in criminal sentences of a lesser sort where truth and justice suffer mightily.

In either case the vengeful conclusion acquires the displacement value of being absolutely 'right' like the moral of a story, even when there is nothing intrinsically right about it. In the blink of an eye it all seems to say, 'See!' 'There!' 'This is how it must end!' One reaps what one sows. 'What goes around comes around.' 'Crime does not pay for sweet revenge (or just punishment) will surely follow.' But here too, the sophisticated revenge plot is especially devious. Having witnessed the punishment, the gentle reader is told, revenge is not so sweet after all. One is reminded to be wise, to be reasonable, that there is no true compensation for a crime, no satisfying revenge, but only *after* having tasted its bitter reward. One is drawn either way to position of the avenger. The movement from terror to pity, driven through by rage and grief, unwilling to face the logic of time, makes its exaggerated claim upon a public stage so that no one – neither oneself nor one's audience – can have the slightest doubt. This, of course, is the authoritarian aspect of revenge, which as we have said from the beginning, is extremely dangerous for a democracy, and which we must now examine in that connection more closely.

4

Revenge and the Fallibility of the State

The Problem of Vengeance and Democratic Punishment Revisited, or How America Should Punish

The effect of these cruel spectacles, exhibited to the populace, is to destroy tenderness or excite revenge; and by the base and false idea of governing men by terror instead of reason, they become precedents. It is over the lowest class of mankind that governance by terror is intended to operate, and it is on them that it operates to the worst effect. They have sense enough to feel that they are the objects aimed at; and they inflict in their turn the examples of terror they have been instructed to practice.
– Tom Paine, *Rights of Man*[1]

It should now be clear that the grief-driven need to remake memory, to overcome the past completely; to destroy one's antagonists utterly is disturbingly authoritarian. On a personal level such vengeance does seem to proceed at the expense of reason and of truth. As it becomes dominant within American culture, altering its practices of punishment and changing its perceptions of justice, it appears to be systemic vengeance of a different order, a vengeance which is at odds with democratic justice itself.

But what can it mean to say that vengeance has this character, or that it is undemocratic when there has clearly been so much of it in democracy? From the French Revolution to the uprisings of New England, the cause of democracy has always had its vengeful side. While democracy has aligned itself with 'reason' and 'rights' against revenge, those very things have justified democratic revenge and revolution. Vengeance, we must concede, now makes entirely *democratic* demands upon the institutions of punitive justice. Americans fight 'wars for democracy' by rallying a vengeful nationalism.[2] We fight 'terror with terror' and punish our enemies and criminals alike with the vengeful finality of death.

It is equally clear, however, that this tendency affects the very character of our political authority – its harshness, its arrogance, the uncompromising nature or 'infallibility' of its judgments, the degree to which it is undemocratic in a deeper sense. The more that authority heeds such

145

popular demands, applying harsh and irrevocable punishments, the more it compromises the elements of American democracy that resist the same impulses. These include the rights of the accused and procedural safeguards that so much concerned the Warren Court – protections against unwarranted police actions, the right to a fair and public trial where evidence is presented in good faith, the extension of due process to a wide range of cases under the Fourteenth Amendment – those longstanding safeguards against the dominance of the majority and the moral hegemony of the state. Like First Amendment guarantees, such things protect the integrity of rights-bearing persons in the variety of their beliefs, opinions, and ways of being, so that ours remains a pluralist democracy and exerts its punitive authority with reasoned consideration and appropriate restraint.

Now it appears that this tension within our justice, this paradox of vengeance and democratic justice, has become a most pressing one for America: Our democracy should reflect the will of the people, but when the people want revenge, they are hostile to those rational legal propositions that make up the fabric of that democracy. To address this problem properly, therefore, we must return to the founding considerations of that system, to Locke again and Thomas Paine, to see how the principles of authority that once animated that cause may yet be instructive. If the 'reason' championed by the cause of democracy has not been enough to contain its vengeance, we must ask whether there are other sensibilities in that tradition that still stand against it. We will carry this question forward as we examine the vengeful authoritarian impulse at work within contemporary legal practice. We will examine the state's presumption of infallibility in this light (as it presents itself in one notorious capital case *State of Texas v. Roy Wayne Criner*). We will see why democratic justice, in the fuller sense, should remain opposed to this – in the character of its judgments, in the quality of its mercy, and by the nature of the accountability it expects of its citizens.

* * *

In the tradition as we have considered it, the problem of vengeful authority first arose for the lawless renegade or tyrant – the prince in relation to other princes, or the 'savage' confronting others in a state of nature. For all of the efforts to set it aside in favor of a more rational principle of 'self-protection,' it seems clear that vengeance is never entirely forsaken. Vengeance lingers in this tradition as an aspect of self-assertion. It would seem to be an inalienable aspect of the will of the people – a righteous expression of indignation at being harmed.[3] The 'self-respect' of sovereign people demands nothing less – as Martha Minow and others have observed. Rights themselves are jealously guarded assertions before they are principles, and vengeance must be counted among the first democratic impulses.[4] In the story of our American origins (in one version at least) the powerless seize the state and cast out its oppressive rulers in an act of justifiable revenge.[5] Their egalitarian regime triumphs first by getting even, as for that "long train of abuses" committed by the English King and set out in the Declaration of Independence.

It is quite apparent, however, that this democracy could not endure its vengefulness for very long. The revolt of the masses has never been far from the retaliation of the mob, or that "sudden and convulsive outbreak against monarchical and aristocratic despotism" that so worried Tocqueville, and which (as Mill feared too) might lead to the "tyranny of the majority."[6] A system based on reason, consent, and the will of the people would soon need to cultivate a kind of force and authority different from that which guided it in revolt. Once the people had asserted their will and won their equality, they would need to calm the very forces they had set in motion and to find ways to treat each other fairly and equitably, so that something greater and more worthy about their will, their consent, their right to self-government might flourish.

Beyond the assertion of the will of the people in revolution, this system must reflect *the fact* of their will, their reason, their capacity for choice and voluntary engagement in society, as a principle of governance. This is why there must seem to be an initial 'choice' by which the people have subordinated their vengeance – even *against* their will – and thereby 'consent' to be governed, so that the will, reason, or choice might be advanced in general.[7] It is why democracy is never just the 'will of the people' – their whim, opinion or belief – but sets their will above such things by institutionalizing its protection (that of various freedoms, ideas, or beliefs as abstract products of the will) and making that protection its first principle of justice.

What a democracy does to establish itself therefore must be very different from what it must do to sustain itself. If its first act is a punitive, reactive one – of the sort that Nietzsche characterized as the "vengefulness of the impotent"[8] – its very next act must be one of restraint. This second act must make its concerns about vengeful authority manifest, whether it is that of a despot, or that of its own majority. If it reflects the "calm reason" by which sovereignty might best be established for Locke, it must also express caution, humility, uneasiness, and doubt concerning its possession of that same authority.

The American revolutionaries would have to struggle with this in the aftermath of their victory, as would their French counterparts who ultimately opposed the guillotine.[9] The Romanian rebels must have been aware of this too when they executed Ceaușescu in the vengeful coup that established their democracy, but abolished the death penalty as their first act of state.[10] This transition to democracy reflects the difference, for that matter, between our own Declaration of Independence and the Constitution of the United States. The latter codifies, and contains the vengeful revolutionary force of popular will expressed in the former, giving it a limited and restrained institutional form. This is why the Constitution permits acts of political protest, for example, but privileges the vote, and why it allows

the right to bear arms, but suggests that this be done only in "well regulated militias." It is why the state has been compelled (eventually and by
amendment) to minimize its 'cruel and unusual' punishments, those that
are most vengeful among them.[11]

It follows that there are two very different principles of authority at
work in the democratic founding and its initial covenants – one which
logically and historically anticipates the other – and two different dispositions toward the will, reason, or liberty that arise with the problem of
vengeance. As Hobbes had observed, in the establishment of a political
state it would be necessary for people who are naturally in a condition of
war to be subjected to a "visible power to keep them in awe, and tie them
by fear of punishment to the performance of their covenants."[12] It would be
necessary to "govern men by terror instead of reason" as was consistent
with the monarchical authority of his time. If their obedience to authority reflects a "tacit covenant" (even for Hobbes),[13] it is driven no less by a
vengeful and coercive authority, and the degree to which a threat of this
kind bears on the initial 'choice' or covenant would be much on the minds
of the democratic founders. For Locke and those who follow him in the
American republic, Paine and Jefferson among them, the state thus retains
the character of a more "voluntary union."[14] Nevertheless, if the people
are subject to an authority that they "ought to obey" (Locke) having first
given their "tacit consent" to be governed, the initial covenant reflects their
judgment and operates *in principle* by their consent, though not thereafter
by their expressed consent, such that a coercive principle is retained in the
compromise.[15]

Two different disciplinary principles and sets of sensibilities follow from
this, which are equally embedded in the democratic experience. The first
is a principle of intimidation and coercion – expressed in those common,
frightful American punishments that Masur portrays, and which Paine so
vividly recalls.[16] This mode of authority finds its chief historical horizon in
the strict religious communities of the colonies (or for Locke perhaps in
the Inquisition), is quite at home in the more authoritarian strains of democratic revolution, and is entirely comfortable with the use of shameful and
humiliating punishments. It lingers in institutions where there is minimal
respect for the will of those within them – authoritarian military schools
and prisons even now. The second principle is one of voluntarism, consent,
and persuasion (expressed by Locke) as it arose in themes of the Reforma-
tion and was borne out in the Quaker prison reforms of the early American
republic.[17] This persists where the will is respected in various covenants and
constitutions, and in policies that maintain the rights of persons against a
coercive authority.

Today, a certain voluntarism is retained in the laws and procedures that
protect individual rights and liberties as we have said – especially those that
protect persons against persecution (the vengeful anger of the majority) for

their actions or their views. Practically this has meant maintaining a right to speak or have representation in court of law, a right to present one's case (habeas corpus), a right to due process in criminal matters, and painstaking equal protection of persons under the law. Intimidation, coercion, the presumption of the majority that it is unquestionably right – these are retained in certain practices of the prosecution, in the manner in which criminal statutes are enforced, in mandatory minimum sentences and capital punishment. Such things persist in implicit agreements between the police, district attorneys, and judges, as we shall see in a moment. They are manifest in the tactics of power of those who occupy such positions of authority and in the attitude of condescension that they bring to the effort – one that abrogates doubt, insists on the infallibility of its own judgment, regards the accused with contempt, and puts its interest in power above its interest in truth.

The Presumption of Infallibility in America

This second principle of authority, this attitude, was much in evidence, for example, for those representing the people of the State of Texas in making their case against one Roy Criner for the rape and murder of Deanna Ogg, a 16-year-old girl whose body was found on September 27, 1986. Mr. Criner, then 20, was sentenced to 99 years for aggravated sexual assault. Though there had not been enough evidence to sustain an initial capital murder charge, the jury found Criner guilty of the assault "beyond a reasonable doubt." As the news program FRONTLINE reports in some detail, however, the verdict, like the initial charge, had been based almost entirely on circumstantial evidence and indirect testimony.[18] After a series of appeals the case would receive national attention, as it typified the problem of zealous prosecution in the face of exculpatory (DNA) evidence.

To begin with, crucial testimony had been given to investigators by three of Criner's male acquaintances. According to police reports, the three maintained that Criner had boasted of having threatened, and had sex with, a female hitchhiker whom he claimed to have picked up on or about that time. The recollections of the men varied substantially on this and other points, however. They were inconsistent with regard to the woman's hair color as Criner recalled it, and the date of the incident. There were also substantial discrepancies in their observations concerning timing of Criner's departure from the logging site where he was working on the afternoon of the murder, and the route he would have taken, that would never emerge at trial.

Conspicuously, the police failed to record testimony by one of the men, a co-worker, that Criner had completed tasks on the day in question that would have occupied him for much of the time during which the murder had been committed. In addition, the co-worker reported that he was repeatedly asked by an investigating officer, "Didn't Mr. Criner tell you he murdered the girl?" in spite of the fact that he had clearly answered "No" and that the officer was "trying to add words to my mouth."

It is worth noting that in 1991, the Beaumont Court of Appeals reversed Criner's conviction for insufficient evidence because it had been based on such unsubstantiated admissions. The conviction would be reinstated, however, in 1992 by the Texas Court of Criminal Appeals on the strength of the remaining evidence. That evidence, significantly, included blood and semen taken from the victim's vagina and rectum. Tests done on them at the time, crude ABO tests for blood type, determined that Criner, like millions of other men, could indeed have been the source of the sample. A reporter recalls how Prosecutor David Walker had put this in the most affirming light during the trial: "[I]s there any scientific evidence to prove that this was Roy? Yes there is, and the blood test is it. . . . Yeah the blood matches. That could be Roy."[19]

In light of all this, in 1997, an appeals lawyer named Mike Charleton prevailed upon the Criner family to have newly available DNA tests done on the semen samples in an attempt to reopen the case. Once it had obtained and processed the samples, the reputable private laboratory engaged by the family determined that they did not in fact contain Roy Criner's DNA. Not surprisingly, District Attorney Michael McDougal refused to accept these results on their face, and ordered retesting at a state lab. The state's results were also negative, but the effect was not as Criner's defenders had hoped. The following exchange is telling:

> FRONTLINE Interviewer (Ofra Bikel): Why, then, did you send the DNA to your own lab?
> District Attorney Michael McDougal: To make sure that what the defense was telling us was in fact true, that it wasn't his. We didn't know that except that they were saying they – "We had it tested. It's not his."
> Ofra Bikel: Okay, so now you know it's not his, so now what?
> Michael McDougal: Well, I don't know that it's not his just because they tell me it's not his. So I've got to test it and see if it's not his.
> Ofra Bikel: So now your lab told you it's not his.
> Michael McDougal: So now it's not his.
> Ofra Bikel: So what are you going to do about it?
> Michael McDougal: Nothing, it's not his.
> Ofra Bikel: But he's still in prison.
> Michael McDougal: He's still in prison.
> Ofra Bikel: And he'll stay there.
> Michael McDougal: He'll stay there.

The official logic appears to be that just because a part of the evidence – the only solid part – on which Criner was convicted does not stand up to scrutiny, that *doesn't mean he didn't do it*. As we shall see, the double negative counts, legally speaking and in the mind of the prosecutor, as a positive, regardless of how it reflects on the original verdict – the juridical equivalent of saying 'that's my story and I'm sticking to it.' Of course, such a conclusion may still "appear to be . . . based on reason rather than caprice or emotion,"[20] on the terms that Justice Powell had required of capital cases. After all, there had been formal proceedings, which *in their own time* had led to a rational assessment of truth and a finding of guilt, and even now the State appears to be on the side of truth in ordering its own test.

By the narrowest of reasoning, that is – reasoning concerned largely with maintaining its own appearance – this is all that seems necessary to meet that condition. The coercive principle that has troubled our democracy from the start and the state's presumption of infallibility are clearly linked in the person of the prosecutor as he engages in a vengeful self-deception. Here, in Governor George Bush's Texas where such appeals notoriously fell on deaf ears,[21] the 'truth' as constituted by the legal process assumes the character of unassailable truth by virtue of its very unwillingness to revisit the truth. The *test* of truth, or 'retest' ordered by the District Attorney, stands in much the same relation to that legal truth as the practice of dunking to an alleged act of witchcraft, since it can be entertained only after the fact to confirm the original judgment.

That official 'reasoning' now appears to be indistinguishable from a vengeful reconstruction of the past and memory. The interviewer persists:

Ofra Bikel: It seems to me that by doing your own test you are admitting that the test was important. Now why would you spend the money to do another test if it doesn't make any difference?

Michael McDougal: Well, just because, to make sure that the defense was correct in their assertion, that that the um . . . that he was not the donor.'

Ofra Bikel: And he wasn't.

Michael McDougal: And he wasn't

Ofra Bikel: And it doesn't make any difference.

Michael McDougal: No it doesn't make any difference. I'm not going to argue with you. I've told you and I've explained to you what it is. It means that the sperm found in her was not his. It doesn't mean that he didn't rape her. It doesn't mean he didn't kill her.

Now there are three possible constructions of the events that might be inferred from this. Criner either raped Deanna Ogg after she had sex with another man, and either did not ejaculate or wore a condom, and then killed her – a theory advanced by Judge Sharon Keller in denying the appeal, though not advanced at the original trial. Or, someone else raped her and then Criner killed her. Finally, though it seems to have no bearing here except in the minds of the dissenting appellate justices, Criner *neither* raped nor killed her – the conclusion born out ultimately by DNA testing of a cigarette filter found at the scene.[22] In all of this it would appear that there is a great deal of "reasonable doubt"[23] of the sort that would have affected the verdict had it been entertained at the time, but which cannot be permitted to gain sway after the fact.

Says Justice Keller in an interview: "The evidence didn't show that he did not have sex with that woman. . . . It can't, just like the absence of fingerprints right here doesn't show that I didn't touch that chair." On this logic, however, the evidence provided by the test could not pertain retroactively to the original finding of guilt (as it was made on the basis of what was *then* "beyond a reasonable doubt"), a finding that can only be (*or appear to be*) confirmed now. That evidence could be offered, presumably, if it were part of another more thoroughgoing case for exoneration in a new trial (as democratic justice requires), but which now after the fact and by virtue of Justice Keller's own decision, it is not permitted to be.

But Keller is hardly alone in this. In a comparable Massachusetts case, prosecutors insist that "[a]lthough the DNA results may be exculpatory, they do not exonerate the defendant. . . . " "Whether he committed these crimes as the jury first determined beyond a reasonable doubt, will never be known with certainty. . . . " In that Massachusetts case at least, if not in Criner's, prosecutors think they can say with a degree of certainty that "facts presented at trial are otherwise convincing of [the defendant's] guilt."[24]

Now for Criner, of course, as always on appeal, the burden of proof shifts to the defendant. A dissenting Justice argued that Criner had met that burden by presenting the DNA evidence in question, but the court's majority offered the extreme interpretation that he must now prove his *innocence* beyond *any* doubt. By this reasoning, it would seem, a mere 'reasonable doubt' cannot be introduced retroactively even to reopen the case, and any doubt concerning the state's authoritative judgment must meet an impossibly high standard of proof.

Again for Justice Keller at Criner's appeal, as for the District Attorney earlier, DNA testing "could be important if it came back positive. It would be important because it would have been more evidence that he did it." But if that is the case, the interviewer persists again, and if the reverse is not just as important, then, " . . . how do you prove you're innocent?" Justice Keller replies: "I don't know . . . I don't know" – the uncertainty would prevail until Criner was finally pardoned in 2000.

So now it seems that the *doubt* or uncertainty of the state's advocate flows freely with regard to any belated attempt to prove innocence, but not retroactively to the proof of guilt. (This doubt has a 'prospective' utility, one might say, serving the interests of power, reinforced by retributive certainty that admits no 'retrospective' doubt.) That temporal block, one can see, is no true imperative of logic, time, or memory. It hardly reflects the 'reason' of the law, but is purely the creation of power – and of the unwillingness of those in power to relent.[25] In this, to be sure, the principle of "beyond a reasonable doubt" has been undone by the shift in the burden of proof that puts Criner and others like him beyond the possibility of a 'reversal by appeal' or (if prosecutors had gotten their capital verdict in the first place) beyond all salvation, precisely as the logic of vengeance dictates.

Of course, one might think that the sheer wickedness of the crime and the extreme concerns for public safety that arise with rape and murder do warrant the extra burden of proof. One suspects, by contrast, that a forger convicted for a forgery discovered after the fact to have been penned by another's hand, would soon be released. Yet in either case one must suppose a degree of constancy in the relationship between the crime and the criminal across time – the criminal only is what he is if the former is still what it was. In cases like Criner's, however, judges and prosecutors are interested to sustain that equivalence and make it stick in *spite* of all proof to the contrary. The identity between the crime and criminal, past and present, is thus constituted by a legal ploy that seems reasonable from the vantage point of a self-assured authority that conflates truth and power, but which is really only an aftereffect of that very power.

If the attitude on the part of the officials involved here is one expression of the temporal block in question, however, their resistance to the retrospective challenge of this kind of testing now reveals its deeper nature. In a recent ruling for the Virginia Circuit Court of Appeals, for example, Judge Keary R. Williams would reject a request by journalists to permit the DNA testing of evidence in the case of Roger Coleman who had been executed in 1992 for the rape and murder of his sister-in-law. The judge maintained that there would be "no benefit to society" in such an inquiry. Unimpressed by the fact that the Coleman case was one of few in which the relevant samples of evidence had been preserved, Williams posed the question: "How can investigation of the death penalty as it was implemented in 1992 be beneficial in scrutinizing the death penalty as it is carried out in 2001 when the processes are so different?"[26] Here again we find the same single-mindedness and unrelenting temporal logic as there had been for Criner's prosecutors. There can be only one time line, and one set of purposes in establishing it. Quite the same logic would be underscored by the 'exception' allowed in the State of Florida that sets a two-year limit for inmates to seek exonerating DNA testing.[27]

The state's infallibility – at least, the rectitude of the state in its own time – must trump any other consideration or judgment of *events in time* as they might bear on justice. It does not seem to occur to Justice Williams, as one critic observes, that "if Coleman was innocent of this crime, there is a murderer still at large." (The reason for the extra burden of proof for the defendant, to 'avoid unnecessary risk,' apparently does not apply to the Court.)[28] But this is only the most glaring danger in Williams' posture in the case. He refuses to entertain the request, because if he did, the very logic of the death penalty itself would be in jeopardy along with the greater claim that the state's judgment is unfalsifiable, even when it is manifestly false. One might ask, by contrast to his ruling, how the *incompetence* of the state to assess the truth, and its unwillingness to be subject to the retrospective test on its own judgment, could *not* be relevant in assessing the state's competency now, especially when so much is the *same* about the case and the process by which it decides. Surely it would be of 'benefit to society' to demonstrate this.

Significantly, however, that presumption of infallibility is now openly defended at the highest level, and in terms that make its true intentions clear. In arguing that delays caused by appeals in capital cases should be limited, for example, Justice Anthony Kennedy, writing for a five-to-four majority, declares: "These limits reflect our enduring respect for the state's interest in the finality of convictions. . . . "[29] The state's interest in "finality," it is reported, "outweighs the inmate's right to further review" – a similar argument to that ventured by Justice White in *Gregg v. Georgia*.[30]

But this is curious. What exactly is the state's interest in finality in criminal cases and why, in a democracy, should finality ever matter more to it than truth? Why, indeed, if there is no statute of limitations on murder, should there be a statute of limitations on the possibility of discovery as it bears on innocence, or might rectify such a mistake? Of course it is impractical for the state to let its decisions be challenged too easily and Justices must be concerned with the great inefficiency of rehearing cases. Treaties must endure. Laws must be laws at least until they are changed. But here it is the finality of *convictions resulting in the penalty of death* that is so cherished.

Finality of that vengeful sort conveys an impression of irrefutable judgment in the very act of disallowing refutation. This, along with the irrevocable punishment itself, is what makes the state's judgment *seem infallible*. It is of course finality by fiat, and to borrow a phrase from Stanley Fish, a "political/rhetorical achievement" of the highest order.[31] Yet it is also an ingenious imposition of authority upon time and memory, a tactic that uses due process (the implication that it must at some point be exhausted) to undo due process, thus altering the relation between certainty and doubt that lies at the heart of such legal protection. To be sure, the due process clause of the Fourteenth Amendment, the procedural home of 'reasonable doubt,' has long been hailed as a bulwark against absolute and arbitrary judgment.[32] It would be ironic, to say the least, if it were redefined in the interest of a 'finality' that amounts to the same thing.

A jury's verdict, one must recall, is final in one sense (the trial being over), but it is *only ever* the best that it can do. This was Beccaria's famous observation in opposing the punishment of death in 1792, namely that "trials at law never achieve a completely certain outcome . . . at the very best they reach what we call 'moral certainty'."[33] What is 'beyond reasonable doubt' for a jury is not the same thing as that which is determined by rational or empirical means to be true – even if the latter may bear upon the former – in the form of evidence – but it is treated nevertheless *as if* it were true.

That observation, of course, is wholly lost on Justice Kennedy and the not-so-hidden agenda of his interest in finality. For him, legal truth must be or appear to be much more solid than it is. Otherwise, he (and the rest of us) must concede, legal truth is only ever *judgment* that has been made convincing on terms that are acceptable to us – on terms that are acceptable, that is, to a plurality of people in a democracy. "Beyond a reasonable doubt" is only the aggregate, conditional sense of 'truth' in which the *as if* becomes the *is* for democratic purposes. It is at one and the same time an admission of the insufficiency of legal truth and the virtual means of overcoming it, of insisting calmly and reasonably that procedure, deliberation, and the cumulative effect of interrogating the evidence has produced something worthy to be taken as the truth, even if it is not the actual truth. By the Supreme Court's current ruling, however, we are in danger of forgetting how tenuous this all is, or indeed, of accepting the terms of vengeful self-certainty over and above the essential *uncertainty* of democratic truth. There is no more 'as if' in the 'finality' of a capital verdict, only the amnesiac verisimilitude of a vengeful conclusion that seeks to put legal authority itself beyond all doubt.

Democratic Doubt

Doubt, then, plays a greater part in democratic thought and judgment than one might think. "Reasonable doubt" is not just a benchmark for the jury. Such qualified certainty is in the nature of collective reasoning overall – in voting, and decisions arising from debate and compromise – it is the best a *citizenry* can do. One might say that the very toleration of others (that "voluntary union" of persons of differing views that Locke and our democracy prize so highly)[34] requires the acceptance, but also the subordination, of such moral self-certainty. A world in which "everyone is orthodox to himself," in Locke's phrase, requires a civil authority that questions the supremacy of any one orthodoxy, as of its own moral supremacy.[35] The principle of voluntarism as it is borne out in democratic compromise (and the punishments that sustain it) requires this much doubt.

Beyond a more general skepticism that is,[36] that democratic authority reflects a specific sort of doubt. If it does not mean doubt regarding the truth of one's moral convictions, it does mean doubt about the prerogative it gives one to impose those convictions upon anyone else, or to exercise authority over them. Says Locke: "Every man has commission to admonish, exhort, convince another of error, and by reasoning to draw him into truth; but to give laws, receive obedience, and compel with the sword, belongs to none but the magistrate."[37] The magistrate's sword, in turn, may be used only to enforce the laws (including a penalty of death), but *not to impose* orthodoxy – we need hardly be reminded of the many bad kings and overzealous bishops (or zealous prosecutors), and the dangers inherent in making 'truth' and 'power' synonymous. In raising such questions in the context of a democracy, no less, we may wish to go further than Locke in restraining the magistrate.

Indeed, doubt of this sort reflects Paine's fresh democratic awareness of the "inability of moral virtue to govern the world."[38] For him too, democratic government itself is an extension of rights by certain powers that are "defective in the individual," and which are only "competent in the aggregate," or when they are "collected to a focus ... to the purpose of everyone." This competence is a practical expression of a voluntarist authority, one arising from rights-bearing persons within a civil society, which by its nature is unlike that of immutable moral laws issuing in absolute final judgments.[39] This seems to be consistent with Paine's own notorious opposition to the use of the death penalty in the case of Louis XVI and beyond.[40]

Doubt, then, is central to that healthy democratic exchange of opinion, which for Mill allows the "opportunity" for self-correction and a "clearer perception and livelier impression of truth."[41] In such a world, "[a]ll silencing of discussion is an assumption of infallibility."[42] For Mill, of course, orthodoxy of any kind is only the "dead dogma" of received opinion until it has been tested – or subjected to doubt.[43] A tolerant democratic society prizes diverse opinion and clings less obstinately to "truth" since, for Mill, "... if the lists are left open, we may hope that there be a better truth, it will be found when the human mind is capable of receiving it...." The best standard of *judgment* here, then, "is the amount of certainty attainable by a fallible being...."[44] It is the standard of imperfect men who are open to persuasion by an authority that is itself open to question. This is because the claim to truth of fallible beings – those powers 'defective in the individual, but competent in the aggregate' for Paine – can and should never be the basis of *infallible* authority that tyrannizes over others.[45]

In this vein moreover, it appears that rights may be less clearly derived from the natural endowments of such individuals (reason, etc.), and more by this recognition of the fallibility of judgment – their own or anyone else's – and consequently of any power of judgment over them. Since all democratic decision-making (not just on moral matters, but on matters of fact, such as guilt) bears this inadequacy, rights are retained in the ongoing and persistent ability to challenge it. This, of course, belies Mill's utilitarian defense of the death penalty, and engages his own defense of liberty against it. It is why democracies that prize liberty have juries that decide upon punishment, and afford protections against undue punishment by the state and its authorities.

That "the lists are left open" is thus crucial to a democracy. And in light of it, the state's "interest in finality" must seem especially odd. As a matter of law, contracts must be binding, but are nevertheless subject to legal challenges and reinterpretation (Fish builds his jurisprudence on this).[46] The decision in a criminal case is open to appeal, or may be reopened for sufficient cause. But not once the penalty of death has been applied – that being the ultimate assumption of infallibility.

To be 'innocent until proven guilty,' of course, is also to have the 'benefit of the doubt' – doubt, that is, as it pertains to *an accuser*, even or especially if the accuser is the state. In matters of blame in a democracy, the presumption of another's innocence is central to maintaining respect and reciprocity. For Locke, one is "not bound to submit to the unjust will of another" in a state of nature, but may nevertheless enter into "promises and bargains" even on a first encounter.[47] The benefit of doubt must be a precondition of trust on such occasions, as it is extended by each to the other to indicate that he intends no harm and might be trusted. There must first be a suspension of certainty on that score and a willingness to proceed without it – an article of faith, so to speak – that presages trust (or for that matter law): one which is the diametrical (and temporal) opposite of revenge.[48]

When there is a breach or failure of that trust, one may resort to punishment, but to do so is also to admit its failure, which is why democratic punishments must be undertaken with reluctance, and should be contemplated with a measure of doubt. To restore trust (respect and reciprocity) one must suspend certainty once more, and be willing to do so in all such encounters. This, of course, is what distinguishes good Americans of faith who adhere to democratic principles from the Taliban and much of the Christian right. Again, it is not that they doubt their faith or the truth of their convictions, but that they share a measure of doubt about how and where to apply it in relations of authority with others. Even if they do not *experience* doubt, they are inclined to accept it as a democratic necessity, as the devout Catholic judge might accept it in recusing herself in a decision concerning abortion, or the family of the victim might in being barred from testimony in a murder case. And if such gestures prevent bias or emotions from hampering a supposedly impartial process, they keep vengeful self-assertion from erasing all doubt as well.

It is not enough, therefore, to say that this institutionalized uncertainty should prevail only *on the way* to certain judgments – like those argumentative challenges, which ultimately lead to truth for Mill. Rather, the formal skepticism of democratic institutions implies that there is room for error within *any* judgment or decision, always room to 'admonish, exhort, or convince another.'

Hence, when Richard Rorty imagines a world divided between metaphysicians and ironists, the former are those who are unquestioningly possessed of a "final vocabulary." It is "'... final' in the sense that if doubt is cast on the worth of those words, their user has no noncircular argumentative recourse. Those words are as far as he can go with language; beyond them there is only helpless passivity or resort to force." Rorty's "ironist," however, is someone who "has radical and continuing doubts about the final vocabulary she currently uses."[49] The ironist is ever aware of the 'contingency' of all final vocabularies and their claims to truth. That ironist one might say is both an *effect* and *cause* of democratic institutions; she is a manifestation of doubt, not just as it is expressed on the way to finding truth, but as an embodiment of the formal and persistent recognition of the fallibility of judgment in which there is *always* "noncircular argumentative recourse."

As a juror, one imagines, the ironist would be a prosecutor's worst nightmare, but she, or what she represents, is no less vital to the function of the jury.[50] The very ideals of democratic discourse, that of legal institutions included – respect, reciprocity, the establishment of acceptable truth claims (Habermas)[51] – imply the adjustably of truth claims and operationalize their contingency. They make permanent the possibility to "exhort or convince" or to find 'argumentative recourse' in a uniquely democratic relation of language to truth that is precisely the function of the jury. The juror must accept an argument as true, even as the exhortation to do so in formal legal terms – 'plea,' 'alleged,' 'determine the facts,' 'disregard,' 'deliberate' with others, 'reach a verdict' – betrays its own contingency. Her awareness of that contingency is central to the process and to the *validation* of the truth she must ultimately accept.[52]

The relation of truth and language in question here is at once a pedagogical one – one in which the possibility of learning (or changing an opinion) is never entirely foreclosed; in which authority and truth are never synonymous, and error, whether as a matter of fact or moral opinion, is always subject to correction or appeal. In this uniquely democratic relation, words and meaning are contested and *coercion* yields entirely to *persuasion*. If it seems that such doubt should pertain only to matters of opinion in this justice, however, and not the determination of criminality or matters of fact, we are reminded that this too is determined discursively. It is only ever a judgment rendered in a verdict or sentence *as if* it were true, which, again, is why a democratic state should never be more interested in 'finality' than it is in truth.

Now when this principle is conceded or taken, as it should be, as something implicit within the constitutional system of law, the terms of authority shift substantially. No authority can dictate the truth to a democratic people. There is no more sin and damnation; no excommunication, no 'outside' (or Guantánamo) to which to banish malcontents who break the state's law or question its truth. With the benefit of the doubt intrinsic to its own proceedings, they are welcomed into the world of reasoned disputation and law where the rationality of the law – its power to convince and *not* its claim to infallibility – should incline them to obey.

Here, of course, the sense in which such people are 'accountable' must shift as well. They do not dumbly suffer the consequences of their crimes at the hands of an unquestioned authority, or accede to its vengeance. Nor does the fact that they 'have reason' or use it make them blindly accountable to 'reason's laws.' Rather, they are made answerable as voluntary agents who explain or account for their actions. Voluntary agents facing a fallible authority, again, are subject to persuasion rather than coercion. As such, they may have advocates. They plead innocent, not always because it is 'true,' but as a tactic that resists the imposition of truth; a discursive strategy that expresses the truth of the very legal position in which they *always* have further recourse.[53]

Indeed, if there were 'appeals to reason' in a society based on consent for Locke, appeals *from* its judgments must always be close behind. It is not merely "tacit consent," then, or some agreement implicit in reason that now gives punitive force to its authority.[54] It is rather something that follows from the argumentative appeals of democratic discourse themselves – consent of the sort given by voluntary agents who have explicit doubts about the infallibility of authority and who must, for that reason, be *convinced* to accept its terms – not tacit but *expressed* consent. Again, this implies a certain pedagogical stance in relation to authority – not obedience to an infallible state, but tentative compliance within a fallible one.

Here it would seem is a standpoint from which to assess democratic authority and punishment. From here, the state is never entirely self-assured in its judgments and never has clear title to, or an unencumbered 'right of punishment.' It no longer teaches its subjects lessons by punitive threats or coercion or imposes its morality by fear and intimidation.[55] It no longer regards them with vengeful self-certainty and piteous distain. Rather, its 'morality' and its 'truth' (legally established fact) are matters of provisional agreement that are subject to doubt and disagreement. It is should be supported by sanctions that are consistent with that process of agreement, such that it exercises coercion only as a last resort. And when it does exercise coercion, even severely, it should neither be irrevocable nor be designed to induce terror. This, again, is not an aggregation of *tacit consent* within that punitive authority of the state, which might allow it to be authoritarian, but of the ongoing *assent* of the people that issues from democratic discussion, which does not.[56]

* * *

This is particularly important, because in judgments of this kind our democratic state is so frequently wrong. Where truth is a function of persuasion, and the imperfectibility of judgment is openly acknowledged, that is, the means of substantiating truth should receive special scrutiny. In this we must acknowledge that the very democratic practices of law that fairly test and establish the facts also raise questions about their ultimate validity – legal representation, the extremes of argument generated by an adversarial system, the entering of pleas – are all in some sense *misrepresentations*.

For all of its procedural safeguards, moreover, and for all the care it takes in finding truth, a state that is the creation of fallible beings is quite capable of distorting truth. Plea-bargaining, the use of 'snitches,' of coerced or 'jailhouse' confessions, all comprise that truth.[57] Now the use of "death-qualified jurors," those who do not oppose capital punishment, may incline the jury to a particular reading of the facts.[58] In cases like Criner's, the skewed interests and abilities of investigators, public defenders, and jurors – not to mention the electoral pressures on judges and prosecutors – all call into question the state's ability or willingness to make valid judgments. Even the most solid foundations of legal truth (laboratory tests, expert testimony) are open to exploitation by persons with questionable motives.

Consider the example of Fred Zain – a "respected crime lab chemist with a compelling courtroom demeanor ... " who testified as an expert consultant throughout the 1990s in West Virginia, Texas, and ten other states, in "'hundreds and hundreds if not thousands' of murder and sexual assault cases." In 2001 Mr. Zain would face five felony-fraud charges following a probe into his work in which coworkers alleged that he had been "calling things that weren't there." In West Virginia, where at least seven convictions based on his efforts have since been overturned, the State Supreme Court has decreed that "as a matter of law, any testimonial or documentary evidence offered by Zain at any time should be deemed invalid ... and inadmissible."[59] In spite of this, Zain's career dates back to the '70s when he was head of the West Virginia State Police crime lab's serology division, and no one knows the extent of his mischief or the degree to which it was rooted in incompetence or malice.

Yet this extreme case is one instance of a more pervasive problem – the unquestioned legitimacy of the state's experts regarding questions of veracity that they are not (and cannot be) competent to judge. Not only is the legal presumption in their favor, but the virtual monopoly of their 'science' in court breeds contempt for anyone who might challenge it and who cannot in any case afford to rebut it. The institutional unwillingness to admit error compounds the problem for a system in which the democratic authority is just barely "competent in the aggregate" to render a truthful verdict, and in which a tainted process of adjudication formally, if often mistakenly, renders the 'as if' as the 'is.'

The convincing presentation of the evidence (legal truth, proof) always involves interpretation, and for all its reliance on science is open to manipulation. Forensic testing at a crime lab like Zain's would seem to be extremely reliable, but not if the state's investigator lies or plants evidence. Sandra Anderson, a Michigan woman indicted in 2003, apparently did just that so that her dog, Eagle, who had tracked human remains for law enforcement agencies in over 1000 cases for 17 years, would appear to be more successful.[60] One Joyce Gilchrist, the Oklahoma City police chemist, had corrupted evidence in 11 known cases since her career began in the '80s, according to investigating officers, causing 196 to be reexamined.[61] In a similar scandal involving its crime lab in 2004, the city of Houston is retesting evidence in 360 cases and may need to reexamine thousands more spanning some 25 years.[62]

It now appears that the technique used for decades to match bullets at the FBI lab is suspect as well. In the many cases where gun barrel markings cannot be identified, chemists 'match' bullets by extrapolating data in a manner that the National Academy of Sciences has deemed to be substantially flawed.[63] Even fingerprints, as Judge Lewis Pollak observed in *United States v. Plaza*, are only as good as the experts who interpret them – Pollak would ultimately side with the prosecution in this case, but only after insisting that this long-established practice constitutes a "specialization" but not a science. Fingerprint testimony has been ripe for abuse according to those who scrutinize it, because there are no uniform tests for establishing expertise in the field, and no established scientific means by which the expert declares a 'match.' In a number of cases, untrained police officers presenting themselves as 'experts' have given testimony that has been successfully refuted.[64]

Confessions and sworn testimony, once the bedrock of legal truth, are frequently distorted under pressure by investigators. The five young men convicted in the Central Park jogger case would be released after several years in prison after it was discovered that their confessions had been coerced, and that another man had committed the crime.[65] Having reproduced the same sorts of 'confessions' in experiments, Saul Kassen elaborates on the process by which police interrogation techniques may yield unfounded positive results with emotionally fragile suspects, arguing that such practices have now become routine.[66]

It was on precisely such grounds that outgoing Illinois Governor George Ryan proclaimed the system of capital punishment to be "haunted by the demon of error," as he commuted the death sentences of 163 convicts in 2003.[67] Blaming "rogue cops" and 'zealous prosecutors,' Ryan berated the system for being "inaccurate, unjust, and unable to separate the innocent from the guilty and at times very racist."[68] He would recall the 12 inmates executed and 13 exonerated during his term, and the 46 inmates convicted on the basis of jailhouse testimony. He also lauded the results of DNA testing, which had proven the innocence of some "beyond a shadow of doubt."[69]

Someday, it is supposed, the state will fix all this. DNA testing will offer 'incontrovertible proof' of guilt, and a process of "melding science with legal safeguards" will lead to a "virtual certainty" of a defendant's guilt – a standard, it is hoped, that will be even higher than that what is now 'beyond reasonable doubt.' Capital punishment advocates in Massachusetts currently maintain that this, coupled with a careful appeals process, will finally provide for a "fail-safe death penalty,"[70] one that is as "infallible as humanly possible."[71]

But this betrays a deeper problem and a more disturbing and fundamental source of untruth within the law. In *truth*, such verdicts are only
ever based on degrees of proof. Yet under the law, *every* finding of guilt
by a jury is taken to be as valid as any other. For legal purposes, the capital verdict of guilt based on indirect evidence, jailhouse testimony, and
so on, is as good that based on a full confession in which the offender is
caught red-handed. While the state weighs the *degree of guilt* therefore –
in filing the charge of first- or second-degree murder, or in the penalty
phase of such a trial – the *degree of proof* represented in a verdict is never in
dispute.

The state's interest in 'truth' constituted in this way, like its interest
in finality, is thus inclined to confirm the forced conclusion and give it
formal validity. The verdict that was beyond a reasonable doubt is taken
to be beyond all doubt (the finding of guilt being irreducible), and the
very practices that should insure the interrogation of truth (improved testing, systematic appeals, etc.) serve the illusion of its perfectibility instead.[72]
When the end of judgment is the end of life, moreover, such 'proof' (irreducible as a matter of degrees; no longer subject to question) is at once
validation of the state's claim to infallibility – or again a fait accompli that
begs any question of the insufficiency of its truth.[73]

It follows that where such judgments prevail, good citizens and their
children are taught the disturbingly undemocratic lesson that every violation of law is a violation of something absolutely right. They may cease to
wonder how many mistaken executions there have been if their newfound
confidence in the perfectibility of judgment, taken together with the finality of the punishment itself, preclude further efforts to determine the "risk
of error."

Under this tutelage, they may cease to question the adequacy of a system that promises fair and neutral judgments, but has been 4.3 times more
likely to assign the death penalty to a black person who murders a white,
than to a white person who murders a black one.[74] They may well accept
the proposition that the death penalty deters violent crime despite evidence to the contrary,[75] or that it balances the scales of justice and can
restore morality, or that a democratic state can or should ever be adequate
to that task. They are likely to regard the state authority as the aggregation of perfectible judgment, not the creation of fallible beings who are
merely "competent in the aggregate" in Paine's clearer vision of democracy. On the presumption of this punitive pedagogy, the democratic *act* of
consensus (debate, consent, majority rule) cedes to the universalization
of its claim to truth.[76] Yet, the will of a majority *without doubt*, as the democratic theorists were wise to remind us, is decidedly undemocratic.

By contrast, of course, such democratic doubt should engender a distinct skepticism about punishment and about what the state can know
in inflicting it. This is the sense in which that thoughtful doubt can be

extrapolated from the tradition of democratic authority, and stands squarely against vengeful self-assertion, and the public anger (or affects of broken attachment) that drives it. The common objections to capital judgments can be reframed in this way:

We doubt that the State of Florida knows whether the twelve-year-old it has tried and convicted of murder as an "adult" is too young to be put to death or to be tried in this way, or what the standard of legal competency should be.[77] On this, good citizens may well *disagree.* We doubt that a judge or jury can really know whether Ted Bundy was "sane" when he brutally murdered so many women or really what sanity is or how it should bear on his three death sentences. Surely we doubt whether most of those who are convicted of murder are so obviously guilty as the confessed serial killer. We cannot know how the disproportionate presence of blacks on death row is affected by bias, or whether this is relevant in the case of Mumia Abu-Jamal, and whether he did the crime or was framed or is protecting someone. We are not sure whether it is fair that the murderer of the well-connected middle class victim whose friends and family give 'victim impact statements' is more likely to face execution than the murderer of a solitary indigent one. We do not know whether Carla Faye Tucker really found Jesus while awaiting execution or was still the 'same person' if she did, or whether that should mitigate the state's action or only concern the hereafter. We cannot be absolutely certain that police investigators did not tamper with evidence against O. J. Simpson, or have in the case of others who could not afford his attorneys and were found guilty on similar grounds. We cannot tell whether a jury was unduly swayed or a skillful prosecutor had twisted the story, or whether Louise Woodward battered a small child to death or panicked in trying to help him. We are unsure whether Lee Boyd Malvo was a troubled teen manipulated to the point of insanity as the defense maintained, or an equal partner in the sniper killings. We doubt that Shawn Drumgold (who served 14 years of a life sentence in Massachusetts after prosecutors withheld exculpatory evidence) should have received his sentence in a state with the death penalty.[78]

The state does not have any idea what really happened in many of these cases, or whether what it has held to be true in crucial aspects of the case is true, or what motivated these people, or how their motives should relate to their worthiness to die or be imprisoned for life. For it to pretend otherwise, of course, is to institutionalize the claim to privileged insight of authoritarian omniscience (and the temporal block that makes it seem possible) that we have identified in revenge. Manifestly, we – our democracy and the culture it has spawned – do not *know* the implications of punishing with such finality. We do not know what death is, or how much anyone suffers in knowing how and when it will come. We do not know what cruelty or evil is, or which punishment truly honors human dignity. These are matters of profound disagreement in a democracy, things viewed differently by persons of different faiths or convictions. And since those matters bear heavily on what constitutes "cruel and unusual punishment," they are better left to the First Amendment than to the Eighth.[79] If punishment is to be undertaken in full awareness of this aspect of democratic authority – that it is the aggregation of fallible judgment and varied opinion, that it can seldom achieve factual, and should never claim moral certainty – the relationship between the individual and the state, accountability and punishment, must shift accordingly.

Restraint and Accountability

Where this much is understood – that such punishment is at best an expression of collective disapproval in a state that should know its limitations – a great deal follows: Because there is doubt in a democracy, and because the relationship between the plurality of voluntary agents and their fallible state demands it, punishment must be conducted with restraint. This, however, must be restraint of a more deliberate and aggressive sort than even the old liberal kind.[80] For his part, Locke had maintained that when the "absolute power" of monarchy is displaced by that of a consenting people, they must immediately concern themselves with "methods of restraining . . . exorbitancies of those to whom they had given the authority over them. . . ."[81] It was not clear, as we have said, what they would consider to be exorbitant or how much they would restrain it.

An idea of 'proportionality' had led both the retributive and utilitarian theories thereafter to limit the excesses of punishment. For Bentham, a punishment must avoid "cruelty even to the offender himself by punishing him to no purpose. . . ."[82] And Mill also sought to minimize the bad effects of too much punishment for the sake of the general happiness. On different grounds, Kant insisted that the intrinsic relationship between the crime and punishment imposes a "principle of equality" or rational limit in determining the kind and amount of punishment.[83] For the most part liberal thinking insists that there be limits to punishment, but does not make it clear how much, or what those limits should have to do with democracy.

While such liberal arguments for restraint are based upon *reason* (either retributive or utilitarian) that may readily be adopted within a democracy, they do not *proceed from* democracy as a first principle. It is not reason as such that dictates proportionality or restraint in democratic punishment, although the people may come to this view when they deliberate, and their reason is implicitly at stake. Yet if we suggest that democratic *uncertainties* rather than such overstated claims for reason should be central to the calculus of punishment in an established democracy – that it is misguided for such a system to contemplate them in any other way – then we may come to suspect that we have been punishing from the wrong paradigm. We may wonder why punishment is not grounded in the realities of a mature constitutional democracy instead of those old liberal theories that sought to give rational attainments the status of religious ones; why indeed the constitutional vagaries of "cruel and unusual punishment," which the states apply willy-nilly, should override that more subtle constitutional instruction.

It is apparent, then, that while our working democracy must entertain those old notions of punishment in debate, it has reined them in with 'rights' and 'due process' precisely because they do not set sufficient limits on their own. Authoritarian states, significantly, lack such safeguards and may *themselves* have either utilitarian or retributive reasons for punishing.

So it would seem that a democratic state that is aware of this difficulty should not simply be restrained in cases where it is vexed or uncertain – 'hard' or ambiguous cases that test the limits of judgment. It would not be enough for its punishments to be checked by a court or fleeting majority only when they are deemed to be disproportionate or 'cruel.' It should be restrained, rather, *in respect of the disputed ground of punishment itself.* It should be restrained in acknowledgment of the fact that it is a plurality of voluntary agents (retributivists or utilitarians or something else) whose opinions are observed in *the compromise that is the punishment* – restrained *within* the punishment as it reflects democratic debate and uncertainty, such that there can never be a mandatory sentence that is beyond dispute or appeal, or an irrevocable punishment that is beyond doubt.

To say that punishment should be restrained in respect of voluntary agents and democratic doubt, therefore, is to suggest something distinctive about rights and legal obligations. It is not quite to say that those agents 'have rights' as citizens under the law, like those enumerated in the Fifth, Sixth, Seventh, and Eighth amendments to the Constitution (though rights have something to do with it). Nor is it to say, as in so many liberal formulations, that a person with rights is accountable to the laws of nature, God, or reason in some abstract sense, or that blame attaches to the intentions of rational agents who are accountable (as such) to rationally discernable laws (Kant). Here, on the contrary, voluntary agents, *whether they are rational or not*, are accountable to laws that are not so surely derived by reason, universal morality, or divine right.

The 'accountability' of such voluntary agents to a fallible authority is less unilateral and more reciprocal. The law-breaker is accountable to the state, but so is the state to the law-breaker. A state that is aware of its limitations in assessing a law-breaker's actions or the status of his will is especially obliged to entertain his own account of both. It may arrest, subdue, or even kill him if he poses a danger to others, but it must listen to him wherever that is possible.[84] This is not religious accountability – reward or suffering for one's deeds no matter what one says or thinks of them. It is not the accountability of *revenge* in which one is held in contempt and 'made responsible' (as by shame or humiliation) in spite of oneself or one's excuses. It is not Lockean accountability in which one is unwittingly bound to the laws of nature. Nor is it that of Kantian or Hegelian retribution, undertaken variously in respect of reason, but with little regard for one's own reasons for one's actions.

On the contrary, this accountability makes the particular agent 'answerable,' as one might be in an equitable, discursive democratic exchange – present at trial, allowed to speak in one's own defense (even if it is unwise), to confront one's accusers, to protest or appeal against prejudice – a discursive exchange in which one might hope to be *understood.* Here one is not 'held accountable' or 'responsible' in the old coercive way in which an authority compels its subjects, and remains indifferent to their subjectivity,[85] but in a way that expects them to take responsibility for their actions. It holds them, as it were, in a *state of accountability*; it does not shame or humiliate them, it does not torture them or employ coercive interrogation techniques,[86] and compels them only as a last resort.[87]

Now, holding a particular individual accountable to the law, regardless of his or her intentions in breaking it, has long been the mainstay of orderly society. Initially at least, that society treats the driver who kills accidentally just like the sniper who kills deliberately, even as the intentions of each may be taken into account in weighing the crime (the 'degree' of murder) and assigning the punishment. Strict liability of this sort is necessary, equitable, and just in one sense, but presumes greatly upon the law's ability to be a discerning rational authority in another. In being abstract and equitable, that is, in holding the individual accountable for a *type* of action, the law is also *indiscriminate* and must judge and punish with indifference to the particular person or case. By virtue of a more democratic sort of accountability, however, and even in an initial charge or plea, a premium may be placed on the individual and his unique motivations, for expressly democratic reasons.[88]

The aim here is not just to assign greater blame to those with the worst intentions, then but to foster the accountability of voluntary agency in general (an avowedly democratic aim) and to offset the authoritarian effects of revenge. For an offender to 'answer' mutely to the law is sufficient for the first purpose. To answer or be permitted to answer in actuality is the accountability of such democratic citizenship. This, then, constitutes a 'public sphere' that is the aggregate of toleration and voluntary agency, which invites responsibility wherever possible, instead of inflicting pain for the lack of it.[89]

To *invite* responsibility must be strictly distinguished from merely 'holding the offender accountable' without expecting him to '*take* responsibility,' since the two are dangerously confused in this system. Harsh punishments that make a mockery of the offender; which inscribe a message or ascribe sensibilities to him *in spite of himself* (the old forced confessions or branding), mandatory sentences, Three-Strike laws, capital punishments – all hold him responsible in that way, but disregard his agency and responsibility in another. In this his responsibility is stripped away *as* punishment for his own lapse in responsibility – yet another vengeful tit for tat that forecloses any possibility of contrition or hope of making amends.

All of those liberal ways of punishing in 'respect of reason' – insofar as they are institutionally or temporally severed from the *process* of accounting, like the prison from the trial – hold one responsible in quite the same way. They equate conformity to standards of rational conduct with 'responsibility,' which – like so many things in that tradition: 'tacit consent,' 'the categorical imperative,' 'the good of all,' the 'veil of ignorance,' and so on – *presents* itself as if it originated within the will, but falls short of or vitiates actual willed responsibility that is grounded in the voluntarism of democracy. It is in those expectations of *un*willed or *un*reasoned conformity to reason, of course, that vengeful and authoritarian tendencies still reign in our practices of punishment.[90]

Liberal punishment certainly seems softer, less invasive, and more respectful of rights and persons than its predecessors. Once those persons have been tried and sentenced, however, the respectfulness quickly vanishes or reverts to something else. Incarceration, as we know, is no longer concerned with their internal states, penance, or the 'betterment' of the will. It no longer intrudes upon individuals in *that* way. Rather it 'reforms,' 'corrects,' or simply penalizes them by an abrogation of the will across time. For the duration of their sentence, in 'doing time' – insofar as this suspension of will and responsibility addresses their absence of responsibility in the commission of the crime by seeming to impose conditions that make them 'responsible' – they are curiously isolated, both in time *and* from their own agency.[91] In this, their confinement is only abstractly related to the past, to their crime or motivation in committing it, and only incidentally to changes in their 'will' or state of mind as they relate to assuming responsibility thereafter. Incarceration is, of course, neither very compelling as a retributive redress for a past injury, nor as a utilitarian corrective for the future – yet it does incorporate the indifference to the will and the appearance of contrition necessary to achieve a perverse and vengeful *replication* of responsibility.[92]

It is not surprising, in light of this, that there is now considerable resistance to that decidedly undemocratic character of incarceration. There are experiments, for example, that would make something different of time and responsibility, which are neither retributive gestures toward the past, nor undertaken simply for a future utility. Rather, they hold the offender accountable *in the present* and engage his will as such in voluntary projects. Restitution, when it is presented as an option in sentencing; making amends in some 12-step (AA, NA) programs for inmates; the variety of reflective therapies for offenders on probation; self-governance in pre-release centers or in prison – these may thus involve discussion of the crimes, the motives, or compulsions that have led to them. Even in highly coercive settings, such efforts may be relatively self-motivated and may reintroduce responsibility to a degree. One might say that they cultivate self-esteem and respect for others, or try to even where that seems futile, in a way that is necessary for the assumption of responsibility.[93] They introduce a relation of authority *within* the punishment that is appropriate to democratic citizenship – which does address the crime, even if it cannot make up for it, and which may also, if incidentally, make it less likely to be repeated.[94]

In this of course, 'knowledge' of the criminal and his crime must assume special importance. It appears to be an obligation of the democratic state concerned with such things to balance its interest in punishment *sui generis*, by understanding *in particular*, which as Martha Nussbaum reminds us, is sometimes called "equity."[95] That is, the aggregate of democratic condemnation expressed in the punishment must be offset by its appreciation both of its own fallible agency and of the particular agency that has led to a crime.[96] It must be tempered by an awareness of the biases in the law against certain classes of people insofar as they bear on the particular agent who stands accused, and its propensity to conceal those biases within its own abstractions.[97] This state's interest in truth, therefore, is at once its interest in the facts of the individual's case uncluttered by bias (yet aware of the bias that affects its perception of them) and in his own account as it pertains to them, which is why truth remains his greatest ally against tyranny. It is also why the 'truth' of the case against an individual cannot register as *democratic truth* until the individual has been heard or understood – even, or especially, if he or she scoffs at the 'truth,' 'reason,' or 'the law.'[98]

That 'truth,' again, is always open to amendment or appeal (to test whether it is false), and the state's interest in pursuing it, if only to refute error, is far more important than its interest in finality. Accordingly, if the state's verdict on the truth of a criminal act and the agency behind it is at best an aggregate judgment, its ability to 'rectify' the injury must be limited too. It stands in *general* opposition to a past action and its perpetrator, but it cannot offer a particular, personal, or vengeful resolution for the victims. The democratic state thus acquires a distinctive duty to the past, to the crime, and to the victims of crime when it punishes, in which its aggregate, pluralist character is clearly at work. It owes particular understanding to the victims, to the criminal, and to the truth, both to the facts of the case and the effects of the crime (which is at best imperfect understanding), but does not have a duty or the ability to redress the crime in a particular way (as by tailored vengeful or humiliating punishments).[99]

In the case of a murder, no less, the democratic state owes understanding to the victims in respect of the crime and its incalculable impact, but cannot assume the vengeful attitude of any one of them. It cannot prescribe the public reaction like the TV expert, or those sheriffs at Tyburn who wanted more pity. It is not the state's job to give the victims solace of one sort or another, 'closure,' or a particular way to mourn. Nor can it prescribe compassion for the offender, or assign a particular attitude to its own necessary restraint.[100] Rather it is to make room in the punishment for every possible reaction on their part that does not preclude others (every reaction, that is, that does not foreclose others by vengeance).

So it must include, but not be limited to, one sort of response that is anything but vengeful, and which has a particular resonance for a secular, democratic people. This is the wish simply to understand the injury and the motive – only *that* truth of the crime. That response entails a tragic awareness (born perhaps from the sense of irony for those who do not have a "final vocabulary" in Rorty's sense) that such a crime may remain unfathomable and that those who have suffered it must endure it nevertheless.[101] There are those in a democracy, that is, who do not demand retribution or rectification, or need public sanction for their sorrow, but who contemplate their loss in other, private ways. One recalls the mother who wished to see the scene of her daughter's murder without the need of public resolution, to find her own way to grieve.[102] The state's punishment must leave room, that is, not only for vengeful feelings, but for such things as mercy, forgiveness, and for this sort of acceptance.[103]

Mercy, Forgiveness, Acceptance

Of course, mercy and forgiveness have long been presented as opposites to revenge, but they must now look very different in light of this democratic accountability and the particular understanding that it owes to the offender and the offense. A democratic authority does not properly 'forgive' or 'have mercy' on the offender, in a strict sense, since such things are undertaken from the vantage point of moral and factual certainty (not doubt) concerning his guilt, and remain oddly dependent upon revenge. God's mercy, the forgiveness of one's sins, seems contrary to vengeance in this sense, but only because the power of damnation remains entirely at His disposal.[104] It is in this spirit too that the usual wish is conveyed upon a death sentence – where the courts have not been merciful – "May God," *at least*, "have mercy on your soul."

Mercy may thus be granted from two distinct points of view. The first retains the condescension that we associate with revenge. To show mercy, after all, may also be an act of *pity* undertaken with as much derision. This mercy must be satisfied that the work of judgment is done, and compensation is under way, and have assurances that some other force (God, honor, the balance of justice, etc.) has, could, or will punish the offender in any case. It does not question the original judgment, or concern itself overly with new information about the offender, but determines that the offender has 'suffered enough' *relative to the revenge* that has occurred or will be forthcoming – a revenge that is not fully taken, because vengeance has been or will be formally or symbolically fulfilled. Mercy in dueling, jousting, boxing; even the executioner's 'merciful' *coup de grâce*, comes when victory is certain, when the game is won or honor served so that the continued pain of the offender seems superfluous. Where acts of mercy 'leave the vanquished to his fate' in this way, his weakness relative to those who are victorious still validates the outcome. This mercy compounds his shame and humiliation, intensifies pity, and dignifies as much as it mitigates the revenge.

Yet another sort of mercy is undertaken with the view that there is some- thing more to the offender (or less in the offense) than has been taken into account in the assigned punishment. It is more like compensatory relief offered instead of or after the punishment than pity expressed during, and is closer to forgiveness. Pardons, clemency, parole, all entail this sort of revaluation. They are applied to compensate where an offender has been misjudged or has changed his character significantly, or when the punish- ment seems disproportionate to his crime. Unlike the other sort of mercy they act as an assessment against the punitive authority itself, and acknowl- edge its own capacity for excess or faulty judgment. This mercy, then, is applied in the spirit of equity as Nussbaum represents it, and apprehends the offender and his offense in a way that is quite different from the first. It is based on a broader understanding of his motives or his actions, miti- gating factors that bear on his punishment in a way that does not reduce him, as he would be, were he just a pawn in a vengeful performance.

If the first sort of mercy is an exercise of power, or is undertaken at the discretion of those in power, and is still caught up in the expectation of vengeful recovery, the second must be an exercise of leniency that abandons the hope of recovery in favor of deeper understanding. The latter implies a sort of humility in which a punishing authority reflects on itself and its failings that is characteristic of a democracy, even if it has no formal, and rather only an exceptional place in democracy.[105] Indeed, and since both sorts of mercy seem to proceed at the discretion of that punitive authority, the first is often taken for the second, which is why we would not want to leave criminals entirely 'at the mercy' of the state or its courts today.

Forgiveness has a rather different connotation. In this, the person or persons who have suffered a wrong obtain a certain attitude toward the perpetrator and the injury that he has caused. To 'let bygones be bygones,' or to 'make peace with the past' are dispositions of forgiveness in that way. Each would seem to be the opposite of the vengeful attempt to hold the perpetrator accountable, to connect him permanently to his deed and quash the memory of it by his punishment. Forgiveness, by contrast, would release him from accountability, dissociate him from his crime and purge its memory in another way, so that to 'forgive and forget,' in this sense, is a tautology.[106]

As with mercy, however, there are at least two types of forgiveness. One proceeds from a position of power in which vengeance could be taken, but pursues the satisfying if lesser catharsis of choosing not to.[107] It is a transcendent effort of will of the sort that is credited in the conversion of vengeance into justice, which is nonetheless dependent on its ability to take revenge. Religious absolution has something of this character as it aggrandizes the punitive authority that grants it, while still admonishing the one who is absolved.[108] It forgets the sin, so to speak, on the condition that it *could* remember, so that the sinner will remember himself, and he and others will revere it in perpetual gratitude. So the formal mechanism of forgiveness in liberal punishment may leave the paroled felon in a forgotten and dependent state so that the forgiveness continues to do the shaming work of vengeance on the forgiven. Even those benevolent souls, who seem to relinquish vengeance and 'forgive' the terrorists of September 11 to achieve a state of peace or closure, may still imagine that the injury is *redressed* and memory rectified by that action on the perpetrators, or that a higher power is appeased in the act of forgiving.[109]

There is, however, forgiveness of another sort, one that relinquishes its power position relative to the perpetrator and the injury, and treats horrific memories rather differently. That forgiveness makes 'peace with the past' precisely in recognizing the futility of the vengeful attempt to correct it. As it is less entitled, and less interested in aggrandizing the authority that grants it, it is more concerned to persuade or invite responsibility, and is better suited to a democratic state. It forgives, that is, as an adult might forgive a child so that she will be more likely to take responsibility for her own actions (unlike the forgiven sinner who only knows to avoid such actions). In abandoning its attempt to remake the offender or the offense (like the absolving authority), this forgiveness does not aim to forget the crime (or the sin) and may address the past (the offender and the offense) rather more fully. It is not focused narrowly on such things as a matter of redress, but on what the offender has been and might become – why she could not or would not take responsibility for the injury, or act responsibly toward the persons harmed. This forgiveness aims both to understand and set aside thoughts of the offender to make room for another sort of grief (that which Oedipus could not allow himself and which the mother above might seek). In pursuing such understanding by way of this forgiveness, that is, the injury may be 'faced' but not forgotten. Both its unalterable effect on one's present life and the unlikelihood that punishment will undo it would have to be accepted, even as punishment may be undertaken for other reasons.

Acceptance, then, is the better part of mercy and forgiveness. Or rather, it is better than either as a benchmark for democratic justice. This is not, of course, to assign a *particular* point of view in grief or indignation to a democratic society. It is only to say that acceptance forms a point of intersection among the many religious and secular responses to injury at the hands of another[110] – a least judgmental common denominator, or aggregate position from which democratic blame might be assessed or forgiveness granted. Moreover, where the question, "why do bad things happen to good people?"[111] is still being asked in a post-secular society, and people still raise the question 'how can they be rectified?' one likely secular response might be to accept that bad things happen without explanation or accountability – that they may never be rectified, or (at the least) that this is a matter for the faiths to resolve and not the state.[112] If democratic justice does not privilege this much of acceptance, it must at least include it so that a salutary response to an acquittal or unresolved judgment remains possible. This insures that the rule of law will endure even if it does not satisfy anyone, that the losers will not just be embittered, and that forgiveness will survive as a part of civility. Civility, in this sense, must have a special resonance for persons engaged in democratic citizenship, since it implies a certain reflectiveness about oneself and magnanimity toward others. If this is not to be mere civility (of a lesser, condescending sort) it appreciates the complexity and fallibility of human agency, and adopts a measure of humility in every attempt to judge it.

It is this sensibility that Nussbaum noticed in Seneca in her meditation on equity and punishment, as he saw fit to "come before himself as judge," so as to "cease from retributive anger."[113] Or, as she expands on this: "Seeing the complexity and fallibility of his own acts, seeing those acts as the product of a complex web of highly particular connections among original impulses, the circumstances of life, and the complicated psychological reactions life elicits from the mind, he learns to view others, too, as people whose errors emerge from a complex narrative history."[114] This kind of self-regard or regard for others, Nussbaum reminds us, is not like the pity or compassion that Aristotle endorsed.[115] It is no ordinary sort of empathy, we may add, but something both particular about oneself and generalizable in the perception of others – not *sympathy* for the offender exactly or compassion, but interest in and insight into his character and his crime – precisely what is opaque to "retributive anger" and so profoundly missing in this culture. This acceptance stands in a different relation to the past and to memory than the first sorts of mercy or forgiveness and is consistent with the second. It recalls an injury or a blamable action in all of its complexity, without the distorting anger that is already looking for a remedy. It would *expose* the crime and the offender without the need for shame and humiliation. It is interested in truth, in the sense that is uniquely important to democratic justice.[116]

Truth and Justice (or if prosecutors stopped taking sides)

This interest in truth could not be further from the interest in finality or manufactured truth that we encountered earlier. As a product of democratic discourse or deliberation, it must be more closely related to honesty. It is not less but more exacting as it approaches the past with its eyes open, and without the self-deception of revenge. That interest in truth, no less, is perfectly consistent with the idea of holding offenders accountable for their actions, in the fuller sense of accountability that we associate with democracy here, or with using deadly force to stop them when they are dangerous, or for that matter with protracted (if less condescending) detention. It is what police and prosecutors ought to pursue in the interest of public safety, and which failed entirely in Criner's case. They ought to pursue the truth, that is, whether it condemns or exonerates, and employ necessarily coercive punishments with the *greater* precision of 'equity.' Such targeted punishments that seek to know the offender and the offence fully are not less, but *more* precise and more effective against crime.[117] And if that interest in truth is respectful of the offender or of his account of his actions (a reason to advise him of his rights and not to coerce a confession), it can still expose his crime and reveal what it must about him, without betraying the voluntarism, the interest in persuasion and rights that are also vital to a democratic justice.

This seems to have been the intention of the New Hampshire Attorney General in refusing to speculate publicly about the murders of Half and Susanne Zantop in their Hanover home in 2001 as in some other well-handled cases like it. Evidently he did not want to prejudice or influence the outcome of a trial by sensationalizing the case, preferring instead to pursue the truth with patience and respect for all parties.[118]

One can appreciate something similar in the decision of King County Prosecutor Norm Maleng to accept a plea bargain in Oregon's Green River Killer case. Melang, who had been a conservative supporter of capital punishment, had vigorously sought the death penalty for Gary Ridgway in 7 of 48 murders in which he was implicated. But the majority of the cases, involving runaways and prostitutes, showed little promise of resolution. After consulting the victims' families and reflecting on the death of his own daughter, Melang chose to abandon the course of retribution and to pursue a fuller truth. He would forego seeking the death penalty and seek a life sentence instead, in exchange for Ridgway's confession and cooperation in resolving the unsolved cases. In reaching this decision, Melang reports that he experienced a kind of revelation arising from his experience as a minister. He recalled a passage from 1 Corinthians: "For now we see in a mirror, dimly, but then face to face." On this occasion, it was reported that "[i]nstead of seeing only Ridgway's face . . . he began to see the others involved: the victims their families and the community."[119]

The importance of truth to a democratic community – truth explored publicly, with patience and honesty – cannot be overestimated. It requires an authority that seeks the truth and a diverse and interested audience to the trial and punishment that is altogether different from the vengeful, self-serving kind.

In South Africa, for example, the procedures of "truth and reconciliation" thus often reclaim the past for those involved without attempting to rectify it for such an audience. The villains of apartheid do not tell of their crimes to repudiate or pay for them, exactly. Their pain or suffering is beside the point in this public reckoning. Yet as others hear, test, and respond to their testimony, they lend it a different meaning and legitimate a different truth.[120] A member of the Truth and Reconciliation Commission offers this observation:

The effect that telling their story has on people, and it's very easy to say glibly that this is a cathartic process, but I think of three mothers for example of young men who were killed, who were completely bowed down by not grief, but long exhausted grief. They were witnesses when some of the police officers who were involved were questioned at a public hearing. They saw the police on the mat, so to speak. I still couldn't understand why it seemed to have such a transforming effect on them because in the final day of the hearing they went home singing and smiling and dancing. It was physically visible in the way they stood and moved, conducted themselves. One of them said to me, 'now everybody knows, my neighbors know, that my son was not a criminal, he was a freedom fighter.' For years she had been looked at as the mother of a criminal, and now she could hold her head up in her own circles, and so for her it was that public acknowledgement that was important.[121]

The "long exhausted grief" of these mothers, it would seem, had been made so in part by the impossibility of accepting their sons' deaths on the terms that had been publicly offered – death without respect, recognition, or legitimacy. But here, in this place of democratic truth telling, the terms have shifted as their murderers are held to account in an extraordinary way. If the proceeding seems indifferent to them as it pursues the truth, it is not a vengeful indifference, and does not enlist their pain unduly to force the truth. The deaths of their victims are not redeemed by their pain or humiliation, and yet they are validated in a sense by their testimony, which now plays a special part in the democratic inversion of power.[122]

This truth, then, is a victory for democratic principles over authoritarian rule – over the murder, torture, and forgetting of a people, which it recalls and reclaims for democratic justice – but nothing more.[123] If there is pride in this for the mothers, it is not the vanity that we associate with vengeful acts. This public acknowledgment does not make their wounds heal, precisely. As the horrors of the past are laid bare there may be no cathartic forgetting, no prescribed moral resolution, and no particular ending for their grief. The dead and those who mourn them are simply recognized in a manner that vindicates a democratic justice and the rightful place of their loved ones in it(leaving each to mourn in her own way with anger or forgiveness as she chooses), which is the best a *democracy* can do.

What a different message this conveys for a new democratic community than the guillotine or the killing of Ceauşescu. What better than to cast democratic justice forthrightly against revenge and mendacity? The truth, it seems, is what a democracy owes to its people, and it is what its people, mindful of their own and their state's fallibility, must make central to their justice. We Americans should therefore be careful about what we ask for in justice. It must pursue the truth of an injury and hold people accountable, but it must be aware that its verdicts are imperfect judgments, not absolute truths, and treat people accordingly. Even where there is agreement about who and what to condemn, it must recognize that there may not be agreement as to how or why, and that its punishments are at best a compromise.

Where democratic justice pursues the truth in the awareness of its own fallibility, then, it is no absolute authority and does not embody a uniform morality. It cannot do what theodicy does to resolve evil or make the world meaningful. It cannot restore values or virtue or register a singular disgust. If that justice exposes the truth, as it should, it cannot undo the past or rectify memory or make the rage and grief go away or transform, or dignify it through punishment. Yet if one values democracy in a way that resists such things, one can see that this does not make it 'morally weak,' and that this seemingly faithless secular justice is not a path to hopelessness and despair. Rather it is a condition of liberty that generates its own moral postures of doubt and equity – an interest in truth, and respect for persons, which is remarkably strong and profoundly anti-authoritarian.

Now, when we 'export' democracy or engage in 'state building,' how difficult would it be to comport ourselves with respect to this? How difficult is it to extend this principle in acts of democratic justice that would renounce vengeful punishment? How difficult would it be to oppose instead of celebrate the rush to execute Saddam Hussein after a single appeal,[124] or to try Osama properly if we could, or extend rights to enemy combatants? What is more democratic, in this sense, than to join the world in banning capital punishment? Or to advance the rule of law in this spirit, in the Middle East, Northern Ireland, Rwanda, Afghanistan, Sudan, or the Balkans? How difficult is it to keep Hess in Spandau, or Manson at Pelican Bay, as living testaments to the truth of their crimes and in homage to a better justice? If we acknowledge that vengeance will not go away, what better reason to resist it than for the sake of democracy – since we have made it abundantly clear that this is the choice? This, it would seem, is the difference between extending an empire 'in the name of democracy,' and advancing what is worth having in democracy. A democracy, that is, which affirms the humility and procedural caution of its authority by its very opposition to vengeance.

Notes

Chapter 1. Liberalism and the Anger of Punishment: The Motivation to Vengeance and Myths of Justice Reconsidered

1 These are very different thinkers observing something similar. See Michael Sandel, *Liberalism and the Limits of Justice* (Cambridge, 1982); Stanley Brubaker, "Can Liberals Punish?", *American Political Science Review*, 82 (September 1988); Jürgen Habermas, *Legitimation Crisis* (Boston, 1973); Alasdair MacIntyre, *After Virtue: A Study in Moral Theory* (South Bend, 1984), 249, 251. MacIntyre argues that we have lost our allegiance to a tradition of virtue that includes a justice of desert.

2 See CNN.com: The Execution of Timothy McVeigh, and "death draws a crowd" at http://www.cnn.com/SPECIALS/2001/okc/

3 In Bonnie Honig's reading of Rawls on punishment, the presumptive rationality of a "justice as fairness" relegates criminality to "bad character" such that it becomes "extrasystemic" in such a way: *Political Theory and the Displacement of Politics* (Ithaca, 1993), Chapter 5.

4 He adds to these "envy, jealousy, mistrust." Friedrich Nietzsche, *On the Genealogy of Morals and Ecce Homo* (New York: 1969). He calls these "reactive feelings," 75, and "reactive affects," 74. For him they are made general in the revenge of *ressentiment*, which is like and yet different from the phenomenon we are addressing, as we shall see below.

5 William Connolly, *Why I Am Not a Secularist* (Minneapolis, 1999). Connolly is concerned that a certain "visceral register of subjectivity and intersubjectivity" has been barred from secular discourse and engages the term to refer to something broader than vengeance. Yet he is well aware of the dangers at that end of the register when he refers to the "visceral attachments to a vindictive nation," which are exploited by the political right (William Bennett, and others), 3, 131.

6 Friedrich Nietzsche, *Thus Spoke Zarathustra*, Second Part, *The Portable Nietzsche* (New York, 1974), 251.

7 Albert Camus, *Reflections on the Guillotine* (Michigan City, 1959), 17.

8 Renato Rosaldo, *Culture & Truth: The Remaking of Social Analysis* (Boston, 1989), 6, (quoting his *Knowledge and Passion*, 33).

9   Rosaldo, 3. (I am aware that this is not my story to tell, and can only hope to do it justice in the retelling.)

10 Rosaldo, 9.

11 In other commentary, Robert N. Bellah et al., *Habits of the Heart: Individualism and Commitment in American Life* (Berkeley, 1985), and Christopher Lasch, *Haven in a Heartless World: The Family Beseiged* (New York, 1977). The sense of loss or emptiness in American culture discussed here misses this.

12 The moderator of the debate, Bernard Shaw, had asked: "Governor, if Kitty Dukakis were raped and murdered would you favor an irrevocable death penalty for the killer?" Dukakis replied: "No, I don't Bernard, and I think you know I have opposed the death penalty all my life. I don't see any evidence that it is a deterrent, and I think there are better, more effective ways to deal with violent crime. We've done so in my own state and it's one of the reasons why we have had the biggest drop in violent crime of any industrial state in America. . . ." Thomas Dumm's transcription of the presidential debate at UCLA, October 13, 1988 from videotape at the Vanderbilt Television News Archive, Vanderbilt University, Nashville, Tennessee, in *United States* (Ithaca, 1994), 83–84.

13 Bill Clinton, by contrast, was able to withstand the Republican challenges based on "family values" for a time by grasping this. Whatever faults he may have, one suspects he would sorely grieve the loss of his wife, which is the pertinent family affect.

14 The point is not that such sentiments should be more central to law and justice, only that they have been bracketed or ignored where they cannot be.

15 This helps to explain the Republican Party's shift from its interest in small government to its interest in a powerful, punitive one.

16 Colin Harrison, *Bodies Electric* (New York, 1993), 14. One can trace the theme in popular culture at least to the 1974 Charles Bronson film "Death Wish" and its sequels. There is undeniably an element of racial backlash or 'white revenge' in this; it is something beyond that too.

17 Thomas Hobbes, *Leviathan* (New York, 1958), Chapter 13, 107. John Locke, *The Second Treatise of Government* (Indianapolis, 1952), [Ch. II] 10. Mill offers: "In savage life there is little or no law, or administration of justice . . . everyone trusts in his own strength or cunning, and where that fails, he is without resource." *Essays on Politics and Culture* (New York, 1962), 46.

18 Rosaldo, 9.

19 The opposition to lynching, especially during Reconstruction, was weakened by other vengeful, racist interests. See Randall Kennedy, *Race, Crime and the Law* (New York, 1997), 42–45.

20 Gouverneur Morris to John Penn, 20 May 1774. American Archives, 4th ser., 1:342–43 *The Founders' Constitution*, Volume 1, Chapter 15, Document 8, The University of Chicago Press. American Archives. M. St. Clair Clarke and Peter Force, eds. 4th ser., 6 vols. Washington, DC, 1837–46. 5th ser., 3 vols. Washington, DC, 1848–53.

21 Hobbes, *Leviathan*, 70.

22 Says Locke: "And thus in the state of nature one man comes by a power over another; but yet no absolute or arbitrary power to use a criminal, when he has got him in his hands, according to the passionate heats or boundless

extravagance of his own will; but only to retribute to him, so far as calm reason and conscience dictate, what is proportionate to his transgression, which is so much as may serve reparation and restraint..." [Ch. II] 6.

23 Locke, [Ch. II] 9.

24 See for example, Judith N. Shklar, *Legalism: Law, Morals and Political Trials* (Cambridge, 1986).

25 John Locke, Ch. II; Immanuel Kant, *The Metaphysical Elements of Justice*, Part I (Indianapolis, 1965), 99–100; G. W. F. Hegel, *Hegel's Philosophy of Right* (London, 1975), 102, 73; Emile Durkheim, *The Division of Labor in Society* (New York, 1984), 58, respectively.

26 Aeschylus, *The Oresteia*, trans. Robert Fagles (New York, 1984), *The Eumenides*. The translation lends itself to this reading of the myth.

27 This recalls Oliver Wendell Holmes' observation that retribution is "only vengeance in disguise." See Holmes, *The Common Law* (Boston, 1923).

28 See for example, V. G. Kiernan, *The Duel in European History: Honor and the Reign of Aristocracy* (Oxford, 1989). Systems of honor still active today are painfully at odds with liberal conceptions of justice: "honor killing" in the Mafia here and abroad and in conflicts in the Balkans.

29 John Stuart Mill, *On Liberty*, in *Utilitarianism, On Liberty, and Considerations on Representative Government* (London, 1976), 64. I am indebted to J. D. Connor on this point.

30 See the discussion of emotion and feeling in John Stuart Mill, *Autobiography* (Boston, 1969).

31 This is not to suggest that Mill should do otherwise. He does not entertain the problem of the vigilante or vengeful individual directly in *On Liberty*, and is concerned with other matters. There is however something of a "private sphere" being constructed here and if grief and revenge were considered to be private matters, there may be a gendered aspect to this too.

32 A consideration of vengeance and the American Revolution will be taken up briefly in Chapter 4.

33 Judith N. Shklar, *The Faces of Injustice* (New Haven, 1990), 93; 5; 54–55; 12 respectively. My emphasis.

34 Judith N. Shklar, remarks at the Spring 1990 *New England Political Science Association* Panel: Ethics, Values and Moral Decisions in Politics: regarding the author's paper, *Revenge and Consent: The Death Penalty and Lockean Principles of Democracy*: "... it is important the paradox that Aladjem has brought out: that democratic consent does not in itself mute revenge, may well keep it alive and well in the very effort to contain it with institutions of procedural justice, and is yet committed to a rights theory that renders the death penalty questionable to say the least."

35 Thomas Hobbes, *Leviathan* (New York, 1958), Chapter 13, 107.

36 Hobbes, *Leviathan*, Chapter 6, 56.

37 Hobbes, *Man and Citizen, On Man (De Homine)*, trans. Charles T. Wood, T. S. K. Scott-Craig and Bernard Gert (New York, 1972), Ch. XII, 57.

38 Hobbes, *Man and Citizen, The Citizen (De Cive)*. Thomas Hobbes, Ch. III, 142.

39 Hobbes, *Man and Citizen*, Ch. III, 142.

40 Hobbes, *Leviathan*, Chapter 18, 152, my emphasis.

41 John Locke, [Ch. II] 6.

42 John Locke, [Ch. II] 7.

43 Adam Smith, *The Theory of Moral Sentiments* (Indianapolis 1982) [II .ii 3.3], 86.

44 Cass R. Sunstein, *Legal Reasoning and Political Conflict* (Oxford, 1996), 8–9, cites Justice Stephen Breyer's account of the United States Sentencing Commission's attempt to resolve conflicting retributive and utilitarian pressures. The commission abandoned "high theory" according to Sunstein, and "it decided to base its Guidelines primarily upon typical, or average, actual past practice." Yet relying on past practice begs the question by returning to former resolutions of the same dispute and allows both principles to find some accommodation.

45 It is suggested below that this claim to punish 'only enough' is disingenuous. The utilitarian may think that it is best to limit the amount of pain imposed, and would denounce the vengeful inclination to increase it unduly. Yet it is impossible to discern how much is minimally enough. This is because even a statistically determined "deterrent effect" is only an approximation – the effects of pain being idiosyncratic and the 'deviation' enormous. There is no means either to determine how much that which deters some people may encourage others (sadists and masochists, or gang members seeking to impress), or how many are indifferent to it when they commit crimes. Moreover, sentences given by judges and assigned by legislatures are often justified on such crude utilitarian grounds, but are seldom set on the basis of data on deterrence even when it is available. Indeed the utilitarian cannot account for the degree to which the very presumption that such a measurement can be undertaken permits excesses in punishment under the guise of precision. Yet even if the proper utilitarian benchmarks for restraint could be found, they would not affect the popular utilitarian sentiment that interests us here – one which says: 'We hope the punishment deters, but since our society should not have to assume the risk of going easy on crime, let's err on the side of caution and punish *more*.' (See Note 193 below.)

46 Emile Durkheim, *The Division of Labor in Society* (New York, 1984), 47, 31. Hegel, 74; Kant, 144, respectively.

47 John Howard Yoder, "Noah's Covenant, the New Testament, and Christian Social Order," in Hugo Adam Bedau, *The Death Penalty in America: Current Controversies* (New York, 1997), connects religious sensibilities of retribution to a belief in the "deep symmetry of things." 430.

48 It is a mistake to imagine that utilitarianism and retributivism can be neatly aligned with a division between secular and religious interests.

49 Both theories purport to measure the initial pain suffered and the pain of the response. Yet a 'quantum of suffering' is immediately invested with other meaning (suffering being a qualitative matter as we shall see) to the degree that it is not just a quantum anymore.

50 Stanley Benn, "Punishment," in Jeffrie G. Murphy, 2nd ed. (Belmont, 1985), [reprinted from the *Encyclopedia of Philosophy*, 1967, 29–35], 11.

51 Murphy, 2nd ed., 6.

52 We shall see how the apparent measurability, seeming equivalence, and proportionality of punishments (both retributive and utilitarian) mask other motives in Chapter 3.

53 John Stuart Mill, *Utilitarianism* (1861) (New York, 1989), 10, claims the first use of the term by way of extending Bentham's happiness principle.

54 Mill, *Utilitarianism*, 64, my emphasis. The pause to reflect, as we notice elsewhere, may counteract a more impulsive revenge, but not that which is savored, like a 'dish best served cold.'

55 Mill, *Utilitarianism*, 63.

56 Mill, *Utilitarianism*, 63, 65.

57 Mill, *Utilitarianism*, 67.

58 Tom Sorell, *Moral Theory and Capital Punishment* (New York, 1987) for one, argues that Mill is not free of the taint of retributivism. 80–84.

59 Hobbes, *Leviathan*, Chapter VI, 56.

60 Mill (in Sorell, 87), *Parliamentary Debates* (Hansard), third series, 21 April 1868. Reprinted in Singer, P., ed., *Applied Ethics* (Oxford, 1986), 97–104.

61 This is the utilitarian inclination to opt for less pain wherever possible that is often questioned.

62 Mill (in Sorell, 89), *Parliamentary Debates*, 101.

63 The problem of such measurement is concealed where the punishment is death, since no one knows "how much" that is.

64 We will meet the "revenge utilitarians" of this persuasion shortly. There are all sorts of ways in which the inclination to punish more and more harshly might arguably serve a general interest.

65 This is intrinsic to the presumption of measurability in the utilitarian treatment of pain and not only a consequence of its improper application.

66 Hegel, 101, 71.

67 Hegel, 100, 70–71.

68 Hegel, 101, 72.

69 Hegel, 102, 73.

70 One might say that it is only ever just *theoretically* possible to banish revenge from actual punishment in Hegel's account. While the theory articulates what retributive punishment could or should be, it is taken here (with dangerous implications) as an expression of what it *is*.

71 Those who punish (the state) may fool themselves or others into thinking that they only obey a higher calling. One wonders whether this "respect" for the offender results in respectful punishment, or becomes a pretext, once 'respects have been paid,' for all sorts of mistreatment.

72 George Sher, *Desert* (Princeton, 1987), ix, 10. It is interesting how the "less-than-perfect consensus" achieves greater status in this "canvassing."

73 Ernest van den Haag, "The Death Penalty Once More," in Bedeau, 451, 445–446, respectively. The circularity of the argument is self-evident.

74 Hegel, 103, 73.

75 If retributive and utilitarian suppositions were really so rational as they claim to be, there would be no facile assumption about the way that inducing pain serves reason for the one, or uses fright to achieve rational aims for the other. Rather, finding the best *pedagogy* to produce accountability would be paramount for the utilitarian, and the right *compensation* to satisfy reason for the retributivist. Neither would have any interest in 'defending' the pain of punishment as such.

76 Nietzsche, *Genealogy*, 77, 66, respectively.

77 Trying to find moral justifications for punishment as the purposive infliction of pain is like trying to justify eating meat. There is nothing 'moral' about it, but a very great 'appetite' for wanting to make it seem moral. Of course, there is more to punishment than this.

78   Sher, 71, cites G. E. Moore's classic attempt at a synthesis, or rather a utilitarian justification of the retributive infliction of pain: "If pain is added to an evil state of either of our first two classes (that is, love of evil or ugliness and hatred of what is good and beautiful), the whole thus formed is *always* better, *as a whole*, than if no pain had been there. . . . It is in this way that the theory of vindictive punishment may be vindicated." *Principia Ethica* (Cambridge, 1962), 214. Attempts at a synthesis are foreshadowed by Kant and Hegel's efforts to allow for the coexistence of the two principles. Marc Tunick, *Punishment: Theory and Practice* (Berkeley, 1992), 94–97; 163–164. Rawls does this too as Danielle Allen characterizes the effort in "Democratic Dis-ease: Of Anger and the Troubling Nature of Punishment," in *The Passions of Law*, ed. Susan A. Bandes (New York, 2001). Following H. L. A. Hart's *Punishment and Responsibility* (Oxford, 1968), practical compromise occurs in criminal sentencing all the time. See Sunstein (note 44 above).

79   Rothman and Garland each offer accounts of the historical cycles of reform and reaction in American attitudes toward punishment. David Garland, *The Culture of Control: Crime and Social Order in Contemporary America* (Chicago, 2001); David J. Rothman, *The Discovery of the Asylum: Social Order and Disorder in the New Republic* (Boston, 1971). Also see James Q. Whitman, *Harsh Justice: Criminal Punishment and the Widening Divide Between America and Europe* (New York, 2003).

80   Margaret Jane Radin, "Cruel Punishment and Respect for Persons: Super Due Process for Death", in Jeffrey G. Murphy, *Punishment and Rehabilitation*, 2nd ed. (Belmont, 1985), 156.

81   Margaret Jane Radin, 156.

82   Margaret Jane Radin, 156, quoting Ernest van den Haag, *Punishing Criminals* (1975), 12–13, counts the latter among the revenge-utilitarians.

83   Stanley C. Brubaker, "Can Liberals Punish?" *American Political Science Review: Journal of the American Political Science Association* 82 (September 1988): 824. MacIntyre (1984) has made similar arguments if not in regard to punishment as such.

84   Brubaker, 825.

85   See Walter Berns, "The Morality of Anger," in Bedau, and the discussion in Tunick (1992) 88–89. Tunick, van den Haag, and Brubaker each pick up the theme in different ways. In Chapter IV we will encounter others who do this (see Bandes) and who lament the absence of "disgust" within expressions of legal punishment.

86   This recalls the "unselfconscious" sorts of moral assertion that conservatives have long found comforting. See Michael Oakeshott, *Experience and Its Modes* (Cambridge, 1933), as carried out in his *Rationalism in Politics* (New York, 1962).

87   Such is the sense of moral superiority, middle-class entitlement, and moral indignation that is expressed in 'road rage,' on talk radio, and TV shows on crime. It is and often ventured as an appeal to victims of violent crime by a superior class or community of the righteous: "We the community, take your loss with the utmost seriousness. We know that you are filled with rage and pain. We know that you may cry for vengeance, may yearn to strangle the murderer with your bare hands. You are right to feel that way. But it is not for you to wreak retribution. As a decent and just society we will do it. Fairly. After due process. In a court of law." Jeff Jacoby, "The unjust logic of sparing murderers," *Boston*

Globe, August 10, 1998. A-15. (Jacoby writes in sympathy for David Gelernter, self-avowed victim.)

88 Retributive punishment obtains legitimacy in a scheme of distributive 'fairness,' Herbert Morris suggests, when punishment negates the "unfair advantage" that a criminal obtains in a distribution of social benefits. But then, punitive adjustments affecting that relative advantage also affect the moral worth of persons and their position in the social hierarchy. In older retributivism a payoff may have come in an afterlife or by attaining virtue; here it is a matter of status adjustment. See Herbert Morris, "Persons and Punishment," in Murphy, 2nd Edition, 26.

89 This refers as well to the affect 'independent of its former content' that we spoke of earlier.

90 That is why the moment of reflection before punishing in which reason should mitigate revenge in the utilitarian logic of Mill is so easily replaced by a pause in which public anger and frustration mount, as when people await a verdict in a capital case.

91 See "Judge Wolf's message to Sampson" by Mark L. Wolf, U.S. District Court Judge, *Boston Globe*, February 7, 2004, A-15 (upon sentencing Gary Lee Sampson to death): "As the Oxford Companion to the Law explains: 'Retribution is one of the purposes of punishment, satisfying the instinct of retaliation and revenge, which naturally arises in a victim, but also to a considerable extent in society generally. It may be controlled and regularized vengeance exacted by society....' (I)n our nation there is another morality that governs judges. It is sometimes called the 'morality of consent.' We live by consent in a democracy...The people, through the jury, have decided that death is the proper penalty in your case...."

92 One refers to a military chain of command, the other to the inviolable rules of a game, the third to autocratic authority.

93 *Miranda v. Arizona*, 384 U.S. 436 (1966).

94 See Martin Kurzweil's Senior Thesis: "The Third Table: The Theoretical Implications and Practical Effects of Victims' Rights in the Death Penalty Process" on the use of victim impact statement in New Jersey for example. Harvard Archives. 2002.

95 Dan M. Kahan makes the case for this use of shame in "What Do Alternative Sanctions Mean?" *The University of Chicago Law Review* 63 (1996). See George Will's column "The Sting of Shame," *The Washington Post*, February 1, 1996, which picks up on Kahan's argument and recalls the revival of chain gangs and the publication of offender's photographs as means of public humiliation.

96 *Booth v. Maryland*, 482 U.S. 496, 508 (1987) (quoting *Gardner v. Florida*, 430 U.S. 349, 358 [1977]).

97 *Payne v. Tennessee*, 498 U.S. 1076 (1991) .

98 *Furman v. Georgia*, 408 U.S. 238, 308 (1972) (Stewart, J., concurring).

99 Quoting *Williams v. New York*, 337 U.S. 241, 248 (1949).

100 *Gregg v. Georgia*, 428 U.S. 153, 183 (1976).

101 *Id.* at 184 (emphasis added).

102 *Trop v. Dulles*, 356 U.S. 86, 101 (1958).

103 The increasing use of lawsuits in matters of domestic abuse and violent crime attests to this and has likely been spurred by Fred Goldman's successful suit against O. J. Simpson.

104 Such efforts may be traced to Title III of the Omnibus Crime Control Act of 1968 (Public Law 90–351, June 19, 1968, 82 Stat. 197, 42 U.S.C. § 3711). "Three strikes" laws of the sort introduced in California with Proposition 184 (1994) were upheld in March 2003, in *Ewing v. California*, 538 U.S. 11 (2003), and *Lockyer v. Andrade*, 538 U.S. 63 (2003). See also the Comprehensive Crime Control Act of 1984. The War on Drugs is explored on FRONTLINE (PBS 1999): "Snitch, how informants have become a key part of prosecutorial strategy in the war on drugs," http://www.pbs.org/wgbh/pages/frontline/shows/snitch/.

105 The truth-in-sentencing (TIS) movement has generally advocated for harsher sentences, the elimination of parole, and judicial discretion in sentencing. "Truth" in this context appears to mean conformity to harsh standards, not the propriety or equity of those standards.

106 This is problematic in the case of criminal sentencing and presents further difficulties in civil judgments where an amount of damages might be assessed with the aid of actuarial or other calculations of harm (see Chapter 2). When there is a disfiguring injury or a death in question, jurors often agree that there can be no true assessment, no real compensation, which is why American judgments can be enormous to register protest.

107 The deterrent calculus in sentencing is never just that. This is underscored by the fact that very little that is called "utilitarian" in the realm of punishment is ever content to leave crimes unpunished, that is, do nothing to a criminal who is guilty even if it is manifestly clear that punishment will neither prevent him nor deter others from such acts. The old criticism that utilitarianism might in principle punish the innocent (which can be rebutted by adjusting the meaning of utility), may conceal a deeper problem: it should not punish the guilty if it cannot demonstrate the efficacy of it, which is of course intolerable to the underlying vengeful prejudices we are considering.

108 Max Horkheimer and Theodor Adorno, *Dialectic of Enlightenment* (New York, 1972), 55.

109 Horkheimer and Adorno, 55, FN 12.

110 Horkheimer and Adorno, 55, FN 12.

111 This is purposive *vengeful* action (and recalls Habermas' notion of "purposive-rational action" set out in response to Adorno and Horkheimer). The point is that vengeance and reason are not necessarily opposed. The rational "patience" with which Odysseus is credited by the latter is not only inclined toward rational law where revenge is patient too, or again "a dish best served cold."

112 Horkheimer and Adorno, 55.

113 Horkheimer and Adorno, 55, FN 12, do note that Odysseus "carries out the acts of revenge later, and all the more thoroughly," but their concern here is his "adjournment of action."

114 Homer, *The Odyssey* (New York, 1963), 156.

115 Homer, 159, 161.

116 Aeschylus, *The Oresteia*, trans. Robert Fagles (New York, 1984), 243, lines 261–264.

117 Aeschylus, 254, lines 514–516; 539–541.

118 Aeschylus, 250, lines 445; 446. The significance of gender in this is another story.

119 Aeschylus, 255, lines 559, 575. The image of Justice with her scales finds its corollary here too.

120 Aeschylus, Robert Fagles and W. B. Stanford in the introduction, "The Serpent and the Eagle." 23.

121 René Girard, *Violence and the Sacred* (Baltimore, 1989), 13, 14, 15, 27.

122 Girard, 306–307, 18.

123 Girard, 17, 21.

124 Girard, 7 (my emphasis), 4 respectively.

125 Girard, 2, 4, 7, 17, 22, 36, 39.

126 See related point in Girard, 15–16, and 21.

127 Girard, 22, 27.

128 Christopher Boehm, *Blood Revenge: The Anthropology of Feuding in Montenegro and other Tribal Societies* (Lawrence, 1984), 192.

129 V. G. Kiernan, citing L. T. Hobhouse, *Morals in Evolution* (London, 1915), says, "In simple communities the 'set fight' or 'duel' . . . generally takes place 'under prescribed conditions': it could be deadly, but might take a quite mild form. 'The public or the chief may look on, and act as judges.'" *The Duel in European History: Honour and the Reign of Aristocracy* (Oxford, 1989), 20.

130 Edward Ayers, *Vengeance and Justice: Crime and Punishment in the 1 9th-Century American South* (New York, 1984), 20.

131 Ayers, 13, 19.

132 Ayers aptly describes the Southern antipathy to the rule of law at the time, 18, but also of republican ideals and the inroads of law elsewhere.

133 Ayers, 16.

134 Ayers, 28–31.

135 Max Weber, "The Social Psychology of the World Religions," in *From Max Weber: Essays in Sociology* (New York, 1970), 274–275.

136 Weber, 275.

137 Weber, 273, 275, 276.

138 The mixed metaphor invoking the essentials food, water, fire as instrumental in the reversal of kindness, guilt, revenge, reflects that extraordinary moral alchemy.

139 See Lewis Hyde, *The Gift: Imagination and the Erotic Life of Property* (New York, 1983), concerning the related moral exchanges in gift economies.

140 Sigmund Freud, *Civilization and Its Discontents* (New York, 1962), 78–79.

141 Freud, 79, 76.

142 Freud has more to say about this, as we shall see in Chapter 3.

143 Nietzsche, *Genealogy*, 59, 58

144 Nietzsche, *Genealogy*, 57, 60.

145 Nietzsche, *Genealogy*, 60–62.

146 Nietzsche, *Genealogy*, 63

147 Nietzsche, *Genealogy*, 64.

148 Nietzsche, *Genealogy*, 65.

149 Nietzsche, *Genealogy*, 75.

150 Nietzsche, *Genealogy*, 74, This, as opposed to a "bad conscience" that internalizes cruelty as guilt. 75.

151 Nietzsche, *Genealogy*, 42.

152 Nietzsche, *Genealogy*, refers to the "enthusiastic impulsiveness in anger, love, reverence, gratitude, and revenge by which noble souls have at all times recognized one another." Insofar as they have *ressentiment*, it is discharged in the "immediate reaction," *forgets* abruptly, and does not "poison." 39. See also "The Wanderer and his Shadow" (1880), 179–182.

153 Punishment, he maintains, is generally in some measure a "compromise with revenge" (Nietzsche, *Genealogy*, 81), even as revenge remains among the "reactive" feelings that comprise *ressentiment* and are less worthy than the purer joys in punishment.

154 Nietzsche, *Genealogy*, 74.

155 Nietzsche, *Genealogy*, he calls this "spiritual revenge," 34, and "imaginary revenge," 36.

156 Nietzsche, *Genealogy*, "... the *last* sphere to be conquered by the spirit of justice is the sphere of the reactive feelings," 74, and "Wherever justice is practiced and maintained one sees a stronger power seeking a means of putting an end to the senseless raging of *ressentiment*.... The most decisive act, however, that the supreme power performs and accomplishes against the predominance of grudges and rancor... is the institution of law...." 75.

157 Nietzsche, *Genealogy*, 64–65. Walter Kaufmann translates: "of doing evil for the pleasure of doing it."

158 Nietzsche, *Genealogy*, 66.

159 Nietzsche, *Genealogy*, 64.

160 Nietzsche, *Genealogy*, 70. One can appreciate the idea of a "cruel" punishment without acrimony (a pleasure in cruelty detached from anger) that is purely instrumental (like retributive and utilitarian claims of that kind). Yet it is hard to imagine more ordinary cruelty (the infliction of pain and humiliation) without it.

161 Nietzsche, *Genealogy*, 66. My emphasis.

162 Nietzsche, *Genealogy*, 65.

163 Nietzsche, *Genealogy*, 72–73. Here he says that the creditor enjoys the "consciousness of power" that is the "noblest luxury" and creditor and noble are momentarily seen as one. We will notice the connection between vengeance and mercy in Chapter 4 in a way that is related.

164 Nietzsche, *Genealogy*, 65

165 He distinguishes the abstract, unexpressed, or "imaginary revenge" of the slave revolt from the "triumphant affirmation" of noble morality, suggesting that a more direct expressed revenge would be closer to the latter. Nietzsche, *Genealogy*, 36.

166 Nietzsche concedes a link between a better, "nobler" sort of vengeance, honor, and law elsewhere. Here, he says, "punishment is revenge." See "The Wanderer and his Shadow" (1880), *Genealogy*, 179–182. He wants to dignify 'the nobles' as a paradigm free of the vengeance of *ressentiment*, not to claim that there are never any vengeful nobles. But that paradigm itself is in question here.

167 Nietzsche is compelling in making the distinction between those noble impulses, and *ressentiment* and revenge. Yet on a different account (or genealogy), that need for rectification underlies both impulses, as we shall see with Oedipus in Chapter 3.

168 Nietzsche, *Genealogy*, 75, clearly identifies fairness with a better justice. Those today who advocate advancement based on "merit," as opposed to affirmative

action, might thus claim to be on the side of this noble fairness, but it is as much a vehicle of *their* revenge.

169 Nietzsche's idea of the "imaginary" revenge of the slaves, *Genealogy*, 36, is suggestively like and yet different from the "imagined" revenge of the Americans that will concern us later. See Note 79, Chapter 2.

170 Nietzsche, *Genealogy*, 96.

171 Nietzsche, *Genealogy*, 57, 60.

172 Nietzsche, *Genealogy*, 80. He puts these things side by side in the list of elements that comprise and make punishment "indefinable," but does not make the connection quite as we do here.

173 Nietzsche, *Genealogy*, 58, 60; 65, 61.

174 Frances Yates, *The Art of Memory* (Chicago, 1966), 10, referring to *Ad Herrenium* (on the uses of memory, unknown authorship; circa 86–82 B.C.). One might explore the relationship between the memory arts and punishments (theatrical displays, see Chapter 3) in the way that Yates has investigated their connection to the plastic arts.

175 Nietzsche, *Genealogy*, 80. He lists these among the many 'accidental' uses to which punishment is put.

176 Nietzsche does suggest the possibility that vengeance may be present in punishment in another way – "Punishment as a compromise with revenge in its natural state when the latter is still maintained and claimed as a privilege by powerful clans." *Genealogy*, 81.

177 The creditor is implicated in this, one might argue, the moment he seeks "recompense." Nietzsche, *Genealogy*, 64, 65. Recompense as a part of punishment is mentioned on page 80.

178 The question of vengeance and self-deception will be taken up in Chapter 3 and the idea that such punishment is an attainment of pity, or again, "cruel" on the way to being "exalted."

179 Nietzsche, *Genealogy*, 66.

180 Nietzsche, *Genealogy*, 77. He offers eleven purposes of punishment including the "making of a memory," but he does not mean it in this sense we do here. 84–85.

181 Nietzsche, *Genealogy*, 83–85.

182 The matter of the vengeful assertion beyond doubt and the importance of doubt in a democracy will be taken up in Chapter 4.

183 Vestiges of this remain where the legal standing of the victim, the witness, or the accuser has the character of the avenger standing over the vanquished. This may occur in the rituals of arrest, arraignment, in the muted presence of the accused in court, and even in the surveillance of prisons. Much of what is justified on grounds of safety (pushing the offender down by the head into a squad car, chokeholds, kicking Rodney King) also has this character.

184 We will take up questions of shame and pity in Chapter 3.

185 George Ryley Scott, *The History of Corporal Punishment* (London, 1959), 37–39.

186 Kant, 101.

187 Aeschylus, *The Oresteia: Agamemnon*, 107.

188 Economy, here as above, being merely the management of things that puts them to use. The phrase reflects the attempt to "balance the scales" and all of the language associated with the repayment of a debt in vengeance. The economy in question is compensation after the fact for something "past due,"

or "long overdue" – to redress, retribute, restore, retaliate, repay – all entertain the questionable proposition in which a debt to memory is repaid in kind, but never exactly. While the economic analogy is apt, and talk about vengeance is full of it, see William Ian Miller, *An Eye for an Eye* (New York, 2005). Yet one should not imagine that it achieves equilibrium any more readily other competitive economies or markets.

189   It seems significant that Nietzsche, who knew the Greeks so well, treats the failure to pay debts and the breaking of promises as the paradigmatic crime, but not the patricide, matricide, or the murder of loved ones that so occupied them, and which involve a very different burden upon memory. The terms of the "debt" in that case shift considerably.

190   For Nietzsche *ressentiment* is abstract vengeance that effects justice in a different sense. *Genealogy*, 36.

191   The "rationality" of rectification operates on its own terms and may confound other rational assessments. Hence, 'precision' in torture or establishing terms of imprisonment only *appears* to be based in a utilitarian or retributive calculus.

192   To 'get the better' is an apt expression for this. I do not mean that this exchange of memories is really just another amoral economy. Getting the better of *this* exchange would confer a certain virtue; it aspires to be 'moral.' Truly commensurate punishment would loose that vindicating edge.

193   See Note 45. Bentham first offers (XIII Rule 5), that the punishment "*ought in no case be more than what is necessary. . . .*" But (XVI Rule 6) "because the profit of an offence is commonly more certain than the punishment . . ." the latter may receive a "proportionable addition in point of *magnitude*" and (XXII Rule 10), " . . . *stretch a little beyond that quantity which would strictly be necessary.*" This reasoning conceals the problem that the magic point at which the punishment deters *only enough* (without adding the burden of its harm unnecessarily to society) is also the point at which its disadvantage must outweigh and *exceed* the advantage – an invitation to excess. Jeremy Bentham, *An Introduction to the Principles of Morals and Legislation* (1823), in Jeffrey G. Murphy, *Punishment and Rehabilitation*, 3rd ed., 31–33.

194   To venture the striking counter-memory may on some level be more important than to find the truth. One thinks of the public anger and eagerness to vilify one William Bennett in the Carol Stuart murder case in Boston in 1989 and the public shock (or perhaps disappointment) at the discovery that her husband was in fact the murderer.

195   This is analogous to the work of repression as Freud described it, although the process of rectification is more deliberate and conscious. Like remediation and revisionism more broadly, rectification is more overtly self-serving.

196   Another way of expressing this is to say that if "justification" depends upon truth, objectivity, *self*-justification often compromises it. This is a problem especially as courts of justice pursue the truth by inviting the testimony of interested parties. Truth and evidence cedes to opinion, impartiality to partiality, a need to get it right, to the impulse to make it right.

197   Susan Jacoby, *Wild Justice: The Evolution of Revenge* (New York, 1983), 1.

198   Pietro Mirangieu and Graeme Newman, *Vengeance: The Fight Against Injustice* (Tatowa, 1987), 159.

199   This need for forgetting in vengeance complicates Nietzsche's idea that the noble man is less vengeful because he does not take "misdeeds seriously for

very long." *Genealogy*, 39. Freud's notion of the 'compulsion to repeat' proves to be conceptually similar to the "obsession" referred to here, though the idea of quieter memory finds no exact parallel in his conception of repression.

200 Christian justice displaces vengeance but keeps it in sight, and thus appropriates its capacity for displacement. In that justice, the crime is effaced by a different, if related, "overcoming."

201 Filming or televising the execution is not permitted (the courts have repeatedly said no to this), see *KQED, Inc. v. Vasquez*, No. C90-1383 RHS, 1995 WL 489485 (N.D. Cal. Aug. 1, 1991). See "*Reel Death*: Disturbing Visions and the 'Illegality' of Televised Executions," by Zoe Tananbaum. Senior thesis, Harvard Archives. 2002.

202 There appears to be nothing other than convention affecting the content of these releases. Inquiries at Associated Press reveal that they are generally brief, 100–200 words, but not governed by formal rules or guidelines – even those in the AP "rule book."

203 Associated Press, "Murderer executed in Arizona," *Boston Globe* April 7, 1992, 15. The announcement continues: "As he waited, Harding gestured as if to urge the executioner to get started. At least twice, once while in the throes of death and with his wrists and forearms in straps, Harding extended his middle finger. Among the witnesses was Attorney General Grant Woods. Harding was sentenced to die for the murders of businessman Robert Wise and Martin Concannon of Tucson, who were robbed, hogtied, beaten and shot in a Tucson hotel in 1980. He also was convicted of killing a man in similar fashion a day earlier in Phoenix motel and was linked to at least three other slayings, one in Arkansas and two in California. It was the first execution in Arizona since 1963, when Manuel Silvas died in the gas chamber for fatally shooting his estranged pregnant girlfriend. Harding became the 168th person put to death since the Supreme Court allowed the states to resume the use of capital punishment in 1976. Late Sunday, the state board of Pardons and Paroles refused to recommend Gov. Fife Symington grant Harding a reprieve or commute his sentence to life in prison."

204 It is common for such death announcements to highlight the idiosyncratic or "obscene" gesture of the person being executed in a way that affirms the practice even as it gives expression to his or her resistance. One AP release is titled: "Killer seen to yell 'I'm human' as he's executed." *Boston Globe*, June 16, 1994, 24. Another, "Child Murderer Davis is Sentenced to Death," reports that Davis, "in a black shirt, smirked as the jury was polled . . . and did not repeat the obscene gesture he made in view of television cameras when he was convicted." [*sic*] Associated Press, *The Harvard Crimson*, August 6, 1996.

205 Says Nietzsche, "Ah, reason, seriousness, mastery over the affects, the whole somber thing called reflection, all these prerogatives and showpieces of man: how dearly they have been bought! How much blood and cruelty lie at the bottom of all 'good things'!" *Genealogy*, 62.

206 The two Latin expressions having somewhat different connotations here, the one colloquial, the other legal, yet both reflect an abiding interest in the state of mind of the offender.

207 Michel Foucault, *Discipline and Punish: The Birth of the Prison* (New York, 1979), remarks at length on the modern concealment of such things.

208 Nietzsche, *Genealogy*, 180.

209 Georg Lukács suggests something of this in *History and Class Consciousness: Studies in Marxist Dialectics* (Cambridge, 1972), 156. Such antinomies notoriously include faith/reason, truth/falsity, fantasy/reality, subject/object, public/private, mind/body, etc.

210 Friedrich Nietzsche, *Beyond Good and Evil*. The translator, R. J. Hollingdale (London: Penguin Books, 1990), 159, prefers the English "deified" to Zimmern's "transfigured." The latter is taken here as it captures the sense of more general transformation. Here too, Nietzsche is referring to a "wild beast" of a different sort. See Friedrich Nietzsche, *Beyond Good and Evil, Prelude to a Philosophy of the Future*, trans. by Helen Zimmern, *The Good European Society*, T. N. Foulis (London and Edenburgh, 1907), The Darien Press (Edinburgh, 1907), Chapter Seven, #229, 177.

Chapter 2. Violence, Vengeance, and the Rudiments of American Theodicy

1 Emile Durkheim, *The Elementary Forms of the Religious Life* (New York, 1965), 475.

2 The phrase is widely in use. Roman Catholic bishops declare in an open letter. "Fundamentally, our society needs a moral revolution to replace a culture of violence with a renewed ethic of justice, responsibility and community." David Crumm, Knight-Ridder Service, *Boston Globe*, November 16, 1994, 3. Sissela Bok, *Mayhem: Violence as Public Entertainment* (Reading, 1998), and James Gilligan's *Violence: Our Deadly Epidemic and Its Causes* (New York, 1996) comment on this as well.

3 Social scientists in the tradition of Durkheim.

4 See the International Victimology Website for example: http://www.victimology.nl/. Since the '70s the use of the term has proliferated.

5 Commenting on Nietzsche's suggestion that punishment is meted out according to the degree of "astonishment" that people feel at the crime in *Human, All Too Human*, William Connolly suggests that "The desire to punish crystallizes at the point where the shocking, vicious character of a case blocks inquiry into its conditions. . . . " *The Ethos of Pluralization* (Minneapolis, 1995), 47. I am suggesting that the point at which "astonishment" becomes "familiar" fulfills a similar function in TV programs of this kind.

6 Stage instructions place the judges between the audience and stage, while the goddess directs the accused, Orestes, to stand at the "Stone of Outrage," and confines the Furies to the "Stone of Unmercifulness" to allow for the possibility of mercy and better judgment. Aeschylus, *The Oresteia – The Eumenides*, trans. Robert Fagles (Harmondsworth: Penguin Books, 1985), 255. On our stages of justice, the audience occupies the seat of judgment and condemns the outrage of the day without mercy.

7 There are those who comment on this shift in justice from the periphery in editorials and some theorists like William Connolly, Wendy Brown, and Bonnie Honig who do, but they would not be seen here.

8 Such is the case for both John Rawls or Jürgen Habermas, as different as they are in other respects. This is not to say that theoretical considerations of a public sphere or democratic discourse should be reduced to this, only that they miss something if they do not consider it.

9   The attack on intellectuals from this standpoint is couched in terms of concern for the "victims of violence" toward whom they are allegedly indifferent. Writing about the "victim culture," Mona Charen blames this on the triumph of the intellectuals of the 1960s (those whom she sees allied with Jean-Paul Sartre, Simone de Beauvoir, Samuel Beckett, and Jean Genet – apparently to prove that she knows some, since none of the four have very much to do with it). She offers praise for Yale Professor and Unabomber victim David Gelernter for being a rare intellectual who is willing to "revile" his attacker. "Triumph Over Victimhood," *Boston Globe*, July 21, 1997, A-11. As she misapprehends the enemy, exaggerates the problem, and overlooks the dangers of her own praise of "vilification," Charen exhibits how the "compassion for victims" (which those intellectuals would doubtless feel as much as she) can become an excuse to express dissatisfaction with liberal justice and to celebrate a more vengeful kind.

10 On the right, Jeffrey R. Snyder, "A Nation of Cowards," *The Public Interest*, 113 (Fall 1993): 40–55, suggests that the increase of violence is due to the failure of citizens to defend themselves, charging that American's have lost their dignity by their unwillingness to fight back against crime. The article accompanied a 1995 national mailing from the "Independence Institute" to many academics.

11 Jeffrie Murphy in *The Passions of Law*, ed. Susan A. Bandes (New York, 2001), 154–161, reprises the view he had once expressed, but here rejects. He discusses resentment and self-respect in *Forgiveness and Mercy*, by Jeffrie Murphy and Jean Hampton (Cambridge, 1988), 16–18.

12 Mark Tunick, *Punishment: Theory and Practice* (Berkeley, 1992), 14, 15, 16, 187. Tunick is quoting G. W. F. Hegel, *Vorlesungen über Rechtsphilosophie* (1818–1831), 4 vols., ed. Karl-Heinz Ilting (Stuttgart-Bad Cannstatt, 1973), vol. 4: 286. He wants to defend a "retributivist ideal" like Hegel's, but to acknowledge that punishment is "essentially contested" such that universal claims are drawn into the realm of the ('less than ideal') particular by his own "immanent critique," which of course Hegel would not do. This is entirely consistent with the American tendency outlined in Chapter 1.

13 Robert C. Solomon, "Justice v. Vengeance: On Law and the Satisfaction of Emotion," in Bandes 127. See also Peter French, *The Virtues of Vengeance* (Lawrence, 2001).

14 Mark Osiel, *Mass Atrocity, Collective Memory and the Law* (New Brunswick, 1997).

15 See Dan M. Kahan, "The Anatomy of Disgust in Criminal Law" (*Michigan Law Review* 96 (1998): 1621, 1623,) reprised in "The Progressive Appropriation of Disgust," chapter 2, in Bandes, 71. Kahan draws upon William Ian Miller, *The Anatomy of Disgust* (Cambridge, 1997) for both. Kahan, like Miller, wants to privilege disgust as a "thought pervaded evaluative sentiment," 64, whereas Martha Nussbaum, suggestively, distinguishes "indignation" from disgust to get away from this, in "Secret Sewers of Vice," in Bandes, 28. If disgust follows upon a moral breach (as tears may follow from a sadness) it is nevertheless distinct from the morality in question.

16 Massaro in Bandes makes this connection in characterizing Kahan, 94. But there are more properly 'democratic' forms of collective disapproval (tempered by a toleration and a recognition of rights). It is one thing to acknowledge the inescapable fact of the "passions of the law" and another to call for the legal orchestration of emotion.

17 It is questionable whether such emotions really lend themselves to a better articulation of the 'virtues.' Where these thinkers suppose that revulsion may be detached from its content, 'appropriated,' or put in service of the good, they are implicated in the problem that we have identified in which affects of broken attachment seek expression without regard for the virtues or any *idea* of the good.

18 The U.S. Supreme Court upheld the constitutionality of the fairness doctrine in 1969 in *Red Lion Broadcasting v. FCC* (395 U.S. 367). The FCC suspended the doctrine in 1987; Rush Limbaugh, and Presidents Reagan and Bush were among its opponents.

19 Jürgen Habermas, *Communication and the Evolution of Society* (Boston, 1979), offers this without sufficient appreciation, perhaps, for this aspect of 'argument.'

20 The function of the "guest" or "caller" on these shows is indicative. He or she is frequently berated, ridiculed, dismissed, or hung up on, and is never a serious interlocutor. If this is not 'democratic discourse' as we noted above, it has certainly changed the character of that discourse. Of course resentment and anger are much a part of democratic discourse, but may be distinguished from such expressions of disgust (see Murphy and Hampton, 1988).

21 The extent to which such invective disrupts the norms of democratic discourse that Habermas and other liberals have enumerated cannot be overemphasized. If argument should achieve agreement and test truth in that tradition, this puts an end to argument and *imposes* agreement and truth.

22 The reaction has the character of striking back. Here too the attempt to detach affects of disapprobation from their content and to reattach them (so that anger finds a new object) in the hope of awakening moral meaning is emblematic of the problem we are addressing.

23 James Q. Wilson, *Thinking About Crime*, rev. ed. (from 1975), (New York, 1983), chapters 3 and 7.

24 William Connolly, *Why I Am Not a Secularist* (Minneapolis, 1999), 126, notices something similar in other of Wilson's works.

25 James Q. Wilson, *On Character/Essays by James Q. Wilson* (Washington DC, 1995), 2, 3.

26 Even as Wilson disparages the impulse to make "assumptions about human nature" in the system of deterrence that he prescribes, he argues for a reassessment of the "nature of man" along traditional liberal lines. *Thinking About Crime*, 3, 145, 249, 250.

27 By contrast, see the discussion in Jennifer Radden, *Divided Minds and Successive Selves: Ethical Issues in Disorders of Identity and Personality* (Cambridge, 1996), 132.

28 Wilson, *Thinking About Crime*, 154. This is emblematic of the tendency to avoid thinking about *thinking* about crime and the extent to which fear and anger have recast its rationalist assumptions.

29 See Peter Dews, *Logics of Disintegration: Post-Structuralist Thought and the Claims of Critical Theory* (New York, 1987). Such antifoundational theories do not address the reactive *want* of meaning that now makes its presence felt within the vengeful response to violence – a defiant, reactive, and vengeful 'foundationalism' in which the problem of 'fragmented identity' is also one of frustrated identity.

This is most pressing where the 'strategies of conformity,' 'technologies of power,' coercive instruction, surveillance, and so on (Foucault) have lost a compelling sense of the 'normal' with which they conspire.

30   This is a distinctive feature of the "real life" crime programs on television. During the chase, the police officer's voice-over remarks "Look at him! Look at him!" or speculates on his state of mind or intoxication of the accused. Upon capture the form of address is formal, yet attempts by such persons to deny guilt are countered by the officer's remarks off camera, "he knows, he knows!" His humiliation is crafted to restore a disrupted "reason" by calling out the apparent lack of it.

31   Agents of crime are punished in ways that pointedly *disregard* their rational being – holding them accountable to reason as it were (Kant) in a way that denigrates them for the lack of it. The accused do not speak for themselves in court, which however it protects their rights also underscores their irrationality. In prison the rights and liberties that follow from that reason are not only "forfeit," as retributivists say, but are strategically withheld to torment or control inmates (the use of "shots" or "incident reports" are indicative). We will take this up in Chapter 4.

32   The subversion of these longstanding dichotomies of western thought is endemic to the inversion of meaning that we are considering.

33   Foucault, *Discipline and Punish: The Birth of the Prison* (New York, 1979). The suggestion here is that for all of the independence that Foucault observes in the emergence of the disciplinary apparatus, it is maintained in relation to such religious and secular assumptions about persons. It is why the separation of church and state is currently so difficult to maintain.

34   Psychiatric testimony to determine aggravating and mitigating circumstances at the penalty phase of a capital case does this, even as the "'CSI effect' has juries wanting more evidence" of this kind. Richard Willing, *USA Today*, August 5, 2004.

35   The polling of blacks or whites to see how many of each thought Simpson guilty or innocent or whether race would affect the outcome (e.g. CNN, O. J. Simpson Verdict Poll, October 4, 1995) proceeded as if to underscore the fact that it should not.

36   A "justice of desert" that claims to be free of bias gives priority to "individual merit" in a way that is also oblivious to the inequities of race. By process too subtle to register in the public debate, such "colorblind" justice would end affirmative action and impose harsh punishment on all felons 'equally,' asserting the priorities of blame and punishment over the concerns of equity.

37   Attorney Johnnie Cochran used the very evidence that would be compelling as a retributive proof of guilt (having Simpson try on the bloody glove) to subvert the retributive paradigm and underscore his theory that the evidence had been planted for racial reasons – in effect employing a justice of desert to revitalize considerations of equity. See CNN "'If it doesn't fit, you must acquit' Defense attacks prosecution's case; says Simpson was framed," September 28, 1995, http://www.cnn.com/US/OJ/daily/9-27/8pm/index.html.

38   See the discussion in Randall Kennedy, *Race, Crime and the Law* (New York, 1997), Chapter 8.

39 Even the apparent backlash in which tough-minded liberals black and white risk racist pronouncements in condemning crime, is also a struggle to move to this level of rationalization and to the comforting vantage point of that other sort of justice.

40 The public response to each case need not be in agreement with the court's determination of guilt or innocence. Public opinion may accept or reject a verdict, or, as with Simpson, have two verdicts (one criminal, another civil) that enable it to imagine the "outcome" as it sees fit.

41 This was evident in the days following the attacks of September 11, 2001 as the media struggled to identify Al-Qaeda as the culprit and explain its "brand of terrorism." The media focus replicates the *process* of revenge from a first insult, to the focus on the details, the naming of the syndrome, and the targeting of blame.

42 See Sam Roberts, "When Crimes Become Symbols," *New York Times*, May 7, 1989, D1, and Michael Kaufman, "New Yorkers Wrestle With a Crime," *New York Times*, April 28, 1989, A1. Reacting to the inflammatory references to the term 'wilding' that informed the case against five teenagers and to "overzealous policing and overzealous prosecutions," a group of black New York City police officers called for a review of the case. Associated Press, "Black officers ask for review of case," *Boston Globe*, August 10, 2002, A-4. DNA samples found at the scene later confirmed the confession by a known rapist, Matias Reyes, to the crime. Subsequently New York District Attorney Robert Morganthau sought a dismissal of all charges. See *Boston Globe*, December 5, 2002 A-3.

43 Christopher Dewing, "The Transformation of the American Frontier: Myth, Meaning and the Hyperreal in the Television News Coverage of the Space Shuttle Challenger Disaster," Senior thesis, Harvard Archives, 1995. Dewing discusses the use of models and other paraphernalia to stand in for the missing evidence in the immediate aftermath of the event.

44 The 'rash' of such incidents involving post office employees in the '80s led to the coining of the term "going postal."

45 The news shows focus on this and scarcely mention that most of Dahmer's victims were black – John Fiske in *Powerplays/Powerworks* (New York, 1993), 237, makes this observation.

46 See "Why the Towers Fell" on NOVA. Original PBS Broadcast: September, 2003.

47 The prevalence of violence in the media does not directly correlate to actual incidents of violence. The Surgeon General's report in 2001 noted the increasing prevalence of TV violence at a time when rates of violent crime appeared to have gone down.

48 The boldness of the clichés seems to have a soothing effect as familiarity and repetition confront and diminish the shock of violence.

49 Inspired by TV shows like *Quincy* in the '70s and its contemporary *CSI*, now this occurs on NBC's *Forensic Files*, the "reality series" that presents actual crime investigations as drama (7). On the news one seldom hears "a piece of rope with blood on it found at the scene," but rather, "the bloody rope used by the killer." Police used suggestive phrasing routinely in the murder case of Jon-Benet Ramsey before charges had been brought. Associated Press reports: "Her parents have maintained their innocence, though police say they remain

'under an umbrella of suspicion.'" See "Ramsey's mother blasts tabloids," *Boston Globe*, September 1, 1998, A-10.

50 This is related to the psychological "closure" now considered by many to be "one of the legal system's most important aims." "A Finding of 'Guilty,' an outpouring of relief" regarding the McVeigh verdict in the Oklahoma City bombing case, by Linda Gorov, *Boston Globe*, June 3, 1997, A-1. Forensic information itself may offer consolation as was said of surviving victims in the Janet Downing murder case at the conclusion of the trial of Edward O'Brien: "In their minds, her loved ones have followed the trail of blood in Dowling's home hundreds of times, speculating on when she was attacked, how long she suffered." Says one, "... I'm so glad it's over. For her sake and ours." Ellen O'Brien, "Closure after Two Years of Pain," *Boston Globe*, October 12, 1997, A-25.

51 Victory in a civil suit notoriously requires a lower burden of proof. As the father of victim Ron Goldman, Fred Goldman, victorious in his own suit, became a media hero and representative victim as the TV host on UPN of "Search for Justice With Fred Goldman." See "Fred Goldman to host 'Justice'," by Brian Lowry of the *Los Angeles Times*, in the *Boston Globe*, February 21, 1998, B-6.

52 "Everyone" of course meaning more whites than blacks. See *O. J. Simpson Facts and Fictions: New Rituals in the Construction of Reality* (Cambridge, 1999).

53 On the use of docudrama, see John J. O'Connor, "Review/Television Murder, Manipulation and Racism," *New York Times*, September 25, 1990, concerning the docudrama of the Stuart murder case, and John J. O'Connor, "Review/Television; Erik and Lyle, The Year's Stand-Ins for Amy and Joey," *New York Times*, April 18, 1994, regarding Fox's "Honor Thy Father and Mother: The True Story of the Menendez Murders," which he calls "a typical exercise in television docudrama, replete with warnings about composite characters and compressed time sequences." There were three versions of the Amy Fisher and Joey Buttafuoco story to which O'Conner refers. A memo from D. R. Reiff & Associates, Inc. to Producers of Docudramas is revealing: http://www.filmmakersforum.org./fmf/articles/docudramas.htm.

54 For this reason, there are much greater strictures on crime reporting by the press in other nations – in Great Britain, for example.

55 Even when cameras are kept from the courtroom to safeguard the search for truth, the still-life drawings that are permitted are shown on the news in a way that gives the "courtroom drama" more coherence than it deserves.

56 This cuts both ways. Prosecutors may find it harder to convince jurors without extremely accurate proof (the "CSI Effect" above), but the public assumes that such proof is to be had and that guilt is thus more certain. Such misperceptions by jurors and strong pretrial prejudices have been the subject of an eleven-state study by the Capital Jury Project. See William Bowers and Benjamin Steiner, "Misperceptions by Jurors Taint Sentencing," *Boston Globe*, November 2, 1997, C-1. See also Michael J. Watkins, "Forensics in the media: Have attorneys reacted to the growing popularity of forensic crime dramas?" http://www.coolings.net/education/papers/Capstone-Electronic.pdf.

57 In a new twist, news programs have franchised the pursuit of criminals. Newsgroups including foxnews.com report that NBC has paid "an organization called Perverted Justice" to perform a sting operation to ensnare pedophiles

for its series "To Catch a Predator." See NBC: "We Paid for 'Dateline' Pedophile Sting," Monday, April 10, 2006, AP.

58 If the former cater to white male audiences there are vehicles for other constituencies to do the same. *The Burning Bed* (MGM, 1984), for example, was among the first "fact-based" TV movies, aimed at women. Farrah Fawcett Majors plays an abused wife who retaliates against her abusive husband by burning him to death. The theme is repeated in the "fact-based TV movie" *Bed of Lies* on ABC, July 3, 1995, the hard-luck story of another woman in which "some names have been changed and certain scenes created for dramatic purposes." The fictionalized retelling of 'the untold story' invites women to join in the vengeful play from another angle. For many African Americans, the film *Amistad* (DreamWorks, 1997) fulfilled a similar function. If there is anyone who has not yet crossed the line between truth and fictive 'justice' of this sort, they can get there on their own by surfing channels from the news to police shows and cowboy reruns, traversing through historic scenes of vengeance to reclaim them.

59 Much of Reality TV openly plays on this with the expectation that audiences accept its vindictive contrivances and vengeful twists as a sort of alternate reality.

60 Judge Judy (CBS, 2006) or Judge Joe Brown (CBS, 2006). The suspension of reality/justice is made palpable by the fact that here "litigants have agreed to settle their disputes in our courtrooms. . . . "

61 Again, the festive treatment of violence and the need to make memories that Nietzsche discerned in punishment (Chapter 1) are resolved in the moralizing story of revenge. We not only make memories through punishment, but remake 'the crime' in such displays as well.

62 For Nietzsche again, the "reactive affects" entail "hatred, envy, jealousy, mistrust, rancor, and revenge." Friedrich Nietzsche, *On the Genealogy of Morals* (New York, 1969), 74, 75. Here, however, reactive feelings are organized to achieve sadistic release and to quash affects of broken attachment. One can trace the affective "formula" at work in such American films.

63 See John Portmann, *When Bad Things Happen to Other People* (New York, 2000), chapter 1. Portmann makes much of the distinctive German meaning of the word *Schadenfreude* – loosely, the enjoyment of the suffering of others – and of the insufficiency of attempts in the English-speaking world to grasp it.

64 For Nietzsche the vengeance of *ressentiment* is likewise "imaginary." *Genealogy*, 36.

65 While the specific nature of masochistic satisfaction is disputed, its public character here recalls "scripting" as a "technique of control," in the way that Robert Stoller and other psychoanalysts have observed it in children: "[T]he child believes it can prevent further trauma by reenacting the original trauma. Then, as master of the script, he is no longer the victim; he can decide for himself when to suffer pain rather than having it strike without warning." *Sexual Excitement: The Dynamics of Erotic Life* (New York, 1979), 119, 125.

66 The imitative coding of "bad guys" as heroes is rampant – from Mafia types to Bonnie and Clyde and the villains of hip hop that make a sympathetic 'pastiche' of violent criminality. Yet pastiche, Fredric Jameson reminds us, lacks the satirical (critical) aspect of parody, "Postmodernism and Consumer Society," in *The Anti-Aesthetic: Essays on Postmodern Culture*, ed. Hal Foster (Port Townsend,

1983), 114. The proposition that such imitative violence has some reflexive, parodic, and therefore critical potential, however, gains currency in John Fiske, *Power Plays Power Works* (New York, 1993). Yet if Fiske sees the emulation of criminality as *political resistance*, this too may be parody without satire where such images are only "parodies of themselves," and reiterate their original content *uncritically*.

67   The costume of many male film heroes is indicative. They rarely wear the black leather of the sadistic villain, but more often the white shirt and tie of the enraged suburban father (Michael Douglas/Bruce Willis), or the likable detective's rumpled street clothes. The familiar attire facilitates identifications with the victim as his tormentor's tormentor in a sadomasochistic reversal that affords a distinct pleasure.

68   *Miranda v. Arizona*, 384 U.S. 436 (1966). It is difficult to find an instance where this is not the case.

69   Jonathan Powell recounts the videotaping of arrests in Austin, Texas since 1998 ("Naked City: Drunk with Power?" *The Austin Chronicle*, July 14, 2000), on controversial attempts by the police in various localities to videotape their arrests for future viewing or presentations on TV.

70   Mark Fuhrman, accused of planting evidence in the Simpson case, claimed to have recorded racist comments in an attempt to inspire a work of fiction. He has written several books, has had his own radio and TV shows, and has served as consultant for ABC, CBS, Court TV, and the Fox News channel. http://www.foxnews.com/story/0,2933,276774,00.html

71   Only recently and in a 5–4 decision has the Supreme Court ruled against the police tactic of conducting two rounds of questioning of suspects, the first without giving the *Miranda* warning to "get a confession," the second to meet the formal requirement of the law. The practice had been "described in some police manuals and promoted on a website on policing." See Lyle Denniston, "Justices question interrogation tactic: Confessions elicited before rights are read," *Boston Globe*, December 10, 2003, A-2. See also Jerry Markon, "Police Tactic to Sidestep Miranda Rights Rejected," *Washington Post*, June 29, 2004, A01.

72   The two cases from New York both involved black men: see Andrew Jacobs, "Judge to Retry Police Officer in '03 Killing of Immigrant," *New York Times*, September 13, 2005, Section B 8, and Michael Cooper, "Amadou Diallo: Officers in Bronx Fire 41 Shots, and an Unarmed Man Is Killed," *New York Times*, February 5, 1999, A 1. Regarding Abner Louima sodomized by police with a baton: See Michael Brick, "Leniency Request Is Denied for Officer in Louima Case" *New York Times*, March 30, 2006, Section B 3.

73   The one-on-one swordplay and dogfights in films like *Star Wars* (20th Century Fox, 1977) are indicative of this. (The fact that the human cast is almost entirely white further expresses the indifference of this sensibility of justice to another working, along with intergalactic characters to neutralize or erase race.)

74   Nietzsche, *Genealogy*, 76.

75   Of course this masks the fact that blacks and others do not have equal access to these roles. Yet there is enough *imagined* access to the heroic paradigm for it to function in this way. Like Bentham's tower, in *principle*, anyone may go there.

76 The cult of the victim thus frequently ignores the actual victims and the variety of possible responses to their condition, portraying them the same way to engage them as symbols as we shall see.

77 This generalized vengeance should not be confused with some loftier ideal of retribution just because it rises above the "standpoint of the person injured" even though retribution may take on much of its baggage.

78 For such characters, race is often a gloss. For black male leading actors the accouterments of race are frequently disposable or are presented as if they do not matter.

79 This is not the "imaginary vengeance" of *ressentiment* that lends itself to the abstractions of the law (see Chapter 1) of which Nietzsche speaks, *Genealogy*, 36, but imagined vengeance that works in precisely the opposite direction (against the abstractions of the law).

80 See Pietro Mirangieu and Graeme Newman, *Vengeance: The Fight Against Injustice* (Tatowa, 1987), chapter 6, here referring to the Sardinian "code of vengeance."

81 Peter S. Canellos, "Texas leads nation as death row population grows," *Boston Globe*, Monday, February 16, 1995, 6.

82 There are countless instances of this. In response to the 1998 slaying of James Byrd Jr. by racists who dragged him behind a truck in Jasper, Texas, Byrd's father, James Byrd Sr., is quoted as saying, "Vengeance is mine, said the Lord" and "All I want is justice, and fair justice is the death penalty." Bob Hohler, "Blacks in Jasper cry for justice: Many back death penalty," *Boston Globe*, June 13, 1998, A-1, A-9.

83 We shall see (Chapter 3) how an equivocation about the present is intrinsic to revenge and is intimately connected to a wish to alter the past and to redeem it for the future.

84 The 'secular' has many implications these days. Here I mean only what liberal formulations have usually meant – an ostensibly 'neutral state' and public sphere that embraces pluralism and makes room for those of various religious and political beliefs. Yet William Connolly, in *Why I Am Not a Secularist*, warns against an orthodoxy of "high secularism" that paradoxically squeezes out other voices. 10.

85 G. W. Leibniz, *Theodicy: Essays on the Goodness of God the Freedom of Man and the Origin of Evil* [1710] (London, 1952), 182. The ingenuity of this formulation is that it allows a place for the "freedom of man" without disrupting essential assumptions about God's omnipotence or good and evil.

86 Max Weber, *The Protestant Ethic and the Spirit of Capitalism* (New York, 1958), 181, 182.

87 Max Weber, *Economy and Society: An Outline of Interpretive Sociology* (Berkeley, 1978), 519.

88 Our lack of a dominant religion and formal division of church and state put us firmly in the secular camp despite the resurgence of religious interest in America.

89 The denominational differences concerning the predestination of the soul that Weber considers must seem relatively minor from the standpoint of the erosion of the dominance of these faiths.

90 We refer here to philosophical retributivists as opposed to religious ones – for Kant, the idea that a murderer must suffer death is an instance of "what [legal]

justice as the Idea of the judicial authority wills in accordance with universal laws that are grounded *a priori.* . . . " Immanuel Kant, *The Metaphysical Elements of Justice,* Part I (Indianapolis, 1965), 104. That law here serves what justice has ordained retains something of destiny and final judgment *without* God's involvement being necessary as such.

91 Secular theories of punishment do not expressly concern final rewards in the way of theocratic theodicy. They do however appeal to future aims (affirming 'right,' 'serving justice,' 'advancing the good of all') in ways that may stand in for destiny.

92 This is not to suggest that Nazi culture provided a full-blown theodicy in opposition to the Lutheran and broader Christian one that it rejects – it was rather more concerned to cast enemies without making appeals of this nature, and was less obviously about vengeance.

93 Interviews with clerics and others on the eve of the first anniversary of the events of September 11 reveal something of this bewilderment. WGBH TV Channel 2 in Boston, NOVA, "Why the Towers Fell," September 10, 2002.

94 Numerous things attest to this, Art Spigelman's black on black cover of *The New Yorker* depicting the World Trade Center towers, September 24, 2001, for example. See also Edward Rothstein, "Defining Evil in the Wake of 9/11," *New York Times,* October 5, 2002, A17 – which is, in part, a review of Susan Neiman's *Evil in Modern Thought: An Alternative History of Philosophy* (Princeton, 2002). Rothstein criticizes Neiman for propounding her own reductive notion of evil even as she accuses others for doing the same. He suggests that a veritable industry of defining evil has sprung up.

95 The attempt to identify victims from their remains and to distinguish them from the attackers has been a chief task of investigators. See Paul D. Colford, "9/11 parts split by good and evil," *The New York Daily News,* October 12, 2005, front page.

96 In the conservative Christian eschatology adhered to by millions of Americans the chosen will soon join Christ in the sky while others "left behind" will perish during the Tribulation, then Christ will lead an army to destroy the unbelievers who remain. Many other Christians dispute this rather vengeful American reading of scripture, or give it a different interpretation. The "Christian right" is a complicated mix of things.

97 William Connolly, *Why I Am Not a Secularist,* 16, among others, uses the term post-secular in a related way.

98 The phrase is not meant to recall the Rousseauian idea that civilization brings its own 'evils' as Susan Neiman calls attention to it ("Modern Evils," paper presented at Political Theory Colloquium, Einstein Forum, Harvard University, September 27, 2002), but to refer to the ways in which secular society itself regenerates a notion of evil.

99 See for example, CNN.com./U.S., Bush: bin Laden 'prime suspect' September 17, 2001. Patricia Williams has made a similar point in "Infallible Justice," a talk at Harvard Law School's Saturday School Program, October 5, 2002. She speaks of a "tremendous literalism" underlying certain uses of the law and religious language that allows for no dissent, interpretation, or sense of irony. She refers to the "evangelical power" that the word "terrorist" has acquired.

100 See Ron Rosenbaum, "Staring into The Heart of the Heart of Darkness," *The New York Times Magazine*, June 4, 1995, from an interview with Mario Cuomo, 58.

101 President Reagan's "Evil Empire," speech to the House of Commons, June 8, 1982; President Clinton's "let us not be overcome by evil" in the Oklahoma Bombing Memorial Address, April 23 1995; President George W. Bush's "Axis of Evil," State of the Union Address, January 29, 2002 are all instances of this. Jimmy Carter had once been cautious in using such rhetoric but would now be seen as deficient if he did not.

102 Already in pre-revolutionary America, as Baylin points out, the "power" of despots was regarded as an evil and anathema to the promise of liberty. For Samuel Adams this put "the worst passions of the human heart and the worst projects of the human mind in league against the liberties of mankind." Bernard Bailyn, *The Ideological Origins of the American Revolution* (Cambridge, 1992), 59–60, 66.

103 Jean Baudrillard, *The Transparency of Evil: Essays on Extreme Phenomena*, trans. James Benedict (New York, 1993), 81.

104 Baudrillard, 84, 85.

105 For all of the questions raised about this by theorists like Michael Sandel, we are at a point where liberal conceptions of 'the good' and pronouncements on 'evil' are advanced regularly. In the movie *From Dusk Till Dawn* (Miramax 1995) for example, the lead character reconstructs the idea of heaven in a rather American way against an unambiguous threat. Addressing a minister who is having a crisis of faith in fighting vampires, he says, "I know that whatever is out there trying to get in is pure evil straight from Hell, and if there's a Hell and those sons-of-bitches are from it, then there has got to be a Heaven, Jacob. . . . "

106 The editors of Jean-Paul Sartre's play *Huis Clos* (1947), Jacques Hardré and George B. Daniel (New York, 1962), offer this suggestive definition: "L'ANGOISSE: Anguish is the normal condition of those who have become aware of their total liberty, and of the fact that there are no universal values that can justify the choices they have made." xiv. We take the implication that such anguish may increase the need to restore universal or other values that inform our choices.

107 Rosenbaum, 1995, quoting Susan Smith's pastor. "Evil" frequently has this connotation today. That pairing of freedom and evil lodges a more explicit charge against liberalism than the older pairing of licentiousness and wickedness.

108 Of course the problem of free will in its relation to evil is a very old one for Christian theology for which Augustine and others have different answers. William Connolly, in *Why I Am Not a Secularist*, considers how the 'Augustinian will' remains a contemporary problem for America, 115–117, and links it to Kant's retributivism, 119–121.

109 Not just the countenance of the villain is now exposed but his psyche or pathology. One finds corollaries to this in the presentation of evil in film, and the wish to expose pure, malevolent will – *Jason*, the shark in *Jaws*, etc.

110 Richard Hoffman echoes the sentiment complaining that the term "pedophile" and its "pseudo-medical" status function like the "disguise" of

a "wolf." He proposes substituting for that relatively benign Greek term mean-ing "one who loves children," the alternative, "peduscele," "from Latin 'scelus,' meaning 'evil deed.'" See "Changing language of sex crimes against children," *Boston Globe*, November 23, 1998, A-13. Tampering with the classical root would reinscribe meaning at the deepest level.

111 Speaking of Iraqi torture during his State of the Union Address, on January 28, 2003, President Bush remarks: "If this is not evil, then evil has no name."

112 Upon the release of videotape showing Osama bin Ladin taking pleasure in having sent others to die in his cause (December 13, 2001), the Ameri-can Administration and media were quick to attribute disingenuous or self-interested motives to him. The American investment in this idea makes it impossible to contemplate other motives and may dangerously misconstrue the danger he poses.

113 Daniel Goldhagen, *Hitler's Willing Executioners* (New York, 1996), has been crit-icized for rejecting more nuanced accounts for the rise of Nazism in Germany at the time, preferring to characterize Nazis as "genocidal killers," 128, and elsewhere.

114 An Internet search reveals a "Profile of a Sociopath" affirms this. This seems fitting since the diagnosis is as much a matter of folklore as a clinical cate-gory. Yet according to the *Diagnostic and Statistical Manual of Mental Disorders*, 4th ed., "The essential feature of Antisocial Personality Disorder is a pervasive pattern of disregard for, and violation of, the rights of others that begins in childhood or early adolescence and continues into adulthood. This pattern has also been referred to as psychopathy, sociopathy, or dyssocial personal-ity disorder. Because deceit and manipulation are central features of Antiso-cial Personality Disorder, it may be especially helpful to integrate information acquired from systematic clinical assessment with information collected from collateral sources....," 301.7.

115 The impulse to think in these terms (as much as anything) accounts for the marginalization of psychoanalysis today.

116 This is a possible verdict of guilt now employed in at least 20 states, which sharply curtails the application of the notion of 'innocence by reason of insan-ity.' FRONTLINE, "A Crime of insanity: Insanity on trial": Airdate October 17, 2002. PBS. http://www.pbs.org/wgbh/pages/frontline/shows/crime/

117 This refers to the famed *M'Naughton* rule. See H. L. A. Hart, "Changing Con-ceptions of Responsibility," from his *Punishment and Responsibility* (Oxford, 1968). The legal standard for assessing sanity hangs on the assessment of a person's ability to 'tell right from wrong.' The related *Durham* rule, adopted from *Durham v. U.S.*, U. S. Ct. App. 1954, states that "... an accused is not criminally responsible if his unlawful act was the product of mental disease or defect." Yet as Bharat Ramamurti points out, Judge Sullivan writing for the Wisconsin Court of Appeals in *State of Wisconsin v. Felicia Morgan* 1995 (441) represents a new trend in suggesting that Felicia Morgan, on trial for murder, "has not shown how in her alleged dissociative state of mind she did not har-bor the specific intent to kill Adams." Here, significantly, culpability attaches to rationality *within* a delusional system. See "Moral Responsibility, Excuses and the Law," Senior thesis, Harvard Archives, 2003.

118 Rosenbaum cites Andrew Delblanco's *The Death of Satan: How Americans Have Lost the Sense of Evil* (New York, 1995), on this point.
119 *The American Heritage College Dictionary*, 3rd ed. (New York, 1993), 476.
120 The nature of associations that people make to different sorts of pain must bear on the utilitarian calculus. One cannot deter those of faith who imagine that certain pain will bring them redemption or that enduring it reflects virtue. The torturers of the Inquisition must have discovered this, although their aim was hardly deterrence.
121 Recalling the Singapore caning of Michael Fay in 1994, Mississippi officials introduced legislation to make that state the first to reintroduce the flogging of criminals. Curtis Wilke, "Miss. flogging debate opens old wounds," *The Boston Globe*, February 21, 1995, 1. In opposing this, others recalled the unjust whipping of slaves in the region. The symbolic import of this particular infliction seems to have been more in dispute than the infliction of pain as such.
122 Elaine Scarry, *The Body in Pain: The Making and Unmaking of the World* (Oxford, 1985), 5 and 4 respectively. If pain evokes a state anterior to language, it actively anticipates its subsequent or mature expression.
123 Scarry expresses this ambiguity: "Pain has no voice" . . . "when at last it begins to find a voice, it begins to tell a story." 4 and 3 respectively. Pain, we might say, takes us into a well of worry that defies explanation yet demands explanation at once.
124 David Bakan, *Disease, Pain and Sacrifice: Towards a Psychology of Suffering* (Chicago, 1968), 57–58; quoted by way of expressing the same idea in David B. Morris, *The Culture of Pain* (Berkeley, 1991), 34.
125 Morris, 34.
126 After suggesting that "Negroes" (in Kaufman's translation) might be taken as "representatives of prehistoric man," and that they are less susceptible to pain, Nietzsche adds: "I have no doubt that the combined suffering of all the animals ever subjected to the knife for scientific ends is utterly negligible compared with one painful night of the single hysterical bluestocking." He is of course ridiculing the latter at the bigoted expense of the former, which does not excuse the racist 'anthropology' at the heart of it. *Genealogy*, 68.
127 Morris, 33.
128 Morris, 71. Of course many others note the lack of spiritual/emotional healing of mind/body problems, from Norman Cousins to practitioners of holistic health.
129 Jean-Jacques Rousseau, *The Confessions* (Harmondsworth, 1965), Book Eleven, 1762, 528.
130 The medical community is implicated in this although it is largely the doing of pharmaceutical advertising. The precise manner in which of many pharmaceuticals work from aspirin to SSRIs often remains a mystery even where there is good clinical proof of their efficacy. See, for example, R. M. Hirschfeld "Efficacy of SSRIs and newer antidepressants in severe depression: Comparison with TCAs," and "Antidepressant-Placebo Debate in the Media: Balanced Coverage or Placebo Hype?" *Commission for Scientific Medicine and Mental Health* 2(1) (Spring-Summer 2003).
131 From the early days of the epidemic it has seemed that distinguishing HIV infection from "full-blown AIDS" might exempt those newly diagnosed from

the stigma of the disease, drawing battle-lines accordingly. Many would say we have not fought that 'war' hard enough.

132 Harold S. Kushner, *When Bad Things Happen to Good People* (New York, 1981).

133 Chronic ailments that are difficult to treat seem especially 'unfair' where so much else can be treated. Americans use this word a lot.

134 The truly empathetic connection in which one feels the pain of others is quite opposite to the self-involved preoccupation with the pain of others that so often passes for caring.

135 Much of youthful Satanism has this character.

136 See, "Self-Directed Violence: Differentiating Between Suicidal, Malingering and Self-Mutilating Behaviours," Correctional Service of Canada, http://www.csc-scc.gc.ca/text/pblct/forum/e043/e043h_e.shtml

137 Of course this is only the public side of the matter, as piercing and self-mutilation can have different aims. What begins as a response to numbness may resolve itself in a different if not ultimately satisfying self-management of pain: "It's saving me from really hurting myself," says one adolescent "cutter." "When I cut I feel calm, relaxed, better," though the effect must be fleeting. And another, "Pain comes out in the blood." See Jenn Abelson, "Quieting a 'storm that rages inside': Some young people try to slice out pain, stress," *Boston Globe*, December 29, 2003, B-1.

138 There need not be pure masochistic enjoyment in this, since either the expression or containment of pain in this paradigm may delimit or control it. Masochism can have this character in any case. See Stoller (1979) and note 65 above.

139 One hardly needs the Protestant ethic to spur capitalism on where this secular one has taken effect.

140 Weber noticed the Protestant (Calvinist) reckonings with predestination in which those "self-confident saints" of early capitalism lived their lives as if to demonstrate that they were among the 'elect' and destined for Heaven. Over Calvin's objection that this would "force God's secrets," people pursued and displayed material success accordingly. *The Protestant Ethic and the Spirit of Capitalism*, 110–112. To seem *lucky*, to hold a winning lottery ticket, provides a secular benefit of the same sort.

141 In conditions of liberty, the problem of fate is exacerbated by the random effects of choice or chance, and one can expect more of luck. This is consistent with the idea that people make their own fortune and might second-guess destiny by increasing their luck. A secular theodicy involves "hedging one's bets" about one's "final rewards" in case one's faith does not come through. Luck, or just wishing, is a postsecular means of underwriting the Protestant gamble as Weber presents it – those who opt to appear as if they are destined for heaven (or now, those who spit on the dice or take other measures to insure their luck) may hope to affect fate or destiny. The prevalence of gambling in America today has much to do with this, and punishing the unlucky criminal would seem to seal the deal. This must be why organized religion in America has so little to say about the sin of gambling of late.

142 The advent of "living wills" is thus continuous with the use of ordinary wills in seeking control and assurance.

143 The funeral directory in the *Yellow Pages* of any good-sized city reveals as much. There are mortuaries geared to specific faiths, but many more of these.

144 Embalming is interesting in this regard. A practice of dubious public health benefit (preserving a corpse, while dispersing bodily fluids, often in public sewers), it nevertheless conveys the impression of 'preservation,' permanence. Cryogenics, if rare, does this even better. See also Jennifer Graham, "Baby boomers remaking once-stodgy funeral industry," on nondenominational commercial innovations in the industry, *The Boston Globe*, August 9, 2003, A-3.

145 Says Mitford: "The emphasis is on the same desirable qualities that we been schooled to look for in our daily search for excellence: Comfort, durability, beauty, and good craftsmanship. The attuned ear will recognize too the convincing quasi-scientific language, so reassuring even if unintelligible." Jessica Mitford, *The American Way of Death* (New York, 1978), 16.

146 Baudrillard, (1993), 81; Morris, (1991), 71; Mitford, (1978) 16, respectively.

147 In a world of contracts and exchanges nothing is 'for nothing.' Every death should have its payback or 'count for something' – donating organs or participating in terminal drug trials may seem to redeem one's death – and in the case of death by violence, 'justice' has the same function. There have long been gift exchanges related to death that that differ from these commercial ones. See Lewis Hyde, *The Gift: Imagination and the Erotic Life of Property* (New York, 1983), 40–45.

148 The SUV and the accessorized casket have much in common here. In a very American way the rich and poor can both partake in this entitlement 'equally' (though the rich are more entitled, the eye of the needle notwithstanding). There is a sense that if you 'can't take it with you,' 'it' will help to get you there in style.

149 Televangelists do this as their TV sermons and infomercials promise to boost the chances of salvation for those who give. Anytime the sermon begins with the old snake oil, "Friends, . . . " one can expect as much.

150 Death being finite and infinite, terminal and permanent, an ending without end.

151 Elisabeth Kubler-Ross, *On Death and Dying* (New York, 1969). Note the five stages of grief as she presents them in this formative book: Denial and isolation, Anger, Bargaining, Depression, and Acceptance.

152 The fact that Kubler-Ross identifies "bargaining" as one of the stages of grief underscores the tenacity of that impulse even where one cannot bargain or plead with God. This aspect of grief carries over directly into vengeance, as we shall see in Chapter 3.

153 I am indebted to Christopher Capozzola's illuminating work on this. The AIDS Quilt had been carefully packed and stored. The items pressed into the wall or left at the Vietnam War memorial are collected and warehoused even though this was not anticipated in the original design. "The Monumental Moment: Recent Monument Design and the Search for Pluralist Frameworks of Memory," Senior thesis, Harvard Archives, 1994. Such practices reflect death rites practiced in many cultures and are available for secular appropriation. See also Mary Leonard, "In Tragedy, a rush to heal: Two years later, Sept. 11 relatives hasten to honor fallen," *Boston Globe*, September 8, 2003, A-1.

154 One thinks also of the inscriptions in the Roman catacombs, and Buddhist and other repositories of written prayers for the dead. The impulse must be very old; the point is that we are reverting to it for the lack of other options.

155 For example the '90s PBS series called "Death: The Trip of a Lifetime," hosted by Greg Palmer. Note efforts by the Soros Foundations to support medical research in this area: Judy Foreman, "Philanthropists set up $15m project to study dying in America," *Boston Globe*, December 2, 1994, 5.

156 Joseph Campbell, lecturing on a variety of religious observances, inspired a generic reverence for mystery of this sort in his audience on PBS. Joseph Campbell and Bill Moyers, *The Power of Myth* (New York: Doubleday, 1988).

157 It would not be enough to conquer Afghanistan or defeat Al-Qaeda if it could be done for example: the airlines must be sued.

158 Aleatory contracts may be continuous with luck and religion here. One knows that one is statistically safer to travel in a plane than a car, but one is wise to have insurance and pray on takeoff anyway.

159 Hence the party that would 'protect business' is also more willing to bring religion into politics and rely on it to rectify harm. So it professes to be more concerned with the victims and supportive of stiff punishment, and seeks damage caps for lawsuits at the same time.

160 A 'tribute to victims' appeared on most TV channels, September 21, 2001. The fundraiser featured performers and athletes who variously pledged their earnings to the New York victims' fund that ultimately earned $534,000,000. A Justice Department fund was established to compensate victims who agreed not to sue the airlines. See Martin Kasindorf, "Some 9/11 families reject federal fund and sue," *USA Today*, July 13, 2003.

161 Richard Rorty, *Contingency, Irony, and Solidarity* (New York, 1989), 147.

162 For Rorty, such moments in literature provide an aesthetic dimension to complement a moral one. Here, the process of making real victims into symbols engages the aesthetic dimension to act *as* the moral one, which is instructively different. David Garland, *The Culture of Control: Crime and Social Order in Contemporary America* (Chicago, 2001), makes a similar point, 143, 144.

163 The victim-hero is uniquely important in a secular theodicy indebted to Christianity. In the figure of the Martyr the crucifixion fuses victim and savior in a way that turns anger into forgiveness and leaves punishment to God. In our secular culture, there are images of victims everywhere with no Savior in sight. There are however, lesser saviors ready to prove, as Christ did in his non-vengeful way, that the sin of our indifference cannot be tolerated. These champions appease us on the ground with "fists of fury," guns, knives, and adrenal calls to action.

164 The "depravity of a crime" is often cited in sentencing, but this still largely refers to the act and not the offender's intentions or character. When the offender's record is weighed in sentencing this does not speak to his motive. Even the "Intentional Infliction of Emotional Distress" as a common law tort claim is difficult to prove or measure.

165 Judith Shklar, *Ordinary Vices* (Cambridge, 1984), 7.

166 Shklar, book jacket.

167 Shklar, 8.

168 Shklar, 44.

169 Despite MacIntyre, Brubaker, and others who attempt this.

170 Shklar, 237. In her eagerness to find the solution within the liberal tradition it is revealing how she has repeatedly had to step outside of it, appealing to would-be intuitions, archaic sensibilities of vice, and arcane political theory. She has appealed variously to Montaigne, Machiavelli, Montesquieu, and Nietzsche, three pre-liberals and an anti-liberal, not to expressly liberal philosophers. The 'dramatists' that she praises for speaking frankly about cruelty are the likes of Euripides, Shakespeare or Hawthorne.

171 Shklar, 238. My emphasis.

172 Shklar, 237.

173 Shklar, 35.

174 Shklar is aware of this too, and takes it up as a secondary consideration as a matter of "hypocrisy" in her second chapter. But it is already a matter of auxiliary concern, as her ranking and the order of her argument implies, and may not be taken seriously enough.

175 "Good Samaritan" laws are an effort to offset this, but capitalism could not do very well without it.

176 Rorty, 144.

177 Martha Minow, "Words and the Door to the Land of Change: Law, Language and Family Violence," *Vanderbilt Law Review*, 43(6) (November 1990), commenting on *DeShaney v. Winnebago County Dep't of Social Servs.*, 109 S. Ct. 998 (1989).

178 On borrowing, lending, and interest: Exodus 22:25; Leviticus 25:35; and Deuteronomy 23:19–20.

179 Shklar, 239. The Patriot Act and other inventions of the Bush administration may be read at this level as an attempt to curtail rights and oppose the particular cruelties of terrorism (remaining oblivious to its own cruelty), and to foreclose further debate about cruelty.

180 Shklar, 237. My emphasis.

181 One recalls the primacy of self-preservation in Thomas Hobbes, *Leviathan* (New York, 1958), chapter 14, 109, and John Locke's *The Second Treatise of Government*, (Indianapolis, 1952), [Ch. II], 5. While such a principle may be said to *imply* a protection against cruelty, this misses its essential indifference to the motives cruel or otherwise of those who threaten ones' person, and its expansive concern for protection against all sorts of dangers.

182 For Shklar the "prevention of physical excess and arbitrariness" of government calls for a "liberalism of fear," 237. Yet even if the latter may 'institutionalize suspicion' in a way that is suspicious of its own power, the condemnation of cruelty as evil remains problematic. One may try to get the cruelty out of punishment (and the revenge too), without supposing that it is superceded by reason (Locke), or making a moral creed of it (Shklar).

183 In a sense Shklar's pragmatic liberalism of fear addresses this paradox and she acknowledges it in having lionized Montaigne's "cruel hatred of cruelty," 248, but the call to put cruelty first still begs the question. To put the uneasy "bargain" and the "paradox" *first* here instead is reminiscent of another liberal pragmatism that Richard Rorty elaborates.

184 Rorty maintains, for example, that Nabokov does an especially fine job of exposing the particular cruelty of "incuriosity," 158.

185 Says Nietzsche, "... all religions are at the deepest level systems of cruelties." *Genealogy*, 61. The same might be said of all theodicies, including our secular one.

186 Much as the liberal justifications for the infliction of pain as punishment try to turn a psychological inclination into a rational and moral one, the denunciation of cruelty would discern a rational moral limit within a psychological morass.

187 See for example, Jody M. Roy, *Love to Hate: America's Obsession with Hatred and Violence* (New York, 2001).

188 This reversal (cruelty organized against cruelties) generates a highly functional micro-theodicy of revenge.

189 Shklar, 238.

190 Hypocrisy is a vice too for Shklar, yet she warns, "To make hypocrisy the worst of all vices is an invitation to Nietzschean misanthropy and to self-righteous cruelty as well." Shklar, 44. Nevertheless, if we remain skeptical about ranking the vices at all, attending to our own hypocrisies might still be prudent, and no more misanthropic than the hatred of cruelty.

191 John Rawls, "The Law of Peoples," in *On Human Rights: The Oxford Amnesty Lectures 1993* (New York, 1993), carried forward in other works.

192 See, for example, Louis P. Masur, *Rites of Execution: Capital Punishment and the Transformation of American Culture, 1776–1865* (New York, 1989).

193 Her unwillingness to put *this* problem first inclines Shklar to defend Bentham's Panopticon for example against his Foucauldian critics as the work of a liberal reformer (which, of course, it is), and downplays the way in which such things conceal their own order of cruelty. She points to Bentham's benevolence and concern for the poor here, but discounts the unintentional way in which cruelties can be perpetrated in the name of benevolence. Shklar, 35–36.

194 Here "retrogression" may be a variation on "transgression." Fascism had something of this character in a way that similarly connotes change and not "progress." See Michel Foucault, *The Order of Things, An Archaeology of the Human Sciences* (New York, 1970).

195 William E. Connolly, panel remarks, APSA Conference, September 2, 1994.

Chapter 3. The Nature of Vengeance: Memory, Self-deception, and the Movement from Terror to Pity

1 Aeschylus, *The Oresteia – The Eumenides*, (Harmondsworth, 1984), lines 391–398, 248. The Furies, revealing their true character just before Athena enters.

2 Friedrich Nietzsche, *Thus Spoke Zarathustra* (Part II), *The Portable Nietzsche* (New York, 1974), 252.

3 "The Politician's Wife" written by Paula Milne, aired on Masterpiece Theatre, WGBH Boston, Sunday, January 19, 1997 (in two parts). Acorn Media.

4 The popular film "9 to 5" (20th Century Fox, 1980) offers a point of comparison. The male villain is trussed, gagged, and suspended in such a way that he is forced to look down upon and witness a vengeful takeover by his female employees.

5 As democratic 'public spheres' suffer the encroachment of the media, one might consider the effect of such appeals.

6 Poe captures the sense in which maintaining the façade is a vital part of the satisfaction of revenge in "The Cask of Amontillado": "It must be understood that neither by word nor deed had I given Fortunato cause to doubt my good will. I continued as was my wont, to smile in his face, and he did not perceive that my smile NOW was at the thought of his immolation." Edgar Allan Poe, *Thirty-Two Stories* (Indianapolis, 2000), 340.

7 One must be cautious about claims that women have had a unique purchase on 'private revenge' by virtue of their place in a 'private sphere.' Yet suggestive distinctions arise in early feminist literature, e.g., Susan Glaspell, "A Jury of Her Peers," in *The Best Short Stories of 1917*, ed. E. O'Brien, 256, and in Kate Saunders, ed., *Revenge: Short Stories by Women Writers* (Winchester, 1991).

8 Poe's opening words in "The Cask of Amontillado" underscore the importance of 'impunity' in acts of revenge: "AT LENGTH I would be avenged; this was a point definitively settled – but the very definitiveness with which it was resolved precluded the idea of risk. I must not only punish, but punish with impunity." 340. See also Benedict Carey, "Payback Time: Why Revenge Tastes So Sweet", *New York Times*, July 27, 2004, D1, which notes the related desire for some to keep the revenge completely secret.

9 See for example Rachel L. Swarns, "Looking for Hope in an Apartheid Monster's Eyes," *New York Times*, May 10, 2003, A-1. Psychologist, and member of South Africa's Truth and Reconciliation Commission, Pumla Gobodo-Madikizela reflects on this process upon seeking out former Police Colonel Eugene de Kock.

10 Exodus 21:23–25.

11 Jacoby, 79–81.

12 Theodor Adorno and Max Horkheimer, *Dialectic of Enlightenment* (New York, 1972). See the discussion in Chapter 1.

13 Friedrich Nietzsche, *On the Genealogy of Morals and Ecce Homo* (New York, 1969), 74–75.

14 This 'unseeing' recalls the anesthetized indifference that we have considered (driving SUVs, etc. – Chapter 2).

15 Thomas Hobbes, *Leviathan* (New York, 1958), chapter 13, 108.

16 Hobbes, chapter 13, 109.

17 Hobbes, chapter 13, 108.

18 John Locke, *The Second Treatise of Government* (Indianapolis, 1952), [Ch. II] 10.

19 While there is more of reason for Locke and more of fear for Hobbes that reigns in such first encounters, it would be premature to call it recognition here. It is more like apprehension (in both senses of the word).

20 Jean-Paul Sartre, "Being for Others – Second Attitude Toward Others: Indifference, Desire, Hate, Sadism," in *Being and Nothingness: An Essay on Phenomenological Ontology*, Part III (New York, 1956), 379–380.

21 Sartre, 379–380. Others note the competitive nature of this. Interestingly Sartre stresses the relation of indifference to agency and choice.

22 Axel Honneth, *The Struggle for Recognition: The Moral Grammar of Social Conflicts* (Cambridge, 1996), 28. Honneth is quoting Hegel's "First Philosophy of Spirit."

23 Plato, *The Republic* (Oxford, 1945), Part II (Books II–IV), Chapter XIII, 137.

24 Mark 9:47.

25 This egoistic aspect of revenge thus confounds the "ethical construction of the self" where it turns on an idea of 'truth.' See Thomas Flynn, "Foucault as Parrhesiast: His Last Course at the College de France, 1984," *Philosophy and Social Criticism* 12 (Summer 1987): 223. The inclination to see what one wants to see in vengeance for example stands opposed to the ethical selflessness one finds in self-abnegating persons (Buddhist monks and other religious ascetics) insofar as they seek truth.

26 Sophocles, *Oedipus Rex, The Oedipus Cycle: An English Version* (New York, 1977), 16.

27 Sophocles, *Oedipus Rex*, 64. Another translation offers it this way: "Time found you out, all-seeing, irrepressible time. Time sits in judgment on the union that could never be...." Sophocles, *Oedipus Tyrannus* (New York, 1970), 28. The timeless justice of retribution will not forgive or forget.

28 Eli Sagan, *The Lust to Annihilate: A Psychoanalytic Study of Violence in Ancient Greek Culture* (New York, 1979), 103.

29 Sophocles, *Oedipus at Colonus*, Scene VIII, *The Oedipus Cycle*, 162–163. Nietzsche says, "Sophocles understood the most sorrowful figure of the Greek stage, the unfortunate Oedipus, as a noble human being who, in spite of his wisdom, is destined to error and misery, but who eventually, through his tremendous suffering, spreads a magical power of blessing that remains effective even beyond his decease." *The Birth of Tragedy and the Case of Wagner* (New York, 1967), #9, 67.

30 Sophocles, *Oedipus Rex*, Scene 1, 14.

31 Vengeance here is not simple personal revenge, but that property of justice that the Prophet identifies as being beyond human reach.

32 Sophocles, *Oedipus Rex*, 67.

33 The presumption in this cannot be laid to Greek sensibilities alone – the act is extraordinary even by classical standards.

34 As Nietzsche distinguishes noble acts of punishment by their lack of *ressentiment* (Chapter 1), Oedipus might seem outwardly to be free of it. Yet if his is a revenge driven by shame (and not the envy of *ressentiment)* and the two seem like opposites, they are quite related in their vanity and need for rectification.

35 Karl Reinhardt, "Illusion and Truth in *Oedipus Tyrannus*," in Harold Bloom, *Sophocles' Oedipus Rex* (New York, 1988), 98.

36 Reinhardt, 71.

37 Sophocles, *Oedipus Tyrannus*, 31.

38 Oedipus expresses this wish. Sophocles, *Oedipus Tyrannus*, 31.

39 Sophocles, *Oedipus Tyrannus*, 31. One might say that at the defining crossroads of his life the actual roads (there is such a place) may represent 'tenses' of this order – one from Delphi (a place of presently discovered truth), the other from Thebes (the city in ruins; the past to be rectified), now the third, to Daulia (a place of future peace or escape if not yet safe internment: says Oedipus: "As I wandered farther and farther on my way to a land where I should never see the evil sung by the oracle."). Sophocles, *Oedipus Rex*, Scene II, 41. On the true location see Sophocles, *Antigone, Oedipus the King, Electra* (Oxford, 1994), 73.

40 Sophocles, *Oedipus Tyrannus*, 31.

41 Sophocles, *Oedipus Tyrannus*, 30.

42   "Let every man in mankind's frailty Consider his last day; and let none Presume on his good fortune until he find Life, at his death, a memory without pain." Sophocles, *The Oedipus Cycle* (Fitts and Fitzgerald, trans.), 78. While the emphasis on memory in this translation may be questionable (an observation for which I thank Elisabeth Mitchell), the contrast between the wish for a life free of suffering and its elusiveness remains. Another offers: "Look at Oedipus – proof that none of us mortals can be happy until he is granted deliverance from life, until he is dead and must suffer no more." Sophocles, *Oedipus Tyrannus*, (Berkowitz and Brunner, trans.), 33.

43   John Gould, "The Language of Oedipus," in Bloom. This is another way of describing the radical isolation that defines Oedipus' experience; his "belonging not wholly among men but also to an alien world, outside our understanding . . . that is the central image of Sophocles' play. That other world is a world outside the limits of the human *polis*. . . ." 160.

44   Sophocles, *The Oedipus Cycle, Oedipus at Colonus*, Scene 1, 86. The Furies, presumably, would there forgive and accept him.

45   In a letter to Fleiss, anticipating his formulation of the Oedipus complex (May 1897), Freud writes of the death of parents in a way that reveals his awareness of this vengeful aspect of grief: ". . . it is a manifestation of mourning to reproach oneself for their death (so called melancholia) or to punish oneself in a hysterical fashion, through the medium of the idea of retribution, with the same states (of illness) they have had. . . ." In *After Oedipus, Shakespeare in Psychoanalysis*, ed. Julia Lupton and Kenneth Reinhard (Ithaca, 1993), 12–13.

46   It is after all the entire course of his existence as it has led to the destruction of both parents that Oedipus is compelled to see; a crime more stark, perhaps, than killing the primal father (Freud), and for which the punishment of castration seems less apt than that of radically disrupted sight.

47   The connection between vanity, vengeance, and self-flagellation might be extended. From a certain standpoint, Oedipus' act has the quality of a self-indulgent, even an 'onanistic' revenge in the cathartic sense that we will take up below. He tries to do the right thing, but what is more, in his self-punishment urgently needs to perceive himself and be perceived as doing the right thing.

48   Martha Nussbaum, in "Equity and Mercy" (reprinted from *Philosophy & Public Affairs*, 22(2) (1993)), in *Punishment and Rehabilitation*, 3rd ed., ed. Jeffrie G. Murphy, 212–248, notices how "Oedipus' particularity" is neglected in the pursuit of *dikê* (justice that turns on retribution, 217), "For he is being treated the same way by *dikê*, as a true or voluntary parricide would be treated, and crucial facts about *him*, about his good character, innocent motives, and fine intentions, are neglected." They are neglected, of course, even as they are made evident, and both come into view as he pursues a seemingly selfless vengeance that aspires to "justice."

49   (Or 'cherry-picks intelligence' and announces victory prematurely from the deck of an aircraft carrier.)

50   This impatience no doubt gives rise to the admonition that "revenge is a dish best served cold."

51   William Shakespeare, *The Tragedy of Othello: The Moore of Venice* (New York, 1993).

52   We have considered the distorting effects of forensic imagination in Chapter 2 and will again in Chapter 4.

53 The *placating* memory is never just a memory – the 'value' attached to memory in the economy of memories of horror considered above must turn on this too.

54 Again, this plays upon hindsight that wishes it had been foresight, as for Oedipus, a feature of mourning that is not limited to revenge. For Orpheus this 'penance' is undertaken in daring *not* to look back and the blindness of his mourning seems to serve the wish of hindsight. In Ovid's version of the myth it is said that when Orpheus sang of his love – "then for the first time...the cheeks of the Furies were wet with tears." See *Bullfinch's Mythology* (New York, 1993), 151.

55 This is the account offered by Dorothy Earnest in a televised segment on "families of murder victims." She expresses gratitude to a man who has taken her to the scene of her daughter's death after a not-guilty verdict in the trial of her accused attackers. "60 Minutes," CBS News, Sunday, October 26, 1997.

56 Immanuel Kant, *The Metaphysics of Morals*, here Mary Gregor's translation is preferred (Cambridge, 1991), 141.

57 For Kant, shame might be used to restore this balance but is not intrinsic to the balancing, 141, emphasis added. Yet if we do not accept his abstract formulation, or the idea that any *pain* that would restore a retributive balance (or the sense in which it is 'fitting') can be conceived in a way that is free of a valuation attributed by others, then someone does the evaluating and the equivalence is never a purely rational one.

58 Stanley Cavell, *Disowning Knowledge in Seven Plays of Shakespeare* (Cambridge, 2003). Cavell is distinguishing shame from guilt here in a most revealing discussion of the play on eyes in *King Lear*, 49.

59 Observation is both intrinsic to the punishment (where shame or public accountability are involved) *and* its valuation such that the latter cannot be separated out. Kant at least allows for the mitigating effect of the "perspective of the justice arising from the people" in matters where honor is at stake, 145.

60 Bentham intended his design as a reform over the more humiliating punishments of the time and not to shame the inmates he would expose to sight. To imagine such exposure without shame, however, would only make sense in a world hardened to shame and degradation.

61 We have remarked on the vengeful and American (distorted Kantian) notion of holding the offender accountable to his rational or better self.

62 Louis P. Masur, *Rites of Execution: Capital Punishment and the Transformation of American Culture, 1776–1865* (New York, 1989), 42. His emphasis.

63 Franz Kafka, "In the Penal Colony," in *The Complete Stories* (New York, 1971), 144–5.

64 Franz Kafka, 150, 154.

65 William Shakespeare, *The Tragedy of Hamlet, Prince of Denmark* (New York, 1998), (19) 1.3. And of course: "I'll observe his looks, I'll tent (probe) him to the quick...the play's the thing wherein I'll catch the conscience of the King." (60) 2.2.

66 The impulse persists in contemporary punishments: "LOS ANGELES – Local lawmakers, responding to the shooting rampage last week by a teenager at a California high school, have passed a law forcing students caught with guns or making threats to view dead bodies and watch autopsies being performed.... 'Young

people need to see the results of violent acts,' Los Angeles County Supervisor Mike Antonovitch said." "Morgue Tour in store for youth offenders," *Boston Globe*, March 15, 2001, A-2.

67 Marcella Bombardieri, "Arraignment eases mother's 15-year pain," *Boston Globe*, August 22, 2000, A-1.

68 Patricia Williams, *The Alchemy of Race and Rights* (Cambridge, 1991), 76. This is Williams' paraphrasing.

69 Patrick Suskind, *Perfume: The Story of a Murderer* (New York, 1991), 282.

70 Shakespeare, *Hamlet*, 4.7 (54–7), 114.

71 Linda Gorov, "As bombing memories churn, a curtain falls: Silent McVeigh executed while survivors watch," *Boston Globe*, June 12, 2001, A-30.

72 Pietro Marongiu and Graeme Newman, *Vengeance: The Fight Against Injustice* (Totowa, 1987), take this occasion to point out how vengeance may redirect the impulse to suicide. 31.

73 *The Iliad of Homer* (Chicago, 1961), Book 22, lines 328–373; 444–445.

74 Poe says "A wrong is unredressed when... the avenger fails to make himself felt as such to him who has done the wrong." 340.

75 One might dispute this if one thinks that there is a soldierly sort of respect for the defeated Hektor in Achilles' address, but then it would be a much quicker and less imploring task.

76 See G. W. F. Hegel, *Philosophy of Right* (London, 1975), ¶100, 71. In this formulation the 'indifference' in question is neutral and unaffected and yet also dismissive of something in the offender.

77 Axel Honneth, *The Struggle for Recognition: The Moral Grammar of Social Conflicts* (Cambridge, 1996), discerns a higher level of Hegelian recognition in which subjects are "socialized in their particularity," or "recognized as concrete universals," yet the pride, self-assertion, condescension so often at stake in honor complicate this. 25.

78 Honneth, 18, is referring to the parent–child relation that forms the foundation of ethical life for Hegel.

79 This is to say that heroic vengeance can readily conceal itself within legitimate liberal self-assertions.

80 V. G. Kiernan, *The Duel in European History* (New York, 1989), recalls the 'condescension' of honor in relation to the duel. 159.

81 Michel Foucault, *Discipline and Punish, the Birth of the Prison* (New York, 1979), 200, 201. See also Gertrude Himmelfarb, *Victorian Minds* (New York, 1968), on the details of Bentham's design.

82 Martin A. Schwartz, "Supreme Court Defines 'Deliberate Indifference'," *New York Law Journal* 212 (July 19, 1994): 3. And see *Farmer v. Brennan*, 511 U.S. 825 (1994), which takes up the liability of prison officials who housed a preoperative transsexual in an all-male population.

83 It is often observed that the use of "cell tosses" and "digital rectal searches" by prison authorities are carried out in retaliation for inmate behavior as well as for the seizure of contraband. In contemporary prisons, selective attention is part of the microcontrol made possible within the general condition of surveillance. See Eric Schlosser, "The Prison Industrial Complex," *The Atlantic Monthly*, 282(6) (December 1998).

84 Foucault, *Discipline and Punish*, 201.

85 *Jordan v. Smith*, 14 Ohio 199, 201 (1846), as quoted in Randall Kennedy, *Race, Crime and the Law* (New York, 1997), 37.

86 Nietzsche, *Genealogy*, 73. "Winking" here obscures vision, overlooks debts, forgives *en masse* what is "owed," thus permitting mercy.

87 See 'Driving while black' – racial profiling under study, CNN, June 2, 1999. CNN.com: http://www.cnn.com/US/9906/02/racial.profiling. Note too the inequities of cocaine and crack cocaine prosecution.

88 The 'Hispanic Store Owner' in *Sleepers*, Warner Brothers (1996). The police are complicit in this all the time: ignoring prostitutes because their pimps will "keep them in line," leaving one territorial gang to contain another, looking away as others look out for their interests, relying on the implicit threat of vengeance.

89 Sartre, 49.

90 In Sartre's view existence is chosen, and one is responsible for one's choices such that seeming self-deception would really entail bad faith (*mauvaise foi*).

91 Annette Barnes, *Seeing Through Self-Deception* (Cambridge, 1997) rehearses this, see for example 98–99.

92 Sartre, 51. In confounding the "id" (which is for Freud a highly complex and principally unconscious agency) with the conscious deceiver here, Sartre begs the question.

93 Sartre, 68. Emphasis added.

94 Philosophers variously take up the question of how "anxious desire" or "wishful belief" affects the possibility of self-deception. See for example Barnes, 3, 34–58.

95 Sartre, 53.

96 In "Mourning and Melancholia" Freud suggests that the presentation within the mind of the lost object in mourning is "in reality...made up of innumerable single impressions (unconscious traces of them), so that this withdrawal of libido is not a process that can be accomplished in a moment, but must certainly be, like grief, one in which progress is slow and gradual." *General Psychological Theory* (New York, 1963), 177. So too, the "obscure comprehension of the end" to which Sartre refers must entail different degrees of obscurity influenced by hidden, affectively charged intentions in an elaborate project of disguise.

97 This might bear on the 'unintentional biasing' in the formation of self-deceptive beliefs that Barnes makes much of, 3. Furthermore, memories that are taken as fact are selected from a host of competitors (as are their recognizable features), the biasing of selective memory in some sense 'precedes' that which is recalled to form the object of intentions – the horse is before and after the cart.

98 See Chapter 1 page 8.

99 If he ultimately opts to accept a truth of loss without revenge, this is by no means assured. There is a tendency for philosophers to regard these things in light of a sort of pure (and perfect) repression, not as a function of the more subtle mechanisms of defense, which may be more apt. See Anna Freud, *The Ego and the Mechanisms of Defense: The Writings of Anna Freud*, vol. 2 (Madison: International Universities Press, 1936).

100 Freud, "Mourning and Melancholia," 171.

101 Freud, "Mourning and Melancholia," 172.

102 Libido here is withdrawn from a "narcissistic object-choice" (a deceased loved one) and applied to a narcissistic "substitute object," i.e. the object of revenge.

103 This duality corresponds to the fact that for Freud, "The melancholic's erotic cathexes of his object thus undergoes a twofold fate: part of it regresses to identification, but the other part under the influence of the conflict of ambivalence is reduced to the stage of sadism...." 173.

104 Says Freud in "Mourning and Melancholia": "One may suggest that mania is nothing other than a triumph of this sort, only that here again what the ego has surmounted and is winning over remains hidden from it...." "When mania supervenes, the ego must have surmounted the loss of the object (or the mourning over the loss, or perhaps the object itself), whereupon the whole amount of anti-cathexis which the painful suffering of melancholia drew from the ego and 'bound' has become available." 175–176. In such cases, grief may be converted into a triumphal sense of 'justice.' Moreover, if libidinally charged (and constituted) objects have no existence outside of that which is potentially self-deceived – love and loss and vengeance here being 'made' of the same substance – then there may be some underlying sense of 'value' that makes this 'just exchange' seem possible (the economy of memories, Chapter 1).

105 The transparency of consciousness to itself is maintained in the denial of its opacity (which it need *not* know very precisely in order to deny it); a point of vanity, perhaps, in all sorts of grandiosity, obsessional thinking, etc., frequently parodied in the use of masks.

106 Here "biasing" confounds the question of intention. See Barnes 78–9.

107 Actors who claim to experience a "split" in consciousness and trance states when they experiment with masks have remarked upon the psychological effect of the self performing for itself. See Keith Johnstone, *IMPRO: Improvisation and the Theatre* (New York, 1979), 151–2. These trance states, like other states of 'becoming, accepting or telling oneself' are neither simple self-deceptions, nor undertakings in "bad faith," but layered attempts to convince the self as if to 'get into character.' Once one is convinced, any gesture one makes to rid oneself of the mask is met by one's compulsion to restore it and one's vanity reigns trance-like over reason and truth. Such impulses are stronger when a wound or scar effaces one's self-esteem, which is why vengeance is supremely an act of vanity. Hobbes distinguishes simple vanity from a sort of confidence "grounded upon the flattery of others" or "vainglory" which is closer to this. Thomas Hobbes, *Leviathan* (New York, 1958), chapter 6, 57.

108 *The American Heritage Dictionary*, 3rd ed. (Boston, 1997), references the "Ojibwa *nindoodem*, my totem." 1429. John Tanner, raised by the Ojibwa, noted the complete identity one might have to one's totem and the difficulty posed in translation, not, "I walk like a bear" (my totem), but "I walk a bear." Private records of Edward Ryerson.

109 An anonymous former prisoner puts it this way: "Yeah, ego, brag, image, that's big. But then again at night after 10 when the doors are shut and the cells are locked, it's a relief, you take your mask off... but seven in the morning and put your mask back on and stand up at the door and the door opens and you gotta come out into the population. I had a murderer's mask on, I was supposed to be the murderer...and I wore the mask since I been in there." Quoted in

Ethan Nasr, "Making Sense of 'Senseless Violence': An Examination of How Prisoners Understand their Punishment," Senior thesis, Harvard Archives, 55 (1996).

110 Susan Youens is referring to certain uses of masks in Mozart's operas and elsewhere. Private communication.

111 Clement Rosset, *Joyful Cruelty: Toward a Philosophy of the Real* (New York, 1993), on Nietzsche's thoughts about masks, 47–49. Rosset is quoting Friedrich Nietzsche, *The Gay Science*, trans. Walter Kaufmann (New York, 1974), 132 as he too alludes to opera – Rossini and Bellini.

112 The absence of a mask for Superman, who is nevertheless unrecognizable to others once in disguise, underscores this idea. The Lone Ranger was hardly seen without his mask, which affirms it too.

113 For A. David Napier, *Masks, Transformation, and Paradox* (Berkeley, 1986), masks are the bearers of ambiguity, paradox, and change: Chapter 1.The ambiguity of the mask is well represented in the two-faced "comedy and tragedy" masks that stand as a symbol for the theatre.

114 Keith Johnstone, 151–2.

115 This may apply to the use of masks in sadomasochistic exchanges as well.

116 Nietzsche refers to something like this when he speaks of "the normal attitude toward a hated, disarmed, prostrated enemy...." *Genealogy*, 71.

117 William Shakespeare, *The Tragedy of Macbeth* (New York, 1963), Act V, Scene viii, Macduff.

118 Greek choruses sometimes have this quality. So much of jurisprudence is stern and imitative – so much of law "speaks through" something else – how much of this is a masking of vengeance?

119 Nietzsche suggests that "... all the celebrated characters of the Greek stage – Prometheus, Oedipus, etc. – are mere masks of this original hero, Dionysus. That behind all these masks there is a deity...." *The Birth of Tragedy*, #10, 73.

120 My thanks to Deborah Foster for pointing out the relationship between ventriloquy and accountability. One suspects that something like this may be true for prosecutors and officers of the court who "speak through" the artifices of the law.

121 Nietzsche knew this well. See Rosset, 47–49.

122 Erving Goffman noticed that in presentations of self, "when an individual projects a definition of the situation and thereby makes an implicit or explicit claim to be a person of a particular kind, he automatically exerts a moral demand upon the others, obliging them to treat him in the manner that persons of his kind have a right to expect." *The Presentation of Self in Everyday Society* (New York, 1959), 13.

123 Sigmund Freud, *The Ego and the Id* (New York, 1962), 34–35; my emphasis.

124 Again, as for Oedipus, the detachment of self-directed anger is instrumental both in the formation of the ego and in revenge. It is also at the root of both the tragic and the comic.

125 Johnathan Swift, *A Tale of a Tub*, in *The Works of Jonathan Swift, with Memoir of the Author*, edited by Thomas Roscoe (London, 1850). Scanned by Deep Singh, http://www.lehigh.edu/~amsp/tubbo-2.html.

126 See Napier.

127 Homer, *The Odyssey* (New York, 1963), 156, 158.

128 This is to say that the rational aspects of legitimation are shadowed by a more self-serving sort where vengeful punishment remains part of the legitimating process. We will pursue this in Chapter 4.

129 John Rawls, *A Theory of Justice* (Cambridge, 1999), 12.

130 Masur, *Rites of Execution*, 47.

131 This "impersonal" inclination and the "impartial" aspect of the law remain distinct, but are related and easily confused.

132 A "put on" face may be offered as a mask to deflect (or satisfy) a vengeful affront. An American gang member speaks of making such an offering as a kind of sacrifice to harassing police officers: "It's not a huge deal. They usually just want to feel big. So make them feel big. If they want to feel like they're beating up on a big tough mother-fucking nigger, give them the nigger face. If they want to feel like you've given in, give them this." Mary J. Hahn, "If We Must Die: The Meaning of Race to Members of an African-American Gang," Senior thesis, Harvard Archives, 111 (1997).

133 Sacrificial substitution engages the power of masks (dressed up offerings; offerings made by those in masks) creating a common identity between the agent and object of sacrifice. For Girard, masks both "arrange" and supercede differences. René Girard, *Violence and the Sacred*, trans. Patrick Gregory (Baltimore, The Johns Hopkins Press, 1989), 166. The avenger and avenged often wear similar masks, the executioner and the condemned wear hoods, combatants in warring camps wear helmets and uniforms that compliment one another. A common medium of facades facilitates the symbolic equivalence in the vengeful 'exchange' (this is not Girard's point).

134 Consider the films *Trading Places* (Paramount Pictures, 1983), *Face Off* (Paramount Pictures, 1997), *The Man in the Iron Mask* (MGM, 1998).

135 Masks figure in mourning in this way – death masks of all sorts may have the character of a vessel that references a loss without capitulating to loss, and may retain and remake the lost object for the present in a way that seems to 'heal time.'

136 Kiernan, 152. My emphasis.

137 Johnstone, 151.

138 Poe's vengeful protagonist addresses himself to "You, who so well know the nature of my soul." 340.

139 David Dolinko, "Some Thoughts about Retributivism," *Ethics*, 101(3) (April 1991): 554, takes up the idea of a message without an audience. An audience awaits when punishment registers in the heavens, or on the balance sheets of justice. An audience is imagined in secret acts of revenge when one says to oneself, "If only they knew!"

140 In vengeful states, the audiences of the mind are often split – one's superego or conscience may *forbid* the vengeful act that such an imagined community *endorses* – there may be two angels on the shoulder, each bearing the authority of a different 'community.'

141 If there is shame in relation to such an audience in honor, the latter is quite different from the internalized audience that is said to be at work in guilt.

142 Nietzsche, *Genealogy of Morals*, 181. His emphasis.

143 David Garland, *Punishment and Modern Society: A Study in Social Theory* (Chicago, 1990), 267.

144 Of the right to present a case, Albert Venn Dicey observes: "*Habeas Corpus Acts* declare no principle and define no rights, but they are for practical purposes worth a hundred constitutional articles guaranteeing individual liberty." *Introduction to the Study of the Law of the Constitution* (Boston, 2000), 195.

145 *Antiphon, Anocides, Minor Attic Orators in Two Volumes*, trans. K. J. Maidment (Cambridge, 1982), vol. 1, 38–41. The text provides elaborate arguments offered by the prosecution and the defense.

146 Antiphon, *Second Tetralogy*, 86–9. Maidment is explaining the "blood guilt" that animates the accuser's side.

147 The representations of vengeance as justice discussed in Chapter 1 may owe a great deal to this initial ambiguity. Girard makes a related point, that "[t]he sacrificial process prevents the spread of violence by keeping vengeance in check." 18 and on.

148 Sagan, 54–55.

149 Sagan, 113–114, is quoting Aeschylus, *Libation Bearers*, in *The Complete Greek Tragedies*, trans. Richard Lattimore, vol. 1, 118–123. Or see Aeschylus, *The Oresteia – The Libation Bearers*, trans. Robert Fagles (Harmondsworth, 1985), 182–3, lines 120–126; 217 lines 888–891; or 221. As he exposes his father's body, Orestes says to Pylades: "Here unfurl it so the Father – no, not mine but the one who watches over all, the Sun can behold my mother's godless work. So he may come, my witness when the day of judgment comes, that I pursued this bloody death with justice, *mother's* death." lines 975–981.

150 Here justice does begin to get beyond revenge.

151 Nietzsche, *Geneology*, 69.

152 Nietzsche, *Geneology*, 69. One sees the consolidation of perspective in the phrasing here as well – the "eyes of God" (a monotheistic audience in the making).

153 Imagining God's justice begins in the ascent that is anticipated in the self-importance of revenge.

154 Alexis de Tocqueville, *Democracy in America* (New York, 1988), 13.

155 John Laurence, *A History of Capital Punishment: With Special Reference to Capital Punishment in Great Britain* (London, 1971). See the caption to the plate depicting "The Condemned Sermon" [facing page 130]. Laurence dates executions at Newgate from 1783–1868, 179–180.

156 Foucault, *Discipline and Punish*, 58.

157 Foucault, *Discipline and Punish*, 68, and Masur, 42–49, discuss French and American versions of this. Attendance began to have formal character of a right burdened by emotional expectations that were quite explicit.

158 Arthur Koestler, *Reflections on Hanging* (New York, 1957), 7–11.

159 George Riley Scott, *A History of Torture* (London, 1997), 235.

160 Tocqueville, *Democracy in America*, 252, recalls an incident during the War of 1812, when a patriotic mob in Baltimore attacked newspaper editors for their opposition to the war such that, "to save the lives of these wretched men threatened by the fury of the public, they were taken to prison like criminals." 252, FN 4.

161 See George Riley Scott, "Religious Flagellation," Part III of *The History of Corporal Punishment* (London, 1996).

162 Quoted in Laurence, 185. Emphasis added.

163 Laurence notes that the bell-man at the parish of St. Sepulchre would intone such statements under Newgate, while hawkers reproduced and sold supposed "verses written in the condemned cell," 185, 186. Masur and Foucault record similar efforts in America and France respectively.

164 Aristotle: "For our pity is excited by misfortunes undeservedly suffered, and our terror by some resemblance between the sufferer and ourselves." *Aristotle's Politics and Poetics* (New York, 1972), Book 2, Chapter 11, 237–238. Evidently pity and terror, like pity and ridicule, are not mere opposites.

165 Such pity would not be 'tragic' in Aristotle's sense.

166 Conscience or superego, put another way, does not require an external object as ridicule or pity does. Yet the latter may induce a reaction quite like it. Shaming others, whether they deserve it or not, may externalize blame for those whose superegos are compromised (a mob) and be experienced as an 'act of conscience.'

167 Garland disputes the importance of this citing P. Spierenburg, *The Spectacle of Suffering, Executions and the Evolution of Repression*, which suggests that such a public reaction was neither so widespread nor significant as Foucault claimed, 108. While there were doubtless other reasons for the change, this does not entirely diminish Foucault's point, 159.

168 Foucault, *Discipline and Punish*, 63–65.

169 Foucault, *Discipline and Punish*, 74. Again, whatever the motivation to reform, this seems to have been its message.

170 Foucault, *Discipline and Punish*, 12; Masur, *Rites of Execution*, 105, respectively.

171 Foucault, *Discipline and Punish*, 13.

172 Foucault, *Discipline and Punish*, 200, and more generally, 173.

173 Tocqueville, *Democracy in America*, 272, 276. Nevertheless, Tocqueville warns of the danger that the jury may serve the tyranny of the majority. 252.

174 One must distinguish between the necessary impartiality of juries and the indifference that this implies. Tocqueville opens the door to a better, impartial, aggregate sort of decision making in democracy, which we will entertain in Chapter 4.

175 *Batson v. Kentucky* 476 U.S. 79 (1986) attempts to rectify the racial bias of juries more recently.

176 There are several ways that juries are kept from knowing the likely sentence or consequences of their verdicts – the bifurcation of jury deliberations in capital cases (super due process), constraints on the prejudicial statements by defense attorneys, juror's instructions to focus only on the question of guilt, etc. The blind that is designed to insure unbiased judgment also allows prosecutors to manipulate outcomes.

177 This is not to say that objectivity and impartiality are not also the aim of this, just that it bears mixed intentions. When jurors are barred from contact with outsiders or from discussing a case among themselves this insures their objectivity, but also allows them to bring their biases to bear.

178 In the same moment the accused is respected, honored, and vilified, depending on the perspective of multiple audiences.

179 Maria Lopez, Associate Justice of the Superior Court, was roundly criticized in Boston for giving a sex offender and would-be child rapist a relatively light

sentence in 2000 and forced to resign in 2003: http://www.mass.gov/cjc/
Lopez-transcripts/Lopez-agreement.htm.

180 Jan Hoffman, "Crime and Punishment: Shame Gains Popularity," *New York Times*, January 16, 1997, 1. This is one function of sex offenders' registries and the displays of capture and humiliation on police shows.

181 There is something of an art involving shame, humiliation, and ridicule on talk shows as well. Some are inclined to ridicule (Jerry Springer, Howard Stern), others are of a more confessional type (Oprah Winfrey, Riki Lake). And here, as on Reality TV, Americans seem happy to humiliate themselves.

182 See for example the Constitutional Rights Foundation's The First Amendment and the Press: The People's Right to Know: http://www.crf-usa.org/lessons/right_to_know.htm.

183 *KQED, Inc., Plaintiff, v. Daniel B. Vasquez, Warden of San Quentin Prison, U.S. District Court for the Northern District of California* (June 7, 1991 U.S. Dist.) (Plaintiff's petition denied). The case received attention because Harris would be the first to scheduled die in a California gas chamber since the reinstatement of the death penalty in 1978. Wendy Lesser, *Pictures at an Execution: An Inquiry into the Subject of Murder* (Cambridge, 1993), 27–28.

184 See Lesser, 25; her treatment of this as theatre, 5. Chapters 2 and 3; the consideration of prurience, 146–7, and her discussion of cases, 28–33.

185 *KQED v. Vasquez* (1991).

186 If "Punishment had gradually ceased to be a spectacle" by the end of the nineteenth century, for Foucault, *Discipline and Punish*, 9, this is hardly true of the public trial.

187 Mark Osiel, *Mass Atrocity, Collective Memory, and the Law* (New Brunswick, 1997), 28–29. The discussion of punishment at this level of abstraction entertains only the most general disposition against wrongdoer and not the particular lessons or principles that such displays might impart.

188 Osiel, 7, 40, 43–44.

189 Osiel, 31. The spectacle of the public trial is 'moral' and affirms a sense of justice not because of the intrinsic worth of prosecuting wrongdoers, but because it fulfills a moral *function* – a utility that might be achieved by any morality or public catharsis, which is not satisfying to the retributivist.

190 Osiel, 14, quoting Paula Speck, 38 (quoting David Garland, 67) on the "didactic theatre," engages the term "monumental didactics" on 40.

191 Oseil, 38, is quoting David Garland (1990), emphasis his.

192 One thinks of the McCarthy hearings which were procedurally constrained at the start, yet became something more.

193 Much of democratic theory emphasizes this aspect of coming to consensus or agreement (there are strands of this in Mill and Habermas) but few appreciate the importance of disagreement in discerning truth (though Mill mentions it), or for its own sake more broadly. This is taken up in Chapter 4.

194 Ingmar Bergman, *The Virgin Spring (Jungfrukällan)* (ACMI Collections Prod Co: Svensk Filmindustri, 1960).

195 William Shakespeare, *The Tragedy of Hamlet, Prince of Denmark*, at the first arrival of his Ghost, the fallen king is referred to in this curious way. 1.1, 5.

196 Durkheim, *The Division of Labor in Society* (New York, 1984), 46, 68.

197 Martha C. Nussbaum, "Equity and Mercy," in Jeffrie G. Murphy, *Punishment and Rehabilitation*, 3rd ed. (Belmont, 1995), 217–218, offers a particularly clear portrait of this idea of balance as it traces to the Greeks.

198 Retributive notions of equivalence often mask this. Herbert Morris, for example, suggests that the criminal as a violator of rules has acquired an "unfair advantage" over law-abiding others by a loosening of self-restraint, and that justice is achieved by making sure this "advantage is erased" in a way that "restores the equilibrium of benefits and burdens." See "Persons and Punishment" in *Punishment and Rehabilitation*, 2nd ed., ed. Jeffrie G. Murphy (Belmont, CA: Wadsworth, 1985), 26.

199 Vengeance commonly reaches a point of no return beyond which it must proceed, yet makes regretful reference to the possibility of return (the wish to undo what cannot be undone).

200 What seems perverse to us about the "trial by ordeal" is precisely the subordination of truth to this theatrical pairing of the criminal and the crime by his or her excessive suffering.

201 Aristotle, *Poetics*, Book 2, Chapter 13, 239.

202 Aristotle, *Poetics*, Book 2, Chapter 1, 230. And also Chapter 7, 235 and Chapter 11, 237. The much considered phrasing is addressed for example in Stephen Orgel, "The Play of Conscience," in *Performativity and Performance*, ed. Andrew Parker and Eve Kosofsky Sedgwick (New York: Routledge, 1995), 134–151.

203 Aristotle, *Poetics*, Chapter 11, 238.

204 From Elin Diamond, "The Shudder of Catharsis," in *Performativity and Performance*, 153.

205 Elin Diamond in *Performativity and Performance*, 153 (my emphasis), is quoting *Aristotle's Poetics: The Argument*, Gerald F. Else, trans. (Leiden, 1957), 407, Chapter 14.

206 In this sense *Oedipus Rex* and the much-compared *Hamlet* are both tragedies and revenge plots. The two heroes move their audiences to a similar place by their efforts at punishment.

207 Aristotle, Chapter 9, 236: "The best sort of discovery is that which is accompanied by a revolution as in the *Oedipus*." See also Adrian Abdulla, "Catharsis in Literature," in Diamond.

208 The Chinese expression for punishment is instructive in this regard. The first character, Cheng of the combined Cheng Fa, contains a radical character that signifies a step with the left foot (to attack or to make submit) next to another meaning upright, correct, or true, both imposed over the (prostrate) sign for "heart" – hence, to "reduce a heart to submission." My thanks to Jim Wilkinson on this point.

209 In an odd way the ordeal of Orpheus would reverse this, and if it had been successful, achieve its aim without vengeance.

210 Again this 'perfect knowledge' as tainted knowledge lends itself to the vengeful self-deception.

211 The plot twist is a recovery from error aided by a deception that undoes a deception – a manipulation of the plot and audience by which the undoing of expectations has the double effect of introducing a shock with the force of 'revelation' and of affirming the possibility of a 'reversal' of the past.

212 Girard notices something like this in fast-paced altercations that call for sacrificial substitutions: "Where formerly he had seen his antagonist and himself as incarnations of unique and separate moments in a temporal scheme of things, the subject now perceives two simultaneous projections of the entire time span – an effect that is almost cinematographic." 159–160.

213 It should not escape notice that this effect, made possible by twists or surprising turns of events to effect a reversal, has the character of a common psychological process. It is in some sense like the 'condensation, displacement, and distortion' that Freud discerned in the unconscious processes of repression. But as a mechanism of self-deception (involving revelation, replication, doubling, and masks) the latter entails more nearly conscious operations upon memory.

214 Foucault, 56.

215 Proverbs 26:27. (Sylvan Barnet refers only to the Hebrew Bible, introduction to *Hamlet* lxxv) but this is readily available.

216 *Hamlet*, 3.4 (210), 93.

217 *Hamlet*, 3.3 (70–96), 85, as noted in Sylvan Barnet's introduction, "he says he wants to damn Claudius's soul as well as kill his body." lxxiv.

218 Such is the fate that has befallen an imagined lawyer whose skull Hamlet mockingly addresses: "This fellow might be in's time a great buyer of land, with his statutes, his recognizances, his fines, his double vouchers, his recoveries. Is this the fine of his fines, and the recovery of his recoveries, to have his fine pate full of dirt? Will his vouchers vouch him no more of his purchases, and double ones too, than the length and breadth of a couple of indentures?" 5.1 (122–3) Does the punning on this deserved destiny both affirm and belie the claim that the double-dealer would really get his due? Is there a double message in the impossible pairing – at once the exact equivalence of desert, and the representation (or double) of improbable recompense – not a tooth for a tooth but rotted dentures for corrupt indentures, the desecrated dirt inadequate recovery for so many double vouchers and double-booked purchases of land? And does this reflect the paradox (and irony) of any equivalence in vengeful punishment or ultimate reward, as of Hamlet's own quest?

219 Hence the *duplicity* of the crime, which has been made apparent in the revelation – its deception, double meaning, and damage to time, is reflected back in the double effect of the punishment and enlisted in the self-deceiving idea that the revenge "addresses" the past. Duplicity is called for to undo deception and duplicity, which heightens the illusory sense that an injury has been "matched."

220 Girard, 79, 159, 160–161, respectively.

221 The play within the play does something of this for Hamlet.

222 *Hamlet*, 3.3, 85 my emphasis.

223 So the villain might best be captured in the state of "rage" (the distorted double of this present state of unacceptable calm; more like the rage arising from the action of the crime), to be dispatched to the blackest hell (which is constituted as a negative double of heaven) – that state and that place together constituting a rightful, extreme destination of vengeance.

224 Marongiu and Newman offer this: "The real feud was then previewed by a series of classic reciprocal minor offenses such as cattle stealing and the publication of lists of spies who were to be killed. But the feud began in February

1954. . . . The first victim was Lussorio Mongili of the Falchi faction, shot down near his village. This first episode was the beginning of an impressive sequel of reciprocal homicides. . . . On the afternoon of January 26, 1956; Antonietta Deiana (the mother of a leader) was wounded by the shot from a handgun fired through the door of her house. Although she probably recognized the aggressor, she gave misleading information to the police in order to reserve for her son the right to avenge the assailant. . . . From that moment on the feud escalated without limit." 78–79.

225　Marongiu and Newman (1987), referring to Antonio Pigliaru's extensive study, *La Vendetta Barbaricina Come Ordinamento Giuridico in il Banditismo in Sardegn* (Milano: 1975). We noticed this in relation to Bentham's a "proportionable addition in point of magnitude," Chapter 1.

226　Foucault, 57.

Chapter 4. Revenge and the Fallibility of the State: The Problem of Vengeance and Democratic Punishment Revisited or How America Should Punish

1　Thomas Paine, "On Public Shaming and Execution," *The Rights of Man*, Part 1 (1791), in *Paine: Political Writings*, ed. Bruce Kuklick (Cambridge, 2000), 78.

2　If not entire wars, many military actions from those of the Indian Wars to Sherman's March and Pearl Harbor have been both strategic and vengeful. The bombings of Dresden, Hiroshima, Hanoi, and Baghdad have arguably had this character, as have plots against Castro, actions against Gaddafi after Lockerbie, the assassination of Al-Qaeda leaders by Drone, etc.

3　We might let Hobbes and Machiavelli have the moment, as they are closer to the American sensibility than Locke.

4　Martha Minow, *Between Vengeance and Forgiveness: Facing History after Genocide and Mass Violence* (Boston, 1998), 10, puts this in a positive light.

5　The vengeful aspect of the American Revolution is of course only a small part of it. Yet it has always been part of the American self-understanding and may be more so now, see for example *The Patriot*, (Columbia Pictures, 2000).

6　John Stuart Mill, *On Liberty*, in *Utilitarianism, On Liberty, Considerations on Representative Government* (London, 1972), 70–73. Mill borrows the phrase from Tocqueville.

7　This is the paradox of consent that Locke precipitously lays to rest.

8　Friedrich Nietzsche, *On the Genealogy of Morals and Ecce Homo* (New York, 1969), 36–37.

9　The Federalist Papers reflect this, and even Robespierre by his own declaration, see "On the Death Penalty," Speech at the Constituent Assembly, June 22, 1791.

10　See BBC: "Romania's 'first couple' executed," December 25, 1989, http://news.bbc.co.uk/onthisday/hi/dates/stories/december/25/newsid_2542000/2542623.stm; *Death is Not Justice, The Council of Europe and the Death Penalty*, Directorate General of Human Rights Council of Europe October 2001, http://www.coe.int/T/E/Human_rights/deathpen.pdfs.

11　The Eighth Amendment to the Constitution of the United States, 1791.

12　Thomas Hobbes, *Leviathan* (New York, 1958), Chapter 17, 139 (emphasis added), 120. Machiavelli expresses this too, as princedoms "pass from the popular to the absolute form of government." *The Prince* (New York, 1938),

Chapter IX, 35, or as a general matter, Chapter XVII, "... Whether It Is Better To Be Loved Or Feared" 54–56.

13 Hobbes, 120, 146.

14 John Locke, *The Second Treatise of Government* (Indianapolis, 1952), [Ch. VIII] 10, 58.

15 Locke [Ch. VII] 50. On the presumption of "tacit consent," such covenants are voluntary *and* coercive. "Democratic" practices like jury duty, the (required) pledge of allegiance, or the draft, reflect this ambiguity.

16 Louis P. Masur, *Rites of Execution: Capital Punishment and the Transformation of American Culture, 1776–1865* (New York, 1989).

17 Thomas L. Dumm, *Democracy and Punishment, Disciplinary Origins of the United States* (Madison, 1987), chapter 3, finds this at work in the early years of the republic and in subsequent penal reforms. The theme is prevalent in John Locke, *A Letter Concerning Toleration* (New York, 1955), as in his *Second Treatise,* and for the American Founders who followed him.

18 FRONTLINE, PBS, Airdate, October 31, 2000, "The Case for Innocence," written produced and edited by Ofra Bikel (there are slight discrepancies between the audiotape and the on-line transcript, here the transcript is preferred): http://www.pbs.org/wgbh/pages/frontline/shows/case/etc/script2.html.

19 Bob Burtman, a reporter who covered the case, recalls the remark. See FRONTLINE transcript.

20 *Booth v. Maryland,* 482 U.S. 496, 508 (1987) (quoting *Gardner v. Florida,* 430 U.S. 349, 358 [1977]) (internal quotation marks omitted).

21 Alan Berlow, "The Texas Clemency Memos," *The Atlantic Monthly,* July/August 2003; http://www.theatlantic.com/doc/prem/200307/berlow; and see Derek Jackson, "Bush's Blind Justice in Texas Executions," *Boston Globe,* July 2, 2003, A-19.

22 The Innocence Project offers: "The DNA recovered from the cells on the Marlboro cigarette filter contained a mixture of DNA from at least three individuals, and at least one was a male and at least one was a female. Criner was eliminated as a contributor of cellular material on the filter. Later, Forensic Science Associates acquired a STR genetic profile of Ogg, from the rectal swab, and from the cigarette butt wrapper. Ogg was found to be genetically compatible with DNA from the cigarette and the male cellular material on the cigarette was compatible with the spermatozoa found on the rectal swab. This was further proof that the spermatozoa was deposited by the person who smoked the cigarette with Ogg very near the time of the murder – her assailant. Criner was eliminated as the source of all of these samples." http://www.innocenceproject.org/Content/74.ph

23 "Beyond reasonable doubt": the common law standard for a finding of guilt in criminal trials.

24 John Ellement, "Victims of Brighton Rape Speaks Out," *The Boston Globe,* May 29, 2001, B-1.

25 In the case of Marvin Lamont Anderson, convicted of a 1982 rape and exonerated under a new Virginia law allowing DNA testing in 2001: "The defense lawyers say the DNA test has strongly pointed to another suspect, now in state prison, who was identified at the time and came forward a year later with a confession that a judge discounted after Mr. Anderson's conviction." Peter

Neufeld comments, "This appears to be the worst case of police and prosecu-
torial tunnel vision in the 10 years we've been appealing these cases." Francis
X. Clines, "DNA Clears Virginia Man of 1982 Assault: First Beneficiary of New
State Law," *New York Times*, December 10, 2001, A14.

26 See John Aloysius Farrell, "Judge Denies Bid for DNA Test to Verify Guilt of
Executed Man," *Boston Globe*, June 2, 2001. Judge Keary R. Williams rejects a
request by *The Washington Post*, *The Boston Globe*, the *Richmond Times-Dispatch*, and
the *Virginia Pilot* of Norfolk to permit the DNA testing of evidence in the case
of Roger Coleman executed in 1992. Testing eventually confirmed Coleman's
guilt: Carol Morello, "Court Rejects DNA Test for Man Killed By Va. in '92."
http://www.clarkprosecutor.org/html/death/US/coleman175.htm

27 Pat Dunnigan, "Fla. Death Row Inmates Face Deadline," *Boston Globe*, July 7,
2003, A-2. This refers to Florida Statutes Section 925.11, 2001, as clarified in
Governor Jeb Bush's Executive Order 05–160.

28 John Aloysius Farrell, "Judge denies bid for DNA test," quoting John Tucker,
author of *May God Have Mercy* (New York, 1997).

29 See Peter S. Canellos, "Justices Dismayed by Execution: Need for 'Finality' of
Cases Stressed," *Boston Globe*, April 30, 1998, A-25. See *Calderon v. Thompson*,
523 U.S. 538 (1998).

30 In his concurrence in *Gregg v. Georgia*, 428 U.S. 153, 226 (1976), challenging
defense attorney's claims that the death penalty arises from a judicial system
that is "created and run . . . by humans" who are "inevitably incompetent to
administer it," Justice White says: "this cannot be accepted as a proposition of
constitutional law."

31 Stanley Fish, *There's No Such thing as Free Speech . . . and It's a Good Thing, Too* (New
York, 1994), 144.

32 Anthony Lewis makes much of this in *Gideon's Trumpet* (New York, 1964).

33 Edmund Cahn, "Preface for Americans" to Arthur Koestler's *Reflections on Hanging* (New York: Macmillan, 1957), xiii, is recalling Beccaria's report for a commission on the penal system of Austrian Lombardy (1792). "The report appears
as an appendix in Cesare Cantu, *Beccaria e il Dirrito Penale* 369 (Florence: G.
Barbera 1862)."

34 Locke, *Second Treatise* [Ch. VIII], 58.

35 Locke, *A Letter Concerning Toleration*, 13.

36 Philosophical skepticism, of course, enjoys a long and complex relationship
with democratic doubt of this sort.

37 Locke, *Letter Concerning Toleration*, 19.

38 Thomas Paine, *Political Writings, Common Sense* (1776), 5. Paine expresses his
opinion of the fallibility of the Bible, the government, and humankind.

39 Thomas Paine, *Political Writings, The Rights of Man*, 87. The "aggregate" here
is the rights of the many collected in the civil power – this as opposed to the
absolute power of the monarch or the Church, and is expressly aware of the
imperfect power of individuals to realize those rights outside of a deliberative
constitutional forum.

40 Paine, front matter.

41 Mill, 85.

42 Mill, 85.

43 Such dogma is, he says, "but one superstition more, accidentally clinging to the words which enunciate the truth." Mill, 103.

44 Mill, 89.

45 This, although the aggregate or majority opinion yields a greater truth for Mill when lists are "left open."

46 Stanley Fish, Chapter 11, "The Law Wishes to Have a Formal Existence," 141–179. The discussion of the parole evidence rule is illuminating in this regard.

47 Locke, *Second Treatise* [Ch. II] 10.

48 One suspends judgment in this way as one lays down arms to establish trust with the stranger. The handshake is said to derive from this and to convey it in the gesture. Here I mean to place democratic doubt in direct opposition to revenge where others so often place forgiveness.

49 Richard Rorty, *Contingency, Irony, and Solidarity* (New York, 1989), 73–4.

50 Democratic appreciation of dissent and dissenting jurors relates to the ironist's doubt and is recalled for example in *12 Angry Men*, written by Reginald Rose, directed by Sidney Lumet (MGM, 1957). And see Austin Sarat, ed., *Dissent in Dangerous Times* (Ann Arbor, 2005).

51 Habermas takes such things to be rather less contingent than we take them to be here.

52 The Supreme Court acknowledged the importance of this validation by democratic doubt in requiring jury sentencing in capital cases in *Ring v. Arizona*, 536 U.S. 584 (2002). See Charles Lane, "US Court Overturns 100 Death Penalties," *Boston Globe*, Sept. 3, 2003: ". . . the constitutional guarantee of a jury trial meant that every fact that might result in an increased penalty for the defendant must be found by a jury beyond a reasonable doubt." A-3.

53 The coverage of Zacarias Moussaoui's court declaration is instructive: "'In the name of Allah, I don't have anything to plead. I enter no plea.' 'I interpret that as a plea of not guilty,' said Judge Brinkema, and Moussaoui's defense team agreed. Declining to plead is legally equivalent to entering a not guilty plea." "Terror suspect enters no plea," 02/01/2002 20:34-(SA). News 24.com, http://www.news24.com/News24/Archive/0,,2-1659_1126515,00.html Presumably Moussaoui did not want to enter a plea because he wanted to tell the world what he really did do with regard to the acts of September 11, which is, of course, not "how it works." Yet his seemingly naive and irrational position reflects a canny awareness of the system – his wish to tell the "truth" as he sees it and not to be caught up in the lie that would be attributed to him in making the proper plea is, paradoxically, what the lie of the proper plea is supposed to make possible.

54 I mean to distinguish between that which is *implicit* in reason or consent in the liberal tradition (from Locke to Kant, etc.) and is taken to establish absolute or universal moral conditions for society, and that which belongs to democratic *reasoning* in which there can be no absolutes. *Democratic* power derived by reason in this sense is not at all the "Political power" that Locke took to be the "right of making laws with penalties of death and, consequently, all less penalties. . . ." John Locke, *Second Treatise* [Ch. I] 4. If the latter was a useful supposition in the face of monarchy and divine right, now it might yield to the more modest democratic principle.

55 The evolution of a democratic pedagogy of punishment reflects this at another level in the shift from spanking and the corporal punishment of children to the use of "time outs."

56 I mean to privilege democratic process of the sort that interrogates truth and debates principle over that which declares principles and merely expresses popular opinion.

57 See FRONTLINE on PBS (1999), "Snitch, how informants have become a key part of prosecutorial strategy in the war on drugs," http://www.pbs.org/wgbh/pages/frontline/shows/snitch/.

58 This refers to the practice of qualifying only jurors who do not oppose the death penalty in capital cases affirmed in *Witherspoon v. Illinois*, 391 U.S. 510 (1968), and in *Lockhart v. McCree*, 476 U.S. 162 (1986). For William Connolly, *Why I am Not a Secularist* (Minneapolis, 1999), that compounds a 'cultural forgetting' this enables the death penalty and constitutes a "public evacuation of self-doubts." 127.

59 Martha Bryson Hodel, Associated Press, "Witness is moved to the dock: Crime-lab chemist faces fraud charges," *Boston Globe*, Tuesday, September 4, 2001, A-6.

60 Robert E. Pierre of the *Washington Post*, "Owner of cadaver dog charged with planting remains," in *Boston Globe*, August 21, 2003, A-5.

61 Deborah Hastings, Associated Press, "Police chemist altered evidence, officials say," *Boston Globe*, April 21, 2004 A-2.

62 Adam Liptak and Ralph Blumenthal, "New Doubt Cast on Crime Testing in Houston Cases," *New York Times*, August 5, 2004, A1.

63 John Soloman, Associated Press, "FBI Bullet Science flawed, independent review warns," *Boston Globe*, November 22, 2003: "One FBI scientist involved in lead bullet analysis has pleaded guilty to giving false testimony, another employee has admitted to improper DNA testing. . . ." A-3.

64 See David Faigman, "Is Science Different for Lawyers?" *Science* 297 (19 July 2002), referring to *United States v. Plaza*, 197 F. Supp. 2d 492 (E.D. Pa. 2002), and *United States v. Plaza*, 188 F. Supp. 2d 549 (E.D. Pa. 2002), notes that the former is based on *Daubert v. Merrill Dow Pharmaceuticals, Inc.*, 509 U.S. 579 (1993). See also CBS News, 60 Minutes, "Fingerprints: Infallible Evidence?" Aired June 6, 2004, on the efforts of attorney Mike Malloy, a Pennsylvania lawyer who has challenged fingerprint evidence. See also Simon A. Cole, *Suspect Identities, A History of Fingerprinting and Criminal Identification* (Cambridge, 2001).

65 DNA samples found at the scene confirm the more recent confession to that crime by a known rapist. Matias Reyes, Associated Press, "Black Officers Ask for Review of Case," *Boston Globe*, August 10, 2002, A-4. In 2002 District Attorney Robert Morganthau sought a dismissal of all charges. The New York Supreme Court vacated the convictions, December 19, 2002. http://www.apls.org/publications/newsletters/winter2003.pdf.

66 NPR's Talk of the Nation, "The Central Park Jogger Case," by Neal Conan, Dec. 10, 2002, focuses on the problem of false confessions, with commentary by Saul Kassin of Williams College who has conducted studies on the matter. http://www.npr.org/templates/story/story.php?storyId=873445.

67 Jodi Wilgoren, "Citing Issue of Fairness, Governor Clears out Death Row in Illinois," *New York Times*, January 12, 2003, A1. (The governor's speech is excerpted).

68   Maura Kelly, Associated Press, "Police torture cited as 4 on death row freed," *Boston Globe,* January 11, 2003 A-2.

69   Jodi Wilgoren, *New York Times,* 22. Ryan, a republican and former supporter of the death penalty, traced his conversion on the issue to the efforts of Northwestern Professor David Portess and his students (which ultimately freed Anthony Porter 48 hours before he was to be executed for two murders). Critics blame Ryan for "making . . . a farce out of our legal system. . . ." and say that for the victims' families the decision is "like we were murdered again."

70   Rick Klein, "Science Key in Building Case for Death Law," *Boston Globe,* September 30, 2003, B-1, B-6. Also, Peter S. Canellos, "Bipartisan Bill Has Funds to Test DNA on Death Row," *Boston Globe,* October 1, 2003, A-3. See Editorial, *USA Today,* August 1, 2002: "Today's debate: Using DNA to fight crime" ("Our view"): "Testing all felons is money well spent: Much potential for abuse" ("Opposing view" by Scott Ciment).

71   Scott S. Greenberger, "Panel Offers Death Penalty Plan," *Boston Globe,* May 3, 2004, A-1. The panel recommends safeguards that would be difficult to implement such as "Controls over prosecutorial discretion," "High quality defense representation," and "independent scientific review system," etc., B-6.

72   The automatic appeal of "super due process" in capital cases detailed in *Gregg v. Georgia,* once hailed as fail-safe in the way that the extraordinary proof of DNA testing is being hailed, maintains the illusion as well.

73   Here again the temporal collapse of retrospective (retributive) judgment into a self-serving consequentialist utility of power makes the past serve the present, and 'truth' serve power in a vengeful absolutist way. Franz Neumann and Otto Kierchheimer make a related point concerning Nazi law in *The Rule of Law Under Siege* (Berkeley, 1996), 152–153.

74   This was the conclusion of the Georgia study introduced by the defense in *McCleskey v. Kemp,* 481 U.S. 279 (1987), which in the words of Justice Powell showed that ". . . even after taking account of 39 nonracial variables, defendants charged with killing white victims were 4.3 times as likely to receive a death sentence as defendants charged with killing blacks." *McCleskey v. Kemp,* 481 U.S. at 287. See Randall Kennedy, *Race, Crime and the Law* (New York, 1997), 328–329, 449, citing David C. Baldus, Charles Pulaski, and George Woodworth, *McClesky v. Zant and McClesky v. Kemp: A Methodological Critique* (supplement to D. Baldus and J. Cole, *Statistical Proof of Discrimination,* 1988).

75   Experts on both sides contest the matter.

76   This tension often seems lost in Habermas' project – a pluralist democracy must entertain 'consensus' that features uncertainty and permanent argument, and only reluctantly advances generalizable moral claims. He knows this perfectly well, but it is not his principal concern.

77   Jill Barton, Associated Press, "Court overturns youth's murder conviction: Was serving life term in death of Fla. girl 6," *Boston Globe,* December 11, 2003, A-2.

78   Dick Lehr, "DA Urges Drumgold be freed: Prosecutor cites flaws in 1989 murder trial," *Boston Globe,* A-1, considering the recanted testimony of one key witness, a homeless man who now claims that he was housed, paid, and encouraged to lie, and the undisclosed brain disease of another key witness at the time of her testimony.

79   This suggests that the states' right to decide on the matter of what is "cruel or unusual" in punishment should not diminish the fact that it is always in

dispute. The sense in which the punishment itself is the locus of democratic debate became clear when as Governor of Texas George W. Bush refused to grant clemency to the born-again Karla Faye Tucker, proclaiming "judgments about the heart and soul of an individual on death row are best left to a higher authority." See Sister Helen Prejean, "Death in Texas," *The New York Review of Books* 52(1) (2005). That highly contestable, essentially theological judgment (which confounds the relationship between church and state and the question of what is cruel or unusual) is made manifest in the punishment, and debate is foreclosed in allowing it to go forward. This is not to say that punishment should always be debatable, only that the punishment is the creation of debate and might better reflect that fact in our democracy.

80   Since democracy here is neither just the will of the majority nor the tacit consent of the people, but the rule of law (conditions of plurality, inclusion, collective decision making, and the neutrality of the state taken together) this calls for particular limits on power and restraint in punishing.

81   Locke, *Second Treatise* [Ch. VIII,], 61.

82   Jeremy Bentham, excerpts from an *Introduction to the Principles of Morals and Legislation* (1823), in Jeffrie G. Murphy, *Punishment and Rehabilitation,* 3rd ed. (Belmont, 1995), 30. Bentham details the occasions in which punishment has no utility: 'when it is groundless; inefficacious; unprofitable; needless,' and elaborates on the importance of proportionality in this connection. 24; 29–35.

83   Immanuel Kant, *The Metaphysical Elements of Justice,* Part I (Indianapolis, 1965), 101.

84   The use of lethal force in extreme circumstances and in the same attitude of caution and restraint is entirely consistent with this understanding of democratic authority. For the reasons enumerated here, punishment by death is not.

85   The 'reason' of the Enlightenment inherits the claims of divine and aristocratic authority in this way.

86   The widely used instruction given to police interrogators in confronting a suspect with incriminating evidence is that they should be prepared to "cut off immediately any explanation the subject might start to offer . . . to permit the subject to offer an explanation will bolster his confidence . . . and this should never be permitted to occur." Fred Inbau, et al. *Criminal Interrogation and Confessions,* 4th ed., (Sudbury, 2004), 8. This pales by comparison to techniques of interrogation used at Guantánamo, Abu Ghraib or resulting from the practice of "rendering" by U.S. intelligence services.

87   This, as opposed to the intention behind shaming punishments. See George Will, "The Sting of Shame," *Washington Post,* February 1, 1996, which lauds Dan Kahan's article "What Do Alternative Sanctions Mean?" *University of Chicago Law Review* 63 (1996), and the idea that shaming punishment should inflict "reputational harm," lower self-esteem in offenders, and reinforce the "expressive function" of punishment. There is restitution and community service that does not aim to lower self-esteem and promotes a different sort of accountability.

88   This suggests a greater degree of honesty in the weighing of criminal charges. It is not "truth in sentencing" of the sort that is called for to thwart judicial discretion, 'time off for good behavior' or parole, as the retributive right would have it, but truth derived in a discursive attempt to make the punishment appropriate

to the crime and respect all parties, which *requires* such discretion. This would discourage prosecutors from prejudicing a case by way of the charge – one thinks of Louise Woodward being charged with first-degree murder after an initial charge of assault and battery.

89 The democratic state that imposes punishment inevitably will inflict pain and negate the will of an offender, but recognizes that inflicting pain cannot 'make one responsible.' It invites citizens to give account and to assume responsibility wherever possible. Pain and privation are a consequence of the refusal to act responsibly in committing a crime or of necessary incarceration, but are not the primary objective of the punishment.

90 Fines are an exception in this regard as they are coercive, but are set in place by democratic bodies that afford recourse or means of protest. Similarly, the compulsions of prison and various sorts of security may temporarily abrogate choice without foreclosing it 'in principle.'

91 Incarceration thus bears out the inversion of the will and vengeful doubling discussed in Chapter 3 – those who lack responsibility seem to 'deserve' to be treated in kind, but where that treatment is protracted and repetitive it mocks them as well. Of course there are other reasons to incarcerate and other ways of doing it.

92 The difference turns on a nuance: to make oneself responsible, to hold one responsible in spite of oneself. Talk of 'accountability' bears this ambiguity.

93 This is a different model of therapy than the coercive sort that abrogates responsibility promoted in the '70s and which Herbert Morris criticizes in "Persons and Punishment," in Jeffrie G. Murphy, *Punishment and Rehabilitation*, 3rd ed. The therapeutic efficacy of such efforts is beside the point, although they have been shown to reduce recidivism rates.

94 This being both 'effective' (as recidivism rates bear out) and 'fair,' would accommodate certain retributive and utilitarian objectives without being another synthesis. Where there are halfway programs or "pre-release centers" for inmates that promote the assumption of responsibility, and coercive "boot camps" that do not, the former is preferred for democratic reasons.

95 Martha C. Nussbaum, "Equity and Mercy" (reprinted from *Philosophy & Public Affairs* 22(2), (1993)), in Jeffrie G. Murphy *Punishment and Rehabilitation*, 3rd ed., considers how for Aristotle the "law must speak in general terms" but contains "gaps that must be filled up by particular judgments." A principle of "equity" calls for this and must therefore weigh the circumstances surrounding a case and understand it in part from the "point of view" of the accused, and is thus related to "mercy." 220–221; 222–223.

96 This is condemnation with the full authority of the law, mitigated by consideration of the intentions and circumstances or the lawbreaker – Nussbaum (in Murphy) recalls Oedipus in this regard. Richard Delgado treats a poor or troubled "background" an excuse in general, which is not the aim here. See "'Rotten Social Background': Should the Criminal Law Recognize a Defense of Severe Environmental Deprivation?" from *Law and Inequality: A Journal of Theory and Practice* 2(1) (July 1985), reprinted in Murphy, *Punishment and Rehabilitation*, 3rd ed.

97 See Randall Kennedy, *Race, Crime and Law*.

98 This is another reason for retaining legal advocates and not always having defendants speak for themselves. It is the democratic (if not liberal) sense in which they must 'have rights' even if they are disdainful of rights. Rights then are not universal principles 'possessed' by all, but a truth-relation that must be realized in practice whenever democratic authority ventures a claim. In this relation, the rule of law trumps the individual will in this respect without ascribing 'true' intentions or 'higher' meaning to it. This is why enemy combatants and the like facing such an authority should have representation and rights.

99 This is why the state's punishments are approximations, like the prison sentence, and not precise acts of retribution. Similarly, restitution is consistent with democratic accountability in some cases where it is presented as an option or general proposition, and not to give victims particular 'satisfaction,' 'closure,' etc.

100 Though a democratic authority must "respect persons" in virtue of this restraint, it is not necessarily more compassionate towards them. While that feeling may motivate many democratic citizens and bear on the punishment in that way, compassion is not the basis of the argument here.

101 Rorty's private ironist (not now as a juror but as a victim) has a different public resonance here.

102 See Chapter 3 page 109. So much of American life has been touched by therapy and the psychoanalytic aim of accepting the past, that it should have a hearing here. Acceptance as a final stage of grieving (and perhaps for this mother) is an instance of this. See Elisabeth Kubler-Ross, *On Death and Dying* (New York, 1969).

103 That broad range of reactions was in evidence in the sentencing of Gary Ridgway to 48 life terms, one for each of the confessed "Green River" murders. Says Tim Meehan, the brother of one victim, "I can only hope that someday someone gets the opportunity to choke you unconscious 48 times so you can live through the horror that you put our mothers and our daughters through." And Kathy Milles, the mother of another says, "Gary Leon Ridgway, I forgive you. I forgive you. You can't hold me anymore. I'm through with you. I have a peace that is beyond human understanding." See Gene Johnson, Associated Press, "'Green River Killer' Apologizes, Is Sentenced to 48 Life Terms," *Boston Globe*, December 10, 2003, A-12. Here the state accommodates both points of view by suppressing vengeful actions, which is why the death penalty would be 'undemocratic' in this sense.

104 Martha C. Nussbaum in "Equity and Mercy" hints at this idea by suggesting that mercy may involve "gentleness going *beyond* due proportion" even on an (Aristotelian) retributivist scale.

105 See Austin Sarat, *Mercy on Trial: What it Means to Stop an Execution* (Princeton, 2005). Pardons and clemency are only the exceptional recourse of an executive authority and a corrective to vengeful excess, but are important nevertheless. Recall Governor Ryan in Illinois.

106 Minow registers concern over that aspect of forgiveness that seeks closure and would forget, citing Friedlander on the Holocaust, among others, 24.

107 We have acknowledged Nietzsche on this point, *Genealogy*, 72–73.

108 Recall Chapter 1, Romans 12:19, 20, and the sense in which beneficence and forgiveness "...heap coals of fire" upon the head of one's enemy.

109 See for example FRONTLINE, "Faith and Doubt at Ground Zero." Airdate: Tuesday, Sept. 3, 2002, written by Helen Whitney and Ron Rosenbaum, produced by Helen Whitney: http://www.pbs.org/wgbh/pages/frontline/shows/faith/

110 Christ's instruction to forgive might thus cohere with the atheist's acceptance. Minow alludes to the ecumenical character of forgiveness, as does Murphy in Jeffrie G. Murphy and Jean Hampton, *Forgiveness and Mercy* (Cambridge, 1990), 5.

111 Harold S. Kushner, *When Bad Things Happen to Good People* (New York, 1981).

112 Recall Weber's admonition in "Science as a Vocation" to those who cannot bear the terms of modern life – go back to church.

113 Nussbaum, 229–30.

114 Nussbaum, 230. This is consistent with Martha Minow's emphasis on "investigating the larger patterns of atrocity and complex lines if responsibility and complicity in the case of South Africa." 9.

115 Nussbaum, 228, FN 42.

116 The observation that criminals who victimize others were often victims themselves might reflect a 'truth' of this sort. It is also a function of the democratic pursuit of truth to reveal the atrocities of oppressive regimes as the Missing Persons Commission has done in investigating mass killings in the Balkans and Iraq engaging modern forensic techniques. See "Answers from the Graves," 60 Minutes, CBS News, November 30, 2003.

117 This better understanding has been lost to the mendacity and incompetence of the prosecution of the "war on drugs" under mandatory sentencing requirements and the improper use of informants is chronicled on FRONTLINE (PBS 1999): "Snitch, how informants have become a key part of prosecutorial strategy in the war on drugs" http://www.pbs.org/wgbh/pages/frontline/shows/snitch/.

118 Then New Hampshire Attorney General Philip McLaughlin and Senior Assistant Attorney General Kelly Ayotte refused to speculate on the motive in the murders of Half and Susanne Zantop on January 27, 2001. See Dick Leher and Mitchell Zuckoff, *Judgment Ridge: The True Story Behind the Dartmouth Murders* (New York, 2003).

119 Gene Johnson, Associated Press, "Prosecutor at ease with sparing killer" *Boston Globe*, November 23, 2003, A-19. In this passage, Melang seems to find the ability to see beyond what vengeance would permit him to see.

120 There is much debate about whether they should also be punished or whether amnesty should be offered in exchange for their testimony. The importance of privileging truth, however, is unmistakable for this new democracy.

121 TRC Commissioner Mary Burton. From National Public Radio: "Hearts & Minds: The Burden of Truth," narrated by Jema Huley. Quoted with permission of Soundprint Media Center Inc.

122 Minow identifies this process as a matter of unmasking "world-denying" atrocities, 18.

123 Here the private makes a public claim in the political rejection of revenge, says Terry Dowdall of the Center for Survivors of Violence and Torture of such observances: "You finally confront the person at whose mercy you lay completely at one stage – you confront that person and the power lies not with him but with you – and yet where he abused the power you are able to use it in a quite and responsible way. You don't torture him back. You don't torture him, kill him, you simply ask him questions which reveal his emotional and his moral impoverishment." NPR, "Hearts & Minds: The Burden of Truth."

124 The requirement to execute Saddam within 30 days of his verdict is a matter of Iraqi law instituted by the Supreme Iraqi Criminal Tribunal (formerly the Iraqi Special Tribunal) established under the Coalition Provisional Authority and endorsed by the Bush Administration. In the eyes of many Saddam's execution (December 29, 2006) was rushed and vengeful and made especially degrading as cameras recorded the taunting of his guards. This stands in marked contrast to the American "super due process" in capital cases.

Bibliography

Adorno, Theodor, and Max Horkheimer. *Dialectic of Enlightenment*. New York: Herder and Herder Inc., 1972.

Aeschylus. *The Eumenides*. In *The Oresteia*. Trans. Robert Fagles. New York: Penguin, 1984.

Antiphon and Andocides. *Minor Attic Orators in Two Volumes*. Trans. K. J. Maidment. Cambridge, MA: Harvard University Press, 1982.

Aristotle. *Aristotle's Politics and Poetics*. Trans. Benjamin Jowett and Thomas Twining. New York: Viking, 1972.

Ayers, Edward. *Vengeance and Justice: Crime and Punishment in the 19th-Century American South*. New York: Oxford University Press, 1984.

Bailyn, Bernard. *The Ideological Origins of the American Revolution*. Enlarged edition. Cambridge, MA: Harvard University Press, 1992.

Bakan, David. *Disease, Pain and Sacrifice: Towards a Psychology of Suffering*. Chicago: University of Chicago Press, 1968.

Bandes, Susan A., ed. *The Passions of Law*. New York: New York University Press, 2001.

Barnes, Annette. *Seeing Through Self-Deception*. Cambridge, UK: Cambridge University Press, 1997.

Baudrillard, Jean. *The Transparency of Evil: Essays on Extreme Phenomena*. Trans. James Benedict. New York: Verso, 1993.

Bedau, Hugo Adam. *The Death Penalty in America: Current Controversies*. New York: Oxford University Press, 1997.

Bellah, Robert N., et al. *Habits of the Heart: Individualism and Commitment in American Life*. Berkeley: University of California Press, 1985.

Bloom, Harold. *Sophocles' Oedipus Rex*. New York: Chelsea House, 1988.

Boehm, Christopher. *Blood Revenge: The Anthropology of Feuding in Montenegro and other Tribal Societies*. Lawrence, KS: University Press of Kansas, 1984.

Bok, Sissela. *Mayhem: Violence as Public Entertainment*. Reading: Addison-Wesley, 1998.

Brubaker, Stanley. "Can Liberals Punish?" *American Political Science Review* 82.3 (1988): 821–836.

Bulfinch, Thomas. *Bulfinch's Mythology*. New York: Random House, 1993.

233

Butler, Judith. *Gender Trouble: Feminism and the Subversion of Identity*. New York: Routledge, Chapman & Hall, 1990.

Camus, Albert. *Reflections on the Guillotine*. Trans. Richard Howard. Michigan City, IN: Fridtjof-Karla, 1959.

Capozzola, Christopher. "The Monumental Moment: Recent Monument Design and the Search for Pluralist Frameworks of Memory." Senior thesis. Harvard University, Cambridge, MA, 1994.

Cavell, Stanley. *Disowning Knowledge in Seven Plays of Shakespeare*. Cambridge, UK: Cambridge University Press, 2003.

Cole, Simon A. *Suspect Identities: A History of Fingerprinting and Criminal Identification*. Cambridge, MA: Harvard University Press, 2001.

Connolly, William. *The Ethos of Pluralization*. Minneapolis: University of Minnesota Press, 1995.

———. *Why I Am Not a Secularist*. Minneapolis: University of Minnesota Press, 1999.

Delblanco, Andrew. *The Death of Satan: How Americans Have Lost the Sense of Evil*. New York: Farrar, Straus and Giroux, 1995.

Dewing, Christopher. "The Transformation of the American Frontier: Myth, Meaning and the Hyperreal in the Television News Coverage of the Space Shuttle Challenger Disaster." Senior thesis. Harvard University, Cambridge, MA, 1995.

Dews, Peter. *Logics of Disintegration: Post-Structuralist Thought and the Claims of Critical Theory*. New York: Verso, 1987.

Dicey, Albert Venn. *Introduction to the Study of the Law of the Constitution*. Boston: Adamant Media, 2000.

DiStefano, Christine. *Configurations of Masculinity: A Feminist Perspective on Modern Political Theory*. Ithaca, NY: Cornell University Press, 1991.

Dolinko, David. "Some Thoughts about Retributivism." *Ethics* 101.3 (1991): 537–559.

Dumm, Thomas. *Democracy and Punishment: Disciplinary Origins of the United States*. Madison, WI: University of Wisconsin Press, 1987.

———. *United States*. Ithaca, NY: Cornell University Press, 1994.

Durkheim, Emile. *The Division of Labor in Society*. Trans. W. D. Halls. New York: Free Press, 1984.

———. *The Elementary Forms of the Religious Life*. Trans. Joseph Ward Swain. New York: Free Press, 1965.

Faigman, David. "Is Science Different for Lawyers?" *Science* 297 (19 July 2002): 339–340.

Fish, Stanley. *There's No Such Thing as Free Speech and It's a Good Thing Too*. New York: Oxford University Press, 1994.

Fiske, John. *Power Plays Power Works*. New York: Verso, 1993.

Flynn, Thomas. "Foucault as Parrhesiast: His Last Course at the Collège de France (1984)." *Philosophy & Social Criticism* 12.2–3 (1987): 194–212.

Foucault, Michel. *Discipline and Punish: The Birth of the Prison*. Trans. Alan Sheridan. New York: Vintage, 1979.

———. *Foucault Live (Interviews, 1966–1984)*. Trans. John Johnston, Edited by Sylvère Lotringer, (New York: Semiotext(e) Foreign Agents Series, 1989).

———. *The Order of Things: An Archaeology of the Human Sciences, a translation of Les mots et les choses*. New York: Random House, 1970.

French, Peter. *The Virtues of Vengeance.* Lawrence, KS: University of Kansas Press, 2001.

Freud, Sigmund. *Civilization and Its Discontents.* Trans. James Strachey. New York: W. W. Norton, 1962.

———. *The Ego and the Id.* Trans. Joan Riviere. New York: W. W. Norton, 1962.

———. *General Psychological Theory.* Edited by Philip Rieff. New York: Simon and Schuster, 1963.

Garland, David. *The Culture of Control: Crime and Social Order in Contemporary America.* Chicago: University of Chicago Press, 2001.

———. *Punishment and Modern Society: A Study in Social Theory.* Chicago: University of Chicago Press, 1990.

Gilligan, James. *Violence: Our Deadly Epidemic and Its Causes.* New York: Putnam, 1996.

Girard, René. *Violence and the Sacred.* Trans. Patrick Gregory. Baltimore: Johns Hopkins Press, 1989.

Glaspell, Susan. "A Jury of Her Peers." In *Revenge: Short Stories by Women Writers,* edited by Kate Saunders. Winchester, MA: Faber and Faber, 1991.

Goffman, Erving. *The Presentation of Self in Everyday Society.* New York: Doubleday, 1959.

Goldhagen, Daniel. *Hitler's Willing Executioners.* New York: Knopf, 1996.

Habermas, Jürgen. *Communication and the Evolution of Society.* Trans. Thomas McCarthy. Boston: Beacon, 1979.

———. *Knowledge and Human Interests.* Boston: Beacon Press, 1971.

———. *Legitimation Crisis.* Boston: Beacon Press, 1973.

Hahn, Mary J. "If We Must Die: The Meaning of Race to Members of an African-American Gang." Senior thesis. Harvard University, Cambridge, MA, 1997.

Harrison, Colin. *Bodies Electric.* New York: Avon, 1993.

Hart, H. L. A. *Punishment and Responsibility.* Oxford: Oxford University Press, 1968.

Hegel, G. W. F. *Hegel's Philosophy of Right.* Trans. T. M. Knox. London: Oxford University Press, 1975.

Himmelfarb, Gertrude. *Victorian Minds.* New York: Knopf, 1968.

Hobbes, Thomas. *Leviathan.* New York: Bobbs-Merrill, 1958.

———. *Man and Citizen: De Homine* and *De Cive.* Edited by Bernard Gert. New York: Anchor, 1972.

Holmes, Oliver Wendell. *The Common Law.* Boston: Little Brown, 1923.

Homer. *The Iliad of Homer.* Trans. Richard Lattimore. Chicago: University of Chicago Press, 1961.

———. *The Odyssey.* Trans. Robert Fitzgerald. New York: Anchor, 1963.

Honig, Bonnie. *Political Theory and the Displacement of Politics.* Ithaca, NY: Cornell University Press, 1993.

Honneth, Axel. *The Struggle for Recognition: The Moral Grammar of Social Conflicts.* Cambridge, MA: MIT Press, 1996.

Hunt, Darnell M. *O. J. Simpson: Facts and Fictions: New Rituals in the Construction of Reality.* Cambridge, UK: Cambridge University Press, 1999.

Hyde, Lewis. *The Gift: Imagination and the Erotic Life of Property.* New York: Vintage, 1983.

Jacoby, Susan. *Wild Justice: The Evolution of Revenge.* New York: Harper and Row, 1983.

Jameson, Fredric. "Postmodernism and Consumer Society." In *The Anti-Aesthetic: Essays on Postmodern Culture*, edited by Hal Foster. Port Townsend, WA: Bay Press, 1983.

Jefferson, Thomas. *The Portable Thomas Jefferson*. Edited by Merrill D, Peterson. New York: Viking 1977.

Johnstone, Keith. *Impro: Improvisation and the Theatre*. New York: Routledge, 1979.

Kafka, Franz. *In the Penal Colony*. In *Franz Kafka: The Complete Stories*, edited by Nahum N. Glatzer. New York: Schocken, 1988.

Kahan, Dan M. "The Anatomy of Disgust in Criminal Law." *Michigan Law Review* 96.6 (1998): 1621–1657.

_____. "What Do Alternative Sanctions Mean?" *University of Chicago Law Review* 63.2 (1996): 591–653.

Kant, Immanuel. *The Metaphysical Elements of Justice*. Trans. John Ladd. Indianapolis, IN: Bobbs-Merrill, 1965.

_____. *The Metaphysics of Morals*. Trans. Mary Gregor. Cambridge, UK: Cambridge University Press, 1991.

Kennedy, Randall. *Race, Crime, and the Law*. New York: Random House, 1997.

Kiernan, V. G. *The Duel in European History: Honor and the Reign of Aristocracy*. Oxford: Oxford University Press, 1989.

Koestler, Arthur. *Reflections on Hanging*. New York: Macmillan, 1957.

Kubler-Ross, Elisabeth. *On Death and Dying*. New York: Macmillan, 1969.

Kurland, Philip B., and Ralph Lerner, eds. *The Founders' Constitution*. Online edition. Liberty Fund and University of Chicago Press. Accessible at http://press-pubs.uchicago.edu/founders/.

Kurzweil, Martin. "The Third Table: The Theoretical Implications and Practical Effects of Victims' Rights in the Death Penalty Process." Senior thesis. Harvard University, Cambridge, MA, 2002.

Kushner, Harold S. *When Bad Things Happen to Good People*. New York: Schocken, 1981.

Lasch, Christopher. *Haven in a Heartless World: The Family Besieged*. New York: Basic, 1977.

Laurence, John. *A History of Capital Punishment: With Special Reference to Capital Punishment in Great Britain*. London: Kennikat, 1971.

Lehr, Dick, and Mitchell Zuckoff. *Judgment Ridge: The True Story Behind the Dartmouth Murders*. New York: HarperCollins, 2003.

Leibniz, G. W. *Theodicy: Essays on the Goodness of God, the Freedom of Man, and the Origin of Evil*. London: Routledge and K. Paul, 1952.

Lesser, Wendy. *Pictures at an Execution: An Inquiry into the Subject of Murder*. Cambridge, MA: Harvard University Press, 1993.

Lewis, Anthony. *Gideon's Trumpet*. New York: Vintage, 1964.

Locke, John. *A Letter Concerning Toleration*. Edited by Patrick Romanell. New York: Bobbs-Merrill, 1955.

_____. *The Second Treatise of Government*. Indianapolis, IN: Bobbs-Merrill Company, 1952.

Lukács, Georg. *History and Class Consciousness: Studies in Marxist Dialectics*. Trans. Rodney Livingstone. Cambridge, MA: MIT Press, 1972.

Machiavelli, Niccolo. *The Prince*. Edited by Charles W. Eliot. Trans. N. H. Thomson. *The Harvard Classics*. Volume 36. New York: Collier & Son, 1938.

MacIntyre, Alasdair. *After Virtue: A Study in Moral Theory*. 2nd ed. South Bend, IN: University of Notre Dame Press, 1984.

Marongiu, Pietro, and Graeme Newman. *Vengeance: The Fight Against Injustice*. Tatowa, NJ: Rowman and Littlefield, 1987.

Masur, Louis P. *Rites of Execution: Capital Punishment and the Transformation of American Culture, 1776–1865*. New York: Oxford University Press, 1989.

Mill, John Stuart. *Autobiography*. Edited by Jack Stillinger. Boston: Houghton Mifflin, 1969.

———. *Essays on Politics and Culture*. Edited by Gertrude Himmelfarb. New York: Doubleday, 1962.

———. *On Liberty*. In *Utilitarianism, On Liberty, and Considerations on Representative Government*, edited by H. B. Acton. London: J. M. Dent & Sons, 1976.

———. *Utilitarianism*. New York: Macmillan, 1989.

Miller, William Ian. *The Anatomy of Disgust*. Cambridge, MA: Harvard University Press, 1997.

———. *An Eye for an Eye*. Cambridge, UK: Cambridge University Press, 2005.

Minow, Martha. *Between Vengeance and Forgiveness: Facing History after Genocide and Mass Violence*. Boston: Beacon, 1998.

———. "Words and the Door to the Land of Change: Law, Language, and Family Violence." *Vanderbilt Law Review* 43.6 (1990): 1665–1699.

Mitford, Jessica. *The American Way of Death*. New York: Simon and Schuster, 1978.

Moore, G. E. *Principia Ethica*. Cambridge, UK: Cambridge University Press, 1962.

Morris, David B. *The Culture of Pain*. Berkeley: University of California Press, 1991.

Mosse, George L. *Nazi Culture: Intellectual, Cultural and Social Life in the Third Reich*. New York: Schocken, 1981.

Murphy, Jeffrie G. *Punishment and Rehabilitation*. 2nd ed. Belmont CA: Wadsworth, 1985.

———. *Punishment and Rehabilitation*. 3rd ed. Belmont, CA: Wadsworth, 1995.

Murphy, Jeffrie G. and Jean Hampton. *Forgiveness and Mercy*. Cambridge, UK: Cambridge University Press, 1988.

Napier, A. David. *Masks, Transformation, and Paradox*. Berkeley: University of California Press, 1986.

Nasr, Ethan. "Making Sense of 'Senseless Violence': An Examination of How Prisoners Understand their Punishment." Senior thesis. Harvard University, Cambridge, MA, 1996.

Neumann, Franz, and Otto Kierchheimer. *The Rule of Law Under Siege*, edited by William E. Scheurman. Berkeley: University of California Press, 1996.

Nietzsche, Friedrich. *Beyond Good and Evil*. Trans. R. J. Hollingdale. London: Penguin, 1990.

———. *Beyond Good and Evil, Prelude to a Philosophy of the Future*. Trans. Helen Zimmern. London and Edinburgh: T. N. Foulis, 1907.

———. *The Birth of Tragedy* and *The Case of Wagner*. Trans. Walter Kaufmann. New York: Random House, 1967.

———. *Human, All Too Human*. Trans. R. J. Hollingdale. New York: Cambridge University Press, 1986.

———. *On the Genealogy of Morals* and *Ecce Homo*. Trans. Walter Kaufman. New York: Vintage, 1969.

_____. *Thus Spoke Zarathustra*. In *The Portable Nietzsche*. Trans. Walter Kaufmann. New York: Viking, 1974.

Oakeshott, Michael. *Experience and Its Modes*. Cambridge, UK: Cambridge University Press, 1933.

_____. *Rationalism in Politics*. New York: Basic, 1962.

Osiel, Mark. *Mass Atrocity, Collective Memory, and the Law*. New Brunswick, NJ: Transaction Publishers, 1997.

Paine, Thomas. *Political Writings*. Edited by Bruce Kuklick. Cambridge, UK: Cambridge University Press, 2000.

Parker, Andrew, and Eve Kosofsky Sedgwick, eds. *Performativity and Performance*. New York: Routeledge, 1995.

Plato, *The Republic of Plato*. Trans. Francis MacDonald Cornford. Oxford: Oxford University Press, 1945.

Poe, Edgar Allan. "The Cask of Amontillado." In *Thirty-two stories/Edgar Allan Poe*, edited by Stuart Levine and Susan Levine. Indianapolis, IN: Hackett Publishing Company, 2000.

Portmann, John. *When Bad Things Happen to Other People*. New York: Routledge, 2000.

Radden, Jennifer. *Divided Minds and Successive Selves: Ethical Issues in Disorders of Identity and Personality*. Cambridge, MA: MIT Press, 1996.

Ramamurti, Bharat. "Moral Responsibility, Excuses, and the Law." Senior thesis. Harvard University, Cambridge, MA, 2003.

Rawls, John. *A Theory of Justice*. Cambridge, MA: Harvard University Press, 1999.

_____. "The Law of Peoples." In *On Human Rights: The Oxford Amnesty Lectures 1993*, edited by Stephen Shute and Susan Hurley. New York: Basic, 1993.

Reinhard Lupton, Julia, and Kenneth Reinhard. *After Oedipus: Shakespeare in Psychoanalysis*. Ithaca, NY: Cornell University Press, 1993.

Rorty, Richard. *Contingency, Irony, and Solidarity*. New York: Cambridge University Press 1989.

Rosaldo, Renato. *Culture & Truth: The Remaking of Social Analysis*. Boston: Beacon, 1989.

Rosset, Clement. *Joyful Cruelty: Toward a Philosophy of the Real*. Trans. David F. Bell. New York: Oxford University Press, 1993.

Rothman, David J. *The Discovery of the Asylum: Social Order and Disorder in the New Republic*. Boston: Little Brown, 1971.

Rousseau, Jean-Jacques. *The Confessions*. Trans. J. M. Cohen. Harmondsworth, UK: Penguin, 1965.

Roy, Jody M. *Love to Hate: America's Obsession with Hatred and Violence*. New York: Columbia University Press, 2001.

Sagan, Eli. *The Lust to Annihilate: A Psychoanalytic Study of Violence in Ancient Greek Culture*. New York: Psychohistory Press, 1979.

Sandel, Michael. *Liberalism and Its Critics*. New York: New York University Press, 1984.

_____. *Liberalism and the Limits of Justice*. Cambridge, UK: Cambridge University Press 1982.

Sarat, Austin, ed. *The Killing State: Capital Punishment in Law, Politics and Culture*. New York: Oxford University Press, 1999.

_____. *Mercy on Trial: What It Means to Stop an Execution*. Princeton: Princeton University Press, 2005.

Sartre, Jean-Paul. *Being and Nothingness: An Essay on Phenomenological Ontology.* Trans. Hazel E. Barnes. New York: Philosophical Library, 1956.

_____. *Huis Clos.* Edited by Jacques Hardre and George B. Daniel. New York: Meredith, 1962.

Scarry, Elaine. *The Body in Pain: The Making and Unmaking of the World.* New York: Oxford University Press, 1985.

Schwartz, Martin A. "Supreme Court Defines 'Deliberate Indifference'." *New York Law Journal 212* (19 July 1994): 3.

Scott, George Riley. *The History of Corporal Punishment.* London: Tallis, 1968.

_____. *A History of Torture.* New York: Random House, 1995.

Shakespeare, William. *Hamlet.* New York: Penguin, 1998.

_____. *Macbeth.* Edited by Sylvan Barnet. New York: Signet Classics, 1963.

_____. *Othello.* Edited by Barbara A. Mowat and Paul Werstine. New York: Washington Square Press, 1993.

Sher, George. *Desert.* Princeton: Princeton University Press, 1987.

Shklar, Judith N. *The Faces of Injustice.* New Haven: Yale University Press, 1990.

_____. *Legalism: Law, Morals and Political Trials.* Cambridge, MA: Harvard University Press, 1986.

_____. *Ordinary Vices.* Cambridge, MA: Harvard University Press, 1984.

Smith, Adam. *The Theory of Moral Sentiments.* Edited by D. D. Raphael and A. L. Macfie. Indianapolis, IN: Liberty Classics, 1982.

Sophocles. *Antigone, Oedipus the King, Electra.* Edited by Edith Hall. Trans. H. D. F. Kitto. Oxford: Oxford University Press 1994.

_____. *Oedipus Rex.* In *The Oedipus Cycle: An English Version.* Edited by Dudley Fitts and Robert Fitzgerald. New York: Harcourt Brace Jovanovich, 1977.

_____. *Oedipus Tyrannus.* Edited by Luci Berkowitz and Theodore F. Brunner. New York: W. W. Norton, 1970.

Sorell, Tom. *Moral Theory and Capital Punishment.* New York: Basil Blackwell, 1987.

Stoller, Robert. *Sexual Excitement: The Dynamics of Erotic Life.* New York: Simon and Schuster, 1979.

Sunstein, Cass R. *Legal Reasoning and Political Conflict.* Oxford: Oxford University Press, 1996.

Suskind, Patrick. *Perfume: The Story of a Murderer.* Trans. John E. Woods. New York: Simon and Schuster, 1991.

Swift, Jonathan. *A Tale of a Tub.* Online edition. Edited by Deep Singh. Accessible at http://www.lehigh.edu/~amsp/tubbo-2.html.

Tananbaum, Zoe. "*Reel Death:* Disturbing Visions and the 'Illegality' of Televised Executions." Senior thesis. Harvard University, Cambridge, MA, 2002.

Tocqueville, Alexis de. *Democracy in America.* Edited by J. P. Mayer. Trans. George Lawrence. New York: Harper/Perennial, 1988.

Tucker, Judith E. *In the House of the Law: Gender and Islamic Law in Ottoman Syria and Palestine.* Berkeley: University of California Press, 1998.

Tunick, Mark. *Punishment: Theory and Practice.* Berkeley: University of California Press, 1992.

Weber, Max. *Economy and Society: An Outline of Interpretive Sociology.* Edited by Guenther Roth and Claus Wittich. Berkeley: University of California Press, 1978.

————. *The Protestant Ethic and the Spirit of Capitalism.* Trans. Talcott Parsons. New York: Scribner's Sons, 1958.

————. "The Social Psychology of the World Religions." In *From Max Weber: Essays in Sociology,* edited by H. H. Gerth and C. Wright Mills. New York: Oxford University Press, 1970.

Whitman, James Q. *Harsh Justice: Criminal Punishment and the Widening Divide Between America and Europe.* New York: Oxford University Press, 2003.

Williams, Patricia. *The Alchemy of Race and Rights.* Cambridge, MA: Harvard University Press, 1991.

Wilson, James Q. *Thinking About Crime.* New York: Basic, 1983.

Yates, Francis. *The Art of Memory.* Chicago: University of Chicago Press, 1966.

Index